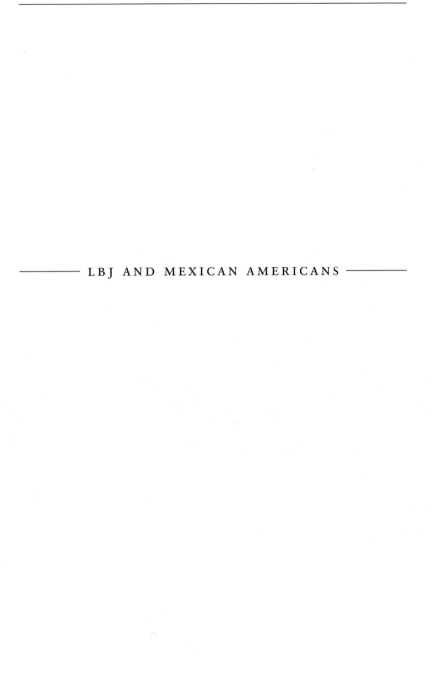

LBJ AND MEXICAN AMERICANS

LBJ

&

MEXICAN
AMERICANS

The Paradox of Power

JULIE LEININGER PYCIOR

UNIVERSITY OF TEXAS PRESS
AUSTIN

Requests for permission to reproduce material from this work
should be sent to Permissions, University of Texas Press, Box 7819,
Austin, TX 78713-7819.

⊗ The paper in this publication meets the minimum requirements
of American National Standard for Information Sciences—Permanence
of Paper for Printed Library Materials, ANSI Z39.48-1984.

Library of Congress Cataloging-in-Publication Data

Pycior, Julie Leininger.
    LBJ and Mexican Americans : the paradox of power / Julie Leininger Pycior.—1st
University of Texas Press ed.
        p.   cm.
    Includes bibliographical references and index.
    ISBN 0-292-76577-0 (alk. paper).—ISBN 0-292-76578-9 (pbk. : alk. paper)
    1. Johnson, Lyndon B. (Lyndon Baines), 1908–1973.   2. Mexican Americans—
Politics and government.   3. Mexican Americans—Texas—History—20th century.
4. Texas—Ethnic relations.   I. Title.
E847.2.P93   1997
973.923′092—dc21   96-48458

For Stan,
Who understands life's paradoxes

CONTENTS

Illustrations follow pp. 22 and 162.

ACKNOWLEDGMENTS

Twenty years ago Virginia Espinosa sparked the idea for this topic when she said that her father had worked at the LBJ Ranch. How fascinating it would be, I thought, to profile this powerful political leader from the vantage point of some of the least powerful people in the nation. I met Virginia (then an Indiana University student) at the Centro de Estudios Chicanos, the brainchild of Gilberto Cárdenas. Gil and I were both in Notre Dame's Mexican American graduate studies program, established by Julian Samora: activist, advisor to presidents, the first Chicano ever to become a sociologist, and our mentor. We also were inspired by his wife, Betty Archuleta Samora, who personified César Chávez's motto, "Hechos son amor" (Deeds are love).

Next came two outstanding people, one from each side of the story, who believed in my work back when I was at home with a preschooler in Queens and far from my historical sources. For ten years Arnoldo De León and Bill Moyers, who set the standard for me in their own work, kept making time in their crowded schedules to offer suggestions and write letters of recommendation. Moreover, Moyers granted me an extensive interview, while De León critiqued the entire manuscript.

James MacGregor Burns, Mario T. García, and Bernard Brock also went out of their way to advise me on this project. Other scholars and writers who have shared their insights with me over the years include Frank Bonilla, Robert E. Burns, Albert Camarillo, Betty Boyd Caroli, Robert Coles, Elaine Crane, Rodolfo de la Garza, Ronnie Dugger, Juan Ramón García, Philip Gleason, Robert Himmelberg, José R. Hinojosa, Robert Jones, Louise Año Nuevo Kerr, Robert Matthews,

Frank Ninkovitch, Cynthia Orozco, J. Gilberto Quesada, Tom J. Romero, Ricardo Romo, Richard Santos, and Emilio Zamora.

The archivists at all of the collections I visited, from California to Michigan to Washington, D.C., were unfailingly helpful, but I would like to single out several, particularly in Texas, who went beyond the call of duty. The Mexican American archivist at the Benson Latin American Collection, Margo Gutiérrez, helped me in so many ways that she became my main link to Chicano sources in general and, what is more, a true friend. Christine Marín, a historian as well as an archivist at Arizona State University's Chicano collection, proved to be another generous colleague and friend. At the Johnson Library, Claudia Anderson found many an obscure source, while Linda Hanson quickly provided answers to my telephone inquiries, even if it meant calling after hours, and Philip Scott pointed the way through the vast photographic collection. At the Texas A&M archives Margaret McKenna first opened the Héctor P. García papers at my request, while Thomas H. Kreneck, the head of special collections and archives there, tracked down photographs and made time to talk Texas politics as well.

I am deeply grateful to the Schumann Foundation for travel funds and, especially, for a semester salary stipend to write the final draft of the book. Grants from the Lyndon Baines Johnson Foundation, the alas now-defunct Institute for Research in History, and Manhattan College defrayed some of my travel expenses.

Over the years the many research trips to Austin came to feel like coming home. Gil Cárdenas and Deeana Rodríguez have always welcomed me, with warmth reminiscent of the late Betty Samora. Other helpful Austinites included Ed Idar Jr., Vivian and Alexandra Mahlab, James Harrington and Rebecca Flores Harrington, Gary Keith, and, above all, *mi verdadera comadre* Jacqueline Kerr. She has sheltered me, fed me, lent me her car for research peregrinations, and in general looked out for me like a sister. Over the years friends from New York to Michigan have come through in ways large and small, but as George Reedy wrote in *Lyndon Baines Johnson: A Memoir*, "I do not believe I need to name names. There are friendships that truly last."

As I traveled around Texas a number of people offered assistance, including Fredna Knaggs Dobie Woods, John Nelson, Mary González, and Nora Mae Tyler, all in Cotulla; Eleanor Butt Crook and William H. Crook of San Marcos; Ernesto González and Maggie Rangel of Duval County; San Antonians Al Kauffman, Kathleen Voight, and Maury Maverick Jr., and John Tiff at the LBJ Ranch. Moreover, this story could not have been told without the cooperation of the more than forty people who generously opened their homes to me, sharing their time, photographs, letters, and, especially, their memories in oral history interviews.

To my good fortune, Theresa May offered me an advance contract with University of Texas Press in 1989, before a single page had been written. Now Assistant Director and Executive Editor, she has contributed much to the project, as have editors Lois Rankin and Kerri Cox.

Securing the book contract helped me land a teaching job at Manhattan College, where Robert Kiernan of the English Department generously offered to read the entire manuscript. The author of several books and a former Fulbright scholar, he gave me valuable suggestions. Other Manhattan College colleagues who encouraged this project include Michael Antolik (who provided the title for chapter 1), Mark Taylor, June Dwyer, Kevin Dougherty, George Schneider, Dean Maryann O'Donnell, and former dean Albert Hamilton. George Kirsch, chair of the History Department, lent me the services of the department's student assistants, and another department colleague, Frederick Schweitzer, enabled me to join New York University's Faculty Research Network, where I benefited from the advice of NYU faculty members Christopher Mitchell, David Reimers, and Susan Ware. The Manhattan College librarians—particularly Maire Duchon, Brother Thomas O'Connor, and Stacy Pober—were extremely helpful, while Ann Campbell and Nancy Cave cheerfully provided occasional secretarial assistance.

As I write this, my children, Anna and Bob, are finding constructive ways to keep busy in the same cooperative spirit as countless other times. Moreover, Anna has shown interest in the book from the time she was small, and Bob helped process some of the notes. My mother, father, stepmother, sister, and brother have believed in this project since its inception; their love has helped me over many a rough spot. As for my husband, Stan, he has been a rock of support—technical, logistical, financial, parental, psychological, moral—never wavering from his loving confidence in my project.

INTRODUCTION

Historian Barbara Tuchman once said, "I did not write to instruct but to tell a story."[1] *LBJ and Mexican Americans* tells the important but neglected story of a close but sometimes contentious relationship that slowly developed from its Texas roots, eventually making its presence felt on the national political scene.

All Johnson biographies mention three occasions when Mexican Americans crossed his path: 1928, when he taught at the "Mexican" school in Cotulla, Texas; 1948, when he won a senate seat with suspect "Mexican" votes; and 1949, when he helped bury with honors a Mexican American serviceman after the local funeral home refused to service a "Mexican."[2] Studies of Mexican American political development, for their part, have examined the effect of Johnson administration policies on Mexican Americans.[3]

The relationship, however, went far beyond discreet events or White House policies. At every stage of their political formation Johnson and Mexican Americans affected each other: sometimes as allies, sometimes as adversaries, sometimes as both. Every single Johnson aide interviewed for this book—including his two protégés, conservative John Connally and liberal Bill Moyers—emphasized the importance of Mexican Americans in Johnson's political thinking. For their part, all of the Mexican Americans interviewed—from traditional political operatives to Chicano insurgents—stated that Johnson profoundly affected their own lives and the lives of Mexican Americans generally. The story is really several intersecting sagas. Texas history played a paradoxical role in the childhood worlds of Johnson and his elementary school students. As the years passed his and their worlds increasingly connected amid the complicated currents of Texas politics, to finally emerge on the national stage, where Mexican Americans influenced the rise and fall of the Johnson administration.

Stylistic influences for this book include the works of C. Vann Woodward and James MacGregor Burns, who develop their themes as much through depiction of historical events as through interpretation of them. In *Thinking Back*, Woodward writes, "Portraying and explaining . . . inevitably go together. . . . *How* events happen can be as important as *why*. . . . The intrigues and plots and hopes that people resort to . . . in their confused efforts to shape the course of history can be as revealing about the meaning of an event as disclosures of the determining factor." More akin to a documentary film script than to a social science treatise, *LBJ and Mexican Americans* weaves together a pattern from descriptions and anecdotes, with the historical actors carrying much of the story along.[4]

Oral history interviews provided much of the eyewitness information used in this study, corroborated by memoranda, letters, and other documents from the time. Several Mexican American archives proved essential, particularly the Héctor P. García Collection, which contains numerous documents about Johnson. They in turn pointed the way to Mexican American references buried among the millions of Johnson Library papers. The papers of George I. Sánchez and César Chávez— who viewed Johnson with more skepticism than did his friend García—served as something of a counterbalance.[5] On the other hand, women—both Anglo and *mexicana*—are almost invisible in the archival records because of their exclusion from high political office and major organizational leadership. Nonetheless, as historians such as Margaret Rose have shown, Mexican American women did act as political agents. Thus oral history interviews with women are particularly crucial, as when Kathleen Voight explains her recruitment of Mexican Americans for the Texas Democratic Party in the 1950s or when Lupe Anguiano analyzes her roles in the Great Society and California politics.[6]

A number of secondary sources that focus on either Johnson or Mexican Americans provide essential background information. Among the Johnson biographies, *The Years of Lyndon Johnson: The Path to Power*, the first volume of Robert Caro's work-in-progress, captures Johnson's complicated feelings as a schoolteacher in Cotulla. A brilliant prose stylist and prodigious researcher, Caro, in his second volume, *Means of Ascent*, paints a convincing picture of Johnson going to any length to curry financial support for his senate campaigns. At the same time the author depicts as a virtuous alternative Johnson's 1948 opponent, Governor Coke Stevenson, but as biographer Ronald Steel writes in his review of *Means of Ascent*, "Conservatives favored Stevenson over the New Deal liberal Johnson because Stevenson was such an exemplar of the white man's Texas."[7]

In *The Politician*, Ronnie Dugger clarifies the complicated world of 1940s Texas politics. Along with historians Robert Dallek and George Norris Green, Dugger has led the way on research about Johnson's role in 1950s politics. (For his part, Caro has not yet reached the 1950s.) None of the major biographers have yet chronicled the 1960s, so part II of this book relies more heavily on primary sources than does part I. Memoirs by White House aides also offered some candid insights into the 1960s, particularly those of Joseph Califano and George Reedy as well as an essay by Bill Moyers.[8]

The field of Mexican American political history has grown steadily since the 1972 publication of Rodolfo Acuña's still-essential *Occupied America*. Mario T. García's *Mexican Americans* is a major overview of the 1930–1960 generation, which made its mark in civil rights history and in the career of Lyndon Johnson. Important chronicles of the Chicano generation—which participated in and protested against the Great Society—include a study by Ignacio García of the Chicano third party that originated in Texas, and by Carlos Muñoz of the Chicano movement in general and the California-based student movement in particular.[9]

Although no one writing about Johnson or Mexican Americans has focused on their relationship per se, a few path-breaking works have explored the history of Anglo-Mexican political relations. Paul Taylor led the way with his interviews with South Texas residents, conducted at the very time that Lyndon Johnson was starting his professional life there. In the 1940s V.O. Key explored the roles of race and class in Texas politics, and in the 1980s Chandler Davidson found that, contrary to Key's predictions, race continues to vie with class as a political factor in the state. Of all such studies, however, *Anglos and Mexicans in the Making of Texas, 1836–1986* provides the most insights into the political background of the Johnson–Mexican American relationship. Here David Montejano demonstrates that South Texas counties that instituted irrigated agriculture excluded the Mexican American majority from voting, while counties that remained cattle-ranching societies continued to rely on paternalistic *patrón* politics and *mexicano* cultural traditions.[10]

David Montejano is a prime example of the younger historians described by Michael Kazin as "increasingly exploring the more political aspects of history 'from the bottom up.'" Thomas Bender points out that by bridging social and political history, such studies are building a network that can lead to a new synthesis of United States history. It is hoped that this process of refining the concept of *e pluribus unum* will be helped along by the connections revealed in the following saga.[11]

PART ONE

THE TEXAS SCENE

THE LADDER OF SUCCESS

Late in the afternoon of March 15, 1965, President Lyndon Johnson impatiently awaited the final pages of what he called "the most important speech of my life." In just a few hours he would speak on behalf of the controversial Voting Rights bill before a joint session of Congress and his largest television audience ever. That morning, when he found out that the speech had been assigned to a Texas staff member, a former public relations man, Johnson had exploded. The president wanted Richard Goodwin, who had experienced discrimination in the form of antisemitism and thus could express more eloquently the yearnings of the thousands of African Americans who were risking their lives daily for the simple right to vote. With the event just hours away, Goodwin sequestered himself in his inner office, giving orders for no one to disturb him. The president vented his impatience on his other aides as he waited for the arrival of each page. Only once did the president call, his "softly modulated, familiar drawl betraying not the slightest concern about the rapidly dwindling hours," according to Goodwin, who recalled Johnson saying, "You remember, Dick, that one of my first jobs after college was teaching young Mexican Americans down in Cotulla. I told you about it down at the ranch. I thought you might want to put in a reference to that." [1]

The final version focused on black civil rights, ending with a daring, stirring evocation of the activist anthem "We Shall Overcome," but in his sole personal anecdote a somber Lyndon Johnson told the nation,

My first job after college was as a teacher in Cotulla, Texas, in a small Mexican American school. . . . They knew in their youth the pain of prejudice. They never seemed to know why people disliked them. But they knew it was so, because I saw it in their eyes. I often walked home late in the afternoon, after classes were finished, wishing there was more that I could do. But all I knew was to teach them the little I knew, hoping that it might help them against the hardships that lay ahead. . . . Somehow you never forget what poverty and hatred can do when you see its scars on the hopeful face of a young child. I never thought then, in 1928, that I would be standing here in 1965. It never occurred to me in my fondest dreams that I might have the chance to help the sons and daughters of those students and to help people like them all over this country. But now I do have that chance—and I'll let you in on a secret—I mean to use it.

Johnson, according to Vice President Hubert Humphrey, "never did forget those days when he taught school to those Mexican American kids. . . . He romanticized it a lot, that I know. And people thought he just used that, but that wasn't true." The president spoke of the Cotulla experience in public, he spoke of it in private, until it became, in the words of a close associate, "almost part of the folklore of the man."[2]

THE PARADOX OF TEXAS HISTORY

In 1928, as the new history teacher in the "Mexican" school, young Lyndon Johnson came to Cotulla with an abiding love of Texas history as recounted by the victors. When his mother read to him as a little boy, he rejected fictional tales, asking, "Mama, did this really happen?" Johnson disliked reading but was a skilled listener, soaking up the stories handed down through the generations. His parents, even more than most Texans, conveyed the past as interesting, important, and best personified by their illustrious forebears. His father, Sam Johnson Jr., loved history, scoring 100 percent in both Texas and American history, while his mother, Rebekah Baines Johnson, was an avid genealogist. Lyndon's great-great-uncle John Wheeler Bunton joined the Texas rebellion against Mexico, signed the Texas Declaration of Independence, and then fought at the Battle of San Jacinto. His captain wrote that Bunton "penetrated so far into the ranks of the defenders . . . that it is miraculous that he was not killed." In gratitude the new Republic of Texas awarded Bunton 960 acres of land. Johnson's great-grandfather George W. Baines was a friend of Sam Houston, and Rebekah's cousin Mary Baines was a founder of the Daughters of the Republic of Texas. With the aid of Lyndon's father, a member of the state legislature, the Daughters persuaded the state to purchase the Alamo as a historic shrine.

Adults referring to the "War" during Lyndon's childhood meant not the Great War or the War between the States but the 1836 Texas Revolt against Mexico. He and his playmates tearfully reenacted the defense of the Alamo in every detail; for them history was palpable, real. At the age of six Lyndon memorized a poem about the Alamo to recite at a Confederate reunion. The event was canceled but Johnson remembered the poem his whole life. As president he bellowed it out for startled White House dinner guests:

> Santa Anna came rumbling as a storm might come
> There was a rumble of cannon; there was a rattle of blade;
> There was cavalry, infantry, bugle and drum—
> Full seven thousand in pomp and parade,
> The chivalry, flower of Mexico;
> And a gaunt two hundred in the Alamo!
>
> "Surrender or die! Men, what will you do!"
> And Travis, great Travis, drew his sword, quick and strong,
> Drew a line at his feet. . . . "Will you come, will you go?"
> I drew with my wounded, in the Alamo.[3]

Johnson thus grew up imbibing a Texas saga that discounted the perspective of Mexican-heritage residents. In any case, few lived in Johnson's Hill Country of central Texas, a land of independent Anglo, Czech, and German-American farmers eking out livelihoods on small tracts of thin soil, each establishing its own community. Johnson's relatives had founded his hometown of Johnson City, which "was just like a big family town," according to a longtime resident, Georgia Commack Edgeworth. Only in relation to African and Mexican Texans did Hill Country farmers of various European backgrounds see themselves as similar: as whites, Americans. Edgeworth remembered that "there were no Latins, none, and no coloreds." One man did open a Mexican restaurant in Johnson City during Lyndon's childhood, "and we thought it was great," she said. "We brought all the newspapers, you know, and he'd give us a few tamales. . . . He just stayed there a few nights, and one morning he was gone. It was terrible. . . . He was run off."

As a state representative Johnson's father voted for the poll tax and for a primary law that, in the words of the bill's sponsor, would stop "the floodgates of illegal . . . Mexican and negro votes." More often, however, Sam Johnson defended the underdog. In the face of threats from Ku Klux Klan members in his own district he supported a bill to curb the Klan by making it a prison offense to wear a mask. He also unsuccessfully opposed a bill outlawing "disloyal" language. Passed during World War I, it targeted his German-American constituents in particular, but it also fanned the animosity toward Texas Mexicans. Moreover, although his uncle had been a Texas Ranger, Representative Johnson supported a bill—sponsored by the lone Tejano legislator, J. T. Canales—to reduce the size of the Texas Ranger force. Canales also called in vain for investigations into Ranger conduct and for his trouble was threatened by a Ranger just two blocks from the state capitol.[4]

Lyndon Johnson often proudly recounted his father's brave stand against the Klan, but in general Sam Johnson's support of minorities, tenant farmers, and workers made him something of a quixotic figure in his son's eyes. Lyndon once remarked, "He was trying to better humanity. He didn't have much to show for it." The elder Johnson had to quit the legislature in 1924 due to rising indebtedness. Lyndon Johnson wanted to be a winner. He admired his uncle, the conservative Democratic judge Clarence Martin, whose business and political connections had enabled him to become financially secure, defeating Johnson's populist grandfather in the process. Eventually Johnson would buy the Martin ranch and there establish himself as a millionaire gentleman rancher.

At the Hill Country college, Southwest Texas State Teacher's College, Johnson majored in history, including several courses on U.S. history and, of course, Texas history. He grabbed the opportunity when his cousin Margaret Johnson, a Cotulla resident, informed him of the position there: to teach sixth and seventh grade history and serve as the principal of the "Mexican" school. Although only a college junior, he obtained a strong recommendation from the college president, who had appointed Johnson as his personal secretary. The school superintendent came from Cotulla to San Marcos and, in Johnson's words, "offered me a job at $125 a month to teach at the Mexican school."[5]

The only people of Mexican background that Johnson met in college were janitors—coworkers on his first campus job. While *he* soon left this menial position behind, immersing himself in presidential errands and campus politics, *they* could not seek promotion or attend classes at the college. In general local policies encouraged Anglo and Mexican Texans to lead separate lives. The colonia—with its open sewers and segregated schools—was on the other side of San Marcos. Some restaurants and drugstores refused service to Mexicans; others did not. Anglo-Texans constituted a clear majority, so Hill Country discrimination was relaxed, lacking what one of President Johnson's aides called the "hard edge" of segregation in towns such as Cotulla.[6]

Cotulla was established in a region known as the Brush Country: south of San Antonio, north of the counties bordering Mexico. After the Texas Revolt of 1836 and continuing into the twentieth century, marauding bands of Anglos and *mexicanos* alike ranged over sagebrush and mesquite that went on forever under a giant blue dome of a sky. One of the most legendary, Gregorio Cortez, was denounced as a murderer by the authorities but extolled as a rebel hero in Mexican ballads, or *corridos*. In 1901 he boldly walked into Cotulla knowing that a posse was searching for him in the surrounding countryside. Several women in the colonia assisted him before he set off again.[7]

Texas Rangers such as the legendary King Fisher came through Cotulla enforcing Anglo justice. A boy once asked Fisher how many men he had killed in the line of duty. The Ranger replied,

"Seven."
"I thought it must be more than that."
"I don't count Mexicans."[8]

A few miles west of Cotulla, another famous Ranger, Captain L. H. McNelly, killed four "desperate outlaws" in an ambush, according to the folklorist J. Frank Dobie, who grew up on his uncle's 56,000-acre La Salle County spread. McNelly, a favorite of Lyndon Johnson's, once ignored an order by the U.S. Army to return from Mexico after his forces entered Mexico searching for a suspect and killed all the adult males on one ranch, which the Rangers had mistaken for another. When a contingent of Rangers came through La Salle [Cotulla's] County asking for the owner of Rancho Buena Vista, the fearful Tejano immediately sold his ranch and moved to Mexico. Meanwhile the *San Antonio Express* reported in 1885 that a masked man took Florentino Suaste from his Cotulla jail cell, lynched him, then shot him. Folklorist and South Texas native Jovita González wrote that the Rangers killed upwards of three hundred Mexican-heritage residents in the early 1920s. The *New York Times* summed up the situation by reporting in 1921, "The killing of Mexicans without provocation is so common as to pass unnoticed."[9] In Laredo, the closest city to Cotulla, *La Crónica* editor protested in 1911, "The Mexicans have sold the great share of their landholdings and some work as day laborers on what once belonged to them. How sad this truth!" By the 1890s Anglo cattle ranchers had acquired most of the Brush Country land through coercion, high taxes, expensive legal challenges, and their growing numbers.[10]

La Salle County ranches traditionally operated in a paternalistic manner. The Anglo ranch managers worked alongside the *mexicano* fence-riders and cowboys. Owners attended employees' festivities, *mexicanas* served as wet nurses for Anglo children, and ranch children of both backgrounds played together until puberty. In this intimate interaction Anglos learned about Mexican food, language, and customs. *Vaqueros*, with their equestrian skills rooted in the cowboy culture, elicited special admiration. "There were really some fine Mexican *vaqueros*," observed Fredna Knaggs Dobie Woods. Descended from a pioneer family, she was related by marriage to J. Frank Dobie.

"Ranch culture [was] like a feudal system," remembered Rita Binkley Worthy, whose father managed the giant Callaghan ranch south of town and whose grandfather, a banker, was Cotulla's first mayor. Ranchers commanded total deference from laborers, who dared not question long hours of backbreaking work, and from sharecroppers contracted into debt peonage. "Sometimes we didn't get" much of a harvest "at the end of the year. . . . It was difficult," Manuela González Contreras said of her sharecropping. (Both of her brothers attended Johnson's Cotulla class.) Landowners and managers could enter with impunity the shacks made of sticks and grass, but they strictly enforced separation in their own houses. Rita Worthy's father "drew a line," she said. He would sit at his kitchen table having coffee in the morning with his main fence-rider, going over the day's assignments, but she noted that Binkley "would never have invited him in to have dinner."

God was also on the side of the winners. Even J. Frank Dobie, who lovingly collected local *vaquero* tales, referred disparagingly to the "priest-ridden" Mexicans. In the 1880s the Reverend J. F. Kimball attempted to establish a Baptist mission among the Mexicans in La Salle County. Kimball, the future father-in-law of Lyndon's cousin Margaret Johnson, unsuccessfully exhorted his coreligionists to "press rapidly" toward the goal of "self-sustaining" Mexican congregations. Mexican illiteracy rates were higher in Anglo-owned counties such as La Salle than in counties with predominantly Tejano landowners.

Uninformed, isolated from each other on the ranches and farms, Texas Mexicans in La Salle County warily looked to the landowner for employment, for credit, and for protection from the vigilantes, the sheriff, and the border patrol.[11]

THE RISE OF SEGREGATION

In the early 1900s the railroad came to La Salle County with the help of Mexican laborers earning less than one dollar per day. In fact, when the company reduced the daily wage from 75 cents to 50 cents in 1906, the railroad workers went out on strike. The sheriff threatened to attack them unless they allowed strikebreakers from Mexico to replace them. (Another strike in the county in 1909 also failed.) With the arrival of the railroad and the establishment of federally sponsored irrigation projects in 1925, much of the rangeland came under cultivation. Anglo families such as Margaret Johnson's migrated from the nearby Hill Country. Others left an East Texas ravaged by boll weevils and exhausted soil, while still others came from the Midwest seeking cheaper farmland. Speculators renamed the Brush Country the Winter Garden, but the land often failed to live up to its billing, particularly for owners of small farms. They barely survived, all of the family members working from dawn to dusk, some of the children attending school in dresses made out of flour sacks.

Although the family farms hired a few Mexicans, most worked on labor gangs for large agribusiness concerns. Labor contractors, many of them Tejanos, began recruiting in Mexico. Thousands came to South Texas, including La Salle County, attracted by job prospects and higher wages. Many also fled the upheaval of the Mexican Revolution (1910–1920). One woman who came to Texas with her family recalled,

> There were hardly any provisions left . . . because the soldiers didn't leave a thing. They dumped over the small pails and fed their horses everything that had been harvested. Many people died of hunger. One of our aunts died of hunger and she had four children and one of them also died.[12]

By the time Lyndon Johnson arrived in 1928, nearly 80 percent of Cotulla's population of 3,000 was of Mexican background. Their presence reinforced the region's Mexican heritage. At the same time, as desperate refugees who had traveled far from their homes in central Mexico, most arrived unfamiliar with Texas and into a job situation where they had even less bargaining power than did sharecroppers, who now often found themselves consigned to work on farm gangs as well. By the end of the 1920s, "Mexican towns were fundamentally farm labor camps," of workers who were hired temporarily when the market price peaked, according to sociologist/historian David Montejano.

While Johnson was teaching there, a Winter Garden laborer's annual wage averaged $375 for an adult male and $600 for a family of four. Many left for better pay in other parts of the Southwest or even the Midwest, often in defiance of restrictive contracts and vagrancy laws. Winter Garden employers and public officials devised the regulations in order to hamper worker mobility. In 1929 the Texas State Legislature buttressed these local efforts by enacting the Emigrant Labor Agent Act, which prohibited people from coming into Texas from other states to recruit farm laborers.[13]

Local Anglos increasingly regarded Texas Mexicans as temporary foreign laborers to be isolated from the "American" residents. As one put it, "We don't want them to be associated with us, we want them for their labor," while another opined, "They were here before we were and they're working for us. . . . We will always need someone to do menial work. They will not be landowners; they don't save." A newspaper in a town near Cotulla editorialized that those with U.S. citizenship were ignorant frauds. Rita Worthy remembered that "They were called 'Mexicans', often in a derogatory manner. . . . There were two separate societies." Throughout the region the Anglo minority disenfranchised the Mexican majority and enforced segregation. One Winter Garden farm woman explained, "We feel toward Mexicans like the old southerners toward the Negroes." John Wildenthal, whose family helped establish Cotulla and who later worked on Senator Johnson's staff, felt "sensitive and embarrassed" growing up in a segregated society, "but you know, it's an awfully big elephant; you never know where to grab hold."[14]

By the time Johnson arrived in Cotulla local family farmers were pressing for an end to Mexican immigration. They faced an increasingly depressed economy and growing competition from an agribusiness that profited from Mexican labor. Segregation, no matter how thorough, did not keep the "undesirables" out. Or as one Winter Garden resident put it, "They don't vote, but they increase like rats. If something is not done we will soon be shoved out of the picture." The writer O. Henry, a former La Salle County resident, expressed these sentiments in his poem "Tamales":

This is the Mexican
Don José Calderón
One of God's countrymen
Land of the Buzzard
Cheap silver dollar, and
Cacti and murderers
Why has he left his land,
Land of the lazy man
Land of the pulque
Land of the bullfight,
Fleas and revolution.

This is the reason
Hark to the wherefore;
Listen and tremble.
One of his ancestors,
Ancient and garlicky,
Probably grandfather,
Died with his boots on,
Killed by the Texans,
Texans with big guns
At San Jacinto.

. . . Dire is the vengeance
Don José Calderón.
For the slight thing we did
Killing your grandfather.
What boots it if we killed
Only one greaser,
Don José Calderón?
This is your deep revenge,
You have greased all of us,
Greased a whole nation
With your Tamales,
Don José Calderón . . .

Eugenicists and a resurgent Ku Klux Klan played on racial fears. The Klan lynched a Mexican resident in neighboring Pearsall, where Johnson's girlfriend Carol Davis taught and where he would teach in 1930. Johnson characterized her father, the mayor of San Marcos, as "an extreme conservative . . . a member of the Klan." Commenting on a spate of lynchings in the area, *El Heraldo Mexicano* of San Antonio complained in 1928 that the Mexican Consulate "has not obtained any success. . . . Therefore we believe that we ourselves ought to leave these places, mainly rural, where we cannot count on justice." In June 1929 the *Comisión Honorífica* of Cotulla asked the Mexican Consul in Laredo to advise Mexican Cotullans; he informed an attentive audience of about 1,500 that the U.S. Immigration Service was increasing its deportations. By October the *San Antonio Express* was reporting "a hegira of Mexican people who were thrown into a panic by deportations, arrests, rumors."[15]

At the same time, agribusiness concerns wanted a steady supply of Mexican laborers, so no sweeping immigration restrictions were enacted. Whatever their views on immigration, however, Anglo Cotullans were united in the belief that the Mexican majority should not have civic or social equality. Segregation practices increased. Public accommodations throughout the Brush Country refused service to Mexicans or restricted them to the lunch counter or kitchen. One restaurant owner stated, "It isn't a question of cleanliness or education, but race." No Mexican Cotullans attended the Protestant churches. "The Catholic church in Cotulla was no problem because you were not socially mingling," Wildenthal explained, unlike the Baptists and Methodists, with their "Sunday school for the kids, youth things in the evening . . . and circles . . . during the week." Catholic Cotullans of German, Irish, or Polish background were buried not with Catholics of Mexican extraction but rather alongside the Protestants. "It was sort of a melting pot if you weren't Hispanic," Wildenthal said. The "American" section was festooned with the occasional Confederate flag and graced with many shade trees, unlike the barren, crowded "Mexican" section. In January 1930 the mayor rejected a request from the local Mexican mutual aid society for expansion of the "Mexican" section but promised to install pipes and other improvements if the society members purchased a plot, which they did a few weeks later.

As for the courts, "If there is a dispute between two Mexicans the courts are all right, but if it is between a Mexican and an American . . . the American gets the best of it," according to a Mexican Winter Garden resident, who added, "You never see them sending an American to the penitentiary for killing a Mexican." In one case during Johnson's tenure there, a Cotulla jury sentenced Carlos Corona to life imprisonment for murder. The local prosecution's case was so flimsy that on appeal the sentence was reduced to five years.[16]

"Discrimination was bad," remembered one of Johnson's students.

The Cotulla colonia originally had included a few Anglo residents, but by the time of Johnson's arrival the town was split in two by the railroad tracks; "the division," Johnson's students called it. Developers could offer Anglos fine frame houses on paved streets with storm sewers. The cousin of one Johnson student described the typical colonia dwelling: a one-room shack with a dirt floor for a family of five. Although their forebears had resided in La Salle County since at least the 1870s, "I got my inside toilet in 1972," she said. According to Johnson's most famous student, Dan García, Anglo Cotullans "were kind of two-faced; they would talk . . . as long as you were working with them but [otherwise] wouldn't give you the time of day." [17]

In the face of growing segregation, some of Cotulla's founding ranch families strove to maintain the paternalism of a bygone era. Several families with children in Johnson's class had friendly ties to the Knaggs family: an old Cotulla clan that made a point of, for example, regularly buying vegetables from the Gonzálezes. "They always took care of my daddy," according to his daughter Manuela. Johnson student Juanita Hernández lived with the Knaggs family and cared for the children when she returned to Cotulla from Illinois after her mother and husband died on the same day. Hernández characterized the Knaggses as "almost like family" and remembered "when the American people ran the town . . . everybody had a job . . . everybody was calm and nice" (if you treated them the same way), she said. For her part, Fredna Knaggs Dobie Woods recalled, "Cotulla was a very nice town, slow moving. We loved the Mexicans. . . . There may have been some [who discriminated], . . . but we loved them . . . and they loved us." [18]

Overall, however, "it was like the blacks in the South. There were just two separate societies," remembered Rita Worthy. In this atmosphere colonia residents relied on each other. Numerous colonia activities occurred during Johnson's stay in Cotulla, according to *La Prensa* of San Antonio, the largest-circulating Spanish-language newspaper in the United States. It reported that a drama staged at Johnson's school during his principalship was "important, stimulating." A number of Cotulla youngsters took part in the production, "El Molino Rugiente," which included an orchestra and chorus. The director, Gilberto Leyva, "was a very good musician . . . very bright and a natural enthusiast," one student remembered. Leyva gave music lessons to a few of Johnson's students whenever the parents could scrape together a little money.

Colonia organizations often sponsored weekend dances. The single men walked up and made courtly bows to young women, who stood with their mothers in the middle of the floor; then the men paid to have the privilege of dancing. Sometimes the dances lasted all night. One young lady, who some years later would have a son in Johnson's class, did not return home until dawn. Her mother, already busy with the housework, ordered her and her sisters to change, to start grinding corn for the tortillas, and then to do the laundry. They did not sleep until that night, but "they didn't say anything, because they loved to dance," according to the daughter of one of the women. On Mexican holidays, colonia residents sold items from canvas booths ringing the plaza in front of the Mexican school. Decorated with sugar cane, the stands offered games and homemade food, including tamales, enchiladas, avocados, and *cabrito*, or braised kid goat, a delicacy prized by Cotullans of all backgrounds. The colonia also mounted Mexican patriotic celebrations, which educator María Romo coordinated. (She had fought in the Mexican Revolution, according to one of Johnson's students.) The children marched with the Leyva band, and representatives of the colonia organizations spoke, including the officers of the *Comisión Honorífica*, the local mutual aid association, and the fraternal group the Woodmen of the World. Johnson student Juanita Hernández remembered the Woodmen activities of her father and, in particular, the solemn funerals of the many members.[19]

The colonia activities caught the attention of folklorist John Lomax, who came to Cotulla and recorded *Los Pastores*, a Christmas musical play performed by Franquilino Mirando and company, which the Library of Congress issued on a 1934 record. Most local Anglos were oblivious to these events; the *Cotulla Record* only reported on the Anglo side of town, except for the infrequent colonia crime.[20]

THE "MEXICAN" SCHOOL

The separate societies extended to the schools as well. A Cotulla teacher, Beryle Rutledge Rock, wrote, "It was believed that the Latin Americans required a different type of instruction from that of the Anglo-American children." In 1926 a modern brick building, the Welhausen Elementary School, was built in the colonia "exclusively for the Latins," in Rock's words. Amanda Burks Elementary School, "limited to Anglo-Americans," followed in 1928. Dorothy Territo Nichols, a schoolgirl who attended Cotulla High School when Johnson taught at Welhausen, later became one of his most important office workers. She recalled that Mexican-heritage children attended the

"Mexican" school in order to learn English, and that "any Mexican student who could speak English and wanted to could attend [Cotulla High School] and some of them did . . . but only the higher-class Mexicans sent their children there, usually."[21]

Although Mexican children attended a separate elementary school supposedly to learn the English language, Germans, Czechs, Italians, and other non-English speakers experienced no such segregation. Also, separation extended to nonacademic activities such as sports and playground use. After twenty-five years comparing "American" and "Mexican" schools, education professor George I. Sánchez wrote in 1951, "I have never found one in which the school personnel, services, and facilities squared up to the implied special offerings upon which the whole idea of segregation . . . rests. . . . A segregated school is an inferior school."[22]

To justify singling out Spanish-speaking children, school officials turned to other arguments: the irregular attendance of Mexican children, the pressure of public opinion, and the lack of space in Anglo schools. Educators also alleged that Mexican children carried dirt, lice, and disease. A 1923 University of Texas report buttressed such arguments, concluding, "In many instances, it must be admitted . . . there is but one choice . . . and that is to put the dirty ones into separate schools until they learn how to 'clean up.'" No thought was given to the poor living conditions, low wages, and lack of medical care that bred diseases such as tuberculosis and diphtheria.

Texas school districts received state aid based on the total school-age population rather than on actual attendance figures. Consequently, "the more you can get to stay at home, the better the school system you would have because you had this X-amount of money for all these cotton-picking children and field laborers," John Wildenthal said. A farmer noted that "the more ignorant they are, the better laborers they are." The children got the message. "In those years the school systems didn't care," according to one Johnson student, while another said that "the prevailing attitude" of Anglos was that the less the Spanish-speaking Cotullans knew, the better.[23]

The majority of Mexican-descent children never attended school at all. In fact, southwestern leaders argued before the U.S. Congress that Mexican immigrants were simply a temporary labor force that did not need to be educated in U.S. schools. The same year that Johnson came to Cotulla a Texas congressman named Olger B. Burtness, testifying before a House committee that was considering restricting Mexican immigration, declared:

I am not going to stand here and tell you that they are the best people on the face of the earth, or that they will have made wonderful citizens or that in a few years their sons and daughters will be graduating from our high schools and soon acting as our preachers and lawyers and doctors and as our professors in colleges or anything . . . of that sort. If they were going to do that I don't know that we would want them.[24]

One of the many La Salle County Mexican children who did not attend school was Julia González de Toro. She remembered picking crops all day because the whole family needed to work; the employers paid very low wages. "There were very few who were able to go to school . . . ," she said, "shopkeepers, people like that." The de Toro family arose in the predawn darkness and worked all day under the blazing sun, moving through the crops as a team. The children pulled the plants; their father, with his big hands, bundled them; their mother put them into crates. Then at sunset they had to go "in a horse and cart to chop wood for the stove." Most of the year they migrated to other parts of Texas to pick cotton, tomatoes, and onions. "We went in rickety trucks," she said. "We had to sleep in them . . . because the next day we had to work." She dreamed of the day when she might quit farmwork and become a seamstress.[25]

About 25 percent of the Mexican American children that started out in first grade had to repeat it; almost 40 percent dropped out by the end of third grade. Even so, the pupil-teacher ratio was twice as high at the Anglo school. Returning to Cotulla later in life, Johnson remembered the difficulties. "We had only five teachers here, we had no lunch facilities, . . . we did not have money to buy our playground equipment." The school board refused to supply school buses to transport children from the farms. As for the few who reached the high school, "they didn't want us," according to two women who attended the "Mexican" school during Johnson's tenure there. John Wildenthal recalled that legally anyone could attend the high school—located on the "white" side of town—but that colonia residents "didn't expect and they weren't expected to, unless they had special ambition." They were allowed in the classroom but not in most social activities. They could never be in the Winter Garden court, where the daughter of Johnson's cousin Margaret served as a princess "dressed in royal purple." For the 1938 graduation procession, the alphabetical order resulted in the placement of Wildenthal alongside Portencia

Rodríguez. "We heard that she was just in tears," he said, ". . . so Dad, mother, and I went over to her house to tell her, 'quit crying,' that we were very happy." In the end "the boys marched down the outside aisle on one side and the girls marched down the outside aisle of the other so it would not be conspicuous who was paired off with who." [26]

While Johnson was teaching in La Salle County, parents in a neighboring district organized a boycott of the Mexican school and of local stores, demanding the replacement of a teacher they accused of bias. The majority of the merchants honored the boycott; "We want their trade and we want them to work for us," said one. A new teacher was hired. Such actions, however, were the exception. Parents feared angering their employers and more often responded by forming their own informal schools, *escuelitas*, which sprouted up throughout South Texas. In Cotulla educator María Romo taught children to read and write in Spanish. In fact, Dan García recalled that his knowledge of grammar from those Spanish classes equipped him with the skills to skip several grades at Johnson's school. Romo supplied workbooks to the mother of two other Johnson students, Felipe and Juan González. Mrs. González in turn taught neighborhood children "English . . . spelling, arithmetic, wherever they were a little bit weak," according to her daughter, Manuela, who, like her mother, tutored for free. "When we were doing all this . . . it was just a matter of having to do something for somebody . . . but now it's history. It's something to be proud of." [27]

No María Romos taught in the Cotulla public schools or for that matter in any other district in the region. Those Mexican Americans that managed to obtain teacher certification found that superintendents preferred "American" applicants. Lyndon Johnson's background was typical; a principal without a college degree was acceptable at a "Mexican" school such as Welhausen, but not at an "American" one. Throughout the region, the Mexican school was often a stepping stone. For his part, one year after his stint at Welhausen, Johnson moved on to the "American" school in nearby Pearsall. Most of the Winter Garden area teachers came from local teacher's colleges, mainly Southwest Texas State, and conformed easily to small-town mores. Southwest Texas State Teacher's College had no pioneering social scientists such as Herschel T. Manuel at the University of Texas. In 1930 Dr. Manuel wrote, "The attitude in general that the Mexican is considered inferior to the non-Mexican is not hard to find. . . . To

Texas readers one could almost say, 'ask yourself' or 'consult your own experience.'"[28]

"HOW DO YOU DO, MR. JOHNSON?"

Lyndon Johnson probably thought that he was coming to Cotulla with a fair amount of background information. After all, he was very close to his cousin Margaret Johnson, who grew up with him in Johnson City before her family moved to Cotulla, and in college he became acquainted with one of the older Wildenthal boys. Johnson had envisioned the Cotulla job as another stepping stone to power, a chance to add references to the resume, to make political contacts for the future, as well as a way to earn money for his senior year at college. That's what America was all about: going to school, working hard, climbing the ladder of success.

Local Anglo attitudes shocked Johnson; they treated Mexicans "just worse than you'd treat a dog," he remarked later in life, and he recalled "the Mexican children going through a garbage pile, shaking the coffee grounds from the grapefruit rinds and sucking the rinds for the juice that was left." Johnson remembered his populist roots; his family had not hired gangs of laborers. In fact, the Johnsons had experienced hard times, and after high school Lyndon had picked crops under the hot sun. No Johnson, however, had been consigned permanently to farm labor, like the families on the trucks leaving town at dawn.[29]

Confronted with students estranged from his dream, Johnson neither rejected his vision of success nor blamed them for failing. Instead he sought to resolve the dilemma with a middle way. From his earliest days—when his refined, devout mother argued with his earthy, populist father—Lyndon Johnson had tried to resolve conflicts, to find some common ground. Now, in his first professional job, he vowed to convert his students into true believers in the American dream by pulling them onto the ladder of success in every way that he knew how. They, in turn, would follow him, giving him the love and respect he craved, and enhancing his professional reputation.

Lyndon Johnson surprised his students. None had ever had a male teacher, and here came this towering, thin man with slick, dark hair and a bright, youthful face, swinging his cane, striding with boundless energy along the dusty dirt road to school. He liked being in charge. The thirty-odd students who had beaten the odds and now sat in his

combined fifth/sixth/seventh grade class soon learned to greet him
with the song,

> How do you do, Mr. Johnson,
> How do you do?
> How do you do, Mr. Johnson,
> How are you?
> We'll do it if we can,
> We'll stand by you to a man,
> How do you do, Mr. Johnson,
> How are you?[30]

In many ways Johnson was a typical teacher of the times. He believed in strict discipline, yelling at offenders, occasionally paddling
male students, and vigorously enforcing a total ban on speaking Spanish. Although Johnson himself knew no second language, saying, "I
couldn't quite understand them; they couldn't talk English and I
couldn't talk Spanish," he was convinced that speaking any Spanish,
even at play, would retard a child's academic progress. In this he was
merely implementing ideas long held by Texas teachers and supported
by state laws since 1905. For their part, the children tended to view
the prohibition of their own language outside the classroom as simply
another aspect of discrimination.[31]

They used a history text that characterized Mexico's 1910 revolu-
tionary leaders as "bandits," while it called the 1836 Texas rebels opponents of a "harsh and tyrannical" Mexican government. The text-
book glossed over the illegal actions of the new Texans—particularly
bringing slaves into Mexican territory—and ignored the Texas natives
of Mexican descent who fought against Santa Anna in the rebellion.
The preeminent historian of the West, Walter Prescott Webb, would
write in 1935: "There is a cruel streak in the Mexican nature, or so
the history of Texas would lead one to believe." During Johnson's year
in Cotulla an Austin newspaper extolled his father:

> Santa Anna took the Alamo
> That was 1836.
> Sam Johnson saved the Alamo.
> That was 1905.

Naturally, Lyndon told his students of the great Texas victory over the Mexican oppressors. For some students in the Winter Garden region's Mexican schools, Texas history was the last straw; they quit for good.[32]

The plucky students who managed to stay in school overlooked such insensitivity, focusing instead on the more positive messages of both cultures. Referring to this emerging generation, folklorist Jovita González wrote,

> Behind them lies a store of traditions of another race, customs of past ages, an innate, inherited love and respect for another country. Ahead of them lies . . . a struggle for justice and equality before the law, for their full rights as American citizens. . . . They are the converging element of two antagonistic civilizations; they have the blood of one and have acquired the ideals of the other.[33]

No teacher provided more inspiration than Lyndon Johnson. Caring, warm, with a magnetic presence, he exhorted them to believe that the history of the United States was summed up in the maxim "that any person could become a president of the United States," as Dan García recalled. Johnson would sit young Felipe González on the hood of a car and declare that this boy would grow up to be an attorney. Unlike the other teachers, who mostly stayed on their side of the tracks, Lyndon liked to stop by the Gonzálezes' bare but immaculate little house to eat, chat, and then stretch out his long frame on the soft cheneille spread of their only bed and take a nap. He convinced a reluctant Mrs. González to let him take her son Juan with him to Johnson City, where Johnson and his mother tutored him in English. The young schoolteacher urged Mrs. González to "keep fighting" to get the Welhausen children into the high school, a rare instance when he acknowledged out loud the societal barriers his students faced. When interviewed by a Cotulla newspaper reporter he put the best public face on the situation, saying that many students had forsaken the cotton fields for the classroom and that they showed much enthusiasm for learning.

Perpetually in motion, he organized declamation assemblies where students recited heroic American poems such as "O Captain, My Captain." He formed a band, a debate team, and athletic teams. He corralled parents and teachers into driving to competitions that he set up all over the county. Often this was the first time that team members had ever set foot in a "white" school. When they won, Coach Johnson bought them treats at the little store across from his school. He took some of the students down by the river, where they cut trees to festoon with Christmas decorations for the classrooms. He paid for playground equipment himself and requested more from the school board, along with books and other supplies. He also ordered the other teachers to help supervise recess games so that the children would stop scuffling in the dirt.[34]

The school board granted Johnson's request for additional playground equipment but drew the line against any further expenditures. They very nearly fired him when the other teachers went out on strike, protesting the playground duty. Many of the leading families saw him as a brash outsider, stirring things up. "He knew he was going to be president. What a ridiculous, silly thing!" John Wildenthal remembered people saying. After all, his aunt, Mary (Mamie) Wildenthal, had set up the first classes for Mexican children in the early 1900s. Now this loud rookie teacher—who became the principal because he was a man—was ordering his staff around and fraternizing with the Mexican families. Mamie Wildenthal and her colleagues threatened to resign, but board member Rebecca Knaggs surprised everyone by suggesting that they accept the resignations. The teachers stayed on, and so did Lyndon, "the brightest man we've ever had in Cotulla," Knaggs told her daughter.[35]

Even while he stood out as a tireless advocate on behalf of his students, Johnson acted for them, rather than with them. He enjoyed the authority his professional position commanded; he would help his students, but on his terms, drawing them into his world. Johnson showed little interest in their community or their individual hopes, fears, and dreams. He ignored the colonia events held in his own school. He loved to eat Mrs. González's tortillas but knew nothing about her tutoring sessions.

Moreover, Johnson had close ties to Anglo Cotullans. He loved his cousin Margaret Johnson Kimball almost like a sister and doted on her daughter, Margaret Ann, swooping her up from her sidewalk play to give her a big kiss. The ambition that drove Johnson to work on behalf of his children also impelled him to curry the favor of the old Cotulla families. He spent many an evening on the Knaggs's front porch, for instance, discussing national issues. For ranchers, if you weren't in ranching, you didn't count, but Johnson won many of them over. A woman who lived on a giant ranch south of town considered him the most handsome man she ever met. When she first saw him at a party in Nuevo Laredo, Lyndon was sitting at another table and she couldn't help staring at this dynamic, charming man with the intent dark eyes. Cotulla superintendent W. T. Donaho, who taught Johnson several extension courses, including Race Relations, called him "one of the very best men that I have ever had with me . . . more than willing to carry out the policies of the school regardless of personal opinion." For years Johnson refrained from speaking publicly about conditions in Cotulla and never did criticize any Cotullans.[36]

Like any ambitious person, Johnson curried the support of those in power. "But while he was a man of time and place, he felt the bitter paradox of both," Bill Moyers has written. What set Johnson apart, according to John Wildenthal, was that "he had the genius to see at an early age that . . . you've got to really be taking care of poor folks, or you are dead in politics." The discrimination and raw poverty that Johnson witnessed in Cotulla inspired the populist, the preacher, the teacher in him. "I think in the best of all worlds he would have liked to have taught in Cotulla for the rest of his life," mused Moyers, "but . . . he was ambitious. And yet he always had some yoke over that ambition."[37] Teaching in Cotulla reminded Johnson that ambition included public service, that strivers like himself must have a heart, that leaders needed to help other people help themselves. He wanted to demonstrate that education was the great equalizer, America the land of opportunity. "He felt that education was the greatest thing that he could give to the people," remembered Hubert Humphrey; "he just believed in it, just like some people believe in miracle cures." Johnson aide George Reedy characterized it as an "abnormal, superstitious respect for education."[38]

Championing the downtrodden might just enable Johnson to take hold of the ambition and compassion that threatened to tear him apart and instead forge these qualities into a vehicle for progress. According to Moyers, "he wanted to persuade and convert and befriend" as many people as he could.[39] Over the years Lyndon Johnson would maintain close ties with both his former students and the Cotulla leadership: to fashion a base of political support, to demonstrate that he could charm people who distrusted each other, and to satisfy his craving for love.

Lyndon Johnson with his class at the "Mexican" school in
Cotulla, Texas, 1928. [LBJL]

Principal Johnson with his Cotulla teaching staff.
Left to right: Elizabeth Woolls Johnson,
Twila Kerr, and Mary (Mamie) Wildenthal. [LBJL]

Conservative Democratic congressman Richard Kleberg of the
King Ranch dynasty inscribed this photograph for Lyndon Johnson,
"To my tried and loyal friend" (1933). [LBJL]

Liberal Democrat Maury Maverick, congressman and mayor of
San Antonio: "To the Honorable Lyndon Johnson who got
me started" (1935). [LBJL]

Emma Tenayuca leading a protest in front of the San Antonio city hall
during Maury Maverick's tenure as mayor. [Institute of Texan Cultures,
the *San Antonio Light* collection]

Mexican American workers on a National Youth
Administration (NYA) project in Johnson City. [LBJL]

Mexican Americans in a San Antonio sewing project
sponsored by the NYA. [LBJL]

Congressman Lyndon Johnson at the inauguration of the
Santa Rosa public housing complex, Austin. [LBJL]

Johnson campaigning for reelection among some of
his Mexican American constituents. [LBJL]

"Favorite visitors": Johnson's cousins Margaret Ann Kimball, left, and her mother, Margaret Johnson Kimball (both of Cotulla), with Lady Bird Johnson, center, and friend, Washington, D.C., January 1948. [LBJL]

Lady Bird Johnson (last of the people facing the camera) at the national convention of the League of United Latin American Citizens, Austin, June 1948. [LBJL]

Coke Stevenson, with cigar, at the hearings he requested concerning the Box 13 ballots in Alice, Texas. [LBJL]

Private Félix Longoria, killed in action in World War II, whose family accepted Senator Johnson's offer of burial with honors at Arlington, after their hometown funeral parlor refused them assistance. [Dr. Héctor P. García] *and Katheria*

Left: Héctor P. García, M.D., founder of the American GI Forum; *center and right*: two LULAC leaders, Professor George I. Sánchez of the University of Texas and attorney Gus García (mid-1950s). [Dr. Héctor P. García]

TWO

THE NEW DEAL

In December 1931 Lyndon Johnson received a telephone call that left him almost speechless with excitement. He adored politics and yearned to enter the Big Time. Now he had his chance: a newly elected congressman named Richard Kleberg had just asked the young schoolteacher to manage the Kleberg congressional office. "We had known the Johnson family for some years," said the congressman's brother. Sam Johnson had been an early supporter of Richard Kleberg, and Lyndon himself had campaigned effectively for the candidate, earning the respect of Kleberg's campaign manager, Roy Miller. Now, on a moment's notice, Johnson left Houston and headed to Washington.[1]

THE KING RANCH

With the Kleberg job Johnson entered two new worlds: Washington, D.C., and the King Ranch. More than any other institution in Texas, the Kleberg family's King Ranch epitomized the feudal *patrón* way of life. Congressman Kleberg, a charming man who spoke fluent Spanish, liked to ride the range with his *vaqueros*, the legendary *kineños*, who had resided there for generations, ever since the congressman's grandfather Richard King had talked an entire Mexican village into resettling on his ranch. The foreman of the King Ranch Las Norias Division, Ed Durham, even married the daughter of a *kineño*. At the same time, Durham's father had been a Texas Ranger, and such Anglo frontiersmen came to symbolize the true Texan, to the detriment of those who did not fit this image, notably women and, ironically, the original cowboys, the *vaqueros*. The story goes that the King Ranch deducted the poll tax from *vaquero* paychecks until the men had voted for the landowners' candidates, under the foreman's watchful eye.

The new congressman's cousin, Richard King, told researcher Paul Taylor, "They are not troublesome people unless they become Americanized. The Sheriff can make them do anything. . . . Educating Mexicans for citizenship is a mistake. . . . the Mexicans, like some whites, get some education and then they can't labor." As for their tenant farmers, King said, "We have oral contracts with our renters on halves but they have all been raised right here. They know what they have to do. They have to do what we tell them or get out." Congressman Kleberg considered his workers fortunate because they received six cents per pound of cotton and earned two dollars per day, rather than the two pesos per day often common in Mexico.

The King dynasty amassed millions of acres of land, a fiefdom larger than the state of Connecticut. Threats and financial pressures forced owners of the original Spanish land grants to sell for bargain prices, particularly in hard economic times. In a typical transaction, the King Ranch bought the Gutiérrez family's 17,872 acres for a mere $240 at an auction for back taxes. As early as 1859 Anglo Americans had acquired nearly all of the Spanish land grants in Nueces County.[2]

Mexicano resentment boiled over in 1915. Rebels called on blacks, Asians, and Indians as well as their fellow Mexicans to overthrow the "Yankee oppressor" and establish their own country, to be forged out of the southwestern states that the United States had won from Mexico in 1848. When sixty of the rebels—calling for "equality and justice"—raided King Ranch's Las Norias Division, a force of Texas Rangers swept through the area, killing 100–300 Texas Mexicans. The bloodshed inspired a *corrido*, or ballad, "Las Norias": "Those King Ranch Rangers say they're very brave; they make women cry, they make people flee. . . . We are going to give a hard time to those King Ranch Rangers."[3] Angry and afraid, Anglo Texans blamed the uprising on Mexican revolutionaries and German agents, particularly after Pancho Villa raided New Mexico in 1916 and when the following year a telegram attributed to the German ambassador in Mexico promised to return the southwestern United States to Mexico if the Mexican nation supported the German war effort. Meanwhile, in the less fertile counties that remained unattractive to agribusiness interests, the owners of the original Spanish grants managed to retain their land and their political positions by wheeling and dealing with politicians such as Sam Johnson and Richard Kleberg. State Representative

J. T. Canales and political boss Deodoro Guerra thus opposed the 1915 revolt and even organized forces to fight the rebels.[4]

In the 1920s segregation became entrenched in those parts of the King Ranch region that shifted to irrigated agriculture. Not able to emulate the Klebergs, who sent their children off to prep schools, Anglo newcomers established segregated institutions, much like those in Cotulla. A school superintendent in a Nueces County farm community said that the parents "would drop dead if you mentioned mixing Mexicans with whites. They would rather not have an education themselves than associate with these dirty Mexicans."[5]

Representative Canales and other reform-minded leaders, mostly middle-class males, organized against the growing segregation and xenophobia. Many were veterans of the Great War; as Corpus Christi leader Andrés De Luna explained, "when they came home they found that they were not served drinks, and were told that no Mexicans were allowed." Veterans formed organizations emphasizing education, citizenship, and equal rights. At the same time, according to De Luna, "The Mexican politicians here made propaganda against us. They were afraid they would lose and could not vote [their constituents] as a mass." In 1933 Canales would run as an independent candidate—in the face of death threats—against the Starr County Mexican political machine.[6] At Corpus Christi—the largest town in the King Ranch region—Canales, De Luna, and other representatives of reform organizations from all over South Texas met in 1929 and founded the League of United Latin American Citizens (LULAC). LULAC began establishing parent-teacher organizations, as in Cotulla in 1932, and started filing suit against school segregation.[7]

Kleberg's congressional district stretched from Corpus Christi on the Gulf Coast up through San Antonio and thus included many Texas-born Spanish-surname residents, but their political voice was muffled. Some counties in the district barred all non-Anglos from voting, while the rest restricted them to local positions. Although he knew about LULAC because it had been founded in Kleberg's district, Johnson worked mostly with those Tejanos who acted as intermediaries between the colonia and the county leadership. Wilson County district clerk José Ximenes, for example, was an honors business school graduate and thus had more formal education than the bankers, the sheriff, and most county leaders, such as John B. Connally Sr. One of Ximenes's forebears had served as Wilson County's sheriff for much of the 1890s. The Ximeneses were one of the "prominent families in

Floresville," in the words of John B. Connally Jr., but the status of the *rancheros* had declined with the influx of Anglos. Ximenes could not aspire to anything higher than district clerk because, in the words of his son Vicente, "we lived in a segregated community." Joe Ximenes warned his sons to avoid interracial incidents, to remain silent in the face of daily discrimination. In Floresville, as in Cotulla, few Mexican Americans reached high school; of the 200 in first grade, only five finished twelfth. At his high school graduation banquet, Vicente was seated with his four Hispanic schoolmates at an isolated corner table, so they walked out. Three of them boycotted the graduation. "We laid our caps and gowns on the steps of the superintendent's house and never went back. . . . You had to endure; at the same time you couldn't give up," the younger Ximenes said.[8]

If the segregation in much of Kleberg's district reminded Johnson of Cotulla, he made no mention of it; he was consumed with advancing his career. The King Ranch mightily impressed the young aide, and why not? It controlled much of Corpus Christi and the surrounding counties, with the attendant colleges, banks, railroads, harbors; the towns of Alice and Kingsville were the family's creations.[9] Johnson dreamed of some day presiding over his own large holding. When he was courting Claudia "Lady Bird" Taylor, Johnson took her on a tour of the vast spread and made a point of demonstrating his close relationship to the indomitable head of the dynasty, Alice Kleberg, or "Grandma," as Johnson insisted on calling her. Like Johnson's own mother, Lady Bird came from the southern plantation tradition. Her father, Thomas Jefferson Taylor, was the largest landholder in Harrison County, where he kept African American workers in debt peonage. Anglo Texans tended to see a willing subservience among rural workers of both minority races. Folklorist J. Frank Dobie wrote, "For his uncomplaining loyalty, . . . [the Mexican] is probably an equal to the 'befo de wah' darkey and as trustworthy." [10]

EMBRACING THE NEW DEAL

Johnson admired the ranch culture, but politics was his life, and Washington, his world. He loved cultivating political sponsors, notably powerful Texas Congressman Sam Rayburn. The young congressional secretary took advantage of Kleberg's preference for golf over politics and ran the office himself. Working twelve-hour days, Johnson pushed his staff to the limit, monitored legislation, wrote to constituents, and even answered the phone as "Dick Kleberg." He later said, "It was the best training you could get."[11]

The Great Depression hit the nation soon after Kleberg took office. Mexican-descent workers were among the first people fired as even menial jobs became attractive to the rising tide of unemployed Anglos. Many colonia residents turned in desperation to the relief rolls, only to be rejected by local public officials. As the only colonia organization restricting membership to U.S. citizens, LULAC emerged as the group best able to withstand the anti-Mexican feeling that reached a fever pitch during the Great Depression. LULAC officials testified before Congress in 1930 to protest the racism of many who called for a quota on Mexican immigrants. At the same time, Lulackers considered Mexican immigration a damper on wage scales and an impediment to LULAC's campaign to present Mexican Americans as respectable, loyal citizens capable of assimilating into the United States mainstream. Fearful of discrimination and reprisals, the organization supported some of the repatriation efforts of the Border Patrol.[12]

For his part, Congressman Kleberg had recruited Mexican workers in the 1920s but expressed no interest in protecting their rights. He only intervened on behalf of important Mexicans such as the grandson of the Mexican Secretary of State. Neither Kleberg nor his chief of staff Johnson had any incentive to learn about repatriation problems. Those people did not vote.[13]

Then in 1933 a new president boldly promised "a new deal" for the American people. Franklin Delano Roosevelt, a cagey, charming political broker, pledged government programs for constituencies at odds with one another: for business *and* labor, for cities *and* farms, for banks *and* the unemployed. Finally Lyndon Johnson had a president who combined ambition and compassion, who advanced his own political career by helping others. As Johnson worked to reconcile the populist goals of his father with his mother's emphasis on social status, he saw in Roosevelt a political model.

Johnson worked tirelessly for the New Deal legislation in the face of opposition from his own boss. Conservatives like Congressman Kleberg considered Franklin Roosevelt a traitor to the Jeffersonian ideal of states' rights. They hated big federal government, equating it with the Yankees who had invaded Dixie and, in the wake of total war, with a generation of Republican-sponsored black male suffrage. Kleberg had called Republican president Herbert Hoover's half-hearted effort to fight the Depression "Hamiltonian" activism. Roosevelt, however, was far worse, creating many more large programs administered by brand-new government agencies. Besides, conservatives loathed the tax increases and the deficit spending they feared would follow.

Undeterred, Johnson pressured his boss into supporting New Deal legislation. Still only in his twenties, with no power of his own, Lyndon Johnson pulled out all the stops. He threatened to quit. He tallied voting counts demonstrating that most of Kleberg's congressional colleagues favored the legislation. He produced stacks of constituent letters urging support of the president. He warned Kleberg that a "nay" vote would be useless, and obstructionist to boot. Worn down, the congressman approved a number of federal programs for his district. After all, how could he reject Camp Kleberg, a New Deal employment project named in his honor? [14]

Moreover, Johnson, like his hero Franklin Roosevelt, detected chinks in the states' rights armor. Traditional Southern Democrats by definition loathed the party of Lincoln. Also, they embraced any government activism that benefited them, as when Kleberg welcomed emergency relief for "major agricultural producers." The congressman came around to supporting a program he had labeled "socialistic," the Agricultural Adjustment Act (AAA), which ended up subsidizing large landowners and accelerating the expulsion of tenant farmers and sharecroppers. The AAA paid growers to reduce their cotton acreage, with the stipulation that the subsidy be split with their sharecroppers, but the landowners often reneged, particularly with Spanish-speaking residents, who often feared appealing to governmental authorities, in view of the mass deportations underway at the time. A landlord-tenant dispute in Johnson's home congressional district is a case in point. When one disgruntled sharecropper asked the Mexican Consulate to investigate, the grower—who also happened to be the local sheriff—stormed into the little dwelling, hit the man's daughter-in-law and fatally injured her child. Another Mexican sharecropper, residing on the 6,000-acre Martindale Ranch, consulted a lawyer, who assured him of his right to a portion of the AAA check but added that legally Martindale could evict anyone deemed a nuisance. Thus the AAA helped trigger the migration of agricultural laborers to the Midwest. [15]

At the same time, many Tejanos signed up for New Deal jobs programs, particularly the Civilian Conservation Corps (CCC). As the only program run by the army, it was immune to local discriminatory practices that plagued other employment programs. Young Mexican

American men seized the opportunity, a number rising to staff positions. Those in Kleberg's congressional district were particularly fortunate because it boasted more CCC camps than almost anyplace in the nation, thanks to Lyndon Johnson. Vicente Ximenes of Floresville became a CCC company clerk at Camp Kleberg. In a letter to Johnson, Camp Kleberg senior foreman James McQueen praised another CCCer, Alex Salinas, for his leadership skills. McQueen added, "I have 33 men and about 20 are Mexicans. I treat them all alike. . . . I honestly think I have the crack crew of any camp." [16]

"Mexican Americans adored Franklin Delano Roosevelt," said Ed Idar Jr., whose family was active in South Texas journalism and politics. In the colonias, many a mother framed a color newspaper portrait of President Roosevelt and hung it on the wall. LULAC joined the emerging New Deal coalition, comprised of urban ethnic groups, minority groups, labor, liberals, and unreconstructed white southerners. While officially nonpartisan, LULAC passed resolutions in support of New Deal bills, calling President Roosevelt "great." The *LULAC News* urged local councils to lobby for federal programs, from education to jobs to housing. LULAC "is not a political club," wrote a LULAC founder, "but as citizens . . . with our vote and our influence we shall endeavor to place in public office men who show by their deeds respect for our people." At the same time, the organization did not hesitate to criticize the New Deal, as when the Civil Works Administration refused to enroll striking sheep shearers in West Texas or when LULAC member Senator Dennis Chávez of New Mexico pushed unsuccessfully for the inclusion of farmworkers in the National Labor Relations and Social Security acts.[17]

Meanwhile, New Deal labor legislation helped spur the activities of Mexican American workers, notably in San Antonio, during a period when Johnson was actively campaigning there for the New Deal congressional candidate. Women in the San Antonio barrio conducted a number of job actions, as in 1934 when various local unions of pecan shellers struck. A New Deal agency negotiated a settlement, but only obtained fifteen cents per hour, so many workers joined the Union of United Cannery, Agricultural, Packing, and Allied Workers of America (UCAPAWA), an affiliate of the Congress of Industrial Organizations.[18] In the midst of this ferment, the San Antonio area got its own congressional district. Lyndon Johnson campaigned for gruff, nearsighted Maury Maverick, who charged into the political fray like a latter-day Teddy Roosevelt. Maverick championed freedom of expression, the right of workers to organize unions, and the delivery of New Deal programs. In particular he promised to help the Mexican West Side.[19]

Richard Kleberg graciously lent his chief of staff to the effort. Although Maverick was known as a liberal, even a radical, he, like Kleberg, hailed from a distinguished old Texas family, and the two men had long been on friendly terms. More important, their political fortunes coincided; in 1931 Maverick had supported Kleberg's congressional bid with the understanding that the Corpus Christi congressman would reciprocate when the new San Antonio district was created. Johnson worked untold hours for both men, and he loved every minute of it. More than Maverick or Kleberg or his own father, Johnson reveled in his ability to play the political game. In this respect he resembled no one so much as Roosevelt himself. By serving both the arch-conservative Kleberg and the radical Maverick, Johnson made a small contribution to the emerging New Deal coalition.

Johnson turned out to be a formidable campaigner, particularly on San Antonio's West Side, where he saw not a sea of brown faces, but rather distinct individuals: here, a boy who reminded him of a Cotulla student, there, a man with the leathery dignity of a *kineño*. The young congressional secretary "pressed the flesh" for Maury, soaking up love and making political contacts. One couldn't help noticing, however, a touch of paternalism on the part of this tall, pale Anglo imparting *abrazos* to one and all. Moreover, Johnson had no qualms about using traditional machine tactics, and Maverick, while courageously outspoken on social reform issues, was ready to fight political fire with fire. So Johnson sat in his bedroom in the Plaza Hotel giving colonia political operatives stacks of five dollar bills: one per vote, paying for the poll tax with a little bonus for each voter.

Maverick put in a good word for his young aide with the White House. Johnson also curried the favor of Texas Senator Tom Connally, House Speaker Sam Rayburn, and First Lady Eleanor Roosevelt. These efforts paid off in 1935 when the Roosevelt administration named Johnson the Texas director of the new National Youth Administration (NYA), which awarded scholarships and hired unemployed youths for federally funded public works projects.[20]

THE NYA

At twenty-seven years of age, Lyndon Johnson was the youngest NYA director in the country and arguably the one with the most energy. He worked ceaselessly and drove his staff, seeking ever more public works proposals and youth applications. Between Johnson's arrival in August 1935 and his departure in February 1937, the Texas NYA provided jobs for almost 30,000 youngsters and built a number of public works, reaching into every corner of the state. In the little Cotulla colonia, for example, workers refurbished the plaza in front of Welhausen school. National NYA director Aubrey Williams called the Texas NYA a model program, one of the best in the country.[21]

The Texas NYA did not keep a count of its Mexican-heritage recruits because, in the words of the agency's final report, "they were properly classified as 'white.'" Roosevelt ordered federal agencies to change the designation when Congressman Maverick told him that the "colored" label kept some of these loyal New Dealers from voting in the "white man's primary."[22] Despite the lack of accurate figures, the NYA estimated that the vast majority of youths hired in South Texas were of Mexican descent. The high rate of Mexican American participation in the NYA reflected their disproportionately high unemployment: 49.51 percent compared to 25 for white youth and 28.1 for black youth. The NYA stipulated that 90 percent of the workers be from impoverished backgrounds, which especially helped minority youth. For his part, Johnson had wanted the figure reduced to 75 percent, which, he argued, "would meet with hearty approval on the part of the general public."

Although many eligible Mexican Americans participated, many others knew next to nothing about government assistance programs. Colonia residents tended to view government officials as agents of deportation. Upwards of 300,000 people went back to Mexico in the 1930s, mostly Mexican citizens, but also some U.S. citizens caught up in the immigration sweep. The most familiar government agency was the Border Patrol. The NYA's sponsoring agency, the Works Progress Administration (WPA), reinforced this fear by eliminating aliens from eligibility, even longtime residents with American-born spouses and children. In San Antonio the WPA allocated 1,800 jobs for pecan shellers, but some 1,100 were disqualified for lack of citizenship papers.[23]

Most of the Mexican-heritage trainees in the NYA worked as common laborers. For example, in the first Texas project, a series of roadside parks, the state highway department supplied the trucks, materials, and supervisors; the NYA paid the laborers, mostly African and Mexican Americans. According to the NYA's final report, many of the trainees "went on to work permanently for the Texas Highway

Department." In San Antonio, 160 men repaired and built fountains, bridges, and bridle paths in Breckenridge Park, and 118 men worked on the city drainage system. A few learned skilled jobs, as in a Laredo metal shop program, or when Anglo and Tejano recruits repaired National Guard glider planes in Houston. A small number received college aid, including Joaquín González, who eventually became a physician. His brother Henry—later Johnson's ally as a congressman—was ineligible because the NYA gave only one scholarship per family.[24]

Mexicanas joined the NYA in large numbers. In Cotulla, Johnson's successor as the "Mexican" school principal, Mamie Wildenthal, used NYA funds to hire Manuela González as the first library aide, while in San Antonio the agency enabled young Mexican American women to work as high school secretaries. By the end of Johnson's tenure, almost as many females as males were signing on to the NYA, often providing the only income for large families crammed into shacks or tiny tenement apartments.

Nevertheless, the opportunities for *mexicanas* in the NYA compared unfavorably with those offered to their *mexicano* counterparts. Usually the only skilled training for women was in the clerical field, where emphasis on proficiency in English put Spanish-speakers at a disadvantage. The NYA did establish training camps for other occupations, but these residential facilities barred black women and hired Mexican American women in numbers far below their actual unemployment rate. Moreover, they often worked in inferior facilities. An NYA supervisor reported to national headquarters that the only sewing room that needed significant improvement was the one with mainly *mexicana* trainees. Local San Antonio officials refused to supply the center, which consequently lacked sewing machines and furniture, so the women brought their own chairs and sewing supplies. Lacking tables, they bent over their laps, sewing by hand in a dark room.[25]

Many had been laid off from pecan shelling, as in the case of Julia, Lucile, and Margarita Fraga, each with less than seven years of schooling. After the camp Julia was placed in a sewing room full time, the others part time. According to Rebecca Masterson, the director of a camp near San Antonio, her staff encouraged respect for all cultures by, for example, having the campers perform their favorite songs. As a result, "there certainly was a decided difference in the attitude of many of the girls. The two groups mixed without question and without a thought of race differences." Furthermore, the counselors encouraged discussion of "topics of current interest . . . the cause of the need for private charity enterprises and for state and national welfare agencies." The campers raised "some very interesting reflections . . . The need for better living conditions and for adequate health and safety protection in employment was a topic of never-ending interest." The report did not indicate whether any campers mentioned the pecan sheller unions that were conducting job actions in San Antonio at the time.[26]

Mexicanas, as women, were excluded from the CCC, where so many *mexicanos* got their first break. In contrast, the NYA operated through the local school system. "It was up to the superintendent to determine who needed it most," according to a Texas NYA staffer. Thus the same people who enforced the segregation selected the trainees. Consequently, Mexican Americans, male and female, often ended up at segregated sites.[27] Moreover, growers and local officials often convinced county agents and New Deal officials to cut off relief during harvest seasons, regardless of job availability, in order to create a surplus of laborers. Johnson complained to his bosses in Washington, "With another month of cotton-picking ahead of us, shall these children be barred from school until the county relief boards put their families back on relief?" Washington officials replied that these young people could be helped if there was enough money left but said nothing about the local policies over which the NYA had no control. Many of the same growers who blocked farm worker relief were, like Congressman Kleberg, themselves receiving subsidies from the Agricultural Adjustment Administration.[28]

Despite its shortcomings, the NYA position gave Johnson an opportunity to translate into action his concern for the plight of Mexican Americans. "For a Texan he had rather a broad tolerance for races, particularly the Spanish-Americans," observed Richard Brown, NYA deputy executive director, who speculated that teaching in Cotulla also contributed to a "closer relationship." Brown recalled that when an NYA staffer used an anti-Mexican epithet, Johnson cut him off, saying, "You can't use that term here." Waiting to speak at a luncheon in San Antonio, Johnson was buttonholed by a club member who said, "all these kids need to do is go out and hustle." Johnson retorted, "Right. Last week I saw a couple of your local kids hustling, a boy and a girl. They were hustling through a garbage can in an alley," an anecdote he also used when describing conditions in Cotulla.[29]

At the same time, Johnson did not hire Mexican or African American staff members. Rather, the NYA looked for Spanish-speaking Anglo supervisors who "know how to handle men, with particular reference to Mexican boys." The NYA operated through the local leaders, be they Anglos who enforced segregation or border Mexicans who worked to enroll as many local youths as possible but who never questioned agency policies.[30]

Johnson established an official administrative channel not for Mexican but for African Americans. Following the lead of the national NYA headquarters, he quietly formed a Negro Advisory Committee and placed fifteen of the NYA Freshman College Center programs in black colleges. One center provided "research into negro local history, folklore, education, and employment needs." Others, however, helped reinforce racial inequities, as in the case of the NYA center at Prairie View A&M College, which emphasized "domestic service training," thereby continuing the pattern of female college graduates working as servants. Such was the case of the Johnson family housekeeper, Zephyr Wright, a home economics graduate of Wiley College, in Lady Bird's home county. Johnson threatened to resign rather than appoint an African American to the NYA Advisory Board because, he said, "I would, in all probability, be run out of Texas." In fact, African Americans served on NYA advisory boards in several Deep South states, but the Texas director had no use for what he considered empty, controversial symbolism that could prove distracting and a threat to his reputation among white Texans. He reminded Negro leaders that there existed

the last 100 years in Texas . . . a definite system of customs which cannot be upset over night. So long as these customs are observed, there is peace and harmony between the races in Texas, but it is exceedingly difficult to step over a line so long established and to upset a custom so deeply rooted, by any act which would be shockingly against precedence.

Johnson considered the NYA not an engine of social reform but rather a jobs program to help the needy and a vehicle to further his career.[31]

Mexican Americans were more integrated into NYA programs, at least officially, in part because LULAC had successfully lobbied for them to be classified as "white" so that they could vote in the "white man's primary." Despite the Caucasian designation, few Mexican-heritage youth could avail themselves of NYA programs at the "white" colleges. At the same time, they had no colleges of their own that could sponsor separate NYA programs. Although the largest minority group in the state, comprising almost 12 percent of the Texas population, Mexican Americans had no place on the advisory boards, entities the national NYA director characterized as "crucial." Categorized officially as white but treated as racially inferior, they had no voice in administering the Texas NYA, which adhered to Johnson's emphasis on relief over social reform.

On the other hand, the national office, by opposing racial discrimination, opened up opportunities for Mexican Americans. For the first time some government agencies were helping, not rounding up, colonia residents. Many jumped on the New Deal bandwagon, particularly young people born in the United States, be they the children of immigrants, such as Cotulla's NYA librarian Manuela González, or CCCer Vicente Ximenes, whose family predated Johnson's in Texas. Thirty years later President Johnson would refer to this common bond, saying, "Mr. Ximenes and I are both graduates of the first antipoverty program in the 1930s. He was a member of the Civilian Conservation Corps and I was a member of the NYA."[32]

MEXICAN AMERICANS AND CONGRESSMAN JOHNSON

Lyndon Johnson and other young, dedicated New Dealers proffered young Mexican Americans a helping hand, but New Deal assisted Johnson even more. "The whole state [NYA] organization was really a Johnson organization," remembered one aide. Johnson also attracted loyal support from the thousands of youths he employed, the local political leaders who took credit for the projects, and the construction firms that profited from the government contracts. Ready to jump at the first political opportunity, Johnson was the first to declare his candidacy on the death of his local congressman in February 1937. Austin Democratic party insider Alvin Wirtz supported him and suggested that Johnson run on the slogan "100% New Dealer." Even though several of his opponents also supported Roosevelt, Johnson's sweeping claim put them on the defensive and spotlighted his own New Deal experience.[33]

The candidate, not yet thirty, kept up a torrid pace, recruiting campaign workers from every group and assiduously courting every possible voter. Reynaldo Garza, from an old South Texas political family, remembered a "tall, lanky" Johnson visiting his room in an Austin boarding house and enlisting his support. That same night the two circulated at a bazaar at Our Lady of Guadalupe Church in the East Austin barrio.[34] The campaign also recruited Vincent Valdes, an East Austin grocer and officer in the local LULAC council, but Johnson paid more attention to the traditional political bosses such as José Salazar, who, according to Johnson aide Sherman Birdwell, "controls 50 qualified Mexican votes" in Kyle.[35]

Johnson advisor Ed Clark remembered paying off political bosses in various ethnic communities with funds provided by the construction firm of Brown and Root. George Brown said of Johnson, "He was for the nigger, he was for labor, he was for the little boys, but by God . . . he was as practical as anyone." So were the Browns. Although they hated minorities, unions, and, in theory, federal programs, they financed Johnson's campaigns in return for lucrative New Deal construction projects. Johnson outspent his seven opponents and sought out voters that the others overlooked, trudging into rural hollows and barrio back alleys. The money and effort paid off. Although less experienced than some of his opponents, Johnson edged them all out by just a few hundred votes, the smallest margin of any congressman that year.[36]

Congressman Johnson drove himself and his staff at an even fiercer pace than in his NYA days. He read and signed each letter, including the few from Spanish-surname constituents.[37] He demanded that correspondence be answered the same day as received, and he pitted staff members against one another in productivity contests. "I've answered as many as eighty letters a night on the typewriter after the office was closed," said John B. Connally Jr., one of Johnson's top assistants.[38]

The new congressman unabashedly courted White House advisors, senior legislators, and innumerable secretaries: anybody who could get him in to see the boss. The president was even more impressive in person, with that warm, hearty voice and big grin; he motioned you in and chatted amiably with "my friend" as if he had all the time in the world, making you forget about the polio that confined him behind the presidential desk. The freshman congressman maneuvered to get Central Texas at the head of the line for government programs. According to New Deal braintruster Tommy Corcoran, Johnson obtained more funds for his district than any other congressman, including 135 miles of farm-to-market roads in Travis County alone. Through the Rural Electrification Administration the Hill Country stepped out of the dark ages. In his first two years in office over $70 million in public works projects came to the district through the Public Works Administration and the WPA alone.[39]

Johnson kept close tabs on NYA projects in his district and encouraged new proposals. In one sponsored by the Austin Public Schools and the Federación de Clubes Mexicanas y Latinamericanas, NYA workers converted an Austin "Mexican" school into the Latin American Community Center, which soon housed a number of other NYA programs, from sewing to hot lunches for NYA workers citywide to recreation for community residents to citizenship programs. One room also served as a weekly clinic and a number of colonia organizations used the center as their headquarters.[40]

The congressman did not hesitate to intervene when problems arose, as in his hometown of Johnson City, where local businessmen protested the hiring of a Mexican American crew. Many of the workers responded to the discrimination by walking off the job. Johnson City gas station owner Dan Rose wrote to the congressman, requesting that the trainees be removed. Johnson reminded Rose that every eligible Anglo had been hired and that many a town in the area would love to have the project. The gas station owner backed down, saying that he had only written to Johnson out of concern that "the disgruntled few . . . might get to talking to some of the boys who come from . . . out of town and they would make some kind of a move against the Mexicans." Now that NYA administrator Sherman Birdwell, an old Johnson City boy, had gotten the support of the Chamber of Commerce, however, "everything will work out nicely." Johnson replied, "Your letter . . . has eased my mind a lot."[41]

Meanwhile both grass-roots organizations such as LULAC and congressmen such as Johnson were lobbying for a public housing bill, which Congress finally passed in September 1937. In fact, Johnson submitted the very first application to the new U.S. Housing Authority: $714,000 for the city of Austin, to replace shacks with garden apartments. He told Mayor Tom Miller and other local leaders, "Now, look, I want us to be the first in the U.S. if you're willing to do this, and you've got to be willing to stand up for the Negroes and Mexicans." He pointed out that the construction would engender profits for local companies and jobs for residents, and he argued that the project would counter radicalism at a time when nearby San Antonio was experiencing a number of strikes, some led by communists. "This country won't have to worry about isms when it gives its people a decent, clean place to live and a job, they'll believe in the government," Johnson declared. At a public hearing in January 1938 all of the 340 people present endorsed the plan. In speeches and in a radio address entitled "Tarnish on the Violet Crown," the congressman spelled out the tragic housing conditions: "within five blocks, a hundred families, an old man with TB, dying, a child of eleven, all of them Mexicans." When a city councilman accused Johnson of exaggerating the situation and creating bad publicity for Austin, the congressman was ready: he named prominent Austin leaders who owned slum housing, including Johnson's own patron, Herman Brown, who kept quiet, knowing that Johnson was angling for a far more lucrative dam project for Brown and Root. (The congressman soon obtained the dam contract, the first of many large federal construction projects that would enrich the Browns.[42])

The U.S. Housing Authority announced that the first three sites would be New York City, New Orleans, and, yes, Austin, Texas. Upon completion of the Austin housing projects, the wire services flashed the news around Texas, complete with a photograph of Congressman Johnson at a Mexican apartment. The family had moved "from a residence where they all lived in one room, with a dirt-floor leanto. Their former rent . . . was almost identical." At the same time, the article considered it worth noting that these particular children were "all in clean clothing," alluding to the hygiene issue, which many municipalities used to justify segregation. The Johnson housing proposal created three segregated apartment projects: one for "Negroes," one for "Mexicans," and one for "Americans."[43]

Johnson was a man of action, impatient with theoretical talk about social issues, particularly controversial ones such as race. He knew full well that Austin segregated African Americans completely and Mexican Americans in part. The Austin cemetery maintained three separate paupers fields. Some restaurants refused service to Mexican-heritage people, who also could not find work near the University. Texas Senator Tom Connally advised Johnson to avoid the political risk of any action that could be construed as supporting racial equality, not that the young congressman needed reminding. Johnson voted against all civil rights bills, taking a cue from the president, who ducked the issue in fear of retribution from powerful southern congressional leaders, particularly from Texas.

Lyndon Johnson was not about to join forces with Maury Maverick, the lone southerner supporting antilynching legislation. Johnson wanted to avoid ending up the butt of a racist pamphlet, such as the one Herman Brown passed on to him alleging that "a whispered conference was held between white Congressman Maverick and black Congressman Mitchell and out of the blending of these two colors came the revival of the Red supported [antilynching] proposal" even though, according to Maverick's biographer, "he did not believe in social equality for the Negro." Johnson voted against the abolition of the poll tax because, he said, "we haven't got the votes." He told black Texans, "I must vote this way, but I'm for you and I will get what I can for you" in the way of New Deal programs, but that "timing is important." He echoed the sentiments of the president himself, who said, "Politics is the art of the possible. . . . at the present time, passage of a law abolishing the poll tax is impossible. . . . I believe you should never undertake anything unless you have at least a 50-50 chance of winning." LULAC did not lobby Johnson on the issue. Reluctant to risk losing the government classification of "white," Lulackers instead mobilized pay-the-poll tax drives. Johnson made a point of getting acquainted with LULAC leaders, but quietly and unofficially, keeping his distance from this group that championed desegregation. When the Austin LULAC council received a flag that had flown over the Capitol dome it came not from Johnson but from Maury Maverick.[44]

Johnson also avoided labor issues. In a rare speech entitled "Sit-Down Strikers," he did not even state his opinion of the tactic. Rather, he vaguely criticized that old populist nemesis, the Wall Street/eastern business establishment. Out of loyalty to the New Deal coalition he voted for labor's agenda, which mattered little to his mainly rural constituents. A 1938 union poll found Johnson "correct" on all of his voting, a better record than that of his liberal friend Maury Maverick. This was the high point of Congressman Johnson's pro-labor record, however; in the following years he increasingly voted against organized labor as the issue became more contentious and as he looked to statewide office.[45]

THE MAVERICK EXAMPLE

Maury Maverick's political demise would serve as an object lesson to the young, ambitious Johnson. "Just remember our old friend Maury Maverick isn't here any more," Lyndon said when he refused to support some liberal social legislation, "Maury got too far ahead of his people, and I'm not going to do that."[46]

The San Antonio congressman lost his seat in 1938 despite a number of advantages. 1936 "Congressman of the Year" for political pundit Drew Pearson, Maverick had a family name emblematic of Texas history. Also, the San Antonio incumbent was more popular than ever among Mexican Americans, for the first time handily outpolling the entrenched political machine on the West Side, where he accused the city health department of playing political favorites at the cost of lives.

A number of LULAC members worked for Maverick, the one leader who treated them as New Deal allies and fellow war veterans, talking to them in English without a trace of Kleberg-style paternalism. LULAC's bylaws forbade political endorsements, so attorney Alonso Perales formed the League of Loyal Americans, which actively worked for candidates such as Maverick.

At the same time, a number of LULAC leaders supported the machine candidate, Paul Kilday. Married to a *mexicana* and not from the landed elite, he was the trustworthy local leader. Meanwhile, despite Maverick's unsurpassed voting record in favor of New Deal legislation, he could not count on White House support to counter the machine. No doubt Lyndon Johnson took note that Roosevelt did not visit San Antonio when he came to Texas to try and unseat Kleberg.[47] Maverick had become too controversial. The local press, Catholic hierarchy, and Chamber of Commerce were vilifying the congressman, blaming him for the labor and radical activity on the West Side. Maverick's opponents pointed to his cooperation with organizations that included some communist members, such as El Congreso de los Pueblos de Habla Española, a new congress of Spanish-speaking people. The Congreso, which called for equal rights and democratic social reform, was brought to San Antonio by Luisa Moreno, one of a number of radical women organizing in the San Antonio barrios. In 1938 she traveled around the country drumming up Congreso support from Cubans, Puerto Ricans, and Mexican Americans, and from sympathetic Anglos such as Maverick, for a national convention.[48]

A number of other *mexicanas* worked for the CIO and for the Communist Party, the only major political party that recruited them. Emma Tenayuca Brooks, whose family had long resided in San Antonio, founded the communist-backed Workers' Alliance. With some 3,800 dues-paying members, it staged sit-down strikes and demonstrations, demanding more relief and New Deal jobs projects. Manuela Solís Sager left the Lower Rio Grande Valley, where she and her husband had been organizing farm worker unions, and came to work in San Antonio for the UCAPAWA and in leftist politics.[49]

Maury Maverick was getting much of his campaign financing from the CIO at a time when pecan shellers were staging a major strike. In fact, while Paul Kilday was challenging Maverick's congressional seat, his brother, Police Chief Owen Kilday, and Mayor C. K. Quin were opposing the strikers. Picketers were harassed, with over 1,000 arrested for "blocking the sidewalk," "disturbing the peace," and "congregating in unlawful assemblies." For her fearless, charismatic leadership, Tenayuca earned the name "La Pasionaria," after Dolores Ibarruri, a communist leader of the Loyalists in the civil war then raging in Spain. Authorities used tear gas seven times in the first two weeks, but a local judge refused the union's request for a restraining injunction. Chief Kilday declared that the walkout was organized by outside communist agitators, so UCAPAWA president Donald Henderson removed Tenayuca and other leftists from leadership posts.[50]

Perales's League of Loyal Americans voted to support the strike, but only if Tenayuca and the Workers' Alliance were purged. The largest *mutualista* organization, Sociedad de la Unión, on the other hand, allowed the UCAPAWA to use its hall, and a group of colonia grocers donated supplies. Less eager than LULAC to shed their Mexican identity, *mutualista* members found little reason to worry about their reputation with the Texas Democratic Party. Governor James Allred finally persuaded union and management leaders to negotiate, and on March 8, 1938, the strike ended. The settlement disappointed many workers; wages only rose by two cents for every hundred pounds shelled, while the Southern Pecan Company earned $500,000 that year.[51]

The agreement was overshadowed by the Wages and Hours Act, which went into effect in late 1938 and set a minimum wage of 25 cents per hour. LULAC had lobbied for the act and Johnson voted for it, in part because Maury Maverick told him that pecan shellers earned about $1.29 per week. Johnson said of the bill's opponents,

> They said it was socialism, statism, communism, would wreck my political career, and would wreck the unions. They said it was government interference and it was. It interfered with that fellow that was running that pecan shelling plant. It told him he couldn't pay that little widow seven cents [per hundred pounds] any more.

Undaunted, pecan processors responded by drastically cutting back the work force through mechanization.[52]

The pecan sheller strike figured prominently in Maverick's run for mayor of San Antonio later that same year. He called Mayor C. K. Quin the "enemy of Latin-Americans." Cesar Compa of the CIO worked for Maverick, as did pecan shellers, who walked the West Side streets distributing Maverick literature. Perales and other liberal

Lulackers also stumped for the scrappy challenger. Not to be outdone, Quin marshaled the more conservative LULAC leaders such as James Tafolla Jr., who organized a rally at which Quin took credit for millions of dollars of federal housing money for the West Side. The mayor said Maverick was not to be trusted. With the Catholic Church leading the crusade against godless communism from Spain to San Antonio, Quin's Catholicism helped him among his Mexican coreligionists. Overall, however, economic issues mattered more to them; Maverick won most of their votes. He also picked up some support among white laborers, but the majority of Anglos voted against him, splitting their ballots between Quin and Leroy Jeffers, a conservative who entered the race as an anticorruption candidate after Mayor Quin was indicted for misusing city funds.

Maverick won, but with only a plurality of the vote. "The election, consequently, was an anti-Quin vote by the Anglo community, but a pro-Maverick vote by many in the Mexican community," historian Richard García has written. The new mayor quickly fulfilled his campaign promises. City police no longer arrested strikers en masse or shooed into paddy wagons the old *mexicanas* who peddled tamales. He persuaded the Census Bureau to change the Mexican classification from "colored" to "white." The NYA awarded the city of San Antonio $100,000 for the wholesale restoration of the old Mexican quarter, La Villita. Complete with a museum, a library, and a cultural center, it showcased, in Maverick's words, "The heritage of early Texas. Likewise . . . of 90,000 Spanish-Mexican-Americans, many of whose ancestors have lived here over 200 years" and who were "justly entitled" to "prestige and dignity." [53]

In August 1939, while the Villita proposal was winding its way through the federal bureaucracy, Emma Tenayuca applied to rent the municipal auditorium for a Communist Party rally. Fully aware of the political risk, Maverick allowed the assembly in the interest of free speech. The meeting came to order in front of a large poster of Stalin, only to be interrupted by a mob, which, "ignoring tear gas and streams of water, smashed almost every window in the auditorium and ripped up the seats," in the words of Johnson biographer Ronnie Dugger. Maverick's opponents, calling him an agent of communist subversion, launched a full-scale campaign to remove him from office. In a letter Maverick wrote to President Roosevelt about La Villita, the scrappy mayor added a postscript, "Don't worry about my troubles. . . . It is not as bad as the war and besides I will win."

Years later, Lyndon Johnson recounted his father advising Maverick that he should allow Tenayuca's meeting and should personally escort her to the stage. "I think it'll beat you, but I think you ought to do it," Johnson quoted his father as saying, but Sam Johnson had died two years before the meeting took place. Lyndon had his father say what he himself could not.[54]

Maverick narrowly beat back the recall challenge, only to be indicted on charges of having paid West Side poll taxes with union funds. Johnson knew that his friend was guilty, but at least Maury did it with panache. In the words of a Johnson aide, Maverick converted the money into silver dollars, "puts them in a sack and marches down the middle of Broadway to a storefront, and sets up a table and the Mexicans line up." At the same time, Johnson, with his NYA background, fully appreciated the Maverick administration's pathbreaking accomplishments such as La Villita. Besides, the poll tax did in fact disenfranchise poor minority people. Maverick's main critics, moreover, supported the indicted former mayor, whose political operation, in the words of a contemporary study "not only pays the poll taxes to its henchmen who vote 5–15 times in each election, but goes so far as to have the tally sheet made up the night before the election."

Maverick's prosecutors played upon the use of *union* money for the *Mexican* vote, much as Anglos in nearby farm areas harped on the "tainted Mexican vote" to disenfranchise the nonwhite majority there. Famed defense attorney Everett Looney—who also was an advisor to Johnson—met the challenge head on. Looney eloquently recounted the famous, heroic Maverick family deeds of yore. Turning the Americanism issue on its head, he looked the jury members in the eye and said with a voice full of emotion, "We're in the shadow of the Alamo." For years New Yorkers had been coming down, taking San Antonio money back to Manhattan, and now, finally, a true-blue Texan brings New York money to San Antone. "Does he use it to build a swimming pool? . . . No! He uses it so poor people can pay their poll taxes. Are you going to send Maury Maverick to jail for *that*?" They acquitted him unanimously.[55]

The rivalry between Maverick and Quin reflected the division in the national Democratic Party. Quin considered the New Deal a radical threat. For years the Quins had been close allies of their fellow South Texan, Vice President John Nance Garner, who in 1940 challenged Roosevelt's run for an unprecedented third term. At first Garner had cooperated with the New Deal, following Sam Rayburn's maxim "You have to get along to go along," but "Cactus Jack" was virulently anti-union. Rumor had it that he paid his Mexican pecan pickers ten cents an hour, saying, "They are not troublesome people unless they become Americanized. The sheriff can make them do anything." Garner became infuriated when Roosevelt refused to condemn strikers. In 1939 CIO president John L. Lewis called Garner a "labor-baiting, poker-playing, whiskey-drinking, evil old man." The Texas congressional delegation drafted a resolution condemning the statement as slanderous. Only Johnson, hedging his political bets, refused to sign it, endorsing a revised version that simply called Lewis' attack unwarranted and unjustified.[56]

Johnson joined the Texas Third Term Committee for Roosevelt, along with Maverick and Austin mayor Tom Miller, but the Texas Democratic Committee and a majority of Texas Democratic leaders supported Garner, as did many local Democratic officeholders. Johnson's cousin Margaret wrote to him that Cotulla officials "would endorse Garner and would instruct the delegates to vote that way," although in the Cotulla delegation "the general sentiment was for the third term."[57]

Roosevelt and his new running-mate, Henry Wallace, won the nomination and the election, but the conservative wing of the Democratic Party, in partnership with the Republicans, blocked most of the remaining New Deal legislation. Meanwhile Garner, the Browns, and others with financial interests in cotton, railroads, ranching, utilities—and, in particular, the growing oil industry—successfully pushed for antiunion legislation in the Texas legislature.

In 1941 former Mayor Quin defeated Maverick with a united Anglo vote. Maury Maverick's political career was over. He wrote to NYA director Aubrey Williams, "I do not weep. The truth is, I have done my best, and San Antonio got its best administration. I was trying to see if decent, local democracy would work—it looks like it didn't." Maverick requested that Williams appoint him to "make a study of the economic and social background of Latin-Americans coming into the NYA." The project never materialized; instead Maverick became an assistant to another friend, federal price administrator Leon Henderson.[58]

By this time Johnson was running for the Senate. Roosevelt wrote to Maverick's son that, just as with Mayor Maverick, "The same thing is true about Lyndon Johnson. I hope he will win, but even if he does not the things for which he stands will eventually win. He will tell you that." Johnson might very well mouth those sentiments to Maverick partisans, but in actuality he had learned a very different lesson. Busy soliciting the victorious Quin's unofficial support, Johnson had learned that he would have to finesse the labor issue and master the netherworld of South Texas politics if he ever hoped to win a Senate seat in Texas.[59]

THREE

THE "LAST HURRAH" FOR BOSS POLITICS

In the 1941 Texas Senate race Lyndon Johnson again ran as an underdog. Together with his campaign manager John Connally and longtime political advisors such as Austin attorney Alvin Wirtz, Johnson mapped out his campaign strategy. He would spend lavishly publicizing his New Deal credentials and the faults of his opponents, and would target minority voters, both Mexican and African American. Prior to Johnson's opening campaign rally in San Marcos, his staff sent a Spanish-speaking aide into the local colonias. A large crowd greeted the congressman, who spoke in positive generalities about the New Deal and called for increased military production, now that Hitler's forces had engulfed continental Europe and seemed poised to conquer Great Britain.[1]

THE "MEXICAN VOTE"

One region where Johnson did hold something of an advantage was South Texas. None of the other main candidates had longtime ties there, while he first learned about the region's politics at his daddy's knee. In the state legislature Sam Johnson had allied himself with Archie Parr, legendary boss of Duval County (in Congressman Kleberg's district), and Lyndon's mentor Alvin Wirtz had assisted Parr in an unsuccessful 1928 congressional race that reportedly included voter fraud.

Later, while stumping for his boss Richard Kleberg, Lyndon saw firsthand the loyalty of laborers for the *patrón* who, regardless of his ethnic background, rejected segregation, classified Texas Mexicans as "American" or "white" on census forms, appointed them to most of the county positions, and gave them financial assistance. Moreover, Anglo *patrones* absorbed the traditional Mexican culture of the region, sometimes marrying into the old *mexicano* elite. Referring to the leaders of the Laredo machine, one Johnson aide said, "I assumed that they were Mexican. I was startled to discover that they were Lebanese!" Or as a Laredoan put it, "The Anglos that came adapted rather than the other way around. They nominally were in charge, but *la raza* was running the show."

Johnson was well aware that the ranching counties contrasted sharply with those counties dominated by irrigated farming. When agribusiness took hold, most Anglos treated Mexican-heritage residents as transient workers of an alien race and barred them from voting, as in the Winter Garden area, where he got to know the local political leaders while teaching in Cotulla. As David Montejano has written about the new grower elite, "Every practice and norm that helped keep the old timers in power was seen as illegal or corrupt . . . speaking Spanish at the polls and having Texas-Mexican election judges . . . and political rallies were outlawed." Archie Parr's son George explained the split among Anglo leaders this way:

> I pick the man and the people here vote for them. They trust me. . . . Look out there in that bank . . . see any Anglos? The Mexicans run the bank. . . . These people vote with me because I've been their friend all my life. My father was their friend. I spoke Spanish before I could speak English. I sit in their homes and talk with the old ones. My wife is Mexican. I live with these people, work with them, play with them. When they need a friend they come to me. I help them get born and I help them get buried. I'm not like my churchified Baptist enemies . . . they're too good to go to a Latin American home. Well I'm not too good.

According to Mexican American Ed Idar Jr., whose family had lived in the region for generations, George Parr "was more Mexican than me, spoke better Spanish than I did. Sure, they stole a lot of money, but they helped a lot of people." A friend of Idar's started a grocery store with a loan from Parr. Duval County resident Ernesto González remembered his mother receiving money for medical prescriptions from a Parr lieutenant, O. P. Carrillo, whose father had known Johnson's father. "I am told they used to hunt together," said the younger Carrillo, who first met Johnson in the 1940s at a Duval County celebration. Carrillo recalled, "He gave me a whole bunch of tickets, and said, 'go buy some beer for your friends.' Actually I was too young to drink!"

On the other hand, only loyal voters could hope to work in city government, on county construction projects, or in the school system. Idar's father took part in an unsuccessful attempt to oust the Laredo bosses, and the younger Idar thought of himself as "a refugee; they controlled everything." In the 1940s Idar witnessed voting fraud, as in the "chain ballot." The first voter would be given a marked ballot, copy the choices onto a blank one, deposit one copy in the ballot box, and hand the other to the next person in line. Ernesto González recalled, "O. P. Carrillo . . . would come to my house . . . and he would ask my mother and father . . . right there to vote for the George Parr machine . . . every time there was an election they would come down; we didn't have to go to vote." Writer James W. Kunetka has observed, "Like Boss Tweed of Tammany Hall and James Michael Curley of Boston, Parr was a savior to some and a bandit to others."[2]

No region in Texas more consistently reported returns of over 90 percent for one candidate. The bosses "wanted to be with the winner; they were not interested in statewide issues or social improvements," said Idar. "We would constantly hear that . . . you got the jobs . . . if you were involved in politics," remembered Ernesto González. One of his uncles was related to O. P. Carrillo, who arranged for the uncle to receive a government check, with the understanding that the local machine would pocket half of it. Meanwhile in the 1940s the Gonzálezes, despite generations of residence in Duval County, still worked as sharecroppers without benefit of modern machinery on a ranch owned by a *mexicano patrón*. For his part George Parr paid his laborers, who lived in shacks, $16 per week while he bought a 57,000-acre ranch with $500,000 of Duval County funds. His construction company had a stranglehold on county projects, controlled two banks, and assiduously bought up county oil holdings. As Johnson biographer Ronnie Dugger has written, "the first requirement of the *patrón*, giving the people small handouts, was the continuation of their relentless poverty." Moreover, Mexican-heritage residents fared worse under Anglo rule than under *mexicanos*. In those ranch counties run by *mexicanos*, Spanish-surnamed residents retained more land titles and attained higher literacy rates than in any of the counties administered by Anglos, whether paternalistic or not.[3]

One *mexicano* boss, Horace Guerra, wrote to Johnson, "Starr County will give you a substantial majority," meaning over 90 percent of the total. The 1941 Johnson campaign manager, John Connally, recalled,

> [Johnson] formed lasting relationships with people like Manuel Bravo in Zapata County . . . the Guerra boys in Starr County . . . Johnson well understood [as] I did . . . the importance of the Hispanics in South Texas and how important [it was] to develop who the leadership was, because we'd seen it develop all our political lives. . . We were constantly keeping abreast of political changes in all these counties.[4]

Connally sent speakers out to a number of Mexican holiday celebrations, and he channeled campaign funds to local politicos, as when Manuel Vela brought a contingent from Laredo to a Johnson rally in San Antonio. Johnson urged Judge Manuel B. Bravo—the political chief of Zapata County and a Roosevelt Democrat—to "contact your friends all over the State and tell them of your interest in this race. Time is very short and I must count on folks like you very heavily. Your kindness and cooperation will never be forgotten." With the election fast approaching the Johnson staff wrote to Bravo, "Let's redouble our efforts. . . . There wouldn't be any question of the results. If you will continue working as you have, Lyndon Johnson will be your next Senator. . . . he will never forget what you have done. . . . Keep in touch with me and let me know your suggestions." The very next day, little more than a week before the vote, Johnson sent Bravo yet another booster letter, writing, "Please know that I shall be forever grateful to you for all that you are doing for me."[5]

Not all of these supporters were political bosses. Judge J. T. Canales supported the campaign out of admiration for his friend the late Sam Johnson, reminding Lyndon to "follow in the straight and narrow path that your Father set before you." Canales proved particularly helpful because his friends included not only traditional Democratic party operatives—such as a relative who ran the Johnson campaign in part of the Parrs' fiefdom—but also Canales's fellow reformers in LULAC. He promised to "do my best to . . . line up the Latin American vote in this section of the state for you." The Johnson campaign reached out to LULAC leaders such as Jake Rodríguez, who wrote that he was planning to set up a Johnson campaign display and needed $500 for "one of the best locations . . . to create the best possible impression in the minds of our Latin American leaders." Other civic-minded citizens supported Johnson, including women such as

María Villegas of Austin, who wrote to her friends and acquaintances, urging them to work for him, "one of Mr. Roosevelt's boys." John Connally was well aware of this motivation, saying, "The Hispanics were basically for Roosevelt."[6]

At the same time, the other New Deal candidate, Gerald Mann, was currying Mexican American support. Earnest, handsome, and just two years older than Johnson, Mann had first gained fame on the college gridiron. Then, after working his way through Harvard Law School, Mann earned a statewide reputation as a diligent defender of consumers while state attorney general. Judge Canales warned Johnson, "I found out about an effort that is being made by a man in Laredo to switch the Latin American vote to Gerald C. Mann," and Mann himself recalled, "In our organization we dealt some with the Latin Americans." San Antonian Rubén Munguía remembered that many young people who admired Maury Maverick looked askance at Johnson. "We were more partial to any opponent" of Johnson's because of his ties to the "oppressive" King Ranch regime and to bosses such as George Parr, "people that our group of *mexicanos* were not in favor of because we were against the *cacique* rule."

Attorney General Mann had ruled that an antistrike bill was "unenforceable and unconstitutional" at the same time that the antilabor firm of Brown and Root was bankrolling Johnson. The 1941 Johnson campaign would spend an unheard-of amount: upwards of one million dollars. George Brown described the thirty-two-year-old as a "dynamo . . . his whole ambition was to get on the next ladder up." Indeed, Johnson used his personal connections with the Roosevelt administration to raise questions about Mann's New Deal loyalty. Although one of the two front-runners statewide, the young attorney general lacked Johnson's South Texas connections. When Mann solicited the support of Canales, the Brownsville judge replied,

> The Hon. Lyndon B. Johnson is the son of the late Sam E. Johnson, who represented his District in the 36th Legislature in 1919, when I made my fight to clean up the Texas Rangers from being used as political agents. It nearly cost my life to do so, but for the loyal support and help that I received from the late Johnson I would have never succeeded and possibly would have lost my life. Now Lyndon B. Johnson is his son, and I would feel it an ungrateful act on my part if I could not, at least, cast my vote in behalf of the son of such a loyal and dear friend.[7]

The other main candidate, Martin Dies of East Texas, had gained fame as the chairman of the House Un-American Activities Committee, where everyone from child star Shirley Temple to Renaissance playwright Christopher Marlowe came under his scrutiny as possible subversive influences. The investigations tapped the undercurrent that confused jingoism with patriotism and feared foreigners and social change, but Dies's lackluster style and inept campaign structure blunted his effectiveness.

Then suddenly Governor W. Lee "Pappy" O'Daniel entered the race, upsetting the political landscape. A flour producer with a popular radio program, "Pass-the-biscuits Pappy" had entertained his way into the hearts of Texas voters through his country music radio program. As governor he failed to deliver on promised state pensions and he allowed the government to drift, but he remained popular, a beloved uncle seemingly above the political fray. Behind the scenes, however, he mobilized on his behalf Democratic leaders such as the former speaker of the House, Lieutenant Governor Coke Stevenson. Johnson used his war chest to counter O'Daniel with brassy rallies featuring stars such as Kate Smith and relegated his own pedestrian speechmaking to short, patriotic paeans.[8]

O'Daniel hurt his chances with Mexican-Texans when he donated a $250 reward for the capture of murder suspect Emilio Benavides. One Texas Ranger who helped in the eventual arrest commented, "We didn't have no damned search warrant." During the Senate campaign Benavides—still denying his guilt—awaited execution, which came three months later, despite protest from the U.S. State Department.

With O'Daniel and Dies both to his political right, Johnson went on record as "unalterably opposed to socialized medicine" and promised, in a nod to supporters such as independent oilman Sid Richardson, that "I shall see that our present [oil] depletion allowances are preserved." While the Senate contest raged, Mayor Maury Maverick was fighting furiously for his political life. Johnson took pains to obscure his own prolabor voting record, declaring that "Strikes must cease!" now that war seemed imminent. He lauded "the FBI as it ferrets out sabotage experts, traitors, and spies." The agency was busy investigating all sorts of groups, including LULAC. A 1940 report characterized the LULAC president of the time, Dr. George I. Sánchez, as "loyal . . . but rabid on the subject of the Mexican minority in Texas" because of his pioneering work documenting racial segregation in the public schools. Johnson literature fed this atmosphere, asserting that "fifth columnists, foreign agents, communists, fascists, proponents of every other ism but Americanism, must be wiped out, not just ridiculed and publicized." Johnson even stooped to question-ing Mann's German-sounding name.[9]

Throughout South Texas Johnson racked up overwhelming mar-gins. Duval County, which had voted 95 percent for O'Daniel for gov-ernor in 1940 gave Johnson that same margin in 1941. Opponents charged that Johnson had used federal funds for "gravy train poli-tics," that, for example, the Brownsville area's lopsided "Mexican vote was silent and bought." A Johnson operations man concurred. San Antonio Postmaster Dan Quill complained, "You had to pay their poll taxes. And then on election day some guy might come along and give them $5 and they'd vote the other way." Quill estimated he needed $10,000 for the West Side precincts alone. Johnson did receive 90 percent of those votes, but only about one-third of the eligible West Siders voted, which in the end contributed to Johnson's narrow defeat overall.[10]

What seemed like Latin passivity to San Antonio political profes-sionals was not that simple. After all, just three years earlier Mexican American voters had turned out enthusiastically in far larger numbers to elect Maury Maverick and to oust the Kilday machine, despite the bribes it offered and even though rumor had it that Owen Kilday placed fifty pistols at the West Side polls at election time as a reminder for people to vote correctly. This strong-arm tactic may have back-fired, and Kilday had alienated many on the West Side by opposing re-form groups such as La Liga de Defensa Escolar/School Improvement League, a coalition of more than fifty barrio organizations.[11]

Moreover, political manipulation also took place in Anglo East Texas, where O'Daniel allies outmaneuvered Johnson. The governor's supporters reported their East Texas votes only as preliminary totals. After the South Texas returns had been announced, Johnson's oppo-nents switched to the O'Daniel column some of the East Texas votes provisionally counted for Dies. Johnson played the gracious loser and did not contest the election. When his brother Sam asked if he wanted an investigation, Lyndon is purported to have replied, "Hell, no, I hope they don't investigate me!"[12]

ON THE HOME FRONT

A few months later the United States entered World War II. Johnson fulfilled a campaign pledge by enlisting in the Navy the day after Pearl Harbor, but he only flew as an observer on one bombing mission. For that trip a politically astute Douglas MacArthur awarded him the silver star. In July 1942 President Roosevelt called back to Washington all members of congress on active duty. Some resigned in order to enlist, a proposition Johnson never seriously considered; despite his campaign rhetoric, he had no intention of forsaking the political life he loved. For their part, Mexican Americans responded wholeheartedly to the country's call. "This war seems to have touched everyone," remarked a Mexican American physician; 373,000 to 500,000 served in the war, including many resident aliens.[13]

LULAC supported military conscription but complained of Mexican American exclusion from draft boards. In Cotulla, for example, the draft board included one of Johnson's distant relatives but no Mexican Americans, although they constituted the vast majority of those conscripted. John Wildenthal, the Cotulla draft board clerk and later a Johnson aide, said that initially most Mexican American draftees were exempt because of their physical condition, "mostly correctable deficiencies." In the end, however, a number of Johnson's former students served, including Dan García, who joined along with two of his brothers. García marched across North Africa as a technician in the 760th Tank Battalion.[14]

Mexican-heritage GIs fought with uncommon valor, earning seventeen Congressional Medals, the most of any ethnic group. By the war's end Mexican-heritage soldiers had sustained disproportionate casualties, comprising over one-quarter of those on the Bataan "Death March," for example. LULAC leader Alonso S. Perales pointedly questioned the War Department as to why 50–75 percent of all South Texas casualties were Tejanos, while they comprised 500,000 of Texas's 6,000,000 population. Perales wrote, "we want to ascertain for sure whether . . . there are not sufficient soldiers of other extractions in South Texas . . . or whether it is because some individuals who are prejudiced against the Mexican people are rushing our boys to the battle fronts in order that they may be the first to get killed and get rid of them that way." Disgusted that the rampant discrimination even extended to soldiers in uniform, Perales sent the Roosevelt administration a list of offending Texas towns. Among others, he cited the McClellan hotel in Johnson's Hill Country, where the management told Mexican American servicemen that they could only eat in the kitchen, while in Cotulla, Mexican Americans who died in the war were buried in the segregated "Mexican" section of the town cemetery.[15]

At the Houston shipyards another LULAC leader, John Herrera, protested against what he called "rampant" discrimination by employers. These included Johnson's main financial supporters, the Brown and Root Construction Company. Johnson tipped them off to lucrative military projects, such as the Houston shipyards, where they landed a contract despite no experience in shipbuilding. Brown and Root also built a number of oil pipelines; they and other pipeline companies routinely excluded Mexican Americans from employment. Moreover, Congressman Johnson refused to support the Fair Employment Practices Commission (FEPC), charged with combating racial discrimination in military production. He knew full well the FEPC was anathema to Anglo Texans in general and the Brown and Root owners in particular.[16]

Washington observers considered Congressman Johnson an ingratiating gladhander with a gift for legislative maneuvering who assiduously avoided making speeches, particularly on controversial issues. Nevertheless Johnson solidified his liberal reputation by siding with the New Dealers when the conservative Texas Regulars wanted the Democrats to oppose the 1944 Supreme Court decision overturning the white-only primary. Johnson got hooted off the stage at the state convention when he called for dialogue between the factions. He, in turn, characterized the Regulars as "all dissidents and die-hards, the Roosevelt haters and the corporation lawyers, and those organizations trying to raise in Texas the ghost of intolerance." After visiting wounded veterans he was moved to tell the members of the Texas House of Representatives, "I want to substitute for free enterprise *equal opportunity*. Every man who has gone through a living Hell for you and for me, and comes out with scars on his body and his soul to show for it, shall have an equal opportunity to get a job when this is over."[17]

In April 1945 Americans received the shocking news that the president who had shepherded them through twelve years of depression and war had died. A teary, shaken Congressman Johnson exclaimed to a *New York Times* reporter, "God! God! How he could take it for us all!" Johnson remembered Roosevelt "like a daddy," a sentiment echoed by people far from the corridors of power. For the first time millions of Mexican Americans loved a president. "I really felt like I had lost somebody in my own family," Ed Idar recalled. When he shipped out to the Pacific, the flag flew at half mast for a month, a mournful sight that the young man would never forget. In San Antonio the Comité Mexicano de Acción Cívica y Cultural erected a Roosevelt bust "to the memory of Franklin D. Roosevelt, 'The Good Neighbor' and in Honor of those who, like him, died for freedom."[18]

A PIECE OF THE PIE

World War I veterans such as Alonso Perales well remembered being treated as foreigners by many hostile Anglo Americans, who regarded Mexican-heritage people as a temporary labor force to use or with whom they competed. Would this new generation of veterans face the same barriers? [19] Not if the returning servicemen could help it. With white supremacy discredited by Nazi atrocities, the "GI Generation" was particularly well qualified to challenge what LULAC called "Wounds for which There is No Purple Heart." Oswaldo Ramírez swore, "if ever the combatants of this war are cheated of the things for which they risked their lives . . . I shall take the stump loud and strong and shall not cease in my condemnation of such fraud." He had survived the Normandy invasion, "a veritable hell. Sniper bullets, machine-gun fire, mortar and artillery shells, and personnel mines, took their toll of victims. I saw many of my close friends—officers and men—get shot right through the head." [20]

In Cotulla veteran Dan García helped establish a LULAC chapter, which led a protest when the high school principal refused to accept diplomas from graduates of the "Mexican" elementary school where Johnson had taught García nearly twenty years earlier. Three Congressional Medal of Honor winners in San Antonio joined LULAC, and in 1946 the Houston LULAC council organized a defense committee for Congressional Medal of Honor winner Macario García after he was arrested for assault when he angrily protested denial of a cup of coffee at a cafe in a nearby county. The following year Lulacker John Herrera cried "foul" when the all-Anglo Houston police department established a unit specifically assigned to investigate barrio incidents. As the first Mexican American candidate from Houston ever to run for the state legislature, he pointed out that the first Houston battle casualty and the only Houston Congressional Medal of Honor winner both had Spanish surnames. LULAC chapters undertook extensive drives to get barrio residents to pay their poll taxes and in San Antonio an African American and a Mexican American, attorney Gus García, won seats on the school board through the organizing efforts of local community groups.

Veterans prided themselves on their political independence. As one put it, "Latin American veterans who were prepared by Uncle Sam to be on their own are figuring to be on their own when the time comes to vote in any election." Another, in his new McAllen newspaper, *El Mundo*, declared, "It is time that our Latin American element, as the

Anglo-Saxons are accustomed to calling us, make use of their rights as citizens. . . . Let us vote as our conscience dictates, then, and not as our friends, who are paid by the political machine, tell us." Rubén Munguía reflected, "We came back in 1945, '46 no longer awed by the father images in most Mexican American families, somewhat away from the Church . . . with new skills, new viewpoints."

Building on the organizing efforts of its predecessors, the "GI Generation" branched out, allying with a new generation of Anglos that was beginning to ask some of the same questions, as when a GI named Humphreys defended his decision to violate a restrictive real estate covenant. "I believe that a GI of Latin-American descent has the same rights as any other American. . . I am convinced I am doing what is right in selling to Puente and I don't intend to back down," he testified. While the Puente case was in process, the Supreme Court struck down restrictive covenants. (One of Puente's legal advisors was Henry B. González, later a congressman and Johnson ally.[21])

At the 1946 Texas Democratic convention, ex-serviceman Jim Wright, a new state legislator, noted to fellow liberal Kathleen Voight the absence of black and brown delegates. "We're going to change that in Texas" he said, and she agreed, "Yes, we are!" Bob Eckhardt, Field Representative for the Inter-American Affairs Committee of the State Department, worked in tandem with Mexican American activists such as fellow student Cristóbal Aldrete. While Eckhardt investigated discrimination in the Austin area, Aldrete founded a new Mexican American student organization, the Alba Club. "To me the GI Bill was the dawn of a new era for those of us poor kids whose parents couldn't afford to send us to school," Aldrete recalled. Alba Club members worked to break down the isolation of Spanish-speaking students at the University of Texas and demanded equal rights there. One of the club's charter members, Duval County operative O. P. Carrillo, was the first Mexican American to join a social fraternity. Alba Club members soon branched out. Under the sponsorship of Dr. George Sánchez they documented the segregation of Mexican American schoolchildren, on behalf of a LULAC-sponsored lawsuit. They targeted a number of school officials, including those in Cotulla and some in Johnson's congressional district.[22]

The winds of change were in the air and Congressman Johnson meant to use them to his advantage. In 1948 O'Daniel was stepping down from his senate seat and Johnson yet again took on a front-runner, in this case the popular former governor, Coke Stevenson, who soon led in the polls by more than 25 percent. If elected, Stevenson most likely would stay for years. This was Johnson's last chance. He needed every vote that he could get, and Mexican-heritage residents comprised nearly 20 percent of the state's population.[23]

Although he sought every possible vote that the traditional border bosses could deliver, it was the young activists who would recruit the new voters so crucial to a Johnson victory. Moreover, Johnson and the veterans shared a common vision: that Texas become more integrated into the national society and that the Texas Democratic Party shed its states' rights heritage and embrace national legislation, from federal rent control to aid to education to public housing to an increase in the minimum wage and in military spending. At the same time they did not ask who would pay, much less seek redistribution of wealth or oppose the anti-Communist crusade. Combat experience predisposed GIs to support the commander in chief's foreign policy. Like Johnson, they considered World War II an object lesson in the failure of appeasement. Most veterans agreed with Johnson that "we'd rather see the Communists stopped at the Mediterranean than to have to stop them at the Gulf of Mexico."[24]

The Johnson campaign benefited from the strong support Mexican Americans gave to President Truman. Roosevelt's heir and the first president ever to establish a civil rights commission, Truman also endeared himself to Mexican Americans in 1947 by laying a wreath at the Mexico City monument to the young cadets who had died defending Chapultepec Castle against the United States in 1847. On his Texas campaign swing some 25,000 people—many of Mexican heritage—cheered the president in El Paso, as did upwards of 200,000 San Antonians. On the long train ride through the Brush Country, small knots of people dotted the way, so Truman told his daughter Margaret to wave from one side and he'd wave from the other. The president told San Antonian Kathleen Voight, "I knew when I got to Texas I was going to win."[25]

Few others did. Truman lacked FDR's handsome visage and warm, mellow radio voice. Conservatism was on the rise, particularly in Texas, where oil and gas money subsidized GOP advertisements, such as the full page ad in the October 1946 *LULAC News*: "Haven't You Had Enough? Enough of the OPA [Office of Price Administration], graft, shortages caused by dreamy-eyed experiments with our national economy."[26] The growing anti–New Deal wing of the Democratic Party leaned toward Truman's conservative challenger, segregationist Dixiecrat Strom Thurmond, and supported the Senate candidacy of Coke Stevenson. Named for Governor Richard Coke, who had helped restore conservative white rule to Texas after the Civil War, former Governor Stevenson venerated the principal of states' rights and represented the farming and ranching elites that had dominated state politics since Reconstruction.[27]

While urging his supporters to register every possible pro-Truman voter, Johnson opened his campaign with a speech designed to woo conservative Democratic votes and funds that he also considered crucial. He criticized labor and decried Truman's civil rights agenda as

> a farce and a sham—an effort to set up a police state in the guise of liberty. . . . It is the province of the state to run its own elections. I am opposed to the anti-lynching bill because the federal government has no business enacting a law against one form of murder than another. I am against the FEPC because if a man can tell you whom you must hire, he can tell you whom you cannot employ.

Johnson attacked the proposals in Austin, Sherman, Waco, Texarkana, San Antonio, and Fort Worth, receiving enthusiastic responses everywhere.[28]

At the same time the candidate quietly curried Mexican American support. He obtained the endorsement of Senate candidate Frank Cortez, who garnered some 14,000 votes in the initial 1948 primary, then gave speeches for Johnson in the runoff. Students Johnson had taught in Cotulla also stumped for him. "People in Laredo were for LBJ because of the Cotulla connection. People from Cotulla came down here to work . . . [they] loved LBJ," remembered Pete Tijerina. He and others in Laredo went "through the barrios, house to house," face to face. At the LULAC national convention picnic in Austin, Lady Bird Johnson was the guest of honor.[29]

Most of the new campaign volunteers, however, were recruited not as ethnics per se, but as *veterans*. This minimized the risk of Anglo backlash and appealed to the young men's pride in their military service. At the same time, it reinforced the prevailing ethos of party politics as an all-male club. For their part, Mexican-heritage veterans wagered that Johnson, like Roosevelt before him, would continue to support social programs and that there was always the chance that Johnson's civil rights position might shift, as Truman's had, if the political climate changed. As Ed Idar put it, "Johnson, as a state politician, could not afford to antagonize these [conservative] elements."

From Del Rio in West Texas to Corpus Christi on the Gulf Coast,

GIs jumped on the Johnson bandwagon. Cris Aldrete, native of Del Rio, had spent most of the war decoding Japanese messages. His easy-going personality belied a fervent organizer. Home for the summer from the university, Aldrete canvassed more than twenty counties for Johnson, speaking of him "as someone who could really help us and that this man went beyond the provincialism of our Texas politicians. He was not prejudiced. He was a man alien to these practices." Through his sister, who ran a grocery store, Aldrete made contact with other grocers. He looked up relatives and acquaintances from Del Rio to Abilene, encouraging them to "get active in the community" for the Johnson campaign. He found a "ready-made welcome" for Johnson among migrant farm laborers and those ranch hands who remained from stock-raising days. They all viewed Coke Stevenson as "anathema . . . for what he did and where he stood. He was for Jim Crow" and against government programs except "wool and mohair incentives . . . weed eradication, anything that will help the rancher, but nothing for the urban, nothing for the minorities, nothing for the poor. . . . The status quo was already breaking up but . . . he was behind the times."[30]

Another Johnson recruit, Raymund Telles, knew firsthand the opportunities that activist government provided. Thanks to a WPA job he was able to finish business school during the Depression, then became a cost accountant at a federal prison. Drafted as a private, he worked his way up to major. Raymund Telles's brother Richard and their father both were active in El Paso barrio politics. Together with many of the *veteranos*, "we started feeling the pressure of social justice; we wanted a little cut of the pie," in Richard's words. They convinced Raymund to run for county clerk. He was the perfect candidate: handsome, articulate, quiet, dignified, and a highly decorated veteran. Richard mobilized everyone from veterans to women's groups to cantina owners, commenting, "When it came down to strategy and all that, very few people knew how to handle South and East El Paso." In the words of a campaign colleague, Richard was a "Mexican Lyndon Johnson—master politician." At the same time the candidate himself waged a nonethnic campaign stressing reform. Raymund Telles recalled,

I was in contact with [Johnson] quite often during the campaign . . . the excitement generated by my own campaign—the first time that a person of Mexican descent had even dared—and I'm using that literally . . . to run for any major office in the county . . . generated a very high interest . . . we had a larger number of Mexican Americans registered . . . in that year than we had in the history of El Paso.

The overwhelming Mexican American vote, coupled with African American votes and Anglo defections, spelled victory for Telles and votes for Johnson.[31]

Meanwhile in Corpus Christi another former major was recuperating from a serious kidney ailment. Dr. Héctor García had not been sick one day during the war, but after months of serving as the only physician in an emergency room, he had been laid low. By nature a man of action, his mind raced as he stewed over the mistreatment of returning servicemen. The Naval hospital refused to admit veterans except in emergencies, and patients often were segregated by race. In bed, listening to the Spanish radio, he heard school superintendents quoted, defending the segregation of Mexican-descent schoolchildren in the face of the LULAC lawsuit. Like some of his fellow *veteranos,* such as Ed Idar, he had married a European woman. Is this the America to which he had brought her home, where they would raise their children? For LULAC he had investigated "horrible" conditions at a Mathis, Texas, labor camp, but now he vowed to do more. "I had no money, I had no political clout; I had only my ability as a doctor," he recalled years later. Nevertheless García promised himself that when he recovered, he would mobilize his fellow veterans and that they would devote their lives to their people.

Proud, confident, with an air of serious commitment, Dr. García threw himself into seeing patients, calling organizers, receiving visitors. He focused intently on individuals, quickly learning each one's name, looking each in the eye. His frenetic, charismatic style was balanced by an ability to attract younger, more methodical people such as Cris Aldrete and Ed Idar. Unlike Lulackers, they did not have to emphasize their knowledge of English and their professional status in order to prove their U.S. citizenship to skeptical Anglos. No matter how poor or how dark-skinned, a veteran had the best possible U.S. pedigree. "We were Americans, not 'spics' or 'greasers,'" García recalled, "because when you fight for your country in a World War, against an alien philosophy, fascism, you are an American and proud to be in America." His American GI Forum proved to be an effective combination of Mexican community roots and U.S. identity; by the end of 1948 the GI Forum had chapters throughout South Texas, except in machine-dominated counties such as Duval.[32]

At the same time, "The men couldn't go out and do anything by themselves; they needed the family; they needed the women to help," recalled the founder's sister, Cleotilde García, M.D., who added, "And everybody got into it. Everybody was interested in jobs and schooling." While Héctor García crossed the state on Forum business, his sister singlehandedly ran both of their medical practices.

> People earned forty cents an hour: no Medicare, no Medicaid, no welfare, no Social Security. I would take care of his patients and my patients, well, I tell you, I got so sick on my feet I couldn't walk. . . . I wore high heels because I didn't want . . . [it] said, 'She looks like a man.' . . . But I enjoyed working; people had confidence in me.[33]

The GI Forum, like LULAC, was officially nonpartisan, but the newer organization encouraged individual members to participate in the political process to an unprecedented degree. Early on García established important political contacts, notably Congressman John Lyle; they had fought together in Italy. Through Lyle, García volunteered for the Johnson campaign "because I'm a child of the Depression," said García, who viewed Johnson as the New Deal candidate. Lyle introduced his friend to other politicians, such as district attorney (and future Congressman) John Young. García set up medical practice next door to Young in the Texas Building.[34]

Forum civil rights lobbying efforts introduced rank-and-file members to the political process, as when the vice president of the Robstown GI Forum chapter asked for Johnson's assistance in getting Spanish-surname people on the local draft board, adding that "Since our Beloved the late F.D.R. gave you his blessing, I have been for you and have campaigned for you." To liberals of every stripe Johnson was, in the words of activist Kathleen Voight, "the more liberal of the two, so of course we all went for him. . . . Racial and labor issues were not important. What was important was: were you loyal to Franklin Roosevelt or a Dixiecrat?"[35]

On the other hand, many Mexican-heritage Texans felt alienated from party politics altogether. When *mutualista* organizations faded from the scene during the repatriation of the 1930s, most former members gravitated toward community organizations such as the Liga Pro-Defensa Escolar in San Antonio. For their part, Mexican Americans who had been active in the Congreso de los Pueblos de Habla Española or the CIO considered Johnson part of the problem, supporting policies that they feared would accelerate the economic integration of the Southwest into a modern industrial America dominated by large corporations at the expense of laborers. Although to the left of Stevenson, Johnson had voted in favor of the 1947 Taft-Hartley bill, which curtailed many of the methods organizers had used to recruit industrial and farm workers, and his main financial supporter, the Brown and Root Construction Company, was known for having successfully lobbied the state legislature for a spate of antiunion laws.[36]

Moreover, Johnson was conducting an anti- "Red" offensive, determined to avoid the "soft-on-Communism" slur. *The Johnson Journal* warned that "the big Northern labor unions, with their leadership which includes admitted Communists . . . have aligned their forces against Lyndon Johnson and in favor of Coke Stevenson. . . . Wake up Texans! Don't let the Reds slip up on you by any such cunning plotting!"[37] At this time the Federal Bureau of Investigation (FBI) was investigating the new Asociación Nacional México-Americana (ANMA) and declared that it was controlled by the Communist Party. In 1948 longtime activists, many of them from the CIO, many of them women, had established ANMA, calling for "first-class citizenship" for Americans of all racial backgrounds. Some ANMA members belonged to the Communist Party, most of them having joined in the 1930s, when it was one of the few groups to espouse racial, gender, and economic equality and had adopted a reformist Popular Front strategy.

Isabel González, the ANMA president, also headed "Amigos de Wallace," which supported the Progressive Party presidential candidate, former Vice President Henry Wallace. (Fully one-third of the Wallace delegates were women.) He supported farm labor strikes, calling agribusiness leaders "absentee landlords, land speculators and oil kings," and criticized Truman's foreign policy, which Wallace considered excessively anticommunist.[38] Dr. Ernesto Galarza of the Pan American Union echoed these sentiments in 1948 congressional testimony before the House Foreign Affairs Committee, where he complained that South American dictators were breaking up legitimate parades and demonstrations with the help of weapons purchased with U.S. foreign aid. When his policy recommendations went unheeded, Galarza left Washington for his native California to become research director of the new National Farm Labor Union, the precursor of César Chávez's United Farm Workers.[39]

The mainstream press vilified Henry Wallace as radical and "soft" on Communism because of support he received from groups such as

ANMA. No ANMA members were ever indicted for illegal or "subversive" acts, but a number were deported.[40] One did not have to be a *mexicana* leftist, however, to be accused of subversion. When Governor Beauford Jester fired the head of the Texas Good Neighbor Commission, Pauline Kibbe, for reporting too critically on farm labor conditions, he warned that "Communists and those of Mrs. Kibbe's ilk are factors in the disturbance of conditions." Without the protective veteran coloration, civilians were fair game.[41]

"LANDSLIDE LYNDON"

It seemed to be politics as usual in other ways. Both Johnson and Stevenson tolerated the practice of excluding Mexican American voters altogether in a number of counties, such as Cotulla's, while in the ranch counties near the border the election results turned in large part on "bloc votes."[42] As in 1941, most South Texas politicians supported Johnson. Bexar County clerk James Knight described to biographer Ronnie Dugger the machine at work in 1948 for Johnson in the key city of San Antonio.

> The only time I ever took money from Lyndon Johnson was the day of the runoff. I took $1,000 and I got those in $1 bills because he, Lyndon Johnson, wanted to go around the polls. . . . Oh, when you got there, why there's people standing around . . . they haven't had lunch. . . . You happen to inadvertently put your hand in your pocket and give them a couple of dollars and move on, you understand. . . . If the candidate personally gives the money, it has to be more. . . . Don't misunderstand me, it's not a payoff or anything, because they've been standing there all day, drumming up votes, putting up posters. $5 for expenses or something like that. It was costing them that much money by the time they ate and bought two or three soda waters around the polls.

Kathleen Voight, although a staunch reformer, made a similar argument: that Johnson people simply paid local residents one dollar to pay the poll tax or as wages for their work handing out information.

As political scientists Dale Baum and James L. Hailey have written, "Paying poll taxes for poorer citizens, treating voters to food and drinks, and making promises should not be clumped indiscriminately with other acts such as ballot stuffing, miscounting, intimidation, and violence." They discount the role of voter fraud in the result, noting that Johnson forces campaigned vigorously for the lion's share of the votes from erstwhile candidates such as Frank Cortez, whose 3,891 supporters probably constituted the majority of Johnson's 5,114 additional San Antonio votes. Stevenson did not make any appearances in San Antonio during the runoff campaign and failed to mobilize his core supporters. Meanwhile Johnson, who vastly outspent him, was helicoptered all over the state.[43]

The Parr machine of Duval County does deserve some of the notoriety it has received for its effect on the outcome. Duval operative O. P. Carrillo carried messages between Johnson headquarters in Austin and George Parr in Duval County while also organizing for Johnson at the University of Texas. Johnson's own Jim Wells County manager—after pointing out that Stevenson people "were stealing votes in East Texas"—acknowledged that some pro-Johnson "skullduggery" took place, that Luis Salas, a Parr henchman, "added a bunch of names and votes" to the totals out of Box [precinct] 13, in the county seat of Alice. Years later a neighbor who lived in one of the pleasant bungalows across from the polling place remembered seeing numerous cars on election night, including one with George Parr, and many police vehicles, with some of the police officers shooing Coke Stevenson supporters away from the voting entrance. This witness voted for Johnson because he thought the congressman would win, then went across town to the Alibi Club for a beer, where folks kidded him, saying, "Boy, it's wild over on the South Side!"[44]

Remembering the delayed voting returns of 1941, Johnson's chief of staff John Connally said, "We've got this damn thing won if they don't steal it from us. And the only way to keep them from stealing it . . . is to make sure they don't know how many votes we've got." Connally spent the evening on the telephone calling supporters across the state, including the Parr people, asking, "What is your vote? Can you hold it? Don't turn it loose until I call you." He sent telegrams to supporters, including one to Zapata County leader Judge Manuel Bravo:

> The man who is going to win tomorrow is going to be the man who has the best friends. I don't believe any man ever had better friends than you are. I hope you will give me tomorrow and work as hard and fast as you can and as you know I will for you when I am senator. Please watch the polls after 7:00 p.m. and get

us a wire or telephone call telling us when we have taken the lead in your county.

In both the Johnson and Stevenson camps, county leaders began sending in revised totals that favored their candidate. The day after the election Johnson telegraphed Judge Bravo, "The race is so close that an honest error in tabulation could easily make the difference. Please check the returns now . . . please wire results of returns to me in Austin." Zapata County sent in a lopsided return of 669–71 in favor of Johnson, who wrote back, "It's too early to say whether we have won or lost this election, but win or lose, I'll always be grateful from the bottom of my heart for the good people of Zapata County." Two days after the runoff election, on Tuesday, August 31, the Election Bureau declared Coke Stevenson the winner by 349 votes, with 40 left to count. Johnson refused to concede and on Thursday maintained that he had won. On Friday Jim Wells officials met in Alice and announced a new official total: 965 to 62 instead of 765 to 60. In later years Parr operative Luis Salas named the people he added to the Johnson column, writing in his memoirs, "that night . . . a President was made."[45]

Stevenson said he was robbed. He sent some college students to Duval County to investigate, including Pete Tijerina of Laredo, who had been recruited by Coke Stevenson's Webb County chairman there. (Tijerina and his friends, although Johnson supporters, were chronically short of money, so the ten dollars a day plus expenses sounded good.) They interviewed a Duval County woman whose poll tax was stamped "voted."

"Did you go and vote?"

"No, the commissioner picked up my poll tax. He always votes for me."

The local notary that they had brought along refused to certify her statement, saying, "No, no, no, I'm not going to get involved in this!" and proceeded to walk back to the county seat alone, despite the sweltering heat of a mid-August afternoon in treeless South Texas. Tijerina remembered that "when we were driving back . . . we were confronted by two or three police cars." The officers said that they had heard that the students were carrying weapons. "Oh, no, sir," Tijerina replied, and he remembered years later, "I was asked to get out of the car, spread eagle, and was frisked." The policemen told him, "We want you out of Duval County by sunset." So Tijerina and his friends got their pay and headed back to Laredo.

Meanwhile in neighboring Jim Wells County the Democratic Party officials refused to show Stevenson's lawyers the ballots, so the former governor decided to investigate in person. He was accompanied by the legendary Texas Ranger Frank Hamer. For many Texans Hamer symbolized the famous Rangers of yore, gallant gunslingers in defense of freedom. This Ranger was renowned for having ended riots in the Lower Rio Grande Valley early in the century; twice he had been left for dead. He had killed fifty-three men in his time, including Bonnie and Clyde, which had earned him a Congressional citation. At the same time, Hamer had worked diligently to break up strikes in the 1930s. Moreover, for many Mexican Americans, Rangers such as Hamer symbolized storm troopers more than heroes. As Stevenson and Hamer walked to the bank in Alice they epitomized an older Texas that was cherished by most Texans but best forgotten by those of Mexican heritage. The two men ordered bank official Tom Donald to open the vault and show them the Box 13 ballots. Sure enough, the last 201 names on the list, 200 of them for Johnson, were in a new ink, all in the same handwriting, and all in alphabetical order. Stevenson's men got busy tracking down as many of these people as they could. All of those interviewed said that they had not voted. Three were deceased.[46]

Stevenson filed suit before Judge T. Whitfield Davidson, who issued an injunction on September 25 removing Johnson's name from the November 3 ballot for the general election. The judge also ordered investigators sent to South Texas. Evidence was hard to track down. In Zapata County, for example, Judge Bravo told them that one of the ballot boxes had been lost. Meanwhile, Johnson (and perhaps Parr) conferred with President Truman on his campaign train in San Antonio. After a series of court skirmishes Johnson supporters appealed to liberal Supreme Court Justice Hugo Black, who was senior justice for Texas. He overturned Judge Davidson's decision and blocked an investigation by the state legislature. A U.S. Senate subcommittee looked into the charges, only to discover that a janitor had illegally burned the Box 13 ballots. The subcommittee certified Johnson's primary victory; the Democratic-controlled Congress wanted to end the issue well before November. Truman Democrats had overwhelmingly supported Johnson and now they obtained his narrow victory at the state convention.[47]

The Senate campaign had disgusted the Texas electorate. Democrats always prevailed in Texas Senate races, so Johnson won the general election easily, but with fewer votes than a controversial Truman.

As a result of the scandal the new senator acquired the sobriquet "Landslide Lyndon." Over the years Johnson poked fun at his reputation by telling this joke:

> Little Manuel was crying and another Mexican came up and asked, "What's the matter?"
>
> "My father was here last Saturday and he didn't come to see me."
>
> "But your father has been dead ten years, Manuel."
>
> Manuel sobbed louder. "That is true. But he was here last Saturday, and he voted for Lyndon Johnson, and he did not even come to see me." [48]

Actually, however, this victory was the *patrón*'s "Last Hurrah." Duval County boss George Parr spent the rest of his life in and out of prison. The federal jobs and housing programs that Truman Democrats such as Johnson and the GI Forum championed undercut the old patronage system. Meanwhile, the farm counties that had enforced segregation lost ground as businesses from the North expanded in Texas cities. Johnson kept apace of the changes, hiring Ed Cázares as the first Mexican-heritage person ever to serve as an aide to a Texas Senator. More important, early in 1949 the new freshman senator and the new American GI Forum both would make their first national headlines over the emerging issue of the era: civil rights. [49]

FOUR

THE POLITICS OF PROGRESS

Soon after Senator Lyndon John-
son took office, his political acumen was put to the test in a discrimination case that captured national attention. Félix Longoria had been
killed by the Japanese while on a volunteer mission in the Philippines
and his wife had planned to have him buried in his home town of
Three Rivers, but the manager of the sole funeral home refused her the
use of their facilities.[1] Her sister, Sara Moreno, president of the American GI Forum girls' division, decided to take action. On January 10,
1949, Moreno consulted Dr. García, who in turn called the funeral
director, T. W. Kennedy. In a notarized statement García recalled
Kennedy saying,

> "Well, you see, it's this way—this is a small town and . . . I
> have to do what the white people want. The white people just
> don't like it."
> "Yes, but Mr. Kennedy, this man is a veteran, I mean, a
> soldier who was killed in action . . . Doesn't that make [a]
> difference?"
> "No. . . . You know how the Latin people get drunk and lay
> around all the time. The last time the Latin Americans used the
> home they had fights and got drunk. I—we have not let them
> use it and I don't intend to start now."[2]

While the Longorias fruitlessly tried to reach an agreement, García
called the *Corpus Christi Caller-Times* and fired off seventeen telegrams to members of the media and top elected officials, decrying the

action as a "direct contradiction of the same principles for which this American soldier made the supreme sacrifice." The next day newspapers around the country featured the incident, including an article on the front page of the *New York Times*. Walter Winchell told his vast radio audience, "The state of Texas, which looms so large on the map, looks mighty small tonight." [3]

Johnson called his old friend Robert Jackson, publisher of the *Corpus Christi Caller-Times*, who confirmed the story, adding that the GI Forum was holding protest meetings all over South Texas. Clearly, this was becoming a major issue, calling for more than the standard answer that a private funeral home was outside of senatorial jurisdiction or a pro-forma promise to study the facts. Besides, according to his top assistant, John Connally, the senator considered the decision "an outrage" and wanted to "right a wrong." Here lay an opportunity to use his sympathy for Mexican Americans as a vehicle for both their advancement and his own, as he had done when teaching at the Mexican school and in administrating the Texas NYA. If Johnson played his cards right, he could solidify his support in the well-organized veteran community and among the growing group of Mexican American voters. This would reinforce his reputation as a moderate Democrat, a prerequisite for any southerner aspiring to national leadership.

Johnson knew Three Rivers, which had been in Congressman Kleberg's district. Also, the town resembled Cotulla in its wholesale segregation practices and reawakened in him the shock he felt at the oppression suffered by the Mexican majority. At the same time, he remembered the self-satisfied attitudes of his friends and relatives among Cotulla's Anglo minority. The new senator realized full well that Anglo Texans gave Mexican Texans the highest negative rating of all racial groups even though most Anglo Texans would take offense at any suggestion that systematic discrimination existed in their state. The Three Rivers funeral director denied discriminating; he maintained that Moreno and her inlaws had disagreed over whether to have the burial there or in Corpus Christi, that he had simply wanted to avoid a family dispute. Many Anglo residents of Three Rivers told Johnson and Connally that the incident resulted from the ineptitude of the funeral director, a recently arrived northerner. The mayor responded to the storm of negative publicity by obtaining assurances from the funeral home and the local American Legion that they would bury the body with honors. He even offered the use of his own home, but it was too late; the die was cast. [4]

FORGING AN ALLIANCE

Johnson told García, "We want to help you and your people. As long as you do everything peacefully, we will help you in every way that you need help." To a protest meeting of over one thousand people Dr. García made the dramatic announcement that Senator Lyndon B. Johnson had just sent a telegram of support:

> I deeply regret to learn that the prejudice of some individuals extends even beyond this life. I have no authority over civilian funeral homes. Nor does the federal government. However, I have today made arrangements to have Felix Longoria buried with full military honors at Arlington National Cemetery, here at Washington, where the honored dead of our nation's War rest. . . . There will be no cost. . . . This injustice and prejudice is deplorable. I am happy to have a part in seeing that this Texas hero is laid to rest with the honor and dignity his service deserves.

Soon thereafter García met Johnson through their mutual friend, Corpus Christi Congressman John Lyle. Just six years younger than Johnson, García shared with him a boundless energy and drive. García's parents had both taught school and, like Johnson's, had instilled professional goals in their children. The physician's first impression of the new senator was of someone "nice, unpretentious, interested in people, polite . . . he had that charisma . . . we appreciate the fact that he was very warm, *muy simpático* . . . spontaneous." Johnson and García instinctively knew that the loyalty issue was the key to success. By honoring Private Longoria they were honoring the armed forces, the flag. García realized full well that if the incident had involved anyone other than a serviceman killed in the line of duty, few in Anglo society would have cared. "A volunteer . . . that got killed in World War II . . . made it possible for us to achieve the momentum to put the beginning of the end of segregation and discrimination not only in Texas but in the Southwest. We made the system work." [5]

Other Texas public officials offered to help the family bury Longoria in Texas, but Johnson had made the first offer of assistance. Beatrice Longoria declared herself "humbly grateful." The family discussed having Longoria interred at Fort Sam Houston in San Antonio, but when they realized that burying Longoria outside of Texas would more likely avoid controversy, particularly for the senator, they decided it would be best. Those attending the Washington burial included Senator Johnson, Mexican and U.S. foreign service officials, the Mexican ambassador, several congressmen, and President Truman's personal advisor, Major General Harry Vaughn.

Forum members were inspired, energized. For the first time a Texas senator had treated them as full-fledged constituents, had responded to their call. Messages, money, and letters of support poured into the Forum headquarters, which in turn helped local chapters with discrimination cases. In Cotulla a former student of Johnson's asked for the Forum's assistance in a case that eerily resembled Three Rivers': the Cotulla funeral home was refusing to bury with full military honors a Cotullan killed in action in Europe. According to Dan García, the Cotulla Chamber of Commerce put pressure on the local funeral director, and when the Forum intervened, local leaders accused the veterans' group of political agitation.

From all over Texas Mexican Americans were inundating their new senator with thanks and advice. For their part, many fair-minded Anglo Americans were upset by this disrespect to a soldier. Editorials in the San Angelo, Texas, *Standard Times* and the Sherman, Texas, *Democrat* praised the senator's action. John Connally recalled, "The phones were ringing off the wall. [Johnson] was talking, I was talking."[6]

Some of what they heard was critical, however, as when the Bexar County American Legion accused Johnson of "causing humiliation and embarrassment for the . . . good people of the city of Three Rivers, and the State of Texas." San Antonio political operative Dan Quill managed to get Council president Homer Long to disavow the resolution because it had been issued without Long's approval, but such proclamations were potentially political dynamite; Johnson could not afford to alienate his core Anglo Texan constituency. While he never wavered from his sympathetic aid to the aggrieved Longorias, Johnson nonetheless chose a solution that in effect removed the controversy, the "problem," from Texas to Washington.[7]

Predictably, the main criticism came from the leaders of the Three Rivers community. The president of the Chamber of Commerce accused the senator of pandering to Mexican American voters. The *Three Rivers News* declared, "no town in South Texas has better relations with Americans of Mexican descent . . . hasty action by Senator Johnson was largely responsible for the unfavorable publicity." According to John Connally, local State Representative J. F. Gray "was bitter as hell. Mean bitter." Dr. García had opposed Gray's reelection and the legislator accused Johnson of, in Connally's words, "pulling a grandstand play to try and embarrass somebody." The representative inquired about negotiations then underway between the State Department and Mexico to renew the *bracero* contract labor agreement "whether or not . . . negotiations . . . were delayed, interrupted, or stopped as a result of the publicity of the Longoria incident."[8]

Connally replied that, on the contrary, the State Department strongly approved of the senator's action as the best way to defuse a potential scandal. The department's Mexican Affairs chief Paul J. Reveley asked Connally to speak to Mexican ambassador Rafael de la Colina. The Johnson aide recalled, "I explained in every way that I possibly could . . . that it was merely an isolated case." The Mexican ambassador did not question Connally's analysis—perhaps out of diplomatic courtesy—even though the Mexican press was rife with stories about Texas racism. Soon thereafter Reveley told Connally that the incident had "complicated" the *bracero* negotiations, but that the situation would have been far worse if the burial had not been at Arlington, in the presence of dignitaries, and with full military honors. The *bracero* program was renewed in July 1949, but not until the governor of Texas visited the Mexican president and apologized for discrimination in Texas.

Longoria already had been buried by the time Representative Gray persuaded the state legislature to conduct hearings in Three Rivers. Historian George Norris Green has written of the "tense setting" reminiscent of an old western standoff: "some townsmen showed up with weapons. . . . Most of the committee were followers of embittered former Governor Coke Stevenson." The controversial 1948 election results remained a live issue in this county near Jim Wells County, of Box 13 fame.

Presenting the Longorias' case was Gus García of LULAC. Brilliant, flamboyant, with eyes that bored into one's soul, Gus García was a master of courtroom debate. John Connally characterized García as "a great debater . . . very aggressive, very articulate, extremely well read, a superb orator. . . . Gus and I had a long relationship and a very close relationship," dating from their time as fellow law students at the University of Texas.[9]

Attorney García wrote to Johnson that the senator's name came up in the proceedings: "But we managed to leave the correct interpretation on the record, . . . The Chairman wanted to establish the theory that you and Doctor García had ramrodded the whole thing for publicity purposes. . . . I had to introduce a letter from you to [Longoria's widow], in which you stated that you would follow her instructions." In a letter to his old buddy Connally, Gus García joked, "I suggest that we adopt the motto of the tool grinders' union: 'illigitimi non carborandum/Don't let the bastards get you down.'" Johnson advised his chief of staff to maintain his distance, so Connally wrote that Johnson was "very interested in your reaction and in the information you gave me" and left it at that.[10]

Several witnesses gave testimony documenting the discrimination, but four of the five committee members voted that there was no discrimination by the funeral director. No other examples of segregation in Three Rivers were allowed as evidence, even though next door to the courthouse a barber told a veteran "We don't serve Latin Americans" while the hearings were taking place. Gus García helped the dissenting member, Frank Oltorf, write a rebuttal so eloquent that another legislator changed his vote. In the end the committee found itself on the defensive. The Three Rivers incident had galvanized the public; most members of the state legislature and most Texas editorial writers did not endorse the majority report, so the committee quietly tabled it. Lyndon Johnson and Héctor García had made their point and in the process established a permanent bond.[11]

AN UNEASY ALLIANCE

Now Johnson tacked to the right. While the conservatives in the Texas legislature were setting up the Three Rivers hearings, Johnson delivered his maiden Senate speech, which took a swipe at civil rights activists, and condemned "mass-produced minorities." He acknowledged that filibusters, or unlimited debate, had killed antilynching, antipoll tax, and FEPC bills, but he argued that these were internal state matters, and he staunchly defended the right of senators to use this debate tactic.[12] Johnson viewed particular issues more as means or obstacles to finding a consensus than as ends in themselves. According to John Wildenthal, who left his law practice in Cotulla to work for the new senator, "my first impression was that of a rather shrewd, calculating type of personality. . . . The wheels were turning in his brain at all times . . . an intensely practical, goal-oriented type person." Johnson's political maneuverings paid off. After just two years in the senate he became minority whip and the following year, 1953, the senate Democratic leader.[13]

In the meantime Johnson concentrated on winning the support of the conservatives who dominated the Democratic Party in both the senate and in the Texas Democratic Committee. Thus, when the executive officers of the League of United Latin American Citizens, the American GI Forum, and "other civic and patriotic groups" telegraphed the senator, urging support of the 1950 FEPC bill and of civil rights legislation in general, he refused, writing to Gus García, "You know, Gus, what my position has been . . . I still feel . . . that such legislation would not serve any beneficial purpose." When GI Forum officials asked for FBI investigations and federal prosecution of alleged police brutality, including, in Ed Idar's words, the "cold-blooded murder" of two servicemen, Johnson forwarded the complaint to the Justice Department without comment. A note of relief can almost be detected in Johnson's reply: "since this is a matter before the courts and before the Department of Justice, it is entirely out of my hands." [14]

Johnson also voted against the Forum on labor issues, refusing to take a stand when Héctor García advised him in 1950 that Texas growers were hiring children during school hours in violation of the Wages and Hours Act. García wrote, "The American GI Forum, which represents the people and the children WHO ARE PICKING THE COTTON . . . want our children in school . . . it is no secret that Texas has for the past 100 years and to a certain extent is still segregating our children hoping to . . . discourage them from seeking higher education so that they would furnish cheap labor." [15]

Although GI Forum leaders actively recruited members among poor migrant workers, the activists—with their emphasis on citizenship and military experience—viewed immigrant workers from Mexico, paradoxically, as a threat. Ed Idar once said that if the United States had cut off Mexican immigration early in the century Mexican Americans would have risen to the middle class like Irish and Italian Americans, that unrestricted immigration played into the hands of exploitative growers. Along with LULAC, the Forum championed assimilation into the American mainstream and watched with alarm as segregationists and anticommunist crusaders pointed to alien newcomers as representative of all Mexican Americans. In publications and slide shows Ed Idar, Dr. George Sánchez of the University of Texas, and Dr. Ernesto Galarza of the National Farm Labor Union, among others, argued that wages and job opportunities for Mexican Americans deteriorated with the influx of unregulated immigrants, or "wetbacks." As María de la Paz Torres wrote to Johnson, "Something must be done and I believe that charging a heavy fine to those persons who insist [on] hiring wetbacks . . . will do it." [16]

The GI Forum passed a resolution criticizing the senator for voting against four million dollars earmarked for the Immigration Service to "continue airlifting of wetbacks" and to expand detention camps for people being deported. The "nay" vote came even though the Forum, LULAC, and others had "communicated frequently with U.S. Senator Lyndon Johnson on the so-called Wetback Problem, [providing] extensive documentation . . . seeking his support for an appropriation." They predicted that with the bill's defeat the area would be "flooded" with "illegal aliens," resulting in low wages and "suffering to native workers." The Forum passed a resolution stating

> Whereas Senator Johnson owes in large measure his position in the U.S. Senate to the votes of thousands of citizens of Mexican descent in South Texas, and in particular to 87 such stalwart votes in Jim Wells county . . . and whereas Senator Johnson's actions have been contributing to the principles of liberalism expounded by the late Franklin Delano Roosevelt. . . . His vote is in utter disregard of the friendship in which he has been held by thousands of citizens of Mexican descent.

Johnson replied, "I am sorry that the friendship that I have shown throughout the years . . . should be . . . cast aside" because of a vote against what Johnson characterized as a belated, excessive, bureaucratic request for appropriations. He continued,

> There is no group for which I have done more and to whom I feel more friendly than the Latin Americans. I have tried to show my friendship in a number of practical ways and I shall not be deterred from continuing to do so by resolutions which, at least to me, seem unfair. . . . The persons responsible for the resolution misunderstood. . . . I would not intentionally disregard the friendship of the citizens of Mexican descent.

When Johnson met with Ed Idar and Héctor García later that month in San Antonio, they told him that while they appreciated the gesture, they remained disappointed with his record on the issue.[17]

LULAC and the GI Forum found themselves outlobbied by powerful Johnson supporters in agriculture and business who wanted a sur-

plus of laborers readily available and thus strongly opposed any restriction on immigration. Johnson's friend and colleague Congressman
Lloyd Bentsen used farm laborers extensively, paying them very low
wages.[18] As the new minority whip, Johnson helped shepherd renewal
of the *bracero* program through the senate. On May 29 he responded
to a telegram from 33 growers, two of whom had Spanish-surnames,
writing, "Delighted to inform you that the Senate and House Conferees have agreed . . . on the Mexican labor bill." Attorney J. C. Looney,
who had coordinated Johnson's senate campaigns in the Lower Rio
Grande Valley, wrote to Johnson, "the people in the Valley who are
handling the situation and who are certainly influential . . . know what
you are doing." He assured the senator that they would express their
sincere gratitude "without statewide and national publicity that could
backfire in union circles."[19] Looney, along with some of Johnson's
other close advisors—including Alvin Wirtz, Ed Clark, and attorneys
for Brown and Root—raised nearly $100,000 in lawsuits against
Texas unions. Johnson "abided by what you told him pretty much,"
according to Looney.[20]

Despite their differences, Lyndon Johnson and Forum members
took pains to cultivate the special relationship they had forged with
the Three Rivers incident. In fact, the alliance dated from Johnson's
1928 teaching job, in the sense that his old student Dan García served
as chairman of the Forum for Cotulla and for that entire region.
Preparing for a radio address, the senator wrote to Héctor García requesting "your suggestions about subject matter . . . in which my listeners have a genuine interest." The senator's minority liaison George
Reedy noted that the Forum founder had "a real sympathetic feeling
for Johnson, but he wanted the whole world to turn over overnight."
For his part García thought that Johnson could not afford to risk his
chance at political advancement by supporting controversial issues.
Johnson's office assisted many Mexican-heritage veterans in obtaining
government benefits, and the senator, supported by gripping congressional testimony on the part of García, prodded Congress to allocate
200 additional beds to the Corpus Christi Naval Hospital.[21]

In 1953 the Forum helped convince Johnson, along with several
other Texans in Congress, to oppose the nomination of James Griffin
as agricultural advisor to the secretary of labor. Forum organizers
complained that Griffin, past president of the American Agricultural
Council, blocked attempts to improve farmworker conditions and
countenanced the hiring of undocumented workers by agribusiness
concerns. Not that Griffin sympathized with these immigrant workers;

La Verdad quoted him as having written that "for every man who works and tries to make an honest living in Mexico, there are ten who try to make it by foul or immoral ways." The nomination was successfully blocked.[22]

Large-scale employers from both political parties wanted open immigration, unlike prolabor Democrats and anti-Mexicans, both Democratic and Republican. In 1954 the Republican administration of President Dwight Eisenhower saw an opportunity to blame much of the growing unemployment on Mexican workers who lacked the proper papers. The White House called it "Operation Wetback," and Forum officials worked with the operation's Texas supervisor, John Holland, a friend of both Senator Johnson and Ed Idar. The Forum group published *What Price Wetbacks?*, which painted a fearful picture of a United States inundated with illiterate, desperate, sometimes criminal foreigners. Every member of Congress received a copy. Meanwhile farmworker activist Dr. Ernesto Galarza and others testified on the issue at congressional hearings, while the *Forum News Bulletin* called on Hispanics to judge political candidates in light of this issue.[23]

The number of people crossing the border into the United States decreased, but at a price. "Operation Wetback" deployed a large-scale military force that struck fear in the hearts of barrio residents regardless of their citizenship, echoing as it did the mass repatriations of the 1930s. As a result, some Mexican Americans expressed reservations about the program, including some leaders of LULAC such as old Johnson friend J. T. Canales.[24]

The most vociferous Mexican American opposition to "Operation Wetback," however, came from labor activists who had been organizing in the barrios since the 1930s. In contrast to labor Democrats, these radicals warned that mass deportations would exacerbate the public's tendency to blame Mexican-heritage people for the recession and to stereotype them as illegal and subversive, dividing the working class in the process. These activists also charged that restrictions did not address U.S. investment policies that they blamed for Mexico's subservient economic position. ANMA charged that mass deportations violated the Treaty of Guadalupe Hidalgo, and the organization asked the United Nations to investigate the treatment of Mexican immigrant laborers. Historian Mario García has written that ANMA asked the United Nations to support what ANMA called "the traditional rights of the Mexican people to migrate to the borderlands without being persecuted." ANMA also railed against the anticommunist crusade abroad, opposing the Korean War in particular.[25]

Radical critics were stilled for the most part by government infiltration and harassment. Senator Pat McCarran of Nevada warned that millions of illegal "Red" aliens threatened the nation's security. Texas editors took up the senator's cry, the *Houston Post*, for one, warning of "alien infiltration." The 1950 McCarran Act forced Communist Party members to register, forbade their employment in the federal government, and gave the immigration service sweeping power to deport them, while the 1952 McCarran-Walter Act gave the federal government increased power to label residents as "subversives" and to deport "undesirable" aliens without due process. Senator Johnson supported the two McCarran acts, both over President Truman's veto. More than ever grass-roots labor organizers—many of them women—were on the defensive.[26]

Meanwhile wives of Houston business leaders were swelling the ranks of the Minute Women, an anticommunist action group that lambasted Dr. George Sánchez for what it called his "affiliation with Communist fronts," after he wished ANMA well. Sánchez was denied a salary increase because the Board of Regents disapproved of his "outside activities," in the words of the University of Texas president.[27] In contrast, Dr. García said that as an independent physician, "I couldn't be touched professionally." The GI Forum condemned the McCarran-Walter Act. That same year local officials in a Central Texas town threatened to report Ed Idar as a subversive for his work on a school desegregation case. He remembers looking at the sheriff and his deputies lining the wall and saying, "I invite any of you to go ahead and file a complaint." Forum members publicized their veteran status and their anticommunist beliefs for their own protection. When the Forum expanded to other states, Idar warned local organizers, particularly in California, of people in their barrios who might be "tainted." In general Forumeers steered clear of ANMA and went so far as to circulate a government list of "subversive" organizations to demonstrate that the GI Forum was not among them. Besides, Forumeers sincerely opposed communism, led by Dr. García, with his close ties to Catholic leaders such as farmworker advocate Bishop Robert Lucey. "We were just trying to . . . keep the opposition from tearing us apart," said Idar; "if they had ever found anything on us I wouldn't be here." He knew that Johnson received letters such as one calling Forum members "tools of a Fifth Column of Communism," allied with "the Communists sent down from Washington to investigate our 'Wetback' labor situation." Meanwhile the FBI placed

LULAC and the GI Forum under surveillance. Referring to the Forum, Carl Allsup has written, "a tenuous balance between manipulating and being manipulated characterized the employment of the patriotic game."[28]

While Mexican American radicals opposed United States actions in the Korean War, GI Forum and LULAC members, like most Americans, staunchly supported the nation's action, sharing with Johnson a bond of reverence for the masculine military tradition and a strong belief in America's mission, as when Johnson voiced his hope that "the same unconquerable spirit which raised the flag of independence over Texas, one day will raise it over a democratic world." In his newsletter the senator declared, "*any*where in the world—by any means, *open or concealed*—communism trespasses upon the soil of the free world, *we should unleash all the power at our command upon the vitals of the Soviet Union.*" The postwar draft exempted college men. Thus poor and minority men served in disproportionately high numbers. Forum members, like ANMA activists, considered this unfair, but the Forum remained in the mainstream and did not question the regulations; rather, the veteran's group lobbied for Mexican American representation on local draft boards, using the Three Rivers case to prod people's consciences. Johnson for his part supplied García with the names of the winners of the Congressional Medal of Honor so that the Forum could demonstrate that Hispanics had earned the most of any group.[29]

Veteran Ernesto González remembered, "We didn't have much knowledge in Duval County about the Korean War. The only reason I went was because my brother had been drafted . . . and my family would cry every night . . . and so I told my father . . . 'As soon as I'm old enough I'm going to join the Army so that I can help my brother win the war, so that he can come back.'" Ernesto refused an assignment in Europe, saying, "I don't want to go to Germany; I want to go to Korea where I can help my brother," and eventually was sent into combat, where he lost an eye. Upon his return he only drew $83 per month in benefits, so he went to the local Veterans Administration official, who helped him apply for disability payments. In the meantime George Parr's nephew lent González $300 to tide him over. (On the other hand, González says that the Parr regime told him to leave Duval County when he and a young Anglo woman fell in love while he was picking cotton at Atlee Parr's ranch.) Like many other veterans, González took advantage of the GI Bill of Rights, taking continuing education courses in order to finish high school. There the teacher told the Hispanic veterans about the Three Rivers incident and Senator Johnson's role.[30]

A staunch supporter of the GI Bill, Johnson also led the Senate in the number of construction projects he brought home to his state. After all, he had first made his mark as a young congressman with a dam that delivered electricity to isolated farmers and also enriched his supporters at Brown and Root Construction Company. He was happiest when his ambition for himself also helped others, when everybody won. Soon after he came to the Senate, Johnson promoted an extensive system of reservoirs to be built across Texas. One of these, Falcon Dam, vividly illustrates the distribution of political and economic power in postwar Texas.

Since the 1920s U.S. and Mexican officials had discussed the need to harness the Rio Grande's tempestuous floodwaters. By 1940 U.S. water projects had advanced to the point that the United States had the technical ability to divert for its own use most of the water that flowed through the Lower Rio Grande Valley. Alarmed growers on the Mexican side called for immediate action to put the river to more equitable use. In 1949 the two nations agreed to build the world's first international dam. The reservoir would control flooding, provide power, and bring water to the agribusinesses on *both* sides of the Lower Rio Grande Valley. The dam also would destroy most of the settlements around Guerrero, Mexico, and in Zapata County, Texas.[31]

Many of the towns in Zapata County, including the county seat of Falcón, dated from the mid-eighteenth century, when local ranchers received title to their land from the king of Spain. These *porciones* remained the primary basis of ownership; the deeds gave each rancher a strip of land stretching some ten miles from the riverbank northward. Most residents of the new Zapata County ignored the boundary line made permanent by the United States after the war with Mexico; residents continued trading with their friends and relatives in Guerrero, Mexico, which by 1880 was the largest town in the Lower Rio Grande Valley. In 1882 the railroad came through Laredo, however, and the Falcón/Guerrero area became a backwater. Although Anglos came to predominate in nearby farm counties—hiring longtime border residents at harvest time and scornfully ignoring them the rest of the year—the original ranchers in Zapata and some of the other cattle counties managed to hold onto their lands. Writer Frank Goodwin observed, "the unpredictable nature of the Rio Grande helps keep the *saxones* away." Into the 1950s 90 percent of the residents were Mexican Americans, most of them landowners. An international bridge built in 1931 tied Falcón to Guerrero more than ever, even as the new road connected each town with its own country's exterior. In the early 1950s a Hollywood film team, looking for an atmospheric landscape for the movie *Viva Zapata*, chose Falcón. Timber, stucco, and stone buildings rimmed its plaza; in the spring a purple haze covered the hills leading to the river; farms and ranches dotted the landscape.[32]

"Now comes Falcon Dam Project," wrote Zapata County resident H. González to Johnson in 1949,

> destroying hundreds of homes, thousands of acres of our best farm land . . . and still many more thousands of acres of pasture land abundant in potential mineral resources. . . . All this is being done in the name . . . of progress. But shall we be among those who . . . will profit . . . or . . . [will we] be discriminated against and deprived of . . . rights for the benefit of others?

Local residents had been flooded out before, but the venerable structures remained. Besides, it was one thing to face nature's whims; it was quite another to witness the obliteration of nearly all of the settlements by conscious public policy. Geologists and engineers selected the construction site with no thought of the local residents. Similarly, the International Boundary and Water Commission (IBWC) limited its report to the size, uses, and ownership of the proposed dam. Johnson advisor Ed Clark got wind of the discontent and wrote to "Lyndon" questioning the purported power shortage. Johnson thanked him and forwarded to him a letter from the assistant director of the Bureau of Power, who replied that, while there might not be a shortage in 1949, the dam was needed "for future power requirements in the market area."[33]

The senator received scores of letters from Anglo investors urging speedy completion of the project. S. H. Holmgren wrote, "I bought some farms and citrus orchards on account of the prospect of getting water from the proposed Falcon Dam." The president of Central Power and Light Company, who was on first-name terms with Johnson, wrote in support of the project, then proceeded to rail against federal domestic spending.[34]

Usually the federal government reimbursed displaced residents in cash, but the reservoir would destroy the county seat and most of the settlements in Zapata County, eliminating it as a political entity. "Zapata County people cannot be asked to scatter to the four winds," one resident wrote to Johnson. In 1950 Congress expanded the authority of the IBWC beyond the acquisition of condemned property to include jurisdiction over the construction of new towns. Johnson expressed his confidence that the IBWC would, in his words, "be interested in the rights of the people." In 1952 local congressman Lloyd Bentsen introduced a bill authorizing the IBWC to replace irrigated farmland with comparable new holdings. Zapata County officials argued strenuously for the bill but IBWC head L. M. Lawson called it "impracticable." The Bentsen bill never reached the senate floor because it did not have the support of President Truman, who did not want to set a precedent of special legislation for specific construction projects.

The IBWC notified Zapata residents to evacuate by November 1, 1953, but the new town was not ready. It lacked sewage and water treatment facilities and adequate residences. In the meantime, torrential August rains forced residents to flee in a panic. The IBWC came to be known locally as "I Bully Women and Children." The Department of Justice blamed the animosity on bad public relations, reporting, "Never in the experience of the Lands Division has there been a case in which so much publicity has been given to irresponsible statements by any and everyone." [35]

The centuries-old deeds caused "numerous title difficulties," wrote IBWC Commissioner L. M. Lawson to Johnson, but Lawson promised the senator that the appraisers, from nearby Laredo, would be fair, that they were "skilled in their profession and conversant with property values in the vicinity." Residents weren't convinced. "They have assured Senator Johnson many times that they intended to be fair, and old Lawson has written . . . that they were going to pay fair and fully for all the land they take, but not one word of it is true," wrote G. Mackenzie. "I know, because I have been fighting with them for two years for what they owe me. They are willing to spend $10,000 of the Government's money, rather than pay a landowner $1,000.00 that he has coming to him." J. Luz Sáenz, a LULAC founder and World War I veteran, wrote, "Many of our people whose homes and possessions are due for removal have but little of anything in life . . . but to them it may be their birthplace and their all. . . . The actual present day value . . . may not even . . . pay legal expenses." Legally the IBWC was bound to pay "fair market value" on adobe and stone dwellings that in many cases had never been sold; consequently, it was difficult to ascertain the market price. The properties were devalued for obsolescence and depreciation with no regard for historic value. When told that Our Lady of Lourdes Church was worth less than when it was built, the Zapata pastor declared, "Since when have churches become 'obsolete'?" He wondered how much the appraisers would devalue the venerable old churches of Vatican City.

Landowners charged that the government assessed them less for their lost land than it paid the company that cleared it. Disgruntled landowners filed suit but in September 1953 Judge James Allred suspended the proceedings until the land titles could be verified. He accelerated the procedure by appointing a court official to process the titles, and in the end the court usually ruled in favor of the plaintiffs, but few of the small owners could afford to file suit. Residents found it ironic that the same federal government that used taxpayer dollars to help displaced persons abroad refused to pay its own citizens the replacement value of their property. A study by University of Texas researchers reported, "The people lost respect for the system of appraisal . . . most of the owners had not been paid for their property by the deadline for evacuation." [36]

Residents protested that the commission even took land beyond the reservoir area. "We are appealing to you, as our Senator to present a most vigorous protest to . . . acquiring more lands than are necessary for the construction of said Falcon Dam," wrote old Johnson supporter J. T. Canales. Commissioner Lawson explained to Johnson that at Falcon, as at other federal reservoirs, extra land surrounding the project was acquired "to prevent pollution of the reservoir" and for recreational facilities. A few weeks later the commissioner assured Johnson that the IBWC would try to limit the amount of land that it acquired. Some 30,000 acres were withdrawn from the flood area, but not until 1953, three years after the initial complaints. Moreover, those ranchers bordering the reservoir who were lucky enough to escape government land seizure could not use the reservoir without petitioning the state, despite their *porciones* rights to use of the river. [37]

To defend Zapata County's interests, the county political leader, Judge Manuel Bravo, retained a formidable special counsel, former Texas Attorney General Robert Bobbitt. Both men lobbied Senator Johnson long and hard on behalf of property rights for their citizens. At the same time, the judge was not about to pick a fight with the IBWC, as it had the support of his powerful Democratic ally Johnson. For his part, Johnson was on friendly terms with the owner of the construction company building the dam. [38]

The company was headquartered in Zapata County, and local Republicans charged that Bravo and his cronies stood to gain financially from the project. These critics pointed out that the new, completely furnished county courthouse was the only structure rebuilt to standard thus far. In 1953 more voters than ever cast their ballots in the county elections, many of them galvanized by their frustration over dam-related issues, such as the plan to consolidate the seven villages and twenty-two cemeteries into one new Zapata. Rival bosses, including the powerful Democratic leader of Starr County, H. P. Guerra Jr., encouraged the anti-Bravo forces and filed a suit charging electoral irregularities after several of Bravo's opponents were jailed. The courts ruled against the suit. Undaunted, the challengers turned to the Federal Bureau of Investigation. Bravo sent an urgent telegram to Johnson complaining that the Zapata political organization was being unfairly targeted. The judge argued that any investigation should look into the practices of both political factions but that, more important, a federal agency had no jurisdiction in local elections. Johnson's office immediately forwarded the telegram to the attorney general, "concerning a certain alleged irregular and illegal investigation by your Department." In his reply to Johnson the assistant attorney general wrote that the FBI had received charges of "numerous irregularities . . . [but] . . . you can be assured . . . that we have no intention of intruding into such areas of State jurisdiction." A relieved Judge Bravo wrote, "Dear Lyndon, The F.B.I. [agents] have not been in Zapata since you went to work for us." [39]

By September 1954 the federal government had moved 488 of the old town's 882 structures to new Zapata and had constructed 122 more. The new county seat boasted its first modern sewage and public water systems, a $150,000 courthouse, and a $272,000 elementary school. Some Zapata boosters predicted "a bright future . . . a modern city on the banks of the lake," attractive to winter residents and outdoor sports enthusiasts. Nonetheless, overwhelming problems remained. The water system was inadequate; electricity was spotty. Relocated homes suffered from cracks in the walls and foundations. Construction of the high school lagged, and the elementary school stood unused due to a dispute over whether the county or the federal government should pay for desks and equipment. In the meantime the children studied in barracks borrowed from a military base. A *Houston Chronicle* reporter wrote, "Anyone remembering the original Zapata on the banks of the Rio Grande will find the newer version a drab, treeless, dusty substitute." According to anthropologists from the University of Texas, "The greater part of the money-making irrigated land is now under water. Few of the farm owners have been paid for their land. The government has not permitted individual farmers to pump water out of the lake." Many of the dispossessed landowners joined the migrant stream, seeking work picking crops in the Midwest. Local businesses suffered, and newcomers dominated the commercial fishing on Falcon Lake. Moreover, the reservoir cut off the town from Mexico. No longer would Zapata be a route south; the new bridge spanned the river in another county.

Residents could not help but contrast their fate with that of their friends and relatives across the river. Mexican government representatives held a series of meetings with Guerrero-area residents, allowing them to vent their frustrations over the loss of their ancestral land and patiently explaining some of the advantages of relocating, including hot and cold running water, indoor plumbing, and reliable electricity. At the meetings officials and local citizens discussed several relocation options. The residents then formed a committee that authorized an independent appraisal of all residential property and advised the government on the location and layout of the new town. True to its word, the Mexican government quickly established Nuevo Guerrero, located at the new border crossing. The town boasted schools, a hospital, municipal buildings, stores, and equivalent-value residences. "[And] we used to say Mexico was one hell of a place to live," said one Zapata resident. The national Mexican administration was anxious to impress international observers with its handling of the entire Falcon Dam project. Moreover, the Mexicans who supervised the relocation came from the irrigation department and thus had experience working with local farmers, unlike the IBWC officials.[40]

Meanwhile Zapata County Special Counsel Robert Bobbitt kept up his lobbying efforts. Referring to Bobbitt, Johnson told his aide Arthur Perry, "I will be happy to see him whenever he wants to," and Perry set up meetings with other members of congress to address the county's problems. In July 1955 Congressman Bentsen and the two Texas senators sponsored special legislation based on a draft by Bobbitt. "Thanks, good friend," Bobbitt scrawled on Perry's memo pad. Nonetheless the bill languished until 1962, when a limited version finally became law. By this time Johnson had left the senate for the vice presidency.[41]

"Initially intended to help a large region on both sides of the river, a goal which it largely accomplished, the dam had unforeseen side effects which proved costly for a smaller group," political scientist and border resident Adela Flores has written. In addition to generating electricity, the dam protected the Lower Rio Grande Valley from flooding in 1954 and 1955 that alone would have cost each country twice what it had spent on building the dam. Also, by 1973 the Zapata County incomes were higher than ever. This was due principally, however, to the exploitation of oil deposits, and some residents wondered whether oil lay beneath the land they lost to the dam. "Zapata is a very wealthy county on the ranches—oil and gas production—but . . . they're owned mostly by outsiders . . . the local people don't share in the wealth," according to one South Texas official. Moreover, the promised tourism never materialized; the U.S. Department of Commerce observed that most of the tourist traffic bypassed Zapata County entirely and that the historic sites were not developed or publicized. Adela Flores has noted, "The population of Zapata County was about 90% Mexican American, a group that was systematically discriminated against and excluded from the political process. . . . Progress was late in coming to the Zapata-Guerrero area. . . . Just when the people of Zapata were beginning to reap its benefits . . . progress took the community by surprise." In the words of one reporter, Zapata was best known as "a town strangled by progress." [42]

Meanwhile Robert Bobbitt joined the Brown and Root Construction Company and eventually worked for the IBWC. When Judge Bravo wrote to Johnson in 1957 about the possibility of employment with Brown and Root, the senator raised the idea with George Brown. Johnson's chief assistant Walter Jenkins advised Bravo on the application process and arranged for the interview, and Bravo was hired. [43]

By this time Johnson had become a wealthy gentleman rancher like George Brown. The Texas senator purchased the 250-acre Martin ranch from his aunt in 1951 and by 1961 owned over 12,000 acres, much of it in others' names. Johnson loved roaming the range and getting to know his ranchhands. There was no question who was boss; the LBJ brand was on everything. He chose many of the paintings in the ranch house, often Hill Country scenes by Texan Porfirio Salinas. Now Johnson could visibly demonstrate his Texas roots, talk cattle breeding with George Brown or Oklahoma Senator Robert Kerr, and entertain in grand style, showing off the latest in modern conveniences. The ranch represented the simple life of the land, the paternalism of the rancher, and the benefits of progress, where a man could dam up his creek and supervise his cattle from a Lincoln Continental convertible. On the ranch Lyndon Johnson held sway in all his paradoxical glory. [44]

DEMOCRATS OF TEXAS

In the 1950s Senator Lyndon Johnson and Mexican American veterans maneuvered for position in a fractious Texas Democratic Party that top Johnson aide George Reedy characterized as "passionate, byzantine, and highly ideological." Liberal editor Willie Morris noted, "These internecine party battles were more than factionalism. They were bitter fights to the finish for outright control. Lyndon Johnson understood this better than any other man." [1]

ADLAI FOR PRESIDENT?

Festering differences within the Texas Democratic Party broke into the open during the presidential campaign of 1952. Conservative Dixiecrats leaned toward Republican candidate Dwight Eisenhower and opposed all federal intervention, except aid to businesses and growers. Dubbed "Shivercrats," after Governor Allan Shivers, they supported segregationist Georgia Senator Richard Russell for the Democratic nomination in 1952. So did Lyndon Johnson and John Connally, who had left the Johnson staff to work for a Texas oil mogul. Johnson could win points with Shivers, a potentially dangerous opponent, and had risen to senate prominence under Russell's tutelage. There is some evidence that Russell and Johnson cut a deal; Johnson would support Russell for president, and Russell would support Johnson for vice president. The liberals, or "Loyal Democrats," supported President Truman's agenda, which included civil rights measures, government social programs, and the Supreme Court ruling upholding federal ownership of tidelands oil. They felt betrayed by Lyndon Johnson.

"I'm pretty tired of that socialized millionaire, who is sucking at the public teat, if you please, who has made his millions from political connections," declared a labor official.

At the spring state convention in San Antonio Maury Maverick asked the delegates to vote for a resolution pledging to support the eventual Democratic nominee. Liberal Ronnie Dugger has written that when Maverick's proposal was ruled out of order, "the great curmudgeon led the liberals out of the hall. . . . The rumpers marched a mile through the rain to Maverick's beloved La Villita . . . and selected a rival set of delegates." Maverick's delegation included a number of Mexican Americans, including Dr. Héctor García, Ed Idar, Cris Aldrete, and Albert Peña Jr., all of the American GI Forum. According to Democratic organizer Kathleen Voight, President Truman had told Maverick personally that the loyalists would be seated, then he reneged. She speculated that the Democratic leadership "thought the power lay with Shivers." Johnson and Sam Rayburn chose the Shivercrats over the Mavericks, discounting liberal warnings that Governor Shivers and his cohorts would later defect to the Republicans. "I believe [Shivers] is going to stick," Mr. Sam told a disbelieving Voight.[2]

As soon as Adlai Stevenson won the nomination, Maverick called loyal Democrats back in San Antonio and told them to get busy organizing. Relaying Maverick's message to Kathleen Voight, Rubén Munguía said, "Tomorrow we have a [local] election. Let's start a Stevenson for President club." She replied that the convention had not even chosen the vice presidential candidate, but Munguía persisted; he would get dressed and run off campaign material in his print shop, ready for distribution by four in the morning. Meanwhile Voight spent the night calling loyal precinct workers, telling them, "Meet me at Ruben's." At seven the next morning Stevenson posters greeted conservative Democrats when they arrived at the polling places to set up their tables.[3]

Sam Rayburn named Héctor García to the Texas steering committee for the Stevenson campaign and asked the physician's advice on campaign strategies "among Mexican American groups in the Valley." The GI Forum, with its nonpolitical stance, did not endorse any candidate, concentrating instead on drives to get people to pay their poll tax and to register to vote. Johnson acquaintance Tom Sutherland, director of the Texas Good Neighbor Commission, wrote in the *Saturday Evening Post*, "The American GI Forum is teaching political action in the tortilla flats of Texas, and they also know García's name, though not so reverently, in the Scotch and soda sections."[4]

Just as the liberals had predicted, Shivers declared his support for Eisenhower. With only two months until the election, the state party machinery was in the hands of Stevenson opponents. San Antonio still had no Stevenson campaign headquarters; Johnson had insisted that the local officials run it, and, being Shivercrats, they had done nothing. Now with Shivers's betrayal out in the open, the loyalists finally got the green light. "We did the best we could," said Voight. An old friend of Johnson, reporter William S. White, wrote, "In Texas this is the day and the hour of the burned bridge, and no one supposes that the Democratic Party in this state will ever be the same again, regardless of the result in the Presidential election."[5]

Johnson hid out, making as few campaign appearances as possible, determined to distance himself from a presidential candidate destined to lose; even a few Mexican Americans such as his father's old friend J. T. Canales had defected to Eisenhower. More importantly, Johnson's most powerful financial and political sponsors opposed the Democratic nominee. When Henry B. González, a newly elected San Antonio city councilman, called him "Lyin' Down Lyndon," Johnson aide Cliff Carter told the councilman that the statement bothered the senator very much, and invited González to meet Johnson. The young San Antonian declined and politely but firmly refused to retract his statement.[6]

When the Stevenson campaign announced that the candidate would visit the Alamo, Mexican American activists insisted that he also visit the barrio nearby, and the campaign coordinators agreed. An elated Albert Peña wrote to Dr. García, "Tell all your friends to be here. . . . It is the first time that a candidate of national importance has taken the time to make a special appeal to the Latino voter." In Cotulla Dan García was stumping for Stevenson because he considered the candidate a very broad-minded, eloquent person, so when the former Johnson student heard the announcements, he and ten to fifteen other Cotullans traveled to San Antonio for the event.[7]

On the eve of Stevenson's arrival, San Antonio loyalists learned that the West Side rally had been canceled. As if to rub salt in the wound, Texas Democratic leaders had substituted a campaign stop at the ranch of arch-conservative John Nance Garner, who had come out for Stevenson only because the candidate did not belong to the party of Lincoln. Furthermore, at the Alamo Maury Maverick might not be the official who escorted Stevenson after all, even though a Maverick ancestor had fought there! Albert Peña declared, "We're not going to go to the Alamo," and Rubén Munguía, who had already printed the

Santa Rosa Park circulars, warned that Mexican American leaders would call for a boycott of the Democratic ticket throughout the Southwest. The regular Democrats caved in, reinstating the West Side rally, but they refused to supply anything: no police protection, no platform, no microphones. "I got busy," Munguía recalled. He prevailed upon a West Side shopkeeper to lend a public address system and the loyalists built a platform on benches from the Munguía print shop. They strung a thick rope around the perimeter of the square, and a Mexican American sheriff deputized some twenty volunteers as security officers for the day.[8]

The master of ceremonies was the first Mexican-heritage member of the San Antonio school board, Lulacker Gus García, who had defended Johnson and the Longorias so eloquently at the Three Rivers hearings. Then in both languages Stevenson warned of a possible Republican depression and extolled the Mexican American heroes, from the Alamo and the Texas Revolution to the two world wars and Korea. The candidate then spoke in English of the five Spanish-surname Alamo defenders and people such as Lorenzo de Zavala and Juan Seguín, who helped found the Republic of Texas. Mexican-origin citizens had suffered too much, Stevenson said, and he called for a domestic Good Neighbor Policy. Afterward the governor donned a charro hat and was showered with rose petals. According to Munguía, Stevenson "had a wonderful time—so good that he did not care to leave the park to go to the Alamo!" The candidate's sister remarked that this was the most enthusiastic audience of the campaign. After Stevenson finally departed, Gus García mounted the platform and called on the audience to march to the Alamo. Two girls in traditional Mexican dress led the impromptu parade, flanked by a United States flag and a Mexican flag that had been presented to Munguía's father by President Miguel Alemán. Munguía remembered that, in a historical turnabout, someone managed to plant the Mexican flag on the roof of the Alamo; "Viva Adlai" signs dotted the crowd.[9]

"The Stevenson Democrats . . . feel that at every cost they must get out the farm vote, the Negro vote and the Mexican vote," wrote William S. White. In barrios around the state people stumped for Adlai, as in Austin, where Mexican American precinct workers sat on the stage with Stevenson's running mate, Alben Barkley. The Forum *News Bulletin* reported, "The younger element were taking the Loyal Democratic stand for Stevenson." Joe Bernal, a young social worker, was typical of this new breed of reform Democrat. Fresh out of college, he ran for precinct committeeman in order to replace what he called "some of the old timers because they used to . . . buy off voters." On the West Side of San Antonio, the Democrats defeated Eisenhower by thirteen to one. Overall, however, the Republican carried Texas and the nation at large, just as a worried Johnson had predicted. Liberals countered that if powerful Democratic leaders such as Johnson had campaigned vigorously, Stevenson might have carried Texas.[10]

STATE ELECTION BATTLES

At a liberal post-mortem meeting, Ed Idar was the only minority person present. He reported to Héctor García, "There were no Negro representatives and no women which I think was a mistake." Idar reminded the others attending the strategy session that Mexican Americans, in his words, "worked hard and stuck their necks out," [and that] "we do not want to be cast out in any process of appeasing the people who knifed the party in the back." Afterward he reported to Dr. García that Maverick and others, in Idar's words, "gave our people lots of credit for the support they gave to the party . . . [and] realize that we're here to stay." Idar urged García to push for Mexican American representation on statewide party committees, "that a definite effort be made to integrate our people in district, county, and precinct levels . . . even if we have to go to Bonham or Johnson City to see Rayburn or Johnson." Idar also hoped that the loyal Democrats would pick their candidates by the middle of 1953 so that Forum members could sound out the possible nominees regarding "the problems of our own people."

Shortly after the election Idar wrote to García, "I am told that Shivers gave his word to Johnson that he would not run against Johnson in 1954," but some political observers "feel that the big money boys are going to put terrific pressure on Shivers to run against Johnson."[11] In the end the governor stayed out of the senate race, opting to run for reelection instead. Johnson's hapless opponent, Dudley Dougherty, tried with little success to woo the Hispanic vote. Alluding to the senator's record on immigration issues, Dougherty said that Johnson "only recently . . . doublecrossed the Latin Americans who were his balance of power in the previous election." The challenger received no support from Mexican American organizations, however; they distrusted this grower who promised "to wipe out existing federal labor laws and start all over."[12]

Disgusted with both Johnson and his opponents, some Mexican Americans, particularly those close to organized labor such as

Dr. George Sánchez, ignored the senate race and worked solely on behalf of the campaign of Shivers's gubernatorial challenger, staunch liberal Ralph Yarborough. Many Mexican Americans, however, strongly supported Johnson as well as Yarborough. George Reedy, the senator's liaison person to minority groups, remembered that South Texas crowds had a special enthusiasm. People would automatically start cheering, "Olé, ain't gonna beat Johnson! Olé, ain't gonna beat Johnson! Tres Ríos, Tres Ríos, Tres Ríos!" The Three Rivers issue remained alive in part because GI Forum members and others had recently defeated the local Representative, J. F. Gray.[13]

Forumeers did not vilify Johnson for his Shivers strategy; they were glad it worked. As part of a whirlwind Texas speaking tour to shore up support, Johnson accepted the Forum's invitation to be its keynote speaker at their 1953 convention. Ed Idar came down to the banquet hall early, only to find the front tables cleared away for television cameras that would record the event for possible use in Johnson campaign films. The rearrangements delayed dinner, and Idar remembered "people were milling about in the lobby wondering what was going on."[14]

"I am among friends . . . of long years' standing," Johnson declared in the speech, which he had shown to García beforehand. The senator reminded the audience of his teaching days in Cotulla, noting, "I learned as much as my students." (At the same time he did not seem to realize that one of his former students, Dan García, was a Forum district chairman.) Johnson characterized the GI Forum as the leader in the "continued progress" of Mexican Americans in Texas. He praised Hispanic servicemen, saying, "I saw the casualty lists . . . evidence that our Latin American citizens were doing their full duty—and more," and he called for continued vigilance against the "Communist aggressors," with "their plan for worldwide conquest." He pledged to work with Forum members for peace, prosperity, and equality, but made no specific promises. After the speech the senator stayed and crowned their queen.[15]

John Connally later said about Johnson, "He realized during his political years that they were a very, very strong element of the Democratic Party [and] potentially had a very significant influence . . . so he treated them with great respect and sought their friendship, and fought to keep it, and he conducted himself in such a way as to enhance the friendship that he had with the Mexican American community." According to Ed Idar, "Johnson was very astute. He knew that in a close election we could be the difference."

Indeed the Forumeers were among the few Democrats connected both to the Johnson faction and to the liberals. "I made good friends with Johnson and with Yarborough," remembered Héctor García. When liberal leader Creekmore Fath placed Ed Idar on the Resolutions Committee with the proviso that the Idar accept all of the resolutions, including one the Forum leader considered critical of Johnson personally, Idar balked, saying, "Look, Creek . . . my organization [doesn't] want to get tied up against Senator Johnson." The Mexican American walked out rather than be, in his words, "a rubber stamp. One thing I hate is somebody outside my group to come and tell me what to do." Forum leaders were "disappointed" with the senator on some issues, but "we were not ready to make an enemy of the man," said Idar. For his part, George Reedy advised Johnson, "the Creekmore Faths . . . are maneuverers who live on the fringes of the labor and minority movements [that] . . . are in a position to cut off the . . . Faths any time they feel like it." [16]

Forumeers maintained close ties to Johnson, "a visceral affinity that went back to Three Rivers," but they also "stayed in the liberal movement" even as it became "ionically hostile to Johnson and he to it," according to Ronnie Dugger, editor and later publisher of the liberal biweekly newspaper *The Texas Observer*. Forumeers stumped hard for underdog liberal Ralph Yarborough against Allan Shivers, charging that Shivers violated immigration laws by hiring "wetbacks . . . placing the almighty dollar ahead of human welfare." [17] Idar has said, "I have good reason to believe that Governor Shivers had us investigated by a former FBI agent . . . to try to destroy us." Citing in particular Shivers's tactics against the Forum, George Reedy wrote to Johnson, "Allan Shivers conducted his campaign with a violence and a fury that is rare, even in Texas." [18]

Lyndon Johnson easily won reelection through his adroit handling of Shivers, his vast campaign funds, and the advantages of incumbency over a politically inept opponent. The senator thanked his friends, writing to his "special friend" Dr. García, "Believe me, I am well aware of all you did to help make our great victory possible. I will never forget it. Please let me know when I can be of service—and I mean that from the bottom of my heart." [19]

HERNÁNDEZ V. TEXAS

In the heat of the 1954 campaign season the Supreme Court made its landmark ruling in *Brown v. the Board of Education*, outlawing segregation of African American schoolchildren with the sweeping declaration that separate facilities were inherently unequal. Needing to be "a chameleon on plaid," Johnson took no stand on the Brown decision. Three out of four Texans opposed the ruling, so their senator continued to criticize "forced integration," as did even liberal Ralph Yarborough. At the same time, Johnson was the only southern senator who refused to sign the "Southern Manifesto" calling for resistance to the Brown decision.[20]

Just two weeks before *Brown* the Supreme Court had struck a blow against discrimination of Mexican Americans in the case of *Hernandez v. Texas*. The LULAC and Forum attorneys argued that Mexican Americans suffered discrimination not as a racial type per se, but as a "class apart." This was LULAC attorney Gus García's shining hour. His keen mind, his quick wit, his passion fueled a presentation so eloquent that Chief Justice Earl Warren extended the allotted time by fifteen minutes. García argued convincingly that Pete Hernández had been tried unjustly because no Mexican-heritage person had been called for jury duty in Jackson County for twenty-five years. Even the courthouse itself had segregated facilities. When Justice Potter Stewart asked whether Mexican immigrants spoke enough English to serve on juries, García used anti-immigrant sentiment to his own advantage: "Your honor, my people were in Texas 100 years before Sam Houston arrived. . . . Sam Houston was just a wetback from Tennessee to the real citizens of Texas but Latin Americans are denied the right to jury service." The Court ruled unanimously that "when the existence of a distinct class is demonstrated, and when . . . laws, written or applied, create unreasonable and different treatment . . . then the guarantees of the Constitution [are] violated." The Hernández case gave activists ammunition for their contention that Mexican Americans, as a *group*, suffered unconstitutional discrimination. Meanwhile, in the wake of the desegregation rulings, Anglo leaders sent out the word, and restaurants and hotels gradually eliminated their "no Mexicans" policies.[21]

While it paved the way for male Mexican Americans to serve on juries, the Hernández decision gave female Mexican Americans this right in name only because statutes and customs excluded most U.S. women from juries. Attorney Carlos Cadena noted that the "class apart" argument could be used on behalf of women, but the main women's organizations had virtually no Mexican American members and thus no knowledge of the Hernández case. By the same token, LULAC and the GI Forum were busy fighting ethnic discrimination and—like most organizations of the time—discounted female issues.[22]

When it came to political leadership, men largely forged bonds with men, particularly during the Cold War with its male military ethos, as in the Three Rivers case that linked Lyndon Johnson and Héctor García. Women conducted much of the grass-roots organizational activity, as when Longoria's sister brought up the issue to Dr. García, but they operated mostly behind the scenes. When in public, they usually served decorative roles. At GI Forum conventions the queen and her court received more attention than any female neighborhood organizers, while Johnson wanted to reward Mexican American loyalty by hiring, in his words, "a talented and goodlooking Mexican or Spanish American girl" as a receptionist or secretary.[23]

The Johnson team increasingly recruited women volunteers in the late 1950s, including a number of Mexican Americans, but many were chosen not for their own ability but because they were married to political operatives, from Luis Salas of Box 13 fame to state representative Oscar Laurel. Cecil Burney, one of Johnson's main men in South Texas, commented, "You sometimes have problems with women who are active in Democratic politics. There's lots of pride and self-denial among them."[24] At the same time, Johnson realized better than many of his aides the importance of Mexican American female organizing at the local level. He kept in touch with people such as his old Cotulla friend Manuela González Contreras, now active in the San Antonio Democratic Party. He telephoned her when he came to San Antonio to visit "the big shots," as she called them. Subsequently Contreras and her husband visited the senator in Washington.[25]

In general the Johnson/Mexican American alliance was still in its formative stages, however, mainly because this ethnic group was feeling its way in Democratic politics. George Reedy noted that Mexican Americans had less contact with Anglo leaders than did their black counterparts, many of whom had moved to the North and wielded some political clout through their elected representatives and as union members. "The blacks were always far better organized, far better financed than we were," according to Ed Idar. Dr. George Sánchez addressed this problem in 1953 by obtaining a grant to establish the American Council of Spanish-Speaking People (ACSSP), a clearing house for organizations such as LULAC, the Forum, and the New Mexico-based Alianza Hispano Americana, but the ACSSP operated haltingly.[26]

To complicate matters, some leaders, such as LULAC cofounder M. C. González, discouraged alliances with African Americans, saying, "We fought our battles by ourselves." When San Antonio City Councilman Henry B. González opposed segregation ordinances, some of his main critics included people long active in the colonia. Most younger leaders, however, agreed with attorney Carlos Cadena that Mexican-heritage people should "be proud to be identified with other minority groups, including the ultra-progressive Negro-Americans, instead of attempting to build a cultural fence." The *Forum News Bulletin* noted that 77 percent of all Mexican Americans said that they favored integration of all the races, compared to 42 percent of Anglos and 62 percent of African Americans.[27]

"LYNDON LET US DOWN"

Senator Johnson was "very familiar" with South Texas political activity and "kept abreast of it. Absolutely," recalled John Connally years later. One night during the poll tax controversy Connally called Ed Idar, saying, "Do you know who I am?" A sleepy Idar answered, "Yes." Connally continued, "Listen, the Senator needs your help. Did you hear what Shivers did tonight?"

Idar had missed the statewide broadcast in which the governor accused the GI Forum and the unions of buying people's poll taxes. To prove his point, Shivers flashed a bank deposit slip in front of the television camera. Connally asked Idar to come over to Austin's Driskill Hotel immediately. When the Forum officer arrived, Connally was on the telephone. Idar later recalled, "From the conversation I gathered that he was talking to Lyndon Johnson, who was in Washington, and they were having quite an argument." Idar concluded that Connally wanted Johnson to criticize the Shivers speech and that the senator disagreed. Idar assured Connally that the GI Forum had the financial records to show that it never paid people's poll taxes. Indeed, no one ever produced proof that the GI Forum had ever done anything more than encourage people to exercise their rights as citizens, while the Shivercrats faced accusations of stealing Forum records and employing smear tactics. In a memo to Johnson, George Reedy pointed out that Shivers in his television address had resorted to the phrase "I hold in my hand," made famous by Senator Joseph McCarthy. Nonetheless Johnson staffers refrained from publicly criticizing the governor's speech.[28]

Governor Shivers was right on one score: although the poll tax drive was nonpartisan, many of the organizers also worked long and hard for the Democratic Advisory Council (DAC), a group of loyal Democrats established by Sam Rayburn in 1955. Initially the DAC had no officers from, in Idar's words, "this one group who can always be counted on when the going gets rough," so Rayburn named Bob Sánchez and his Forum colleague Cris Aldrete to the DAC's Steering Committee and placed three other Forum officers, including Ed Idar, on the National Advisory Council of the Democratic National Committee.[29]

DAC director Kathleen Voight worked tirelessly to link local loyal Democrats such as Mexican American activists to the state DAC. In later years she speculated that she received the nod because "Mr. Rayburn liked me, but I was not labor, I was not black, I was not brown." Perhaps as a female she also seemed less threatening to him than some of the other liberals. For its part, the Johnson camp, not wanting to alienate conservative Democrats, avoided the DAC. George Reedy called Voight "immature and neurotic" but acknowledged that she "made a complete sale" in West Texas.

Voight compiled, in her words, "names and names and names. I traveled all over Texas. In San Antonio we already had the blacks and the browns and labor and the intellectuals working together. . . . Héctor was doing his thing in Corpus. . . . The big cities did not need me. . . . You had to go to the smaller places." In each town she would take down the names of the volunteers, help them elect a chairman, tell them to keep in touch, and move on. Up in Lubbock Dr. Robert Abernathy brought one Mexican American man to a loyalist meeting and Voight buttonholed the professor, asking, "Why can't we get some more tomorrow night?" She was impressed with the younger Mexican Americans: "They were more educated and they were rising in the movement then. They did not like the county courthouse either." Voight thought to herself, "Some day they will take over."[30]

Mexican Americans, whether old or young were "great Lyndon Johnson people," according to Voight, so when she went to the Lower Rio Grande Valley she let people think she was also working at the senator's behest, even though, in her words, "we didn't have anything to do with Lyndon." When Sam Rayburn proposed Johnson as a favorite son presidential candidate Voight was "horrified," as were other liberals, while conservative Governor Shivers called Rayburn an enemy of Texas akin to Santa Anna. Voight found that Mexican

Americans, on the other hand, generally approved of the favorite son candidacy. Soon after Rayburn issued the announcement but before Johnson accepted, Dr. García asked Johnson's permission to begin organizing support for the candidacy. The senator's stock answer to such suggestions was "I am giving Mr. Rayburn's proposal a great deal of thought and study," but at the bottom of the letter Johnson's top aide Walter Jenkins added in longhand, "You may start contacting our friends on favorite son. It's OK. Let's get them all."

Thus Mexican Americans helped create what political scientist Chandler Davidson has called "a marriage of convenience" between the DAC and Lyndon Johnson. Connally told Voight, "I've got to raise you some money, Kathleen; you're doing all that work down there." She never asked him for it, she said, "because I was getting all the money I needed in five and ten dollar" donations. Out in West Texas Forum leader Cris Aldrete was busy organizing the loyalists in Val Verde County, but Voight remembered, "The powers that be were against us." Connally told her, "I'll take care of it." Voight recalled, "He picked up the phone and he called the county judge and said, 'You want that Amistad Dam, don't you?' . . . And Val Verde fell into line." [31]

At the spring 1956 convention Johnson helped seat the loyalists who in turn voted for his favorite son candidacy. Afterward he wrote to Cris Aldrete and others thanking them for their help in this campaign against "demagoguery." The liberal/loyalists then proceeded to eject the Shivercrats from the State Democratic Executive Committee (SDEC), arguing that the Democratic Party could hardly expect to survive if its own officers refused to pledge party loyalty, but Johnson considered the action a radical purge and marshaled conservative Democrats to reverse the action. Liberal differences with Johnson were again played out in the gubernatorial race a few weeks later, when Ralph Yarborough came within 3,500 votes of defeating Johnson's unofficial gubernatorial choice, Senator Price Daniel. Yarborough had the strong support of Forum members and George Sánchez, "a coalition kind of liberal," according to Ronnie Dugger. The embittered loser charged that, as in 1948, Johnson operatives in South Texas delivered tainted results. [32]

Despite growing disenchantment with Johnson the loyalist Texas delegates kept their pledge and voted for him as favorite son at the 1956 Democratic National Convention. Adlai Stevenson won the nomination on the first ballot, then opened the vice-presidential nomination to the delegates. Johnson asked Gus García to make the case for John Kennedy at the Texas delegation caucus. The flamboyant San Antonio lawyer was proud of his Johnson connection, telling friends, "I can talk to Johnson any time I need him." Fellow delegate Kathleen Voight remembered, "Gus was great. He was a genius. He must have had an IQ of 150, 180. . . . He jumped on the table and made the finest speech I ever heard in my life." Voight recalled, "The English just flowed out. Nobody could speak like that." Some say that as the votes began to slip away from Kennedy, García sidled up to Johnson and joked, "What we need here is another Box 13," but that the senator was not amused.[33]

Concerned about his national image and about retaining a Democratic majority in Congress, Johnson pledged to stump for Stevenson and advise him on campaigning in Texas. George Reedy warned the Stevenson campaign, "The civil rights issue should be handled solely on the basis of not inviting trouble," but he added, "It must be remembered, however, that there is a fairly important 'minority group' vote in Texas made up of Negroes and Latin Americans." Reedy thought that speeches on Stevenson's behalf by "some prominent Catholic layman" such as Senator Kennedy "would probably go over big" in South Texas. Johnson personally suggested this to the Stevenson campaign and accompanied Kennedy on a ten-stop tour of South Texas.[34]

Worried that Yarborough would try to control the state party with the help of the "Red hots," as Johnson privately called them, the senator turned around and allied with the Shivercrats at the fall state convention. In the words of historian George Green, "Johnson discarded his pledges . . . given his corporate power base in the state and the fact that Establishment financing was more important for his future ambitions than the (at best) uncertain support by labor-liberals." Conservatives surrounded the convention center with a barbed-wire fence, and police barred the two largest liberal delegations, Houston and El Paso, from entering. John Connally remembered, "They were all contested delegations and so that began to form a little bit of a schism . . . the pretty much more militant Hispanics versus the old-line conservative Hispanics who were very, very loyal to Johnson, basically those counties in South Texas." Johnson, according to Ronnie Dugger, "felt threatened by independent political organizations" and wanted to have overall influence over Texas delegations in the tradition of House Speaker Sam Rayburn. "But of course Lyndon wasn't benevolent. If you were against him he was malevolent. So Johnson's position had to count against the Mexican leaders who were part of the urban-based liberal coalition." According to Connally, "many of the young soldiers who came back, educated under the GI Bill and so forth, they moved to the big cities . . . and they became the more militant Hispanics in a political sense."[35]

The disenchanted Bexar County [San Antonio] delegation composed new lyrics to the "Battle Hymn of the Republic":

> . . . They have stolen votes from counties
> Which they never stole of yore
> Van Zandt, Hidalgo, Harris, and a half a dozen more
> There has been no steal so flag-a-rant since 1954
> As Lyndon let us down . . .

San Antonio City councilman Henry B. González—mobilizing family members, friends, and other political amateurs—became the first Mexican American ever elected to the Texas senate, edging out Owen Latimer by 200 votes. Johnson's old Cotulla friend Manuela Contreras served as a precinct leader and fundraiser for González on the mostly Anglo North Side. She persevered in the face of vitriolic criticism from Anglo residents, later remembering, "They said, 'well, you're probably a tamale and an enchilada lover.' . . . It didn't hurt me because I knew that Henry was very, very qualified . . . defending what he knows is right." At the same time, Latimer was "absolutely" a Johnson man, according to Rubén Munguía; "It was a case of the power and the money." Newly elected County Commissioner Albert Peña cracked it was fortunate that Lyndon Johnson was in the senate because it kept him out of San Antonio politics.[36]

George Green has written, "From that point on in Texas's political history, it was an article of faith among Texas liberals . . . that Johnson could never be trusted." In December 1956 they formed the Democrats of Texas (DOT). With Johnson, Rayburn, and Governor Daniel allied against it, the DOT found itself shut out of the state democratic machinery. At the same time the party leaders realized that the liberal coalition represented a significant number of voters. Former Johnson aide Jake Pickle, the conservative gatekeeper at the State Democratic Executive Committee, described the DOT as "a large group of the more liberal Mexican American leaders, some of the Negro leaders, and primarily financed by the labor group . . . a good-[sized] force" when combined with "the so-called loyal Democrats."[37] Johnson took pains to maintain his good relations with liberal Mexican Americans. When Raymund Telles was elected mayor of El Paso, Johnson promptly sent off a letter: "You seem to be as good at getting votes for yourself as you were in getting them for me in 1948. I will never forget what you did for me then."[38]

GIANT

Lyndon Johnson "had to engage and survive at a time when the regional speech was dying and when, more and more, Texas was coming to be different from the rest of America only as a wide color screen is different from an ordinary black and white one," observed New York journalist Murray Kempton. In 1956 Hollywood depicted South Texas in the movie *Giant*. A blockbuster film starring the movie icons Rock Hudson, Elizabeth Taylor, and James Dean, it ranged over the region for three hours, retelling Enda Ferber's bestselling novel of the King Ranch.[39]

Héctor García had helped the novelist with her research, taking her to GI Forum meetings throughout the region and introducing her to problems in the barrios. Ferber wove much of it into her book: the locked gates "so they won't go out" and vote for the "wrong" candidate; the migrant camp with its open latrines and stifling hovels; the war hero refused local burial and interred instead in Arlington National Cemetery.[40]

Millions of Americans read the novel, and millions more watched the movie version. At the same time their televisions were showing antisegregation marches led by Dr. Martin Luther King Jr. and their radios were blaring Elvis Presley's subversive mix of white country music and black rhythm and blues. Many Mexican Americans, for their part, found *Giant* painful, as in the case of young Tino Villanueva. He spent most of the year following the crops around Texas with his family, then they returned for a few months each year to their home base in Johnson's Hill Country. There, in San Marcos, Tino watched the screen with a horrible fascination as an Anglo cafe owner ejected a family of "Mexicans." Years later in Boston, when Villanueva happened to see the movie on television, the emotions came flooding back, inspiring the prize-winning poem *Scene from the Movie GIANT:*

> He stands there like God of the
> Plains country, heavy-footed like a troglodyte,
> And what he says he says with the weight of
> A dozen churches behind him: "You're in the

Wrong place amigo. C'mon, let's get out of
Here. Vamoose. Andale." The old man, whose
Skin is second-stage bronze from too much sun
That's gotten to it and won't pull back its
Color, has feebly searched among the
Threads of his pocket and extracted the sum
Of his need. In quietude (etched in raw umber):
Reliquary hands are endlessly making a
Wordless offering in a coin purse. Then the
Very way the tight wound voice of Sarge
Echoes through the cafe walls, out into the
Street, and back inside the Holiday Theater
Where I sit alone in the drop shadows of the
Back—: "Your money is no good here. Come on,
Let's go. You too," he says to the women,
Their torment half inside me. And with that:
He plops the old man's hat on his head and
Picks him up by the lapels. *Put the film in*
In reverse (I think). Tear out those frames
From time-motion and color; run the words
Backwards in Sarge's breath and sever the
Tendons of his thick arms in bold relief.

. . . I could not break free from the event that began
To inhabit me—gone was the way to dream

Outside myself. From inside, a small
Fire began to burn like deep doubt or

A world fallen . . . I held on. I held on.

For his part, Dr. García has pointed out that the final scene depicts
Rock Hudson as the ranch owner gazing with amazed affection at his
two grandsons: one white, one brown. "It was a very good movie,"
said García. "It was a happy ending and I hope we have a happy ending ourselves." [41]

Johnson had become the majority leader of the senate, the second
most powerful politician in the land. Perhaps he could, indeed, fulfill
his dream of becoming the first southern president since the Civil War.
If so, he would need to strengthen his position in the national Democratic Party. By the end of 1956 George Reedy had come to the conclusion that "some effort should be made to produce legislation along the
civil rights lines. . . . A civil rights bill—no matter how mild—would

take care of the minority groups," while inaction would allow liberals to convince Americans "that the current Congressional leadership is purely sectional and that would be dangerous." At the same time Reedy warned that a heated debate over the issue might alienate the majority of white voters.[42]

All his life Johnson yearned to bring people together, to fashion consensus out of warring factions and emotions. He considered a civil rights bill "a true starting point for reconciliation of North and South," according to Reedy, who remembered years later, "virtually single-handed, he kept a large body of very strong-minded and willful men concentrating on a purpose most of them thought could not be achieved." In the end this precedent-setting bill became law, but most of the enforcement provisions had been excised in committee.[43]

In this same year, 1957, Texas legislators were debating proposals to block implementation of the *Brown* decision. Senators Abraham Kazen and Henry B. González stalled the segregation bills by means of unlimited debate, defying what community organizer Ernie Cortés has called "oppressive racist backlash." For over twenty straight hours González lectured his colleagues, drawing on a lifetime of experience. As a boy, to rid himself of his accent, he had aped Demosthenes by reading Carlyle aloud with a mouth full of pebbles. Now González quoted with passion from his intellectual storehouse: Churchill, Lincoln, Horace, Herodotus. Himself having endured racial epithets and ejection from pools, picnic areas, and restaurants, González now cried, "Who speaks for the Negroes? What about them? . . . Is Texas liberty only for Anglo-Saxons?" In the *Texas Observer* Ronnie Dugger wrote that González "started roaring, he roared on, and he closed roaring; never has his like been seen here before." Johnson sent González a congratulatory telegram and an autographed copy of *The Lyndon Johnson Story*.[44]

In 1958 González ran for governor against the Democratic incumbent, Price Daniel. The "NAACP Man of the Year," González was carried into the Democrats of Texas convention on the shoulders of his enthusiastic supporters. He galvanized the DOT delegates with his call for liberal activism. At the same time, he had no organization and no state headquarters: just energy, idealism, and his old automobile. Dugger remembered, "Gandhi might as well have run for governor of South Africa before he returned to India." Daniel had the support of all the powerful party leaders, including his old ally Lyndon Johnson. According to Jake Pickle, who had worked for both men, Governor Daniel conferred with Johnson "before he took action . . . this included appointments . . . conventions . . . policy positions."

Nonetheless Johnson managed to establish cordial relations with González; the senator prided himself on winning people over, spending more time and effort on the disaffected than on his supporters. At the 1958 DOT convention the delegates fell into a stunned silence when González praised Johnson and Sam Rayburn, who, in the words of a *Dallas News* reporter, "helped Daniel control the 1956 September state convention of Texas Democrats." In April 1959 Johnson reinforced his ties to González by inviting the state senator to stay at the Johnson home and attend a dinner at the Mexican Embassy, where González sat next to Chief Justice Earl Warren. The following month Robert Kennedy asked González about the Texas prospects for a presidential candidacy bid by his brother, Senator John Kennedy. González asked Robert what he would think "if I go to Massachusetts and ask you, 'How do you think Lyndon Johnson will run in Massachusetts?'" Robert Kennedy replied, "I get it. Thank you very much."[45]

Johnson also was careful to maintain cordial relations with LULAC, stopping by their 1958 convention to make some remarks and "press the flesh." That same year GI Forum officer Arturo González introduced a motion at the Val Verde County Democratic convention "urging the State Democratic Executive Committee . . . to adopt a resolution supporting the candidacy of Johnson for President." In February of 1959, Héctor García met with Johnson in Washington and invited the senator to address the Forum convention that year, but Johnson said that congress might still be in session. When 400 Forumeers endorsed a resolution praising Johnson, the senator responded, "I have enjoyed my many enlightening talks with you." By the end of the decade the senator was addressing the Forum leader by his first name.[46]

BRACERO POLITICS

At the same time, García and Johnson's advisors eyed each other warily. The Forum founder considered John Connally more conservative than the senator. For his part, Connally called Dr. García a radical, and George Reedy characterized the physician as "a pretty wild man." In particular the two groups continued to disagree on the recruitment and treatment of *braceros*, temporary farm laborers from

Mexico. Forumeers and Lulackers complained that growers were not paying the prevailing wage as required by the *bracero* law, and the activists called for immigration restriction. Most growers wanted uninterrupted access for *braceros* and no labor regulations. In this debate, the voice of the Mexican laborers, particularly those entering the country without government authorization, went unheeded by the lobbyists for both sides.

Johnson told Forum officials that members of the Department of Labor were meeting with representatives of the growers, adding, "I am keeping in close touch with these developments," and he forwarded to García assurances from the Labor Department that the government would "make sure that the wages are fair." At the same time the officials ignored the representatives of the farmworker unions.[47] Overall, however, Johnson continued to respond favorably to the growers, as when the labor department required them to pay a piece-rate equal to the minimum wage rate of fifty cents per hour; Johnson chief of staff Walter Jenkins appealed to the labor secretary to rescind the order.[48]

Public Law 78, which authorized the entry of *braceros*, came up for renewal in 1958. Growers—including 10 percent with Spanish surnames—together with their influential allies inundated the senator's office with telegrams and letters demanding that the program continue and even expand. The president of a county cotton growers association wrote, "Since I understand you are a [*bracero*] user yourself, I know that you, even more than most, will be able to appreciate our position."[49]

One telegram came from a grower in Johnson's old bailiwick of Cotulla, who wrote, "*Braceros* must be made available to fill jobs." On the other hand, just three months earlier Cotulla grocer Tristan Ramírez had wired Johnson that he and other grocers in the Cotulla barrio had incurred a $100,000 debt feeding some 300 families who had been unemployed for six weeks. "When work is available *braceros* and wet-backs are hired," wrote Ramírez. He added that county officials claimed that they had no funds available for relief assistance, and had said this to a group of barrio residents, including former Johnson student Dan García. Meanwhile a former Johnson staff member, Cotulla attorney John Wildenthal, wrote to the senator corroborating Ramírez's story. Wildenthal remembered being "persona non grata when Johnson said something in the newspapers to the effect that there was hunger in Cotulla . . . people would just turn away when I would walk down the street after that." Many of his acquaintances thought that Wildenthal had sent the original telegram; he never said otherwise.[50]

Wildenthal had left Senator Johnson's staff to set up a law practice in Cotulla because Johnson "was killing himself, and while I realized a person like that never demands as much of his employees as he puts in himself, being conscientious you feel like you have to approach that level of activity." Plus, Johnson "had the ability to erupt and give everybody else ulcers. . . . He didn't protect himself from heart problems"—Johnson had a massive heart attack in 1955—"but it did protect him from ulcers." Besides, Wildenthal wanted to go home, in his words, "to find out what was going on in . . . my little corner of the world."

Wildenthal wired Johnson, "Thanks for your letter, you have done worlds of good by bringing [the issue] out in the papers. The situation was ignored until then." Johnson had alerted the Texas Department of Public Welfare to the Cotulla crisis; the department sent La Salle County Judge J. W. Martin a list of the available surplus food: at the time only dry milk, cheese, rice, flour, and cornmeal. "It looks like we have done too good a job in eliminating our farm surplus," a Johnson staff member wrote. Wildenthal warned the senator, "the Commissioners Court and several leading citizens obtained some job offers to show that the food program is unnecessary." Meanwhile the Cotulla mayor wrote to Johnson "at the request of the City of Cotulla City Councilmen and the citizens of Cotulla and La Salle County. It was unfortunate, we feel, that the papers carried a story about 33 families in Cotulla [that] were starving, since we can find no one here that will agree that this statement is correct."

The Cotulla Chamber of Commerce decided to hold a job fair to demonstrate the availability of jobs but ended up with over one thousand applicants for a handful of gardening assignments lasting only a few days each. Years later Wildenthal recalled the prevailing attitude as "an imaginary, an illusionary thing." The local hardware store owner, a prominent Baptist layman, did not believe that anyone was truly hungry. He asked Ramírez to prove his charge, so the grocer drove the man into the barrio and stopped at a house at random. After seeing the cupboard, bare except for a little cornmeal, the hardware man asked Ramírez to take him down the street house by house. After just three houses the Anglo visitor had seen enough; he bought a load of groceries for the three families.[51]

Senator Johnson could not have been surprised at the prevailing attitudes. After all, his dear cousin Margaret Johnson Kimball was related by marriage to County Judge Martin. The Martins were "staunch supporters and workers" for Johnson, according to their daughter.[52] While anxious to help the Cotullans of Mexican descent, Johnson knew where the power lay. The Department of Labor authorized 5,000 additional *braceros* for Texas after the senator talked to the secretary of labor "in an effort to be helpful in working out an adequate solution," according to Johnson. The senator's aides came to the conclusion that he should "favor growers and users over organized labor, if necessary" in order to balance the presumably prolabor stance of Senator Ralph Yarborough and to help people such as "Billy Sol Estes, in whom we are very interested . . . [who] has 26,000 acres and stands to lose $250,000 if labor is not available for harvesting." Majority Leader Johnson quietly supported the renewal of Public Law 78 and unofficially sided with those opposing a minimum wage for farm workers.[53] Nonetheless, Mexican American leaders were optimistic. More and more religious and civic activists (many of them women) were lobbying for termination of the *bracero* program; by 1959 Johnson's mail was nearly evenly divided. Only with the rise of the Chicano movement in the late 1960s, however, would the views of immigrants themselves begin to receive national attention.[54]

"TOO MANY PARADOXES"

By the end of the 1950s Johnson had managed to fashion a network of supporters from varied, often adversarial constituencies. He valued his connections to Dr. García and State Senator González and liked nothing better than seeing his former Cotulla students do well and become politically active. At the same time Johnson cemented his ties with growers, businessmen, and conservative Democrats who opposed Mexican American activism.

Johnson took immense pride in his ability to understand and please people who detested one another. He wanted to be a powerful, wealthy reformer and political broker like his hero Franklin Roosevelt. Ronnie Dugger once wrote of Johnson, "No one could say whether his love of the poor or awe for the successful rich is the stronger. . . . He is neither proletarian nor plutocratic, but yearns to be both. . . . He is as good as he thinks his own interest lets him be, which is also to say that he compromises principle to keep his own voters and financial support." [55]

According to George Reedy, Johnson "was a man of too many paradoxes. Almost everything you find out about him you can find out a directly contrary quality immediately." This is what Billy Brammer discovered. While a Johnson aide in the late 1950s, he took notes on his boss in order to use Johnson as the model for a political novel, *The Gay Place*. Published in 1961, it featured a towering Texas politician who "hadn't a selling price; he sold things . . . people . . . but never himself. There was a point in [his] code beyond which existed neither profit nor pleasure. He'd developed his own set of values; there seemed none like him, anywhere, for weighing ends against means." Then Brammer plunged into the character's very soul, finding there "Mahatma Ghandi and Rasputin . . . The Prince of Darkness and the goddamn Mystic Angel." [56]

PART TWO

THE NATIONAL SCENE

VIVA KENNEDY!

As the presidential election year of 1960 dawned, Lyndon Johnson remained the "Number One enigma of American politics," according to an article in *Look* magazine. His whole life had pointed toward the presidency, and he knew that this was the moment to run; he was the most powerful Democratic leader in the land, and the winner most likely would stay in office for eight years. Nonetheless, Johnson was "locked in the vice of indecision," in the words of political pundits Rowland Evans and Robert Novak. Johnson's acute antennae sensed that Americans hardly knew him and that many would reject anyone with a southern accent; no candidate from the old Confederacy had won since the Civil War.

Moreover, he had emerged from the bitter political battles of the 1950s a suspect figure to both liberals and conservatives in Texas. As Evans and Novak noted, "Johnson had no solid *Johnson position* in Texas (as, for example, John Kennedy had in Massachusetts or Hubert Humphrey in Minnesota.) This lack of independence emphasized the split in his political personality and heightened his ambivalence beyond the borders of Texas." So Johnson vacillated, encouraging supporters to work on his behalf but refusing to announce his candidacy officially. To complicate matters, Johnson viewed his 1955 heart attack as a harbinger, a reminder that the men in his family died by the age of sixty. He raged against this fate by drinking, womanizing, and throwing tantrums—what George Reedy called "some kind of colossal midlife crisis." [1]

LBJ OR JFK?

With an eye to national office, Johnson increasingly supported liberal legislation. "Maybe I voted wrong on some civil rights bills in the past, but I'm learning all the time," he told a reporter. "The difference between me and some of my Northern friends is that I believe you can't force these things on the South overnight. You advance a little and consolidate." In a closed-door session with African American leaders he spoke of his moral responsibility to protect every citizen's right to vote, and he shepherded through congress the 1960 Civil Rights Act, albeit once again a law with no teeth.[2]

By the end of the decade Johnson was voting labor's way on nearly all legislation. One conspicuous exception was the *bracero* contract labor program, an issue close to home. (The tide was slowly turning against it.) When the program came up for renewal in 1960, the senator's mail on the subject for the first time was almost evenly divided as more and more church and civic leaders lobbied against the agreement and as growers mechanized much of the harvesting and thus relied less on laborers. Mexican American activists were hopeful; Senator George McGovern had introduced a bill to phase out the program over a five-year period.[3] On May 18 Dr. García wrote yet again of his opposition to the *bracero* program but assured Johnson, "I am still praying for your victory. I am 100% for you." The senator replied, "I was deeply moved by your letter. I know that your interest in *bracero* legislation is motivated only by a high sense of public duty and a strong feeling of compassion." As originally drafted by an aide the letter continued, "You know I share these feelings," but Johnson's chief of staff Walter Jenkins excised the statement, concerned that the sentence would "commit us to Hector's position." Johnson steered through Congress a stopgap measure on this "controversial matter," as he characterized it to García; Congress renewed the *bracero* program, but for only six months, pending the outcome of the election.[4]

As soon as Johnson supporters began organizing, Rubén Munguía began printing bumper stickers, "the first ones," he said: "LBJ for DC." Munguía and fellow San Antonian Henry B. González supported Johnson as someone who knew their situation well and as an adept power broker who could deliver what he promised. State Senator González wrote to Johnson complaining that the San Antonio "Johnson for President" organization had excluded him. Johnson steered clear of the controversy, replying, "As you know, I have not handled the organization of these clubs. . . . I am honored that you have confidence in me."[5]

The unofficial Johnson campaign took up Héctor García's suggestion that he assess the candidate's strength in the Southwest, particularly among Mexican Americans. García concluded, "I believe we can win but we must make some changes," noting that while Johnson staffers were spending most of their time courting political leaders for endorsements, workers for Massachusetts Senator John Kennedy were drumming up support in the neighborhoods. García strongly recommended similar grass-roots organizing, writing Johnson, "you have wonderful appeal . . . but you are not selling it down to the level of the little guy." The materials García brought from headquarters "did very much good," he wrote, and he urged Johnson to disseminate a campaign biography in Spanish. The doctor offered to make promotional tapes in Spanish for broadcast nationwide, but particularly for California, site of the upcoming Democratic National Convention. In his own sales pitch the Forum leader was emphasizing the Longoria case, Johnson's stint at the "Mexican" school, the probability of high Mexican American appointments in a Johnson administration, Johnson's friendship with Latin American leaders such as the president of Mexico, and "the fact that the Texas delegation . . . would have several Latin Americans while the Eastern States would not."[6]

Most of the Mexican Americans that García met thought that Johnson would win the nomination with the help of the convention chairman, House Speaker Sam Rayburn, but most still leaned toward Kennedy, considering Johnson, in García's words, "too 'Southern.' They believe that he is for the Latin Americans but believe he is against Negroes." Or, as San Antonio activist Joe Bernal put it, "Many of us associated with eastern liberals mentally rather than with Texas." Herman Gallegos of San Francisco, a leader of the Mexican American Political Association (MAPA), said of Kennedy, "he gave to all Americans a sense of renewal, a sense of new vision, a sense of hope, inspiration . . . of belonging to the nation." Most Mexican Americans, like Kennedy, were Roman Catholic, but García reported that people did not mention this as a factor. They hesitated to trumpet a religious identity that had become the most controversial issue of the campaign, and one which many Southerners viewed with opprobrium. Moreover, Mexican-heritage Catholics often felt alienated from a mostly Irish-American church hierarchy. In spite of this Johnson campaign officials continued to consider Catholicism Kennedy's only link, discounting Mexican American liberal political attitudes.

García advised Johnson to avoid a divided Texas delegation by inviting some Kennedy Democrats to serve under him, "that if you approach a man or woman to work for you not one single individual labor or liberal would say 'no' to you." Reminding Johnson of California's large minority population, García urged the senator to include some Mexican and African American delegates and suggested that Johnson arrange a banquet for himself during the convention to be sponsored by some minority organization, adding, "I could help there."[7]

The Johnson campaign did not follow up on these suggestions, continuing to focus on important political leaders in hopes that they, in turn, could deliver delegate votes, particularly in the event of a dead-locked convention. Besides, no Democrat had ever won a majority of delegates through primary victories. Times were changing, however; with his West Virginia primary win over Hubert Humphrey, Kennedy was well on his way to sewing up the nomination. Kennedy supporter Richard Goodwin has speculated that if Johnson had waged an active campaign in this semi-Southern, Protestant, rural state that idolized Franklin Roosevelt, he might very well have eliminated his main rival.[8]

Finally, just days before the Democratic National Convention, Lyndon Johnson formally announced his candidacy. As convention time approached, García warned that Kennedy led overall, with a two-to-one advantage among Mexican Americans. The Forum leader suggested that Johnson consider the vice presidency. A Johnson staff member complained about the report, and García remembered replying, "'I don't get paid by Senator Johnson. It's my obligation to be honest with him. You work for him. I don't work for him.' This put me in cold storage" until after the convention.[9]

The Texas delegation excluded most liberals, notably Senator Ralph Yarborough. One of the few selected was Albert Peña. At a caucus in Los Angeles, when Governor Price Daniel announced that the Texas delegation would oppose the civil rights plank, Peña replied, "Governor, the majority leader promised me that this delegation would go for the majority plank." Daniel, startled, asked, "What do you know about it?" At that moment Speaker Rayburn came in, and everyone rose. "Ask him," replied Peña. So Daniel said, "Mr. Sam, this delegate from Bexar County says the majority leader says that we're supposed to vote for the majority plank on civil rights." Rayburn replied, "That's right," and sat down. Johnson's support for the civil rights plank had earned him liberal loyalty at the state convention that spring and now strengthened his national reputation as a moderate.[10]

Although most Mexican American delegates supported Kennedy, a few organized "Americanos con Johnson," among them Raúl Morín, an officer in the GI Forum and MAPA. Born in Texas, Morín had worked in the Civilian Conservation Corps there before moving to California. During the war he was wounded in the Battle of the Bulge and like many of his comrades encountered discrimination when he returned home. Now, as the 1960 campaign got underway, he was finishing a book manuscript that would document Mexican American heroism in U.S. wars, and he hoped to have Johnson write the foreword.[11]

John Kennedy's nomination was something of a foregone conclusion. The big surprise was majority leader Lyndon Johnson's acceptance of the vice presidential slot, an office that fellow Texan and former vice president John Nance Garner had characterized as "not worth a pitcher of warm spit." Johnson and some in the Texas Democratic leadership thought otherwise. If the Republicans won the White House, Johnson as the Senate leader would continue to be the most powerful Democrat in the nation; if the Democrats won, Johnson would reap much of the credit. On the other hand, if Kennedy won without Johnson on the ticket, the Texan would remain majority leader, but no longer would be the most important Democrat in Washington. Johnson also harbored the hope that as vice president he might continue to influence the Senate in his role as its presiding officer. Moreover, a White House office would divert attention from his southern roots and connect him to constituencies beyond Texas. Before almost anyone else, Johnson sensed that in this new television age the vice presidency would become a highly visible national pulpit. Besides, Richard Nixon had demonstrated that the vice presidency could serve as a launching pad for a presidential nomination.[12]

"I think Mexican Americans, mainly in California, had a lot of questions about Johnson. . . . I wasn't too keen on him," remembered Armando Rodríguez, a delegate to the 1960 Democratic National Convention. "I was a precinct walker, part of the crowd. . . . I worked every Democratic campaign." Rodríguez had immigrated with his family to San Diego from Mexico when he was a boy. After serving in the Signal Corps in World War II, he graduated from San Diego State University and worked on the Truman campaign of 1948. By 1960 he was teaching school in San Diego. He belonged to the local MAPA and GI Forum chapters and supported the efforts of César Chávez to organize a union of farmworkers. Rodríguez remembered, "I began to see what was happening in Congress . . . I was influenced by all the information I'd received on Johnson . . . the things he was alleged to have done in Texas in the early years of his political career." Rodríguez feared that Johnson's policies resembled those of conservative Republican Barry Goldwater more than those of liberal Democrats such as John Kennedy and Adlai Stevenson.[13]

CAMPAIGNING FOR KENNEDY

The new nominees conferred at the Kennedy compound in Hyannisport, Massachusetts. Among other things, Johnson mentioned his problematic civil rights record but also spoke of "his long friendship and support from the Mexican-American community in Texas," according to some political observers. For its part the Kennedy campaign had already established ties to Mexican American leaders. At a civil rights conference in New York City, Kennedy, along with his then-rival Hubert Humphrey, had met with black and Hispanic activists from around the country, and in June the Massachusetts senator had become a member of the American GI Forum. Now on the eve of the fall campaign the presidential candidate asked Henry B. González for his assessment of the ticket's chances in the crucial state of Texas. The state senator said that Kennedy would win San Antonio by a landslide that would offset losses in North Texas. Meanwhile in Washington Dr. García met Bobby Kennedy, who asked,

> "Will you help my brother?"
> "Well, we're going to help set up an organization."
> "What will it take?"
> "You give me a couple of credit cards . . . and in two weeks, maybe less, I can set it up for you."
> "How much work can you do?"
> "I think we can give you close to 98% of the vote."
> "Dr. García, what happens to that other 2%?"
> "Well, we've got those damned machines now; we don't quite understand them." [14]

García suggested that Carlos McCormick of the Washington GI Forum chapter work with the Kennedy campaign. During the Forum convention in August Dr. García, Ed Idar, and Cris Aldrete met with McCormick, who broached the idea of an organization by and for

Hispanic voters, to be called "Viva Kennedy!" Idar remembered, "Well, we had been around long enough to realize the value of this slogan. The slogan and the personality combined tremendously." The vibrant, youthful candidate would lead a young constituency eager to join the national political game.[15]

Many Viva Kennedy leaders distrusted the conservatives who ran the state Democratic Party machinery, particularly in Texas. A Johnson operative characterized these new volunteers as "not too much politically in line." Albert Peña agreed to coordinate Viva Kennedy activities in Texas only under certain conditions. First, Viva Kennedy had to be a freestanding organization. "We wanted to be recognized as a group," he said, or the regular Democrats "would sell us down the river." Second, he asked for assurances that the Kennedy administration would make what he termed "significant" Mexican American appointments and, third, that the poll tax would be eliminated. McCormick got Bobby Kennedy on the telephone and the candidate's brother agreed to the conditions, so Peña signed on. "The local Democratic organizations did not want the Mexican Americans to become politically active, informed, and organized," according to GI Forum leader Rodolfo Ramos, who said, "The best thing that we did with the Viva Kennedy Clubs was that we organized independent local Democratic institutions." Ramos thought that the Kennedys "understood it much better than anybody else before and after. . . . They said, 'Set your own up and we will provide the material.'" Organizers also raised money themselves by selling memberships for one dollar. They refrained from asking for money from state party headquarters not only to maintain their independence but also to avoid accusations of machine politics.[16]

Within twenty days Viva Kennedy clubs were operating in some thirty states. "The thing just spread like wildfire," said Ed Idar. Every town with a GI Forum chapter spawned a Viva Kennedy group and a number of LULAC leaders such as John Herrera of Houston worked zealously as well. Viva Kennedy speakers stressed that a Kennedy/Johnson administration would be the first ever to address the social and economic problems facing Mexican Americans. Like the Kennedy people in general, however, they rarely mentioned John Kennedy's Catholicism. In one notable exception, Viva Kennedy campaigners commented approvingly on the candidate's speech to Baptist ministers in Houston, where he finally faced the religion issue directly. Referring to the Alamo, the candidate declared, "Side by side with Bowie and Crockett died Fuentes and McCafferty."[17]

Héctor García delivered radio addresses and sent out some 300,000 mailings nationwide, including 100,000 sample ballots to Mexican Texans alone. In California Viva Kennedy cochairman Edward Roybal, a Los Angeles city councilman, made liberal use of, in his words, "very well done" radio spots produced by McCormick. Rodolfo "Corky" Gonzales coordinated the Colorado activities, registering more new voters than anyone else in Denver. At a Kennedy rally in Chicago, placards proclaiming "Viva Kennedy" and "Arriba Kennedy" dotted the crowd. In San Diego Armando Rodríguez raised money for the campaign. In the process he became acquainted with some of the influential people in the state Democratic Party and held a campaign event in his home featuring John Kennedy's brother Ted. State Senator González stumped for Kennedy in eleven states.[18]

When John Kennedy spoke in San Antonio, Viva Kennedy people were there in force. One, Manuela González Contreras, who had known Johnson since 1928, said, "I enjoyed every minute that I worked for Henry B. González, Lyndon Johnson, and J. F. Kennedy." She passed out literature, posted signs, attended committee meetings. "It was interesting. . . . I supported them wholly." She persevered despite the ridicule she encountered from people who called Kennedy a "nigger lover" and a "Mexican lover." Many women campaigned for the ticket, providing much of what historian Margaret Rose has called "the invisible backbone" of barrio organizational activity.[19]

The activists occasionally ran into problems with the South Texas establishment. According to Idar, GI Forum people organized a caravan of 100 cars that snaked through the towns in the Lower Rio Grande Valley, bringing hundreds of people to an Hidalgo County rally, only to find that county boss J. C. Luna relegated them to the sidelines. To the extent that local politicos such as Luna worked with Viva Kennedy, they did so out of loyalty to Johnson; the region was "strictly LBJ country," in the words of Duval County operative O. P. Carrillo. John Connally remembered, "Some of the 'Viva Kennedy!' signs and slogans were used among the Hispanic communities, but largely because of the symbiosis of Catholicism. The basic core of the Johnson adherents in the Hispanic community were all still there and still loyal to him."[20]

Eighty-three-year-old Judge J. T. Canales of Brownsville met with a number of longtime Tejano residents, including the Cavazoses of the King Ranch. Canales presented, in his words, "a solid front" against the Republicans, writing to Johnson, "It is a great satisfaction to pay a debt I owed to your good father when I managed the Ranger Investigation in 1919." Canales advised the campaign to emphasize fiscal restraint, particularly in military spending, and he published an article to counter charges that the Catholic Church would dictate public policy. "The religious issue is a booger in order to confuse the voters, by fear of something that is not really true," he wrote to Johnson, adding that this statement would appear in publications from Corpus Christi to Laredo. Canales's frail health limited his campaign activities, but his sister and her friends were, in his words, "Hooting for you and working very hard," while his brother-in-law was responsible for the mariachi band that greeted the Johnsons in Harlingen. Canales predicted that the ticket would carry Texas by a thin margin and would prevail mainly because of Johnson's popularity.[21]

Although wary of Johnson's conservative friends in the state Democratic Party, Dr. García remained staunchly loyal to the vice presidential candidate himself, making sure that the Viva group was, in García's words "a Johnson organization," replacing "Viva Kennedy" bumper stickers with "Viva Kennedy/Johnson" ones. For his part, Johnson asked García to accompany him and Senator Chávez on a campaign swing and sought García's advice on speeches to "our Latin American friends," as Johnson called them. The bond between the Forum leader and the Texas senator tenuously linked the three factions of the Texas Democratic Party, with García straddling the liberal and moderate camps, Johnson the moderate and conservative ones.[22]

The senator spent most of his time trying to keep conservative southern Democrats in the fold. He was a thoroughgoing professional, delivering some fifteen speeches per day all over the South even though he detested playing second fiddle to a young whippersnapper of a presidential candidate who had never amounted to much in the United States Senate. Johnson vented his frustration on his staff, berating them in drunken tirades and threatening to quit, but "on the stump he had very few peers," George Reedy recalled. The candidate himself devised the dramatic entrance used at each stop; the train's loudspeakers would blare "The Yellow Rose of Texas," reaching a crescendo just as the engine roared into the station. Then he would ask his audience what the Republicans had ever done for their little southern town and remind them of the legacy of Franklin Delano Roosevelt. Sometimes Johnson touched people so deeply that Reedy thought they seemed entranced. "It was deeply moving. . . . We could feel minds change as he spoke."[23]

Johnson even tried to reach those disaffected whites who held up signs vilifying his racial tolerance. Johnson's main campaign organizer Bill Moyers recalled one particularly poignant night in Tennessee.

When the local dignitaries had finished the last bottles of bourbon and branch water and departed, he started talking about those signs. And long past midnight with an audience of one, he was still going on about how poor whites and poor blacks had been kept apart so they could be separately fleeced.[24]

Kennedy carried Texas and the nation by razor-thin margins. While the president-elect was visiting the LBJ Ranch, Judge J. C. Looney sent him election figures from several South Texas districts that Looney thought "could probably rightfully claim that they were responsible for the Kennedy-Johnson ticket carrying Texas." Kennedy wired Albert Peña, "Congratulations on the magnificent job turned in by the Viva Kennedy Clubs in Texas. The margin of victory in Bexar, Nueces, El Paso counties and the Rio Grande Valley was [of] prominent significance in carrying Texas."[25]

Texas Observer editor Ronnie Dugger called Viva Kennedy "a jumpin' deal, no minor thing," but said that Mexican Americans mainly came out on their own in vast numbers because of Kennedy's charisma and the ties of Catholicism. John Connally remembered, "Viva Kennedy signs and slogans were used among the Hispanic communities, but largely because of the symbiosis of Catholicism." When Arthur Krock of the *New York Times* discounted Mexican American activism and emphasized the Catholic connection, Ed Idar responded that Mexican Americans voted for Kennedy because he was a Democrat, not because he was a Catholic. Idar cited Mexican American registration drives that had vastly increased the number of eligible voters by the end of 1959, long before Kennedy won the nomination. The Forum leader also pointed out that the barrio residents voted overwhelmingly for Adlai Stevenson in 1952 and 1956.[26]

As for Viva Kennedy, George Reedy remembered, "I didn't think it was too well handled, frankly, from the results that I saw," adding that Mexican Americans would not have voted Republican in any case. "We would have lost Texas," said Reedy, "without the Dallas incident" (when a group of well-heeled Republicans yelled and spit at Mr. and Mrs. Johnson in a hotel lobby). "That turned everything around; that was it," said Reedy. The next day he attended a South Texas rally where the crowd took up the Three Rivers chant—"Tres Ríos! Tres

Ríos!"—and people said to Johnson, "This is your country. All of Texas is your country." Bill Moyers recalled, "I knew there was a group called Viva Kennedy but I didn't know what it meant." With the Mexican American leadership working to avoid the Johnson people, perhaps it was inevitable that his camp knew little about Viva Kennedy activities.[27]

PLAYING NATIONAL POLITICS

"Mr. Kennedy rode the Mexican burro into the presidency," proclaimed the *Forum News Bulletin*, adding that there was "much watchful waiting" to see if the new administration would deliver on its promises. On November 28 a number of activists and public officials—including Dr. García, State Senator González, Commissioner Peña, Dr. Sánchez, and Judges Salinas and Benavidez—met to plan postelection strategies. They decided to support González in his expected bid for the United States Senate and to lobby the Kennedy administration for the appointment of Salinas to the federal district court for South Texas. Many of these same people reconvened in January. They called for a meeting to have "the Viva Kennedy movement continue as a political organization," Albert Peña wrote in a letter sent to Mexican American Democrats throughout the state.[28]

Activists from across Texas met in Victoria on February 5, 1961, and formed the Mexican American Political Association. Californians had organized MAPA in 1959 to combat discrimination in the California Democratic Party. When Los Angeles City Councilman Ed Roybal ended up being the nominee for lieutenant governor in 1954, the Democratic Party chairman told him, "You dare not run . . . you won't be good for the ticket," Roybal later recalled. "Why not?" asked Roybal, and the chairman replied, "Because the people of California will not support two Catholics on the same ticket." As far as Roybal was concerned, this was a smoke screen for anti-Mexican sentiment, that if he had been a Catholic of any other extraction the issue would not have been raised. Roybal also recalled that the party gave no support to Hank López when he ran for secretary of state in 1958. "He was the best qualified of all the candidates: Harvard graduate, top of his class, law review and everything," said Roybal. Nonetheless some Democratic officials refused to join him on the campaign platforms; López was the only statewide Democratic candidate to lose that year. He turned to writing articles for national periodicals such as *Life* and *Harper's*, eventually serving as editor and advisor for Sam Houston Johnson's memoir, *My Brother Lyndon* (see chapter 11).[29]

In Texas a number of MAPA members objected to using the word Mexican, which segregationists had employed for years, and they said they wanted to appeal to Hispanics of various backgrounds, so the Texans renamed their group the Political Association of Spanish-Speaking Organizations (PASO or PASSO.) PASO and MAPA would endorse political candidates and lobby for legislation such as the elimination of the poll tax, equal educational and employment opportunities, and a minimum wage for farmworkers.[30]

Meanwhile the new administration in Washington made good on a few of its promises, notably with ambassadorships for both Henry B. González and Héctor P. García, but neither the state senator nor the physician could abandon professional responsibilities for a permanent diplomatic post. García did serve on the United States delegation to the United Nations and as special ambassador to the West Indies. He attended the White House concert by Pablo Casals, "a beautiful, romantic, enchanting evening," he remembered. "There was Mrs. Kennedy in her regalia and beauty." After one event, according to García, President Kennedy told him, "Thank the Mexican American people for electing me president."[31]

Nonetheless, Dr. García wondered why the White House did not seek out other Viva Kennedy veterans for federal appointments. At a February press conference a reporter said to President Kennedy,

> Mr. President, the Mexican Americans are very concerned because you have not named one of them to a high place in your administration. They say that they are the only ethnic group that worked for you nationally . . . and they have not been recognized. I wonder if you plan to give them some recognition?

The president cited Dr. García's work for the administration and added, "I quite agree with you that we ought to use what I consider the great reservoir of talent, and I think this is particularly true in our relations with Latin America . . . we will continue to see if we can . . . associate them with our administration." The White House made a few appointments, such as Dr. George Sánchez to the National Advisory Council for the Peace Corps and to the committee on "New Frontier Policy in the Americas."[32]

The Forum and PASO's desire for appointments, particularly that of Judge Salinas to the federal district bench, ran afoul of the bitter patronage battle between Senator Ralph Yarborough and Vice President Lyndon Johnson. As John Connally put it, "Ordinarily the senior senator controlled state appointments, . . . Johnson, though, got a commitment from Kennedy that he could have half of it. That infuriated Yarborough." People in Texas soon got wind of the controversy. Ed Idar wrote to George Sánchez, "I certainly agree with you that Kennedy may strip us of our leadership. I think he would like to give us appointments in this State but unfortunately, Johnson, Yarborough and other Texans appear to be in the way." García and Idar began lobbying Lyndon Johnson—"the key man," in Idar's words—on behalf of Salinas.[33]

In January the South Texas county leaders met at Johnson's suggestion to nominate a candidate for the judgeship. Salinas had the westernmost counties in the region behind him, in addition to support from several state supreme court justices and the head of the State Democratic Executive Committee. On the other hand the Rio Grande Valley was split between two Johnson people: J. C. Looney and Cecil Burney. While in Washington for the inauguration Looney showed the three names to the new vice president but not to Senator Yarborough. According to Ed Idar, upon hearing about Looney's visit with Johnson, "Senator Yarborough felt that Salinas was a 'Johnson man.'"[34]

Soon thereafter rumors began to circulate that Brownsville Judge Reynaldo Garza was in the running. Garza swore on his mother's grave "that he WAS NOT making any bid for it," according to Idar, but Garza acknowledged that Johnson had told him during the campaign, "You carry the county (Cameron), and it will be good for me and good for you." At the same time Johnson was telling Salinas supporters that he could not get involved in the nomination decision because he was leaving the Senate. "As you know, my hands are pretty well tied in this matter," he wrote to García, but the Forumeers did not believe it. After all, most of the Salinas opponents, in Idar's words, "have been identified for a considerable period of time with the political career of Senator Lyndon Johnson." Garza's relationship to Johnson dated at least from 1937, when, as a college classmate of John Connally, Garza campaigned alongside Johnson in that first congressional race. In addition, J. T. Canales, the old friend of Johnson's father, supported Garza, calling the candidate "a gifted young Latin-American lawyer, very popular throughout this section." A few weeks later GI Forum contacts in Washington confirmed that Johnson spoke on behalf of Garza to the Kennedys. Meanwhile Yarborough refused to oppose Garza even though, Idar reminded the senator, this candidate was "an Eisenhower Democrat, a supporter of former Governor Allan Shivers in every campaign and one who is counting on the friendship of Vice President Johnson." George Sánchez warned a Yarborough aide, "the Senator has jeopardized the support given him by about 400,000 'Mexican' voters."[35]

"I was the one who went to Garza to see if he would receive it," said Duval County operative O. P. Carrillo, "I was the messenger from Lyndon Johnson and President Kennedy." Kennedy appointed Garza on March 23, and the Senate confirmed the nominee on April 13. In a typical GI Forum reaction, Teodoro Estrada wrote to Dr. García that Mexican Americans were "fools" for having trusted Johnson. "We sure were taken for a ride. And Yarborough, the man whom you have been photographed hugging, what has he done for his Texas Latin friends?" Referring to Johnson and Yarborough, a disgusted Héctor García wrote privately, in a rare use of Spanish, "Estos desgraciados no nos quieran dar ni agua. [These good-for-nothings don't want to give us a thing.]" García felt that the Viva Kennedy people had been used, and he warned, "we are just beginning to revolt." Bobby Kennedy, sensing the discontent, called Judge Garza to Washington and told him to address the GI Forum convention in July, even though Garza, in Idar's words, "hated the Forum." Senator Yarborough also reached out to the Forum by agreeing to speak there.[36]

Appointment squabbles were overshadowed by the contest for Johnson's senate seat. On December 4, 1960, State Senator Henry B. González declared his candidacy. Around the state Mexican Americans rallied behind him. In a typical announcement, the Civic Action Committee of Houston trumpeted the news, urging its members to register and pay their poll taxes; the Committee listed some fifty people, all Spanish-surnamed, one-quarter of them women, who had been deputized to receive poll tax payments. González faced the governor's conservative interim appointee William Blakley and moderate Congressman Jim Wright. After González had announced, fellow San Antonio liberal Maury Maverick Jr. entered the race. The liberal coalition was breaking apart, and González feared that Johnson had a hand in it, but other observers saw no evidence that the vice president was a spoiler. In any event, Johnson seemed to favor Bill Blakley.

Meanwhile a united Republican Party nominated John Tower, who went on to win the senate seat. The divided San Antonio liberals trailed the other candidates. Maverick edged out González statewide by 9,000 votes, but back home in Bexar County González beat him by 17,000. Maverick teased Bexar County Commissioner Albert Peña,

"Albert, one of these days I'm going to convince you I'm a better Mexican than Henry Gonzalez," but when speaking seriously Maverick said that he had come to the conclusion "that as candidates, Anglo liberals were finished in South Texas politics."

In June, a little over two months after the senate election, Henry B. González announced his candidacy for Congress. Maury Maverick quickly pledged his support "in an effort to unify all Loyal Democrats." Governor Daniel, Senator Yarborough, and President Kennedy followed suit, with only Lyndon Johnson still uncommitted. The vice president yelled at reporters for having the nerve to ask about an endorsement when he arrived at the San Antonio airport for a speaking engagement. Later at the hotel, however, Lalo Solís and Albert Peña each visited the vice president's room and obtained an endorsement. Peña explained that the campaign was generating a lot of enthusiasm but precious little cash and he recalled Johnson replying, "Commissioner, we're going to come in with money, marbles, and chalk," then picking up the telephone and calling people around the state with the news of his endorsement; he arranged to enlist, in Peña's words, "all the money people." Johnson told the commissioner to call the reporters up to the suite. When Peña said to Jim McCrorry of the *San Antonio Express-News*, "The vice president is going to endorse Henry, wants to talk to you," the reporter sputtered, "Hell, no. He just cussed us out." Peña reminded him, "Jim . . . it's going to be a good story." So the reporter came. Peña watched as Johnson smiled and said warmly, "Hi, Jim, I'm glad you came, I haven't seen you for a long time." McCrorry remarked, "Son of a bitch knew I'd talked to him earlier!" The next day Johnson issued a formal written statement endorsing González.[37]

Once on the bandwagon, Johnson went all out for González. "Johnson has been watching the González campaign closely," reported the *Dallas Morning News*. Lady Bird Johnson attended a testimonial dinner for González, and when the Republicans sent former President Eisenhower on a triumphant visit near election day, Johnson retaliated. Vice presidential aide Cliff Carter spent the last week of the campaign with González, and Johnson himself came down for the final three days. The vice president had campaigned for many a Democratic candidate, but this was a watershed. Johnson made it clear, according to Carter, "either we were going to be for racial justice or we weren't, . . . that a Latin American should be elected from there if that's what the people wanted." The vice president taped campaign speeches for the candidate, urged him to buy more media time, and spoke on his behalf at events around the district. According to the *Dallas News*, "In his speeches during his three days of the campaign, Johnson told voters to prove that a person of Mexican descent could be elected to high office." Republicans seized on this, charging that he was playing racial politics. Undeterred, Johnson kept stumping; at a reception on the north side of town he ran into his old Cotulla friend Manuela González Contreras, who was busy working for Henry B.[38]

The vice president came to the conclusion that his candidate was trailing and needed a boost. So Johnson called the president of Mexico and asked him to send the most popular Mexican movie star of the day, Cantínflas, to San Antonio on election eve. Sure enough, the comedian ended up in the middle of a United States congressional campaign. They grabbed the actor and put him on a flatbed truck, saying, "You're going to go down there and people are going to cheer 'Viva Cantínflas!' and you say 'Viva Gonzalez!'" George Reedy heard the entertainer sputter, "They're crazy people up there!"[39]

The entourage visited "this very elegant northside shopping center and I don't think over 250–300 people were there," remembered Terrell Maverick Webb, the widow of Maury Maverick Sr. Johnson spoke vigorously in praise of González as a defender of the principles of the Democratic Party, but Webb could tell that the senator was concerned. "I saw that look in his face," she said, "where his lips kind of purse and his chin comes up to sort of meet that nose . . . real determination and a little bit of worry." They headed for the West Side, where they encountered "frantically large crowds," Cliff Carter recalled. The Secret Service people had to hold hands and form a circle around Johnson, González, and Cantínflas, slowly edging them out through the excited throngs. The next day as the results trickled in, Vice President Johnson visited several polling places and smelled victory in the air. González won by 10,000 votes, to become the first Texan of Mexican descent in the United States Congress. Democratic National Chairman John Bailey called the victory "a rebuke to those who sought to inject racial issues into the campaign and a hopeful harbinger that religious and racial prejudice is on the wane in American politics."[40]

Johnson intervened "much to Henry's distress," according to González aide Fred Schmidt, who said, "[González] thought he had the race won" before the Cantínflas appearance, "that was his private feeling at the moment," and he feared that Johnson would get much of the credit for the outcome. "Johnson sees it as trying to do the good and righteous thing and González sees it as 'Jesus, they're patronizing me again,'" said another González aide.[41]

When Congressman González announced that Fred Schmidt would be his chief administrative assistant, Cliff Carter called, concerned that Schmidt was not a Johnson man. Another aide to the congressman, Kelsey Meeks, said, "There were some feelings perhaps of personal animosity between Cliff and Fred, and Fred did bring some political baggage with him." The next day Schmidt brought in his last piece of anti-Johnson material: an "I Loathe Lyndon" bumper sticker left over from the 1956 state convention. González laughed, "Nobody woulda found it—now you're bringing it here—you're exposing me!" González held firm. Schmidt, the former education director for a union, had long worked for González, staying up all night with the state senator, handing him books during the civil rights filibuster of 1957. "I loved him," said Schmidt; "I thought he was great." [42]

That first week in office Johnson invited González over. "Any meeting you were in with Johnson he was going to dominate," said Schmidt, who remembered the vice president as someone attentive and courteous but absolutely at the center of the discussion. The congressman and his chief assistant heard a vice presidential lecture on the fine art of reelection. "You've got to start now," Johnson said, telling González to respond promptly to constituent requests and to "buy give-away pens with his name on them," remembered Schmidt. "They'll never get you out of here if you'll just pay attention to these things," said Johnson.

Soon thereafter González and his staff visited the vice president at his ranch, where they discussed ways the new congressman could obtain favorable press coverage. "Look, if there's good news, I want to announce it jointly with you," Johnson told the new congressman. Soon the two staffs were socializing and exchanging political gossip. [43]

González craved a seat on the Armed Services Committee, given the many military bases in his district. No longer a congressional leader, Johnson could not deliver. Veteran Texas congressman and lifelong Johnson friend Wright Patman said, "Henry, you just stay on this [Banking] Committee and quit making a wave about Armed Services and you'll end up chairman." When business people even hinted at ways for him to cash in on his banking committee connections, González dismissed them from his office outright. The freshman congressman might take the vice president's advice about caring for constituent concerns, but he did not emulate Johnson's cozy relationships with corporate behemoths. Years later the congressman recalled having thrown out of his office a Daniel supporter who had the temerity to offer energy company money, in cash, in return for an endorsement.

González quickly established a reputation as a person of integrity, a liberal, something of a loner, but outgoing, with a quick wit and, on occasion, a quick temper.[44]

EQUAL EMPLOYMENT OPPORTUNITY

Lyndon Johnson chafed at being vice president. He missed the power he had exercised in the senate and had forsaken for ceremonial duties at a president's bidding. Only as head of a few committees did Johnson run the show, as in his role as chairman of the President's Committee on Equal Employment Opportunity (PCEEO). Modeled on the Fair Employment Practices Committee established during World War II, the PCEEO forbade racial discrimination by businesses holding federal contracts and by federal employers themselves. Unlike its predecessor, the new agency had the authority to revoke government contracts, but Johnson believed that persuasion and publicity would work better in the long run, that business people would cooperate if given the opportunity, particularly with negative press coverage and government sanctions lurking in the background. Loath to become an opponent of business leaders and powerful conservative Democrats, he also thought that punitive government action could trigger a white backlash that would undo civil rights advances.[45]

In the very first year a number of companies agreed not to discriminate, as in the case of Lockheed, which promised equal opportunity for "minorities," although in practice this meant African Americans only. "The emphasis appears to be all on discrimination against Negroes," stated an internal GI Forum memo that concluded that the PCEEO needed to hire "a capable Latino or Latinos." A number of Mexican Americans nominated their colleagues or themselves. Peña wrote to Carter that Johnson had promised to name him to the commission, but "if my appointment is not possible, I would recommend that a Latin American be appointed." Carter advised Reedy that the vice president had told Peña that the latter's name would be considered, "but did *not* assure him." Reedy responded, "This is a very touchy matter" because "every Latin American of any stature" belonged either to LULAC or the GI Forum "and to appoint a member from either group would alienate the other group." Carter replied, "I am of the opinion Peña should not be appointed . . . but rather a Latin American recommended by Henry González." As a member of congress González was the ranking Mexican-heritage public official from Texas and he belonged to neither LULAC nor the Forum. In

November 1962 Johnson appointed González's brother Dr. Joaquín González.[46]

Forum president Louis Tellez requested a statewide investigation of employment discrimination in New Mexico. Both Albert Bonilla of LULAC and Héctor García of the Forum wrote about employment problems at the Corpus Christi naval base. Johnson responded by meeting with the secretary of the navy, who then asked civil service officials to confer with García, the commanding officer, and the employers. The regional civil service director wrote to García, "Your unselfish dedication and sacrifice for the benefits of your people make me think of you as one of the few truly Christian Gentlemen I know." Nonetheless problems persisted. One year later a Mexican American electrical engineer resigned from his position at the base "because of continued unfair employment . . . but apparently your committee still doubts our true statements," he wrote to Johnson.[47]

Discontent grew. Not one business in the entire country lost a government contract because of discrimination. The PCEEO vice chairman, Texas labor leader Jerry Holleman, wanted action, as did Attorney General Robert Kennedy, who was facing constant complaints from African American leaders. Civil rights activists were on the march throughout the South and even affecting the administration's main priority, foreign affairs, as George Sánchez discovered when he read Mexican magazines featuring articles about the civil rights movement. In California dissatisfied Mexican Americans founded the Equal Employment Opportunity Foundation. One member wrote to Johnson that they "greatly appreciated" his efforts and invited him to address the group but complained that Mexican Americans were "misunderstood and too little represented." To such letters the PCEEO issued the most general of responses. Johnson replaced Jerry Holleman with his friend Hobart Taylor, a black businessman originally from Texas and a firm believer in the power of persuasion.[48]

The Washington Forum leader, Rudy Ramos, watched the Committee's moral suasion campaign with growing frustration. Born into poverty in the little town of Weslaco near the Texas-Mexican border, Ramos earned a law degree at American University and stayed to set up practice. Long interested in public issues, he had observed the 1956 Democratic convention in Chicago and had served as deputy director of the Viva Kennedy campaign. In response to a Ramos questionnaire, the PCEEO indicated that 98 percent of its cases dealt with the twenty million African Americans, while fewer than 2 percent concerned the eight million Hispanic Americans. Hobart Taylor replied,

I gather from the tone of your letter and the questions you ask that you feel the Committee has neglected the problems of the Spanish-speaking and has concentrated on the problems of the Negroes only. I assure you of our deep concern with the problems of the former as well as the latter.

He offered to meet with Ramos "and with other leaders of the American GI Forum at any time."[49]

Meanwhile, Vice President Johnson accelerated his own public relations campaign. In August 1963 he addressed the Mexican American Education Committee, comprised of representatives from various community groups around California, including the GI Forum, LULAC, the Community Service Organization, and the Mexican Chamber of Commerce. The night before, the leaders of the various groups caucused to hammer out a common list of complaints, "the usual litany of problems," according to Herman Gallegos, who remembered his first impression of Johnson in the flesh as someone of large physical size, with big ears and a direct manner of speaking.

Congressman Roybal introduced Johnson, having been briefed by the vice president's office about Johnson's long association with Mexican Americans, starting with Cotulla and continuing with electoral campaigns where Mexican-heritage votes often made the difference. After the congressman's warm introduction Johnson spoke of his determination to combat job discrimination and said that his committee had processed 4,334 complaints in two and one-half years, with 75 percent of the rulings in favor of the plaintiff, but had only received 90 formal complaints from Spanish-surnamed people. Johnson urged his audience to send in evidence of discrimination, even if just on a postcard. "I started to get a different impression" of Johnson, said Roybal, who remembered that in the 1950s, "[Senator] Dennis Chávez told me that I was making a mistake, that Lyndon Johnson actually had a heart, that he knew what the problems of the Hispanics were and would be more responsive than Adlai Stevenson." Mexican American Education Committee chairman Carlos Borja thanked Johnson for his "heart to heart luncheon remarks and, later, the exchange of ideas and information with our leaders. . . . Your coming to Los Angeles . . . has given us renewed hope that there is someone in the Federal Administration that is . . . willing to try and help us." Borja pledged that his organization would "be of service to the President's Committee on Equal Employment Opportunity" and requested details on the upcoming regional EEO conference.[50]

The Regional Conference of Community Leaders on Equal Employment Opportunity convened on November 14, 1963. On the list of proposed workshops Johnson wrote, "Nothing specific on Mex. here." No Mexican American-oriented sessions were added, but at least for the first time they were included. Dr. Joaquín González cochaired the conference, and a number of Hispanic leaders took part. At his session Dr. George Sánchez told the participants, "The *mexicano*, the American of Mexican descent, has not had the spokesmen and the financial backing that either the Negroes or the Indians have had. So, in the Southwest, the question of equal employment opportunity and the question of education and training is most urgent when we think of the American of Mexican descent." [51]

CONNALLY FOR GOVERNOR?

Meanwhile Johnson kept one eye on Texas politics, particularly when his protégé John Connally decided to run for governor in 1962. In fact, the state Democratic executive director of the time has written that Johnson's close friends suggested the candidacy as a way for the vice president to regain some political influence in the state. The race was yet another wild and wooly Texas political contest, with numerous Democratic hopefuls vying for the prize. Connally faced incumbent Governor Price Daniel as well as liberal Don Yarborough. The fact that this Yarborough liberal was no relation to liberal Texas Senator Ralph Yarborough only added to the confusion, as did the entrance of two dark horses: former attorney general Will Wilson and arch-segregationist retired General Edwin A. Walker. [52]

"I think that if we can stick together that we will be able to elect the next governor of the State of Texas provided Lyndon Johnson doesn't try to get into the act," Héctor García wrote to George Sánchez. When Albert Peña visited Washington, Johnson sent a limousine to bring him over to the White House. The vice president saw him ahead of Henry Ford II and "some general," Peña remembered. Conducting one of his famous monologues, Johnson kept him for almost an hour, cajoling, regaling him with stories, in a subtle effort to woo PASO into supporting Connally. Peña kept quiet, knowing that PASO people would not endorse the vice president's man. Undaunted, Johnson people were putting out the word that Mexican American leaders had committed to Connally, according to charges by Don Yarborough and George Sánchez. If the accusation was correct, the tactic worked; the liberals turned on one another. In the *Texas Observer* Ronnie Dugger editorialized that Peña and other Mexican Americans might support Connally as "status seekers" in exchange for "a mess of pottage." GI Forum attorneys Ed Idar and Bob Sánchez fired back that, among other things, the *Observer* did not help fellow liberal Henry B. González's two statewide campaigns and that Dugger had "no conception of what Latins desire and little respect for the political judgment of Latin leaders." For his part, Connally told González that Peña had pledged to support Connally, only to disavow it. "I just called to tell you that he's no friend of yours, either," Connally added.[53]

As the date of the PASO convention approached, members lobbied for the various candidates. According to Peña, Henry B. González kept calling San Antonio PASO people, urging them to support Connally. The congressman would probably come to San Angelo to talk up Connally, wrote local resident Ed Idar, who added that on a previous visit González had "lauded the Vice President as one of the most generous men that he has ever known."[54]

Meanwhile Sánchez was pushing hard for Don Yarborough, writing to Idar that the liberal candidate was

> *not* a Dugger type of liberal . . . more practical, less academic, and more genuinely identified with social problems that mean something to our people. . . . What has LBJ done for us all of these years? He has cut our throats at every turn. I do not swallow the fiction that Connally is his own man. He is LBJ's man, and nothing but—and we can expect from him, no matter what he promises, just what we have gotten from LBJ in the past: nothing. . . . What benefit have we ever received from the LBJ machine? LBJ-Rayburn-Daniel have always treated us like dirt. Are we so naive, so immature politically that we believe that their *alter ego*, John Connally, is going to turn over a new leaf? It is a laugh! . . . If we endorse Connally he will win; and, once in office, he would become so entrenched and the LBJ machine would become so all-powerful, that he wouldn't need us anymore. So, poof, to hell with the social reforms and the political changes for which we stand! We would be back to Allan Shivers, Price Daniel, and the good old political serfdom. Let us not mistake this: LBJ has been making goo-goo eyes at some of us for a purpose—his purpose, not ours. . . . Suppose we endorse Yarborough and LBJ gets mad at us. What do we lose? Nothing! . . . LBJ . . . will know that without *performance* on his

part we will vote the other way! So, we are faced with a situation in which we cannot lose *if only we do not endorse Connally.*[55]

Idar replied that he was not convinced. After staying up until two in the morning talking to Don Yarborough, Idar was certain of the candidate's progressive stands, but feared that Yarborough was "a little too ready to promise everything. . . . I fell for that line of gab with Ralph Yarborough years ago. I do not want to make the same mistake twice." GI Forum members had campaigned long and hard on behalf of the liberal senator, only to see him oppose the Salinas nomination and, more important, vote for the continuation of the *bracero* contract labor program, virtually the only piece of antiunion legislation that he endorsed. A Forum official, probably Idar, wrote in an internal memorandum

> It seems to me that since [Ralph] Yarborough is *unable* or *unwilling* to help, we should reestablish cordial relations with Johnson. . . . It might not hurt to see if we could get one or two Forum leaders on his staff. He may want support for Connally— if so, we could consider same if he makes it worth our while by helping us with some of our problems and also by seeing that we get a little patronage.

Idar also noted that Johnson's speeches defending Hispanic voting rights during the González congressional campaign demonstrated that the vice president "is now pretty well identified with *la raza.*"

Idar also questioned Don Yarborough's electability, "whether the boy is going to have sufficient backing financially," particularly from organized labor. Noting that union official Jerry Holleman supported Connally, Idar concluded, "It is basically a question of whether we ought to make an all out effort to win with an all out liberal or whether we ought to work out the next best thing with one of the other candidates." He strongly agreed with Sánchez "that in the past Johnson has helped us little if at all on the problems that affect our people," but Idar thought that the exodus of conservatives from the Democratic Party meant that Democratic leaders of all persuasions "for once in their lives . . . are going to have to really cater to our people."[56]

At the PASO convention Daniel "made a tremendous presentation,

the best of all of them. A number of us, mostly the Forum leadership, decided to go with Daniel," according to Idar, who said that as
attorney general Daniel had opposed the poll tax, while "Connally
wouldn't even take a stand on the poll tax question." Peña leaned toward Don Yarborough but said, "There was strong pressure for Price
because he promised *mexicanos* some jobs." Although Daniel had
conferred with George Sánchez before the convention, "Sánchez kept
pushing Yarborough," said Idar. While the PASOites argued over
the merits of Daniel and Yarborough, the Connally forces kept up
their own lobbying efforts. Viva Kennedy founder Carlos McCormick,
now working for the Kennedy administration, pushed for Connally at
the PASO convention "at the behest of Johnson," according to Idar.
McCormick avoided the convention floor, instead inviting various
PASO leaders up to his room. In the end the convention endorsed
Price Daniel.[57]

PASO backed the wrong horse. The Daniel campaign never caught
fire and was hobbled by voter resentment over a new sales tax. The
governor lost to Connally and Yarborough, who now faced each
other. "I believe it would be most unfortunate if Connally were to win
the run-off," wrote Sánchez to Idar, adding, "the LBJ crowd will never
do anything for our people." Idar replied, "You must be kidding! Like
all liberals, you assume your judgment is . . . infallible. You could have
campaigned for [Yarborough] without impugning the motives of those
you did not agree with. . . . You help to make PASSO fail . . . and now
you think it can be made to work." Idar wrote to Dr. García, "the
man must be nuts . . . maybe he thinks we are now ready to swallow
Don." Most GI Forum people, remembering Three Rivers and Johnson's friendship with Dr. García, supported Connally.[58]

A divided PASO made no endorsement for the runoff election. "If
they had helped, Don Yarborough would have beaten John Connally,"
said Peña. Connally won by a mere 26,000 votes, with Bexar [San Antonio's] County playing an important role. The *Texas Observer* credited Peña's "potent Democratic coalition" with effective work on
Yarborough's behalf but posited that Connally's "connections with
the Kennedy administration as Navy Secretary" brought the county
into the Connally column by the narrowest of margins. On the other
hand Washington pundits wrote that Connally won precisely because
he distanced himself from the Kennedy administration in general and
Vice President Johnson in particular. When Connally ran against his
Republican rival PASO endorsed him, only to withdraw its support
when Connally refused to meet with the PASO leadership.[59]

REFORMING THE BRUSH COUNTRY

After the endorsement fiasco a number of PASO leaders decided that they should emphasize grass-roots organizing. A crowd of PASO supporters cheered lustily when their state executive secretary, Albert Fuentes Jr., announced that he had just returned from Washington, where the Kennedy administration had given its blessing to the PASO voter registration drive. "We organized poll tax drives and before we knew it we had more poll taxes than the whites. We concentrated on the white-dominated counties," remembered Peña. In the Brush Country/Winter Garden District, where as a young schoolteacher Lyndon Johnson had first encountered wholesale racial discrimination, overt segregation in public facilities was breaking down, but very slowly. One of the younger Cotulla businessmen tried to recruit the few Mexican American shopkeepers into the local businessmen's service clubs, but with little success, perhaps because many of the basic inequities remained.[60]

Throughout the Winter Garden region the Anglo minority continued to hold virtually all of the political offices, as in Cotulla's county of La Salle, where Judge J. W. Martin still presided. Martin was the uncle of Johnson's young cousin Margaret Ann Kimball. Both of her parents had died, and the vice president said that he would be honored to give Margaret Ann away in marriage but did not know if his schedule would permit it. On the wedding day Cotullans anxiously waited at the Martin home until, finally, the call came from the airport, "Please send a car for the vice president and his wife." The bride entered on Johnson's arm. Afterward the Johnsons greeted their old Cotulla friends with gracious warmth. La Salle County historian and Martin relation Annette Martin Ludeman noted, "Thirty-two years had passed, but Lyndon Baines Johnson remembered the friends of his youth." While in Cotulla the vice president brought together two political opponents: Judge Martin and Dan García. The former Johnson student was a leader in the barrio voter registration drive and recalled, "There was a certain amount of friction between the Anglo administrators in the city and the Latin American people there."

Some time later Ludeman's husband, owner of Ben's Western Wear, presented a custom-made Stetson hat to Johnson at the LBJ Ranch. With the Ludemans came Judge Martin, the local sheriff, other Cotulla officials, and several of the students from the "Mexican" school, including Dan García. Annette Ludeman remembered, "Johnson was more interested in his former students than in the new hat." When interviewed for a *Look* magazine profile, Johnson made a point of emphasizing the Cotulla experience because, in the words of Cotullan and former Johnson aide John Wildenthal, "he wanted his relationship and his concern for the Mexican-Americans in the clutches of poverty there in Cotulla to be highlighted in this story. . . . He related it to political power."[61]

Meanwhile the newlyweds settled in neighboring Crystal City. Margaret Ann wrote, "Dearest Lyndon, You will never know how much it meant to me to have you give me away." Two years later a nineteen-year-old activist named José Angel Gutiérrez challenged the Crystal City elite, declaring, "They say there is no discrimination, but we have only to look around us to know the truth. We look at the schools . . . the houses we live in . . . the dirt in the streets . . . and we know." PASO and the Teamsters Union supported an effort by local Mexican Americans to take over city hall through the ballot box. "I had to be very careful because the newspapers would say 'What is the county commissioner doing out of town?'" said Albert Peña, so he only organized in Crystal City on the weekends. He charged that whenever he came to a meeting there, so did the police and Texas Rangers.

The insurgents won a resounding victory. Soon thereafter the voters of Cotulla elected Dan García the first Mexican American councilman in the city's history. The Anglo minority, however, continued to dominate these counties. In Cotulla they retained control of the city council, while in Crystal City the five Mexican American winners promptly lost their outside jobs. Mexican American officials lost in the next election due to inexperience, infighting, and harassment. They were replaced by a slate comprised of Anglos and of Mexican Americans acceptable to the Anglo leadership. "I never forgot those kinds of dynamics," said José Angel Gutiérrez, who would stage another Crystal City revolt in 1969 (see chapter 11). "It's not just important to take power; you've got to be able to hold power and govern effectively. So I learned by watching."

Meanwhile, an incident in Crystal City fed the feud between conservative and liberal Texas Democrats. During his tenure as mayor, insurgent Juan Cornejo got embroiled in an argument with an Anglo councilman. Texas Ranger Captain Y. A. Allee told the mayor, "Come here, I want to talk to you." The Ranger and a sheriff took the mayor into an office, slammed the door, and kept him there for twenty minutes. Cornejo filed a $15,000 damage suit against Allee for assault and intimidation; the case was dismissed for lack of witnesses.[62] John Connally issued a statement in support of Captain Allee. George Sánchez retorted that he was "very disturbed" at the governor's stance, adding, "If Mr. Cornejo says he was 'roughed up,' I tend to believe it—for he has no reason to malign or libel Mr. Allee. . . . The Rangers, better known as *'rinches'* among my people, are sorry representatives of law-and-order when 'Mexicans' are involved; or Negroes, for that matter." The professor reminded Connally, "the *mexicanos* and the Negroes wield compelling political power in Texas," and warned that the Ranger incident would not "be forgiven or overlooked." The following month, when Governor Connally announced "GI Forum Week," lauding the organization for helping Spanish-speaking Texans "in their adaptation to the American way of life," an incensed Sánchez wrote,

> How sweet! How superciliously condescending! What is the "American way of life"? The LBJ way? Governor Connally's education has been very sadly neglected, in so far as the Americans of Mexican descent are concerned. While the GI Forum deserves recognition, and while it has done a very commendable job in a number of areas, that organization has never sought to adapt "Mexicans" to the American way of life. . . . This for the very simple reason that we have never accepted the accusation that we were anything but Americans—in fact, that some of us have been here, in what is now the good old U.S.A., long before Mr. Connally's folks came to Texas or even to the Western Hemisphere.

Senator Yarborough reacted to the Crystal City incident by issuing a statement that criticized "men wearing pistols . . . a relic of a primitive age in Texas . . . not a part of a city government, but breathing down the necks of duly elected city commissioners."[63]

KENNEDY IN TEXAS

The animosity between Yarborough on the one hand and Connally and Johnson on the other worried President Kennedy. In the 1964 presidential election Texas would again be crucial, so Kennedy decided, against Johnson's advice, to visit Texas in order to raise money, shore up support, and, in particular, try to get the two sides on speaking terms. The odds for cooperation among Texas Democrats looked slim. The Texas that John Kennedy visited in November 1963 ranked thirty-third in average income among the states, forty-fourth in adult literacy, last in child welfare spending, while the oil boom was creating millionaires. Just two days before the visit Congressman González wrote to Governor Connally to make sure that funds raised at the presidential dinner to be held in Austin would not be used by any Democratic challenger to the senator. On the Texas trip Yarborough avoided Johnson, who had been looking for a suitable candidate to run against the liberal senator in the 1964 Democratic primary. Yarborough stood next to González in San Antonio and refused to ride with the Johnsons in the motorcade from the Houston airport to the business district. That day in Houston, November 21, the president huddled with leaders of both political factions.[64]

Meanwhile LULAC was holding a convention in Houston. According to John Connally, "the LULACs got word that [Kennedy] was going to be here so they immediately sent up a huge crowd and demanded that he come by and visit them and he decided to do it." After the president said a few words Jacqueline Kennedy briefly addressed the group—in Spanish. A trio performed Mexican ballads composed by one of the LULAC members in honor of the two Kennedys:

Buenas tengan sus mercedes
en la ciudad progresista,
todo el pueblo se orgullese
y le da la buenvenida.

Kennedy, Kennedy, Kennedy,
hombre de fuerza y valor,
todo tu pueblo te aclama
porque eres su salvador . . .

[Or]:

Greetings to the honored ones
in the city of progress,
The people are proud to welcome you.

Kennedy, Kennedy, Kennedy,
man of strength and valor,
All of your people acclaim you
because you are their savior.

This strong people united
and here present,
Openly offer their affection
for the President.

Kennedy, Kennedy, Kennedy, . . .

"It was a rip-roaring reception," said Connally. The president, according to the *Dallas News*, "sought to cement his support, which contributed heavily to his election in 1960, among the Latin-Americans." Most likely the Kennedy team also wanted to make sure it touched all the Hispanic bases. In September Robert Kennedy had been the featured speaker at the GI Forum national convention in Chicago; that same month LULAC leader John Herrera had written to Carlos McCormick, now an assistant to the chairman of the Democratic National Committee, "practically every LULAC president at this banquet and ball will be a Viva Kennedy booster and the sooner we get the ball rolling the better."[65]

Although enthusiastic crowds greeted the Kennedys everywhere, it soon became clear that the reconciliation mission was failing. A squabble arose over whether Senator Yarborough would be seated at the head table at the banquet scheduled for the next day, November 22, in Dallas. Then came the great tragedy that obliterated all other concerns. The assassination of John Kennedy shocked and saddened people everywhere. Julian Samora, the first Mexican American sociologist, was having lunch with a surgeon in Bogotá, Colombia, when his host informed him that President Kennedy had been murdered. Samora recalled, "I went downtown. Theatres were closed, everything was flag-draped . . . Oh, they loved him down there." Guadalupe Saucedo renamed his *corrido* "A Kennedy en vida" (To Kennedy, While Alive). Some two dozen other people composed *corridos* to honor the slain president. Kingsville native Willie López, author of "Recordando al President [sic]" ("Remembering the President"), wrote numerous *corridos* with political themes, including one critical of the Texas Rangers. He gave a copy of the Kennedy ballad to Congressman González, who personally delivered it to Jacqueline Kennedy. In the fall of 1964 López wrote another, "Recuerdo Eterno: Homenaje a J. F. Kennedy" (Eternal Memory: Homage to J. F. Kennedy), which expressed the hope that Johnson would carry on the Kennedy legacy. Meanwhile, a friend of the GI Forum, Fr. Moses Gallegos, wrote an elegiac poem, "Los Caballos Blancos":

The bells ring at eleven in the Washington morning
White horses slowly walk
Black children's faces cry for their president
Only the Chief's horse twists in disobedience
Impatiently hoping its chief will mount and ride . . .

At the same time GI Forum members heard an alarming rumor that some news commentators referred to their organization as a communist front tied to a Spanish-surnamed acquaintance of the chief suspect, Lee Harvey Oswald.[66]

The day after the funeral Forumeer Raúl Morín offered his assistance to the new president, particularly for the election campaign of 1964. "I do not want to sound presumptuous," Morín wrote to George Reedy, "but I can safely say that I am very well acquainted with most of the Spanish-speaking political leaders, both Democrats and Republicans, in the major cities of the Southwest and Midwest." Morín credited his network to his book *Among the Valiant*, "with a Foreword by President Johnson," and to his work as a GI Forum organizer. A few days later Morín wrote to a colleague, "The tragic death of President Kennedy has left the whole picture of the Spanish-speaking in the Southwest jumbled," but one thing was certain; the Forum would play "a prominent role" in reorganizing the Viva Kennedy clubs "due to the closeness of Dr. Héctor García to the new President."[67] The question now was, What would be the new president's agenda?

LAUNCHING THE
GREAT SOCIETY

O n January 6, 1964, Dan García of Cotulla, Texas, appeared on the television program "I've Got a Secret." His secret? He had once been spanked by the man now President of the United States (albeit decades earlier). During the broadcast Johnson called his former student, and the next day García spent two minutes with the president in the Oval Office. García, now Cotulla's first Mexican American city councilman, managed to find time to ask for federal funds for several projects, including improvements in the very school where Johnson had taught and had served as principal. The chief executive promised that Cotulla's application would go to the top of the pile. Speaking of the Cotulla experience, special assistant Bill Moyers noted years later,

> It obviously had a strong impact upon his resolve to act when he could on behalf of the disenfranchised, the disinherited in our society. . . . He would use it in a stump speech or when he was trying to persuade a member of congress. . . . trying to sell the War on Poverty or . . . talk about the importance of education . . . or the imperatives of democracy. . . . With some recalcitrant political tyrant he would try to loosen their heartstrings with this story. . . . It was this same experience, this teaching at Cotulla, used to support different aspirations that fitted into the overall strategy in his mind of the Great Society, which was a place for everybody.[1]

"WE MUST NOT DROP THE BALL"

Late one evening Johnson summoned Moyers to the living room on the second floor of the White House. The president was thinking about the approaching date of March 4, when Franklin Delano Roosevelt was inaugurated in 1933. "It wasn't an anniversary for anyone except President Johnson, who seemed to never forget that," remembered Moyers. Johnson had been doing some calculations on a notepad. "Look, I've just been figuring out how much time we would have to do what we want to do," he said. "I really intend to finish Franklin Roosevelt's revolution." Johnson sensed that Americans yearned for something positive to emerge from John Kennedy's murder and would unite behind the slain president's legislative program. The new president knew that he would have to act quickly. Feelings were fleeting, and, in any case, voters tended to favor the opposition party in off-year elections, such as those slated for 1966.[2]

In a speech at the University of Michigan on May 22, Johnson issued a clarion call for a Great Society. Government would champion equal rights for blacks, educational opportunity for all, health care for older people, urban improvements, and protection of the environment. Johnson asked the students, "Will you join in the battle to give every citizen the full equality which God enjoins and the law requires? Will you join in the battle to build the Great Society, to prove that our material progress is only the foundation on which we will build a richer life of mind and spirit?" To each question they thundered, "Yes!"[3]

Answering the president's call, Americans from business, labor, higher education, and local government worked together on task forces that shaped hundreds of legislative proposals for the war on poverty. "He longed to integrate us all," remembered Moyers. Johnson wanted to bring the disenfranchised into the American system, he said, "to take tax eaters and make them tax payers." Unlike Woodrow Wilson, who ruminated over abstract ideas, or Jimmy Carter, who concerned himself with bureaucratic details, Johnson preferred working with people face-to-face, always searching for common ground, according to White House aide Jack Valenti, who said, "[Johnson] had existential motivation more than intellectual or political; he thought that if you got groups together . . . that by listening and sifting, you could come up with solutions." Laws passed at such a fast pace that the task force meetings kept getting interrupted for bill-signing ceremonies. War on Poverty administrator Dr. William Crook, although a Hill Country resident himself, said, "The real LBJ is not to be found on the Pedernales . . . but in the legislation he passed and the price he paid to pass it."[4]

An aide to Congressman Henry B. González recalled, "So much was happening so fast that all, at least in retrospect, seems more like a hurly-burly than an organized effort." González cooperated with the Johnson administration's efforts to steer legislation through Congress, particularly as a member of the Housing Subcommittee. Johnson facilitated the process by using techniques he had perfected as Senate majority leader. "He worked hard on behalf of every piece of legislation," remembered Edward Roybal, the first Mexican American representative from California. The president thought nothing of leaving the Oval Office sanctuary to argue the merits of a bill over a cup of coffee in the congressional dining room, and Roybal noticed that when Johnson chatted with members' wives at social functions, he made a point of asking about children and grandchildren by name. Late one night, on the eve of an agriculture bill vote, the president called Roybal, saying,

"I need one more vote to pass that . . . will you give me that vote?"

"Mr. President, I can't because I've already submitted a questionnaire and overwhelmingly the people in my district are against it."

"Well, in that case, you vote your district . . . they sent you out here, not me or anybody else. But in the event that I need that vote, would you be the last one to vote?"

Roybal recalled, "I said 'yes,' . . . and he had already won by one vote by the time I voted. . . . That goes to show you how closely he monitored the whole thing. . . . That man was an expert on legislation, and we haven't had another one like him."

One day when Johnson was discussing congressional bills with Roybal the conversation turned to the New Deal. The congressman said that he considered the greatest New Deal acts to be Social Security, the Homeowner's Loan Act, and the Civilian Conservation Corps (CCC). Johnson replied, "I don't disagree with you," and he asked the congressman about his experience as a young CCCer. Roybal explained that chopping all those trees caused strong muscles to develop all along the right side of his chest. Intrigued, Johnson said, "That's hard to believe. Why don't you take your coat off and show me." So

Roybal proceeded to strip to the waist. "Now, who else would have asked you to do something like that in your own office but Lyndon Johnson? He loved that program."[5] (At the same time, Johnson may have had a secondary motive for the strange request. He often tested male reactions to physicality; be it stripping to the waist, skinny-dipping in the White House pool, or riding horseback at the LBJ Ranch, he was always on the lookout for any hint of unease.[6])

Despite the excitement generated by the Great Society legislation, some skeptics continued to question Johnson's sincerity. "Lyndon talked about the New Deal when he wanted to seduce liberals," remarked Ronnie Dugger of the *Texas Observer*. Professor Julian Samora recalled, "Johnson was a crook. . . . When he became president . . . he cashed in what people owed him and he made things work." Mexican Americans had no voice in the task forces. The few who had beaten the odds and established themselves in business, unions, or universities had yet to be recognized nationally. In general, White House staff members favored northeasterners, which further worked against people such as Samora at the University of Notre Dame and George Sánchez of the University of Texas. To his credit, Johnson noticed the preponderance of Ivy League professors and demanded more geographic diversity; by 1966 both Samora and Sánchez were consultants.

Samora's skepticism was outside the mainstream. His own university president, Father Theodore Hesburgh, saw things much differently. The priest told a Johnson staff member that the president came in, "stretched out on a couch, saying he was worn out dealing with the British all day . . . and how the test of his presidency would be how much he could do for the poor and particularly for the Negroes, Chicanos, and Puerto Ricans." To this end Johnson directed his aides to compile a list of Mexican American leaders in California.[7]

The alliance Lyndon Johnson had formed with Mexican Americans, particularly those from Texas, reached its apex with the Great Society. No organization seized the initiative with more enthusiasm than the American GI Forum. "I feel we can be of great help to you," Dr. Héctor García wrote to his old friend Lyndon Johnson. "We have a lot of qualified experienced men . . . in approximately twenty states." The head of the Forum's Washington, D.C., office, attorney Rodolfo (Rudy) Ramos, swang into action, aided by other Washington Forumeers and several LULAC members, whose own organization had not yet established a Washington chapter.[8]

Just five days after the Great Society speech Ramos wrote to an administrator at the Commerce Department, offering the services of the Forum for job training programs. The next month he attended a White House meeting for members of various ethnic groups, where he told presidential advisors Jack Valenti and Lee White, "Federal programs have not been implemented effectively or at all in areas with large concentrations of Spanish-speaking Americans." Ramos gave them twenty-five pages documenting inadequate federal hiring practices in agencies ranging from the Post Office to the State Department. "The President's aides agreed that the 'War on Poverty' must be expanded," Ramos reported in the newsletter he sent out to Forum chapters. He spoke at several Great Society conferences, including one in May 1964 on migratory labor, where he explained that Mexican Americans suffered from educational levels, income levels, and employment rates at least as low as those of blacks. At the National Citizen's Conference on Community Relations several Forum officers talked briefly with the president and with Sargent Shriver, the head of the new Office of Economic Opportunity (OEO), which administered the War on Poverty.[9]

As the omnibus OEO bill worked its way through Congress, Ramos sent copies of the legislation to the local Forum chapters, explaining it title by title and declaring, "The American G.I. Forum has had its war on poverty for almost twenty years. We must not drop the ball now." He urged Forum chapters to take the lead in forming community action groups to implement War on Poverty programs, and he sent information on programs and pending legislation to Forum chapters throughout the Southwest and Midwest, as well as to some 2,500 individual Hispanic leaders. Ramos sent every member of Congress periodic newsletters outlining GI Forum activities. "What he was doing was to me the right thing," recalled Congressman Roybal, who hosted a reception for members of the Forum to meet administration officials, other members of Congress, and Democratic National Committee (DNC) staff members. In Washington "we had some very key people," the congressman recalled, such as Manuel Velázquez, who worked for the chairman of the House Appropriations Committee.[10]

García conferred regularly with Congressman González to plan strategy, as in the campaign to terminate the *bracero* contract labor program. The Johnson administration supported this effort wholeheartedly—"went all out," according to Ed Idar. Now the president of all the people, Johnson no longer needed to curry the favor of powerful growers such as his erstwhile political rival Allan Shivers. "They were going to be with him because he was from Texas. They were not about to undercut him," said Idar. California community leader Herman Gallegos, who lobbied Labor Department officials for repeal of the *bracero* program, observed, "This pulled us into the magnet of national politics. We had access." In December 1963 Congress voted for the termination of the *bracero* program at the end of twelve months. Ramos, who had testified in support of the bill, wrote to Labor Secretary Willard Wirtz, "We are happy for you that you had the courage of your convictions." This legislative success brought Mexican American organizations to the attention of liberal leaders.[11]

Mexican Americans overwhelmingly supported the 1964 Civil Rights Act. This landmark legislation changed the face of the Deep South by forbidding racial discrimination in public accommodations, from hotels to restaurants to movie theaters to parks. By the 1960s Mexican Americans had gained admittance to most public venues, but they placed great hope in Title VII, which sought to end racial discrimination in employment through its Equal Employment Opportunities Commission (EEOC). The Forum passed a resolution commending President Johnson for the act. Meanwhile, older LULAC leaders such as M. C. González—who had lobbied in the 1930s and 1940s for the "Caucasian" designation and had warned against alliances with blacks—had faded from the scene, replaced by civil rights activists such as Judge Alfred J. Hernández, who was elected LULAC president in 1964.[12]

White House press secretary George Reedy noticed that Mexican American leaders were becoming "somewhat more sophisticated." Senator Joseph Montoya of New Mexico asked the secretary of labor to make sure that the administration addressed the employment discrimination problems of all minority groups, and passed along Ramos's offer to supply statistics documenting the lack of Mexican Americans in the federal government. Between June 1964 and June 1965 nearly 2,000 were added to the federal job rolls, with a 23.7 percent increase at the top levels of the government. GI Forum members participated in the establishment of the Community Relations Service Board of the Department of Justice "to bring about solutions to the problems of racial relations," according to García. Title VII also included a provision against gender discrimination, potentially a potent weapon on behalf of the many Mexican American women who suffered from double discrimination on the job, but women's issues were systematically ignored by both the men in the Mexican American organizations and the men in the EEOC.[13]

Efforts to insure equal employment of Mexican Americans were stymied in part by a lack of accurate statistics, an ironic by-product of LULAC success in obtaining a "Caucasian" designation from federal agencies during the 1930s. Besides, Johnson administration officials, like most non-Hispanics, viewed civil rights solely as a "Negro" issue. The 1964 "Status Report on Efforts of the Department of Commerce to Improve Employment Opportunities for Members of Minority Groups," for example, dealt exclusively with blacks, and only African and Anglo Americans attended the "To Secure These Rights" conference called by the White House after the passage of the Civil Rights Act.[14]

In spring 1964 several Mexican Americans, including George Sánchez and members of the GI Forum, did attend the State Department Conference on Equal Employment, which focused exclusively on African American concerns, so Ramos complained to the State Department and he urged Forum chapters to do the same. In December 1964 staff members from the State Department, the EEOC, and Congress met with GI Forum officials and Puerto Rican leaders to work on ways to increase the number of Hispanics in the Foreign Service. Soon thereafter the State Department established a summer intern program for Hispanics. Meanwhile Ramos reported, "I got wind that the White House is interested in hiring a Mexican American"; he suggested that he and Dr. García meet with officials of the DNC. The Forum wanted someone, according to Idar, "if not in a policy making position, at least in a position that he would be able to influence policy . . . not just a title."[15]

VIVA JOHNSON

In a March 1964 magazine article, "The President and the Spanish-Speaking Vote," Henry (Enrique) López warned the Johnson administration not to take these loyal Democrats for granted, writing, "*Will* they turn out in huge numbers for Johnson as they did for Kennedy?" The author had barely lost his bid for California Secretary of State in 1958, and was a leader of the Mexican American Political Association. As such he knew many of the leaders of the Texas counterpart, the Political Association of Spanish-Speaking Organizations (PASO). López cited PASO's "disagreements with Johnson and his close associates such as Governor Connally," and speculated, "It remains to be seen how fervently PASO men will man the precincts in 1964. Certainly Johnson's immediate call for action on civil rights should have impressed PASO's adherents as strongly as it impressed the nation's Negro leaders."[16]

PASO people did sign up, but GI Forum leaders ran much of the campaign operation. Héctor García urged the Democrats to reactivate Viva Kennedy, warning Robert Kennedy that Johnson's Republican opponent, Senator Barry Goldwater, was angling for Mexican American voters. In response to a July request from the White House, Ramos created a pamphlet publicizing every conceivable Democratic public official of latino or latina heritage, everyone from Senator Montoya to a consul in Morocco, as well as any and all federal programs of particular benefit to this constituency.[17]

Although the point man for GI Forum lobbying, Ramos was passed over as head of the Viva Johnson effort in favor of Vicente Ximenes, then residing in Ecuador. Ramos remarked sardonically, "I was the natural person to handle the Viva Johnson campaign but instead, through García again, we had . . . Vicente Ximenes. . . . That's how politics works." Ximenes was a close associate of Héctor García's and had ties to Johnson that dated from the 1930s, when Ximenes's father worked as a loyal political operative in Congressman Kleberg's district. Moreover, the younger Ximenes grew up in the same town as the president's close ally, Governor John Connally, who named Ximenes's brother the first Mexican American on the University of Texas Board of Regents. The White House recalled Ximenes from his State Department post. "I wasn't particularly anxious to come back," Ximenes said. "I was doing what I wanted to do, but it was President Johnson who made the request through the Democratic National Committee." Ramos became the deputy director.[18]

Like Viva Kennedy before it, Viva Johnson recruited prominent public officials as cochairmen, including Congressmen Roybal and González and Senator Montoya, but relied on the state cochairmen for most of the day-to-day planning. García ran the Texas operations and Bert Corona headed the California effort. Since the 1930s Corona had been active in union organizing and Mexican American groups, particularly the Congreso de los Pueblos de Habla Española (see chapter 2) and the Community Service Organization (CSO). Then in 1959 he helped establish the Mexican American Political Association (MAPA). As a Democratic Party organizer he campaigned for fellow CSOer Ed Roybal and was a member of the Northern California Democratic Campaign Committee. In 1960 Corona helped direct the Viva Kennedy national campaign and in 1962 worked in Edmund G. (Pat) Brown's successful gubernatorial race against Richard Nixon.[19]

As in 1960, the Viva organizers avoided the states' Democratic machinery. In order to reassure one county chairman, a Viva Johnson leader wrote that the organization aimed "not to conflict with any other pro-Johnson-Humphrey campaigning; this is to complement other efforts." To his dismay, Ximenes discovered that the Kennedy people had not saved any of the Viva Kennedy records: no volunteer lists, no budgets, no Spanish-language media contacts. Starting from scratch on September 14, he quickly established a full-fledged national operation. Ximenes and Ramos worked in conjunction with fellow GI Forum attorney Cris Aldrete, who had just been appointed to the DNC. Some 500 local leaders founded 300 clubs throughout the Southwest, the Midwest, and in Florida. Viva Johnson developed its own campaign material and, according to Ximenes, "created, programmed, and carried out the National Mexican-American ads" for more than twenty radio stations and newspapers as well as producing a constant flow of press releases. A profile of the oldest registered Democrat, a Viva Johnson member, caught the attention of the national media. Ximenes delivered more than 100 speeches while he and Ramos distributed two million pieces of campaign literature, including one million copies of a Democratic campaign edition of the New York newspaper *El Diario/La Prensa* that Aldrete helped produce.[20]

Ximenes actively recruited women, calling them "the best source of grassroots campaign work." Half of the Viva Johnson volunteers in Austin, for example, were female, as were most of the marchers in Chicago's Viva Johnson procession. As in party politics generally, the higher the organizational level, the fewer the women, but a number did advise the Viva Johnson campaign, including Fran Flores of California, Polly Baca of Colorado (head of GI Forum Ladies' Auxiliary), and Dr. Cleotilde García of Texas.

Dr. García headed Viva Johnson in Nueces County and was a great Johnson asset, according to John Connally. She organized several rallies every weekend, with bands, speeches, and Viva Johnson girls. Like the cheerleaders of the Kennedy campaign, they led crowds in chants, such as "The eyes of Lyndon are upon you . . . til victory's his own," "Hey, hey, what do you say, all the way with LBJ," and "A la bi, a la ba, a la bim bon ba—Johnson, Johnson, Ganará [will win]." She also spearheaded large-scale voter registration drives. Her single marital status and professional expertise insulated her from political reprisal. "You had to be free and independent," she said. "They would come over and tell your husband not to do this or for you not to . . . or you'd be out of work. . . . They didn't want to open up the eyes of the people to come and vote for our candidates." At the same time, as a single mother with a busy medical practice, she had less time to spare than most people, but she persevered because, she said, "When you're needed and people depend on you, you just do it." [21]

Volunteers canvassed door-to-door explaining the issues and distributing material. They compiled lists of registered voters to visit on election day and, if necessary, to transport to the polls. "We turned out about 80 percent of the eligible voters," remembered Armando Rodríguez, who coordinated four precincts in San Diego. Offices in the heart of the barrios operated from early morning to late in the evening; residents could pick up material in English or Spanish. Local clubs assisted the national office in planning large rallies. In East Los Angeles 15,000 people came to see Cantínflas and Viva Johnson speakers. Even at events arranged by the regular campaign apparatus, often half of the signs in the crowd read "Viva Johnson." In October Héctor García regretfully declined an invitation to an LBJ Ranch barbecue, writing, "I had two previous commitments here involving a Television program with the Viva-Johnson Girls [and] a regional meeting with the Viva-Johnson Clubs." [22]

Not all Mexican American activists operated under the Viva Johnson umbrella. In California the CSO registered thousands of new voters, as it had done in 1960. Most of these organizers were registered Democrats, but the campaign was conducted on a strictly nonpartisan basis; whether the Democratic candidates won or lost, Mexican Americans would lobby for their own agenda. Besides, CSOers considered themselves catalysts, not power brokers; let the citizens themselves choose. Meanwhile César Chávez and his National Farmworkers Organization, while campaigning for Johnson, did not operate under Viva Johnson auspices. Herman Gallegos, allied with the CSO and the farmworkers, preferred to operate directly with the California State Democratic Committee. "I was used as a whip to turn out the troops for rallies for Johnson," Gallegos recalled. "I didn't want to be the 'house Mexican' for the Viva Kennedy or Viva Johnson organization. . . . you've got to get involved where the decisions are made." He worked for Johnson's election alongside staff members from local congressional offices as well as Maclovio Barraza of the Steelworkers, Henry Santiestevan of the United Auto Workers, and Larry O'Brien of the DNC. To Gallegos, this meant that Mexican Americans were becoming serious players in the national political game. [23]

On the campaign trail candidate Johnson pledged to fulfill the slain president's legacy. His listeners, enjoying a period of peace and unprecedented prosperity, roared their approval. Mexican Americans remained overwhelmingly poor in this land of plenty, but they placed their hopes in the War on Poverty and sensed that Johnson loved swapping *abrazos* with them. People cheered in Albuquerque as he greeted them in fractured Spanish, plugging Senator Montoya and other Democrats. Later that day Johnson told a Los Angeles crowd that the nation needed Ed Roybal in congress to "continue to fight the people's battles." Meanwhile Lady Bird Johnson addressed the GI Forum convention.[24]

"Amigos de Goldwater" and "Arriba Goldwater" countered that Barry Goldwater spoke Spanish and that vice presidential candidate William Miller was Catholic, but the Republicans could not exploit inconsistencies in Johnson's civil rights and labor records or his coziness to big business leaders, because Senator Goldwater's record was far more conservative on all of these issues. The Johnson campaign played on this, characterizing the Arizona senator as a right-wing extremist bent on eliminating Social Security and unleashing the atomic bomb.[25]

Mexican-heritage voters turned out in unprecedented numbers for Johnson. Ximenes proudly reported to national headquarters that in many Mexican American precincts his organization reached all of the Spanish surname voters and that the results ranged from 10–1 to 20–1 for LBJ. Ximenes suggested that the DNC capitalize on this support by continuing the monthly newsletter sent to hundreds of key local leaders. He got nowhere; Viva Johnson was dismantled, like Viva Kennedy before it. Moreover, the Mexican American results were ignored in the landslide victory.[26]

THE BIG CHANCE

Lyndon Johnson emerged confident that the American people supported his Great Society, even that they loved him. This administration would gain fame not for victory over a foreign foe but for conquering hunger, ignorance, and deprivation. To emphasize this point with antipoverty director Sargent Shriver, Johnson spoke emotionally about having seen his Cotulla students coming to school hungry.[27]

From job training to education to health to housing, new programs sprang up overnight. Mexican Americans grabbed the Big Chance. Finally the second-largest minority would have a voice and be represented at the highest levels of government. Congressman González supported 96 percent of the administration's legislation in 1964, more than any other member of the Texas delegation. "I don't have to worry about Henry," Johnson used to say; "Henry's for the people." Chief Johnson domestic advisor Joe Califano witnessed "genuine love"; "González is the same kind of populist LBJ was."[28]

González regularly hitched rides back to Texas on Air Force One, where the two swapped political intelligence. Some afternoons the president, weary of listening to reports from government bureaucrats, would invite his old Texas buddy to come over for a chat. Like Johnson, González came from a distinguished background but grew up in precarious circumstances. The wealthy González family fled Mexico during the revolution and came to San Antonio, where the congressman's father became the editor of *La Prensa*. Even so, the Gonzálezes had lived no better than their working-class neighbors. Henry never forgot seeing his friend's mother go blind stitching clothing in her dark shack for piecework wages, and he knew that Johnson was seared by his experience in segregated Cotulla.[29]

At the same time, their relationship remained a complicated one. As a youngster González, unlike Johnson, had to face the discrimination and ridicule of Anglo neighbors and often fought them. Moreover, stories circulated of a few instances when the president himself engaged in stereotyping. According to one account, the President defended U.S. military activity in Latin America by saying,

I know these Latin Americans, I grew up with Mexicans. They'll come right into your back yard and take it over if you let them. And the next day they'll be right up on your porch, barefoot and weighing one hundred and thirty pounds and they'll take that too. But if you say to 'em right at the start, "hold on, just wait a minute," they'll know they're dealing with somebody who'll stand up. And after that you can get along fine.[30]

According to longtime González aide Kelsey Meeks, the congressman "was not a White House insider," but "it was a warm relationship, no question about it." The president enabled González to obtain a large number of poverty programs. "The big thing that Lyndon was able to help him on was the Hemisfair. That involved heavy federal appropriations," said González aide Fred Schmidt. The Kennedy administration officials, including Vice President Johnson, had first encouraged the congressman's proposal: a great international exhibition to showcase San Antonio's bicultural heritage and to diversify the city's economic base, which depended on the military for 40 percent of its revenue. The business aspect particularly appealed to another powerful politician, Governor John Connally. Although the fair-related jobs did not last, the exhibition gave a permanent boost to the tourist industry.

Johnson did other favors for González, notably refusing to allow the complete abandonment of a San Antonio air force base. Chief domestic advisor Joe Califano called the decision "a pure gift." If a government grant excluded San Antonio, González would call Johnson, saying, "Look, hey, what's going on here?" Soon San Antonio would be added to the project. "Those were the days when presidents could far more easily bend regulations than they can now. . . . It wasn't seen as necessarily untoward to cut a deal. And that was Johnson's operating style; it was whatever it took to get what he wanted," Meeks recalled.[31]

Organizations throughout the Southwest implemented the Great Society blueprint. In California MAPA used federal funds to establish community service centers. LULAC administered a federal housing program and together with the GI Forum proposed SER (Service Employment Redevelopment) Jobs for Progress, Inc., which would tailor job training, counseling, and placement to the particular needs and talents of barrio residents. The administration had forced the two rival organizations to pool their proposals in the interest of unity, according to a Mexican American SER official not affiliated with either group. LULAC had access to the president when needed, according to LULAC official Pete Tijerina, who cited the "tremendous" effect of the poverty programs: "People were helped, educated, moved up."[32]

Ramos met with OEO aides to get "the Forum into active participation," he said, and he created bilingual OEO brochures, complete with photographs of barrio programs.[33] Ramos also managed to establish contact with top White House staff members such as Cliff Carter and Jack Valenti. In January 1965 the GI Forum cosponsored a national conference on poverty in the Southwest, featuring speeches by Sargent Shriver, Archbishop Robert Lucey of San Antonio (a longtime farmworker supporter), the governor of the host state, Arizona, and President Johnson. The conference's "citizen hearings" provided an opportunity for community workers and representatives of religious, labor, ethnic, and nonprofit groups to make suggestions to OEO administrators, who in turn explained the resources available.[34]

Meanwhile Ximenes sent Carter a list of ten Mexican Americans who would accept appointments. The following month Ximenes and several other Forum leaders sent congratulatory telegrams to Carter's hometown mayor on the occasion of Cliff Carter Day. Nonetheless Ximenes was concerned. Two months had passed since the election, and still the administration had said nothing about appointing any Mexican Americans to important posts or including them in program decisions, so he requested a White House meeting. In a blunt memorandum Ximenes wrote that the same president who taught in Cotulla well knew that Mexican Americans comprised the majority of poor people in their neighborhoods and that Johnson realized better than anyone the importance of consulting Mexican Americans for program advice. Ximenes warned, "Do not take action and then ask the Mexican American if the approach is the correct one." A few weeks later, in March 1965, for the first time in the history of the United States a president met a group of Mexican Americans: professionals, business people, organizational leaders, male and female, from the Southwest and the Midwest. Johnson saw them briefly, then they conferred with the secretary of labor.[35]

The following month scores of Mexican Americans attended a Great Society conference. Ramos repeated the complaint that Washington knew next to nothing about the Spanish-speaking community, which thus participated only minimally in the War on Poverty. In an effort to educate the participants he presented statistics documenting the low income, education, and employment levels; he submitted an OEO employment roster that contained almost no Spanish surnames and a list of Forum-sponsored social programs that demonstrated the group's long commitment to barrio community development. Ramos explained that the GI Forum wanted the OEO to take what he called "affirmative action," including regional offices in Spanish-speaking areas, clearer guidelines for local program applicants, and recruitment of poor and minority residents so that money funneled to cities and school districts would not be controlled by "unfriendly elements" opposed to social change. "One can honestly demand, 'Sargent, praise the Lord and pass the troops along with the ammunition.'"[36]

The administration was beginning to get the message. Shriver's special assistant acknowledged that only eight of the 1,139 OEO employees were Mexican American and Southwest director Dr. William Crook wrote of "the concern this office has for adequate representation . . . with particular reference to the American GI Forum." In June Presidential Appointments Secretary Marvin Watson gave orders to be informed of "anything pertaining to the Mexican-American situation," then passed the information on to the president, as when nine Mexican American leaders wrote to thank Johnson for talking to them. Watson included their letter in the stack of papers that the president scanned at the end of the day; Johnson wrote back to the aide, "Respond and thank." At the same time, both Watson and Johnson realized that thank-you notes would not suffice. Within weeks the OEO was hiring Mexican Americans in earnest, such as Lorenzo Ramírez, one of the people who had corresponded with Watson; Ramírez became an OEO area coordinator. Soon OEO officials were able to inform Rodolfo Ramos that the agency had hired fifteen people from a list he had provided. Forumeers in the OEO included Cris Aldrete, Southwest manager of the Community Action Program, OEO inspectors Ed Terronez and Ed Idar, and Rodolfo "Corky" Gonzales, who headed the War on Poverty in Denver. Corky Gonzales in particular made his mark. In 1965, one year after the Denver appointment, he was also named to the steering committee for antipoverty programs for the entire Southwest and, in 1966, was elected president of the National Citizens Committee for Community Relations.[37]

According to Congressman Roybal, "Lyndon Johnson and his programs absolutely benefited Mexican Americans," citing in particular Medicare, which provided health care for millions of indigent and elderly people, including many of Mexican heritage. When asked twenty-five years later to name the most important OEO program, Judge Albert Peña thought and said "food stamps"; for the first time the federal government made significant strides in protecting its poorest citizens from the ravages of malnutrition.[38]

Ramos and his colleagues in the Washington GI Forum office successfully appealed for an extension of the Head Start proposal deadline after Ramos discovered that Head Start administrators had not sent applications to most of the barrios. The Forumeers personally delivered to OEO headquarters mailing labels for some 1,000 barrio organizations. In the end these neighborhoods had the largest percentage of Head Start programs. "That was fantastic," remembered Ramos. The following year, in July 1965, OEO allocated one of its largest community development grants to towns along the Texas/Mexican border, and that November LULAC and the GI Forum were among the sponsors of a War on Poverty/Migrant Labor Conference. In his keynote address Crook lauded the social activism of organized labor, the GI Forum, LULAC, and PASO. He characterized the SER Jobs for Progress proposal as "the type of cooperation that is needed," and he urged the conferees "to volunteer in these local community wars as you have in the past World Wars."[39]

Programs for migrant farmworkers—from job training and housing to day care and rural health clinics—disproportionately helped Mexican Americans. Rural legal aid proved particularly effective. United Farmworker president César Chávez wrote, "I commend these young attorneys and I want to encourage any possible extension of this form of service of the OEO." According to the farmworker leader, many a California legal aid lawyer educated migrant workers about their rights, from dealing with government agencies to inviting guests to the migrant camp, filing lawsuits when necessary. Joe Bernal, then a Texas state legislator, considered rural legal aid attorneys important allies of the Texas farmworker movement and he referred many of his constituents to legal aid for assistance in dealing with agencies. "That helped me a great deal because I was overwhelmed with cases." Bernal also credited the Johnson administration with scholarships that enabled people to attend college and for encouraging these new professionals to return to the barrios to work in OEO social programs such as the Neighborhood Youth Corps.[40]

One South Texas teacher who jumped at the chance to work in OEO was Ernesto González. "I had fifty cents in my pocket because schoolteachers at that time made $4,200 a year," he said. Moreover, the local school authorities had forcibly transferred him from the high school to the elementary school when, as vice president of the local teacher's organization, he had canvassed for a bond issue that the largest landowner—of Mexican descent, like 70 percent of the population—had opposed. The courts eventually found in González's favor. He was celebrating the victory at a barbecue when he got the call from Job Corps. González recalled, "They said, 'You have a perfect story for the guys here: you're a minority, you were poor, you went to the service, you got educated through the GI Bill without a high school education. We want to have you here.' They doubled my salary!"[41]

The Job Corps supervisors asked González to work with the Mexican American youths in particular. "At the beginning we had riots; we had to be on duty twenty-four hours a day: fights between the blacks and the whites and then between the whites and the Hispanics." He supported the overall philosophy of strict discipline. At the same time, he introduced Mexican food and *conjunto* music: "We'd buy them records, those kinds of things, started buying their dedication to the Job Corps by giving them a little of their culture." In conversations with other teachers, he explained the obstacles that the trainees faced. "When you live in the country or the barrio, you don't have magazines, you don't have newspapers."

Pleased with his efforts, González's supervisor said, "Listen, Johnson is going to come down here next year and [the Johnson people] want us to have Mexican Americans and blacks in administrative positions and I wanted to know if you're interested." The teacher replied, "I'm not ready; I like the job I have and I just don't think that I could be an administrator." His superior kept urging González to take the job and finally asked him as a favor, saying that they were having difficulty finding another good candidate. "So I agreed to try it out; I became chairman of Job Corps communication skills." He helped supervise a number of programs, including high school equivalency (GED) classes, and he was proud that the trainees then enrolled at Southwest Texas State Teacher's College. The slowly rising number of Mexican-heritage students on the campus contrasted sharply with Johnson's undergraduate days there, when such students were rare indeed.

These changes pleased Johnson, who visited the college and ate with some of the Job Corps people. González remembered, "They announced that they were selecting fourteen of us to have lunch with him, and I was one of them because of the color of my skin, because he had told them—I remember reading memorandums that his administration sent to the Job Corps people—'We want to know what you're doing, what minority, what is their role in the Job Corps.'" González sat across from Johnson, slightly to the left, as the president asked various people about the Job Corps. "He came to me, and I introduced myself, and I said I was from Duval County. He looked at me and he said, 'I'm familiar with Duval County.' He did ask me about Job Corps and how I felt about it, but that's the comment that I recall. . . . He had like a smirk on his face." [42]

Of all the OEO programs, southwestern OEO director Dr. William Crook thought that the Community Action Program (CAP) probably introduced the most barrio residents to the role of an active citizen. He watched approvingly as neighborhood people who at first deferred to him soon took over the meetings, insistently presenting their own agendas. San Antonio activist Joe Bernal called it "real political involvement." The War on Poverty took the unprecedented step of stipulating "maximum feasible participation of the poor" in the planning and designing of its projects, thus giving poor Mexican Americans a major voice in half-million dollar budgets for their neighborhoods.

In this vein the *Rocky Mountain News* reported, "It is an open secret . . . that Washington delayed approving Denver anti-poverty programs for months because it wanted an 'indigenous' person at the head of the organization." When Corky Gonzales took over as head of the Denver OEO, the newspaper wrote, "This kind of leadership can fairly be said to be what Sargent Shriver's office demands." Gonzales said, "You have to live among the people, hear what they're saying," and he declared, "I'm an agitator and a troublemaker. . . . They didn't buy me when they put me on this job."

In southern California community college student Gil Cárdenas learned to write proposals for youth projects, developing recreational programs at community centers for gang members and other young people. "Without these programs . . . I doubt that that leadership would have emerged," he said. On the other hand, traditional political machines belittled organizing efforts not under their control. Long-time Duval County political operative O. P. Carrillo ignored the leadership aspects of CAP, characterizing the program as an effort to build community centers and, as such, a "luxury."[43] Cotulla applied for CAP funding, led by superintendent of schools Helen Storey. Mayor W. P. Cotulla and County Judge Jay W. Martin supported the application as long as it focused on literacy programs and bringing sewers into the barrio.

Job training programs were added eventually, according to the local CAP director, none other than former Johnson student Dan García. "The CAP program was very good," he said. "It involved a lot of local people." Alfredo Zamora, another Cotullan active in the program, noted that the CAP centers served as organizational bases and that the War on Poverty enabled Mexican-heritage Cotullans to become governmental administrators for the first time. Some faltered, he said, due to inexperience and lack of professional training, "but in the end if it hadn't been for those programs I don't think that we would have gone into management and . . . had leadership roles." The Cotulla Anglo leadership would oppose the insurgents, particularly when Zamora ran as Cotulla's first Chicano mayoral candidate in the early 1970s (see chapter 11).[44]

WOMEN IN THE GREAT SOCIETY

John Connally thought that Johnson had an ambivalent attitude toward a woman's role. The president would sometimes bark, "Get those women out of here!" when he wished to talk to his advisors without their wives present, but he also ordered his staff members to seek out women for important federal positions; by 1966 some 130 had been appointed. Overall, however, the males—whether Mexican

American or not—lobbied on behalf of males. One exception was Rudy Ramos, who sought out female as well as male applicants for the talent bank list that he sent to the White House.[45]

The Job Corps trained many young women, mostly in traditional female occupations, as in the case of Rebecca Torres, who took business and clerical courses at a Job Corps center, then landed a job as a secretary for the Department of Health, Education, and Welfare in Washington, D.C. Subsequently she participated in the Upward Bound program. "It was really neat and I enjoyed it very much," she told Iris Alicia, a reporter for the Job Corps newsletter. In Upward Bound's eight-week college preparation session Torres studied mathematics, science, English and "group concepts," then entered Cochise College to study social work. Some Mexican American women taught in the Job Corps and a few, such as Dominga Coronado of the GI Forum auxiliary, served as Job Corps advisors. Ernesto González remembered that at the San Marcos center, "We didn't have a single administrator who was a woman, except the head librarian." When he became a supervisor in part because of his ethnic background, the administrators passed over his Mexican American wife. "She was very resentful that she had a master's degree and I had a bachelor's degree and that I was her boss," he said.[46]

Dr. Cleotilde García established nursing programs with OEO seed money. Beginning with ten students, the first one grew rapidly and branched out into training for laboratory and X-ray technicians as well. She spoke on behalf of OEO throughout South Texas, encouraging people to apply for the various programs, from food stamps to Head Start. After the talk she would circulate at the barbecue or tamalada, sometimes joining the local residents for Mass, all the while answering questions. Many in the crowd, both women and men, were local leaders, often with the GI Forum, and they in turn passed on the information to scores of other neighborhood residents.[47]

In the education field, María Urquides of Arizona served on the National Advisory Council on Extension and Continuing Education, while Californian Henrietta Villaescusa served as a liaison between the Department of Health, Education, and Welfare and local community groups. Both women were active in local organizing: Urquides for the Mexican American Political Association, Villaescusa for the Community Service Organization. Even more *mexicanas* worked as Head Start teachers. María Carrizales of Weslaco, Texas, was one. She attended Texas Women's College, on a scholarship, then taught in the Weslaco schools. Carrizales also was active in local civic affairs, serving as a Democratic precinct committeewoman in 1962, organizing a Young Democrats Club, and volunteering in presidential campaigns. In November 1965 she wrote to Louis Martin of the Democratic National Committee, "This past summer I had the unique experience of being head teacher of our local Operation Head Start and . . . we were able to reach some of the most disadvantaged and culturally deprived children in our small town." That autumn she became the supervisor of six elementary schools; in that capacity she observed a number of Head Start programs. She reported that the youngsters were progressing "astonishingly well," in part due to the active involvement of many community volunteers.[48]

Lupe Anguiano coordinated OEO's community youth projects in East Los Angeles. Born in Colorado, she picked crops alongside her mother and other family members in the California fields while her father worked as a railroad laborer. The mother had owned a little store in Mexico and eventually scraped together enough money for a business selling ice cream and other items to farm laborers, but died of cancer about the time that Lupe was elected president of the eighth grade. At twenty Anguiano became a member of Victoryknoll, an order of nuns that emphasized social service. "Pope John XXIII advocated that Catholic nuns . . . get out of the convent and serve the people. . . . It was a great time for me. I just blossomed, along with a lot of other priests and sisters." She became active in the campaign for open housing legislation and picketed the cathedral, urging the conservative cardinal to support the cause. When the archdiocese ordered her to stop these activities, she left the convent, as did many other women at that time.

Anguiano became a counselor for an OEO youth training and employment project, advising junior and senior high school students of career opportunities and serving as a role model. Because of her efforts, many decided to stay in school. Young people landed jobs previously closed to most Mexican Americans, such as cashiers and telephone customer service representatives. Many young women confided in her. "They really did not know what was happening to their bodies or to them. I'm glad those days are over for women. I remember them just opening up and crying, and of course they didn't want to tell their mothers and their fathers." She offered more than a sympathetic shoulder, advising them about their pregnancy options and helping them piece together their educational and career plans. Word of her success led to her appointment as the teen post coordinator for East

Los Angeles. "That was really up my alley," she remembered. Anguiano supervised twenty teen center directors, all Mexican American, about five of them female. She emphasized leadership training, modeling the centers on city and state governmental structures. The young people quickly learned to debate issues and master parliamentary procedure. Joe Gámez, who was elected "governor," went on to work for a member of congress. "Oh, the news of what Joe Gámez was doing in Washington, that just lifted the whole teen post program and the whole community," Anguiano remembered. "The one elected as a senator is now a state representative."[49]

Mexican American women attended OEO conferences, as in May 1967 when five came to Washington: "ranking representatives of their women's organizations," according to a White House memorandum. Nonetheless, almost no women—of any background—directed OEO operations above the local level. One notable exception was Graciela (Grace) Olivarez. "Graciela to me was the best communicator," said Anguiano. "She could get to the point, build an argument, and be very funny." Born in Sonora, Arizona, a company town that has since been destroyed by an open-pit mine, Olivarez attended segregated schools there. In Phoenix she gained fame in the barrio for her popular women's radio show, became the first female radio announcer in the state and the program director of a radio station, then helped found a neighborhood association and organized local residents against juvenile delinquency. From there she joined the Choate Foundation, coordinating their youth careers program. She served on the National Advisory Council on Economic Opportunity while working her way up the OEO bureaucracy as the field coordinator in Arizona and then as acting state OEO director. She said, "I have a mission now, and that mission is to help my people organize on a national scale so that they can use the system."

Olivarez caught the eye of Marie Barksdale at OEO national headquarters, who wrote to a female colleague recommending the Arizonan for a White House conference on civil rights, "in the event Mexican-Americans are invited." Despite her ability Olivarez was not named the permanent state OEO director; instead the governor chose Eugene Marín. At that point George Sánchez recommended Olivarez for the Equal Employment Opportunity Commission. For his part the head of the Civil Service suggested her to President Johnson, "in case you desire to add to the Commission . . . another lady with good ethnic credentials. . . . She has been an active organizer and worker on behalf of women, Mexican-Americans, and poor people, and combinations thereof. She is described to me as a 'very sharp, know-how person.'" [50]

"I SAW IT IN THEIR EYES"

Johnson administration officials worked hard to implement the Equal Employment Opportunity Commission and the other provisions of the 1964 Civil Rights Act. No new civil rights legislation was in the cards, however, according to that master of political timing, Lyndon Johnson. The 1964 Act had barely squeaked through Congress, and a white backlash could already be detected. Undeterred, Dr. Martin Luther King Jr. led a march from Selma to Montgomery to highlight the demand for federal legislation guaranteeing the right to vote. When Alabama State Troopers attacked the marchers on March 9, 1965, the nationwide television audience recoiled. One week later, as the procession approached Montgomery protected by the National Guard, Johnson introduced a voting rights bill to a joint session of congress and a nationwide television audience.

The president made history as he intoned in his soft southern accent the civil rights anthem, "We shall overcome," but it was his description of Cotulla that galvanized many Hispanic viewers. He talked about his students

> who knew in their youth the pain of prejudice. . . . I saw it in their eyes. It never occurred to me in my fondest dreams that I might have the chance to help the sons and daughters of those students and to help people like them all over this country. But now I do have that chance—and I'll let you in on a secret—I mean to use it.

Dan García telegraphed his hearty congratulations to the president, as did a number of other Mexican Americans. Reflecting on the Cotulla anecdote, Joe Bernal said, "The fact that he would say it as president became something very dear to us, because . . . he was really with us." [51]

The growing participation of barrio leaders in federal programs and national politics accelerated their integration into American life. Paradoxically, however, the successful lobbying efforts of the GI Forum, LULAC, MAPA, and others also reinforced a separate, minority identity that would culminate in the antiestablishment Chicano movement. [52]

Viva Kennedy meeting at the Waldorf Astoria Hotel, New York City, October 31, 1960. *Left to right:* Ralph Estrada of Tucson, president of the Alianza Hispano Americana; New York state assemblyman Felipe N. Torres; Texas state senator Henry B. González; John F. Kennedy; Dr. Héctor P. García, founder, American GI Forum; attorney Henry López; New York assemblyman José Ramón López; unidentified. [Dr. Héctor P. García]

In Cotulla, Texas, the vice president–elect gives away the bride, his cousin
Margaret Ann Kimball (holding his hand), in the home of the
bride's uncle, Judge Jay W. Martin (second from left),
the chief political leader of the county. [LBJL]

The vice president and Lady Bird Johnson with members of the
American GI Forum, Omaha, September 1962. [García Collection]

November 21, 1963: Jacqueline Kennedy speaks in Spanish to the Texas
LULAC convention, Houston, while President Kennedy watches (to her left)
and Lyndon and Lady Bird Johnson applaud (to her right). [Courtesy
Houston Metropolitan Research Center, Houston Public Library]

The National Citizens Conference on Community Relations, August 18, 1964. *Left to right:* Dr. Héctor P. García, President Johnson, unidentified, and Rodolfo "Corky" Gonzales (who would break with the Johnson administration and the Democratic Party in 1967).
[LBJL; photo by Cecil W. Stoughton]

Congressman Henry B. González of San Antonio conferring with
President Johnson, May 25, 1966. [LBJL; photo by Frank Wolfe]

The next day, May 26, leaders of the main Mexican American
organizations (facing camera) expressed their concerns to Johnson
(back to camera). [LBJL; photo by Yoichi R. Okemoto]

Los Angeles congressman Edward Roybal speaking at a White House meeting, March 10, 1967. [LBJL; photo by Yoichi R. Okemoto]

President Johnson shaking hands with Pancho Mansera, Head Start child of the year, March 13, 1967. [LBJL; photo by Frank Wolfe]

Vicente Ximenes is sworn in as a member of the Equal Employment
Opportunity Commission, June 1967. [LBJL; photo by Frank Wolfe]

Commissioner Ximenes (also head of the Interagency Committee on
Mexican American Affairs) with President Johnson, 1967. [LBJL]

Vicente Ximenes speaking at the Cabinet Committee Hearings on Mexican American Affairs, El Paso, October 28, 1967. Those behind him include Governor John Connally, President Johnson, and John Gardner, Secretary of Health, Education, and Welfare. [LBJL; photo by Yoichi R. Okemoto]

Dr. Ernesto Galarza, an organizer of the rump conference at El Paso, which he dubbed "La Raza Unida." [Galarza Papers, Special Collections, Stanford University Libraries]

EIGHT

PROBLEMS WITH
THE GREAT SOCIETY

Just a few weeks after President Johnson signed the Voting Rights Act, riots broke out in the black Los Angeles neighborhood of Watts. When the Johnson administration responded with extra federal programs for that ghetto, Rudy Ramos cried foul, pointing out the need for more attention to East Los Angeles, the area with the lowest incomes in the city. He also warned that Mexican Americans would demonstrate vocally if not invited to the June 1966 White House civil rights conference. Armando Rodríguez, who was working for the California Department of Education at the time, recalled, "I don't think the ties to the Johnson administration were as good as they could've been." The White House, bowing to African American wishes, kept the conference focused on them; Johnson officials told Mexican Americans that they would have their own conference.[1]

As for federal appointments, LULAC President Alfred Hernández scoffed at the idea that the government could not find qualified Mexican American applicants, writing, "What does it take? What must we do? While I do not condone violence, it may be that we too should resort to marches, sit-ins, and demonstrations." The GI Forum was engaged in "a one-way dialogue with . . . the President, the Attorney General, and the Postmaster General," according to the leaders of the kindred organization MAPA.[2]

Twelve leaders, including Johnson's old friend Héctor García, wrote a joint letter to the president, accusing the administration of excluding Mexican Americans from positions in the federal government. Johnson scribbled all over the letter, writing that the charge was "not true" and that the correspondents should "give us a list of men and women" applicants. As for a presidential assistant, he wrote, "We designate García!" The president's reply, drafted by aide Jake Jacobsen, expressed Johnson's "distress" in learning about Mexican American problems with job bias. In a handwritten postscript to García the president added, "I'll tell Jake after you all discuss matter and get your proposals together to bring you all to see me anytime." [3]

THE WALKOUT

Matters came to a head over the EEOC, which had no Mexican American commissioners, only 3 Hispanics out of a staff of 150, and which investigated only a handful of Hispanic discrimination complaints each year. Barrio leaders considered EEOC chairman Franklin Roosevelt Jr. a sincere man in the New Deal tradition and thus were disheartened at what they perceived as his insensitivity to their problems. On February 17 Mexican-heritage members of Congress told the White House that they "vigorously opposed" Roosevelt's plan to form an ad hoc committee on Mexican American affairs. Rather, the EEOC needed to address all racial discrimination with equal vigor. Congressman González noted that few of his constituents were hired even by the government's own departments. When Chairman Roosevelt addressed the Congress of Mexican-American Affairs in Los Angeles on March 8, 1966, the United Press reported, "He walked in with 250 friends and walked out with none." One week later in San Francisco EEOC Executive Director Herman Edelman blamed "the disorganization of Mexican-American groups" for the fact that only 12 of some 300 complaints since 1965 came from Spanish-surname individuals. Angry Mexican American leaders accused Edelman of prejudice. George Sánchez wrote to Roosevelt, "The number of complaints, and the ratio of Negro to Mexican-American, is a very lame and illogical excuse for inaction. By this line of reasoning we would render public health service only to those who called in a doctor!" [4]

That same month Senator Robert Kennedy sent aides to confer with MAPA members. Although most Mexican Americans, particularly outside of Texas, had supported John Kennedy over Johnson in 1960, Johnson had delivered for Mexican and African Americans as the Kennedys never had, and the Texan resented the adulation that poor minority people showered on the Kennedys. Moreover, from the moment he took office Johnson feared that the Kennedys and their supporters would maneuver to make him a one-term president sandwiched between John and Robert Kennedy. [5]

As a member of the Senate Subcommittee on Migratory Labor, Robert Kennedy planned to hold hearings in California, and MAPA officer Herman Gallegos suggested Delano, the headquarters of the National Farmworkers Association (NFWA) strike against grape growers, as the site. Leaders of MAPA, the CSO, the GI Forum, and other Mexican American organizations testified. Then, with the TV cameras running, Kennedy sharply questioned opponents of the union. The county sheriff explained that he had arrested NFWA organizers because a grower representative threatened to "cut their hearts out." Kennedy replied, "How can you arrest somebody if they haven't violated the law? . . . Can I suggest that during the lunch break the sheriff read the Constitution of the United States?"

Afterward on the way to the airport Kennedy told the activists, "Anything that I can do for MAPA and CSO I want to do." Soon thereafter Kennedy spoke to an enthusiastic MAPA crowd in San Francisco. Bert Corona of MAPA got the distinct impression that the senator was seriously considering a run for the presidency in 1968. Nevertheless, when Kennedy became the first national political leader to support the farmworker strike, César Chávez did not consider the action a political maneuver. The NFWA founder worried only that Kennedy, in Chávez's words, "endorsed us so straightforwardly, without straddling the line. . . . he didn't have to go that far. Instead of that awful feeling against politicians who don't commit themselves, we felt protective." [6]

With pressure building, the EEOC commissioner announced a conference in Albuquerque to be devoted entirely to the concerns of the Spanish-speaking community. The delegates gathered for the March meeting in a pessimistic mood that was confirmed at a cocktail party on the eve of the opening session. "Word got out that Roosevelt wasn't going to be there," according to Armando Rodríguez. Only one EEOC member had shown up: Republican Richard Graham. "He was just brand-new on the commission," remembered Rodríguez. Curious, Rodríguez asked the new commissioner, "What was your impression? We're here at the call of the Chairman and in good faith we all came." Graham replied, "You're absolutely right; I don't know why you should stay." Rodríguez then chaired a meeting of the Mexican American leaders. "We decided we would have a demonstration, a walkout . . . and have a meeting of our own. . . . We told [Graham] exactly what we were going to do," Rodríguez recalled. "Sounds reasonable to me," Graham replied. [7]

The conference opened with introductory remarks by Graham and by Executive Director Edelman. Several Mexican American leaders reiterated the charge that the EEOC ignored them on all levels of its operation. Suddenly one of the speakers, Albert Peña, announced that he was walking out of the meeting until the EEOC responded to the grievances and he called on his colleagues to join him. Nearly all of the delegates left, including Graciela Olivarez, one of the few females invited (perhaps the only one). Commissioner Graham sent word that he was willing to listen, so the protesters invited him to their meeting. They pledged to support an umbrella lobbying organization in Washington christened the National Organization of Mexican American Services (NOMAS, or "no more"). "The walkout was a defining moment for NOMAS," said NOMAS founder and Forumeer Raúl Yzaguirre. Soon thereafter LULAC held a banquet, attended by four hundred people, to honor those who had walked out of the hearings. At the dinner LULAC President Alfred J. Hernández declared, "In spite of our number we are America's invisible minority. Because we have not demonstrated, because we have not cried out when we have been abused and exploited, we have been ignored." [8]

Meanwhile the president instructed his chief domestic advisor Joseph Califano to investigate possible responses. There was "no question," Califano said, "but that Johnson had a very special place in his heart for Mexican Americans." The president realized that remedies were long overdue. In this he was ahead of his staff, instructing Califano, for example, to ask Mexican American leaders about their backgrounds and concerns. "He told me I was from Brooklyn; I didn't understand." At the White House press conference two days later a reporter asked, "Mr. President, have you heard anything to the effect that Mexican Americans feel they should have more attention?" Johnson replied,

> Yes, I have heard that all my life. And I agree with them. I think they should have more attention. I am going to give them all the attention I can. I haven't given them enough. I want to give them more. I think they are entitled to more consideration in Government employment than they have received. I think they have been discriminated against in housing, in education, in jobs. I don't think we can be very proud of our record in that field. . . . If they are ready for a conference, I will be ready.

Califano, recalling the event years later, thought that the White House itself had planted the question. "If it wasn't a plant we were ready for it," he said. At the same time, Johnson refused to commit himself to specifics, deflecting the reporter's question as to whether Mexican-heritage people would be invited to the June Civil Rights conference. Chairman Roosevelt praised the president's responses, but the White House could take little solace in this compliment from an official with such faulty political antennae, who could report, "We planned the Albuquerque meeting with great care. . . . There was no indication of dissatisfaction." [9]

Meanwhile the leaders of the Albuquerque walkout, calling themselves the "Mexican American Ad Hoc Committee on Equal Employment Opportunity," immediately filed an employment discrimination complaint with the U.S. Civil Rights Commission against the EEOC, the very agency charged with combating job bias. The author of the suit, Rudy Ramos, charged that he personally had delivered to the EEOC commissioner fifty-nine applications from experienced, qualified professionals but that not a single Mexican American had been hired. He also accused the commission of inaction regarding 800 companies accused of discriminating against Mexican-heritage people. Congressman Roybal thought the suit justified, saying, "A lot of lip service was given to the Hispanic community."

The White House considered the problem one of administrative oversight, not bias; consequently, the government's personnel agency, the Civil Service Commission, handled the complaint, rather than the Civil Rights Commission. A Civil Service staff member assured Ramos that the EEOC would be required to report on its hiring procedures, then the Civil Service would decide on the appropriate action, if any. Pleased that he had elicited a response from the White House, Ramos also worried about the consequences of filing a complaint against the most powerful administration in the world, saying, "You feel you're the captain of an aircraft carrier and you just sent all your airplanes up in the air and you're waiting for contact." [10]

Within days Roosevelt announced his resignation. He planned a "very personal" farewell party with "no press." Alfred Hernández of LULAC suggested that either of two EEOC members, Richard Graham or Sol Linowitz, replace him, but instead the White House nominated another commissioner, Luther Holcomb. According to some Washington pundits, Holcomb, "a prominent white Dallas clergyman," had voiced displeasure when Commissioner Roosevelt, in a Texas speech, vividly described the discrimination faced by Mexican Americans. Civil rights activists decried the nomination, but to no avail. Dr. Holcomb would spend the rest of the year visiting groups such as the GI Forum in an attempt to mend relations. If the president was trying to protect his right flank by choosing Holcomb, it did not work. Republican Senator John Tower of Texas took advantage of the discontent by introducing a bill to expand the EEOC by two members so that other ethnic groups, "particularly Americans of Latin Heritage," could be represented.[11]

For his part, Commissioner Graham offered to resign because "I am increasingly convinced that this Commission should have a Mexican-American Commissioner," he wrote in a personal letter to White House Special Assistant Bill Moyers. That same month the Graham family joined Mexican Americans picketing in front of the White House on Easter Sunday. The marchers called their action both a "huelga" (strike) and a pilgrimage, in solidarity with the striking National Farmworkers Association. That same day thousands of NFWA members and supporters reached Sacramento, the climax of a 300-mile "pilgrimage march" from Delano. NFWA founder César Chávez called the march "an expression of penance and of commitment." He prayed for the farmworkers to "set themselves at peace with the Lord, so that the justice of their cause will be purified of all lesser motivation."[12]

On April 13, the same day that Graham offered to resign from the commission, an antipoverty conference convened in Washington, sponsored by the Citizens Crusade Against Poverty (CCAP). This coalition of 125 religious, labor, civil rights, academic, business, student, and farm organizations aimed to insure that poor residents, not local political leaders, controlled community action programs. Ramos served as vice-chairman of the panel on "Maximum Feasible Participation of the Poor," which passed a number of resolutions, including motions in support of the huelga and the Albuquerque walkout. The *Washington Post* reported that "the poor—ranging from Washington youths with 'Rebels with a Cause' sweatshirts to California grape pickers wearing 'Huelga' (strike) buttons—declared their independence from the 'power structure.'" Delegates complained that too much of the two billion dollars spent thus far by OEO ended up either in its own bureaucracy or in the pockets of local officials. Speakers also criticized the agency for scaling down its budget requests in 1966. Sargent Shriver cracked, "I'm not sure I was invited here for lunch or as lunch!" Regional OEO director William Crook approved of GI Forum participation in CCAP, but Johnson considered CCAP a pro-Kennedy group, bent on causing trouble.[13]

On April 25 Corona and Ramos both wrote to the White House.

Corona warned Moyers, "A new current of discontent and defiance is stirring in our people"; they planned to picket the White House Civil Rights conference on June 1. Ramos gave a backhanded compliment to Johnson, praising the recent presidential visit to Mexico and expressing hope that the administration would devote similar attention to the millions of Mexican-heritage residents in the United States. Neither of the activists realized that at that moment the White House was making plans for the president to meet with Mexican American leaders. In fact, Johnson had discussed the issue with Mexican American congressmen while flying to Mexico. The White House issued a press release—on May 22 in English, on May 23 in Spanish—announcing the upcoming meeting.[14]

On May 26, 1966, officials from the GI Forum, LULAC, and MAPA made history. For the first time a president met at the White House with Mexican American leaders for a meeting solely devoted to their concerns. All of the ad hoc committee members were invited except for Ramos. "I was persona non grata," he said, as was Raúl Yzaguirre of NOMAS, who called the invited guests and reminded them of their pledge to support NOMAS. Yzaguirre urged them to present the Albuquerque demands and to consult with other leaders who had not been invited, such as Albert Peña of San Antonio and Rodolfo ("Corky") Gonzales of Denver. In contrast, Héctor García said, "No, you don't call them demands."

Politely but firmly the guests voiced their concerns to the presidential assistants, then after dinner Johnson arrived. He greeted everyone warmly and talked about his lifelong connection with Mexican Americans. Then he said, "Tell me about your complaints and problems." They mentioned their difficulties with the EEOC, their exclusion from White House conferences, and their need for a Mexican American White House aide. The president responded, "I'll give you all of these, however, don't ask me for a fellow in the White House." Otherwise, every ethnic group would want one. When someone complained that SER Jobs for Progress was still in limbo, Johnson asked, "It's not been funded yet, Héctor?" García replied, "No sir." Johnson turned to Jacobsen, saying, "Jake, talk to the labor people; find out where this thing's at." The aide came back five minutes later to report, "Mr. President, it's funded."

Johnson showed several films, including one of his recent trip to Mexico, and gave them a whirlwind tour of the living quarters. "He loved it," said García. At the president's urging they tried out Lincoln's bed. Corona remembered Johnson as "sort of a cornball type. He wasn't very sophisticated, but he was shrewd as hell." On the other hand, Califano characterized the guests as slightly "agog"; "they moved from room to room in wide-eyed amazement, raising their glasses as they shouted, 'Viva LBJ!' Johnson, who was the only one among us not drinking, was completely relaxed, relishing the chance to open the White House to these men." [15]

Everyone left the meeting full of hopeful expectation. At a press conference a few days later, Johnson said, "We hope that we can arrange a meeting to invite the Mexican American leaders and others to the White House to meet with members of the staff and probe more deeply into their problems and the actions that can be taken." He also instructed the Civil Service to get busy on a Mexican American candidate for the EEOC. Looking back on the meeting thirty years later Corona said, "It signaled a new and national political position for Mexican-Americans." Lupe Anguiano agreed. "Those were very exciting times," she said; "Mexican Americans were starting out, communicating with Washington for the first time." [16]

The hope engendered by the White House meeting soon dissipated; the very next month Rudy Ramos organized picketing of the White House Civil Rights Conference. Many Mexican American leaders refused to endorse the Ramos action, fearing accusations of racism. Ramos discounted such concerns, saying that the black conference organizers had excluded Mexican Americans, not the other way around. Besides, he added, some African Americans in the Citizens Crusade against Poverty planned to participate in the picketing. "The least we could do is join them," wrote Ramos, who did not trust the president because of what the Forumeer called "his Texas background. . . . Johnson knew the problems but in my opinion was not going to provide services to us unless we pulled teeth." The Washington-based activists began to feel the weight of White House ostracism. Ramos feared that he and perhaps others were under government surveillance. Raúl Yzaguirre remembered, "They came after us." He noticed that Labor Department funds dried up and friends told him of White House telephone calls to congressional staffs asking for the dismissal of some Mexican Americans employed there. As Yzaguirre put it, "We became radioactive. . . . I'm talking hardball politics here." [17]

OEO BALANCING ACT

Undeterred, Ramos wrote to Secretary of Labor Willard Wirtz to complain about the lack of Mexican American staff members in the

Neighborhood Youth Corps (NYC) and added that grass roots lobbying, not the administration, was responsible for increased OEO funding.[18] Ed Idar found fault with other aspects of the Great Society. He suspected that "at a very high level" OEO officials decided to employ volunteers from the outside to organize the barrios rather than GI Forum people. He watched with dismay as workers from the Volunteers in Service to America (VISTA) would come to a neighborhood as total strangers, hold a few meetings, and then want to march on city hall. In his view CAP's mandate was to educate local residents in the workings of the city council, in voting requirements, in concrete ways to make the government respond to them. He also faulted legal aid attorneys for working on class action suits at the expense of individual cases that he said they considered "too humdrum." The Forum leader also questioned the concept of the "culturally disadvantaged," saying, "They may be educationally and economically disadvantaged, but . . . they have a language, they have a religion, they have a food, heritage, customs." Idar did not fault Johnson, saying, "He instituted what I think was a good idea but it was subverted, in my opinion. . . . What did Shriver know about the poor?"[19]

Herman Gallegos of MAPA, now working for the Ford Foundation, faulted the community action projects for paying people to organize. He feared that the organizers would be looking over their shoulder at their bosses and would never establish lasting community ties, in contrast to his old friend César Chávez, who lived alongside his fellow farmworkers and derived his income from them.[20]

"The OEO programs were . . . helpful but they were very difficult because of all the infighting among the various community groups," remembered Kelsey Meeks, an aide to Representative Henry B. González. In one case, however, the congressman blamed the president for obstructing a program. "San Antonio had a food stamp application in the pipeline. González had been working for months, just beaten the city council to a bloody pulp to get them to agree to do food stamps," said Meeks. "So he sees his application tied up as a consequence of Johnson wanting to put food stamps into Mississippi and other places" in response to the CBS News broadcast "Hunger in America." Meeks explained, "Johnson gets all excited by the CBS piece and he decides wherever in the country there was not a program . . . he would put in food stamps."

A few days later administration staff members called González to make sure that the congressman would be voting for the income tax surcharge to finance the Vietnam War, but González refused to speak to anybody from the White House. Then, about six in the evening the receptionist answered the telephone and froze.

> Receptionist: "Congressman, it's the president *himself*!"
> González: "I don't give a damn; take a message!"
> Receptionist: "I'm sorry, Mr. President; he just stepped out."

Having made his point, González called Johnson shortly thereafter. The president said,

> "Henry, I hope you're all right on this tax bill. That Wilbur Mills [chair of the House Appropriations Committee] has made my life miserable. I need your vote, Henry; I know I can always count on my friend Henry González."
> "Well, Mr. President, I don't know how I can help you. I can't even get a goddamn food stamp program in San Antonio and here I am excoriated on CBS television."
> "What??"[21]

So the congressman explained how CBS mentioned San Antonio in its report, even as the White House was tying up funds already earmarked for that city. In a warm, friendly voice, Johnson replied, "Henry, don't you worry. Don't you worry at *all*." Within the hour the secretary of agriculture called, "How's my good friend Henry González? Henry, I'm here to tell you there's been a terrible mistake." San Antonio got its food stamp program.

Those OEO programs that did manage to empower local residents often ran into another problem: opposition from local officials. Corpus Christi physician Cleo García repeatedly ran into resistance from local political leaders. When the county trustees refused to allow the OEO to implement the food stamp program, she gave a presentation to the trustees and convinced them to change their mind. One time trouble was averted when she happened to replace her brother as the speaker at an OEO event. Hostile Anglo ranchers milled about, waiting to meet up with Héctor, oblivious to the female García up in front, who was telling the ranch employees how to apply for various programs. On several other occasions, however, she found herself hooted down by hecklers. Looking back on those days, she said, "We weren't doing anything wrong; we were just practicing democracy, helping people get out of poverty and ignorance." In Delano, California, the

Chamber of Commerce sent Johnson a resolution opposing an OEO self-help grant for the National Farm Workers Union.

Meanwhile the director of Denver's War on Poverty, Corky Gonzales, created a stir by participating in the walkout at the EEOC meeting in Albuquerque, according to Dan Thomasson of the *Rocky Mountain News*, who added, "While OEO has no policy against antipoverty officials demonstrating on their own time, the agency watches each case closely." The reporter wrote that the "action also has added to friction between Spanish Americans and the Democratic Party." The next day Thomasson quoted OEO official James Kelleher as saying, "In Denver, the big problem is between Mexican-Americans and Negroes" and as calling Gonzales "quite a wild man." Kelleher responded by sending telegrams to the news media saying that the Thomasson quotes were inaccurate. Gonzales went further, accusing the newspaper of libel and trying "to discredit and destroy the War on Poverty." Supporters of Gonzales picketed the *Rocky Mountain News* office and called on readers to cancel their subscriptions.

The *Denver Post* reported that "Senator Gordon Allott, a Republican and frequent critic of the administration's 'war on poverty,' wants an investigation" of Gonzales on charges of incompetency, but meanwhile the mayor fired the Denver OEO chief. Gonzales responded by declaring, "This day a new crusade for justice is born." Rudy Ramos asked Secretary Wirtz to investigate, calling the firing "one hell of a situation." [22]

The first governor to veto an OEO program turned out to be none other than Johnson's own political protege, John Connally, who canceled an NYC project in May 1965. The Texas governor did not oppose the Great Society in theory; he had provided state support for LULAC's "Little Schools of the 400," and Texas led the nation in Head Start enrollees. The issue was control; Connally demanded that state and local officials administer the programs. He complained that county officials had no voice in the program, which would pay rural trainees the minimum wage. [23]

In Connally's home county farmworkers earned only one-third the minimum wage, so a local priest, Father Virgil Elizondo, eagerly helped sponsor the NYC program. When he met resistance, Father Elizondo did some soul searching. "Didn't they trust me? Didn't they want their children to get ahead?" He asked them to explain, so they reminded him that they depended on the large landholders for their employment. The priest concluded, "As long as the people did not make trouble they were safe to enjoy their simple life. But if they started to work for any change in the status quo, one or two members of the Mexican-American community would simply disappear." [24]

In February 1966 the Connally administration appealed a court decision that ruled the Texas poll tax unconstitutional and the governor called for annual registration of voters. Black and Hispanic Texans immediately protested, saying that the proposal would worsen the state's already dismal registration rate—less than half the eligible voters. Connally's political enemy—albeit a fellow Democrat—Senator Ralph Yarborough, accused the governor and other Texas officials of dooming the Great Society in South Texas. In the *Congressional Record* the senator, quoting Bexar County Commissioner Albert Peña, spoke of "The Cactus Curtain." [25]

According to Joe Califano, Johnson used to tell Connally, "you could be president someday but you don't have the compassion." The president quietly supported Yarborough's successful bill providing for an OEO override of gubernatorial vetoes. Local political leaders needed to be accountable to their poor constituents, Johnson told his staff. When Connally demanded that Johnson fire William Crook, the president told the governor, "I don't know how I ended up with that Bill Crook!" Then Johnson called in Crook. When the OEO administrator walked into the Oval Office, Johnson was watching his three-screen television console. He inquired after Crook's wife and her father, the head of a major Texas grocery store chain, then asked about the VISTA volunteer programs. Johnson walked Crook to the door and lifted him off the floor in a big bear hug, setting him down just as John Connally came by. Crook was not fired; rather, he got "total backing from the White House," he said. In 1990 Bill Moyers said to Connally, "I haven't figured Lyndon Johnson out all these years later, John . . . why he would say to me, 'John Connally is the most conservative man I know,' and why he would say to you, 'Moyers is the most liberal guy I've got on my staff,' because it was both his genius to make us all think he was like us, but it was also his trap." [26]

In this balancing act the president was leaning more and more toward old political supporters such as Connally. Johnson wondered whether "a bunch of kooks, Communists, and queers" were taking over the OEO; he told Shriver that local elected officials such as Chicago's mayor Richard Daley should run the programs rather than "liberal outfits" such as the Urban League. In May 1966 Johnson named career civil servant Bertrand Harding as Shriver's assistant.

Harding said Johnson "was ranting on about . . . how the war on poverty got out of hand . . . all of a sudden these radicals got ahold of the system and created C.A.P. agencies." While Shriver continued to push for increased spending on community development to buttress "maximum feasible participation of the poor," some Cabinet members and Vice President Humphrey disagreed. They warned—reading the president's mind—that controversies over local control could scuttle the whole Great Society, caught between conservative local leaders and liberal activists allied with potential presidential rival Senator Robert Kennedy. Someone leaked the White House debate to the *New York Times*, reinforcing Johnson's suspicions. The Democratic Party was splitting apart, with Robert Kennedy voicing increasing criticism of the Vietnam War. That Sargent Shriver was Kennedy's brother-in-law did not help matters.

By the end of 1966 the president was seriously considering dismantling OEO and parceling out the programs to Cabinet agencies. In his memoirs Johnson press secretary George Reedy observed, "The blacks, the Chicanos, the people left in economic dead ends in Appalachia thought major assistance was on the way. Middle-class whites thought that everything was being done for the minorities." Reedy knew that both sides were underestimating the role of the war in diverting both government funds and White House energies.[27]

LABOR DAY IN AUSTIN

Meanwhile problems were accelerating between Governor Connally and Texas farmworkers. In 1966 the National Farm Workers Association, newly rechristened the United Farmworkers Organizing Committee (UFWOC), led a 490-mile pilgrimage to Austin for a Labor Day rally demanding that the state government enact legislation protecting the right of farmworkers to organize and establishing a $1.25 state minimum wage. The procession began in Starr County, site of a bitter dispute between melon workers and the giant La Casita farm operation, which replaced the strikers with workers from Mexico and brought in Texas Rangers to harass the picketers.

"I was district judge when they had the march. . . . I gave the restraining order against the Rangers," O. P. Carrillo said. An old Duval County friend of Johnson and Connally's, Carrillo was also close to a number of Starr County growers, but he had no love for the Rangers. "My mother's brother was whipped and tied to a tree and left there to die. . . . My dad got in the car and drove to Austin and told Governor Allred, 'If that Ranger is in my neck of the woods when I get back I'm gonna kill him.'" The Rangers were gone when Carrillo's father returned from Austin, but some thirty years later they were out in force throughout Starr County.[28]

En route to Austin the farmworkers picked up supporters and endorsements. Although the most visible leaders were male, nearly half of the marchers and many of the organizers were female. "The ladies played a very important part in the overall success of the march," reported the *LULAC Extra*, and Dr. Cleo García noted that many of the women were less tied to earning a livelihood and thus less fearful than the men of losing their jobs. San Antonio Archbishop Robert Lucey called the minimum wage the very least that the state government could do, and Dr. Martin Luther King pledged his support.[29]

When the marchers passed through Connally's hometown of Floresville the Methodist congregation served them a meal. Then outside of New Braunfels, less than fifty miles from the state capital, the governor—accompanied by Attorney General Waggoner Carr and House Speaker Ben Barnes—drove up in a limousine to meet the dusty marchers. Months earlier Connally had told Texas labor leaders that he opposed a state minimum wage, that it would not pass, and that he would not be in Austin on Labor Day. When the march proceeded in any case, he considered it political grandstanding on the part of the Texas Federation of Labor. Years later Connally recalled having told his staff, "The least I can do is go down there and say hello to . . . these poor people . . . who have marched in this hot sun all this way and are being used as pawns by labor." In New Braunfels Connally told the organizers that they should not proceed further, that he did not "want to lend the prestige and dignity of the governor's office to dramatize the march." The governor's actions brought "the eyes of the nation on the problems of the farmworkers," in the words of LULAC President Alfred Hernández. "The press tore it all up," complained Connally.

At the state capitol the crowd, now numbering some ten thousand, cheered the various speakers. Some thought they saw tears in the eyes of Senator Yarborough. In a voice full of emotion, he declared, "Amigos, compadres—fellow marchers . . . as our senior U.S. Senator, I *hold* the highest elective office [20-second ovation] and with all the power and good will which the people of Texas can give . . . I welcome you with open arms. . . . A hundred years ago we ended physical slavery. We are here today to end poverty and economic slavery."[30]

The president ducked the issue, according to J. C. Looney, a Johnson operative in South Texas, but Bill Crook speculated that if Johnson had been the governor, "he would've had chicken and tortillas," that the marchers just wanted someone to listen. A few weeks later the *Wall Street Journal* reported that the differences between Connally and Johnson were becoming more intractable, that Connally "frequently takes stands on Texas issues—stands the President doesn't particularly like." At the same time the article noted that liberals regarded the disagreement as largely cosmetic; they still considered Connally the president's man in Texas. In fact, the governor maintained close contact with the White House. He spoke to presidential aide Marvin Watson about the *Journal* article, saying that he did not mention the president or any federal programs and that he studiously avoided the whole topic of a split within the Texas Democratic Party.[31]

The 1966 elections that Johnson long had feared now loomed before him. He attempted to shore up his various constituencies, including Mexican Americans. At one press conference a reporter asked an inviting question, probably planted by the White House: "Sir, I know you have been interested in doing something for the Spanish-speaking of the country, but could you fill us in on your plans, somewhat?" Johnson replied, "Well, I have been interested in seeing that the Spanish-speaking people of this country were treated equally ever since I have been in public life." He then spoke in general about having appointed a number to high offices and of legislation benefiting them. Then he concluded on a personal note, saying, "I have a very special fondness for Spanish Americans, because I grew up with them. I learned to speak their language as a child. I went to school with them. I taught them. I have been getting them to vote for thirty years."[32]

Many a Democratic leader worried that Hispanic voters would stay home or even defect. "Their major complaint in Colorado and other Western states, where they are the largest minority, is that they are being ignored by the Democrats once the polls close," reported the *Rocky Mountain News*. In Texas, Democratic senate candidate Waggoner Carr fought an uphill battle against incumbent Republican John Tower. William Bonilla, who had long been active in LULAC, announced the formation of "Democrats for Tower." Bonilla explained that the senator supported a farmworker bill, the appointment of a Hispanic to the EEOC, and immigration restrictions. "Waggoner Carr . . . has done nothing," said Bonilla. Moreover, the Democratic candidate's involvement in the New Braunfels confrontation made him anathema to many Texans of Mexican descent. The Labor Day marchers "gave the thumbs down sign as they passed the headquarters of Waggoner Carr's Senate campaign," according to one account. In the end Carr lost badly.[33]

PLANNING A CONFERENCE

A number of California Mexican Americans also voted Republican. Democratic Party operatives attributed this to antiblack sentiment in the wake of the Watts riots, ignoring the other concerns voiced over the previous two years. DNC official Louis Martin sensed this lack of political intelligence and suggested that the administration "do some planning and extensive digging" to ascertain the concerns of the various Mexican American organizations. Meanwhile the White House assigned someone to focus solely on Mexican American issues: David North, formerly of the Department of Labor. On September 8 North suggested that the cabinet officers appoint Spanish-speaking program coordinators for their departments, writing, "We are . . . faced with a restless Spanish-surname community." The head of the Civil Service, John Macy, responded immediately with a Model Plan of Action, in which the EEOC would recruit barrio residents to serve on EEOC advisory committees and would survey poverty programs for "the extent to which they focus on problems of the Spanish-American." Macy met with the managers of government agencies ranging from OEO to the Veteran's Administration to Treasury to the Post Office, in his words, "to communicate the urgency of the situation and the need for action now." He promised to initiate a talent search, evidently unaware of the extensive talent bank compiled the previous year by Rudy Ramos with the assistance of Louis Martin.[34]

With reporters once again raising the issue of a Mexican American White House conference, North began organizing a "preplanning conference" to draw up an agenda. About sixty leaders received invitations to the October session, including Héctor García, Alfred Hernández of LULAC, George Roybal of SER Jobs for Progress, Lupe Anguiano of the Los Angeles OEO, and Herman Gallegos of the Ford Foundation. Absent were activists deemed too controversial, such as Corky Gonzales and Bexar County Commissioner Albert Peña, leader of the EEOC walkout the previous spring. Others were invited despite past involvement in activities deemed radical by the FBI, including

Bert Corona and mine union leader Maclovio Barraza. Senator Hayden's office advised that "Barraza is a potential source of trouble," but neither he nor Corona had stirred up protests against the Johnson administration itself. César Chávez and other UFWOC people refused to participate. A White House memo quoted longtime farmworker activist Dr. Ernesto Galarza saying, "This pre-planning conference is a political move. No good will come of it. I refuse to be party to this kind of thing."

The absence of farmworker leaders let the administration off the hook. The FBI was investigating Chávez for subversion. Also, two California congressmen opposed inviting him. A member of Pat Brown's staff informed the White House that the California governor had "no trouble with the list," but did not want to go on record as having cleared the names. Or as North put it, "We have been trying to do as much as we can for the American farm worker while keeping the political headaches within reason." As far as the farmworkers union was concerned, according to Johnson's chief domestic advisor, Joseph Califano, "We obviously were on their side, if you will. . . . But I think [Johnson] regarded César Chávez as a Bobby Kennedy agent." The White House supported the successful passage of a minimum wage bill that for the first time included farmworkers, but "probably would let percolate" any other legislation, said Califano. According to sociologist Julian Samora, "Johnson wanted to be on the right side, but he also had people pressing him from the other side and . . . the other side would win because they had the money." For his part, Congressman Roybal blamed Congress, not Johnson, for the failure to include farmworkers in labor legislation.[35]

One week before the preplanning conference twelve leaders of PASO, MAPA, LULAC, the GI Forum, and the CSO caucused in Albuquerque, New Mexico.[36] They issued a statement calling for greater Mexican American participation in Great Society programs, from housing to education to community development. The caucus reiterated the demand for a Mexican American EEOC commissioner and for a voice in administration policies generally. On farm labor they called for a minimum wage of $2.00 per hour, rural legal aid, abolition of the Farm Placement Service, the amendment of the National Labor Relations Act (NLRA) to include farm workers in collective bargaining, and the administration of immigration laws "to cause minimal disruption . . . of domestic farm workers." In addition, the leaders listed several women's issues that had been raised by Anita

Ramos, chairman of the Berkeley MAPA chapter. The Albuquerque meeting declared:

1. That more Mexican American women should be involved in the planning and operation of the proposed Conference.

2. That more Mexican American women should be considered for top level employment positions, especially in the Federal Government.

3. That OEO initiate some programs geared to the training and development of Mexican American women.[37]

Five days before the Mexican American leaders caucused in New Mexico, Hispanics in the northern part of the state began occupying some 1,500 acres in Kit Carson National Forest, renaming the area the Republic of the Rio Chama. Federal authorities responded by arraigning the leader, Reies López Tijerina. Born in a small town southeast of San Antonio in 1926, as a child Tijerina attended some twenty different schools as he traveled around Texas picking cotton with his parents, during which time his grandfather narrowly escaped a lynching. After a stint as an evangelical minister, Tijerina took up the cause of the heirs to Spanish land grants in northern New Mexico. In 1959 he led a delegation of 107 families to Mexico City; they asked the Mexican government to support a petition calling on the U.S. Department of State to comply with the treaty of Guadalupe Hidalgo, which guaranteed that the Mexicans residing in land acquired by the U.S. in the 1846–48 War would retain their property. Mexican President Adolfo López Mateos listened but did not raise the issue when he visited Washington or during his stay at the LBJ Ranch later that year.

Undaunted, Tijerina studied land records in the archives of Mexico, the United States, and Spain; in 1963 he established the Alianza Federal de Mercedes (Federal Land Grant Alliance). Three years later, in the summer of 1966, Tijerina led a march to the state capital and gave Governor Jack Campbell a petition asking him to look into the landownership issue. Campbell promised to forward the petition to President Johnson, but nothing came of the request. "We do not demand anything; we just want a full investigation," Tijerina said, adding, "We have written to the presidents—Eisenhower, Kennedy, Johnson—and to the State Department, all with no success." Matters came to a head when the U.S. Forest Service forced more than 20,000 residents of northern New Mexico off their land between 1965 and 1967, while logging firms received permission to cut thousands of acres on the same land. Now, with Tijerina sought by the authorities in the wake of his occupation in the national forest, Alianza members increased their campaign of arson and vandalism against local Anglos. Tijerina was convicted of assault but was out on bail while he appealed the verdict.[38]

While tensions mounted in northern New Mexico, Mexican American leaders gathered in Washington. On the eve of the preplanning conference, according to Lupe Anguiano, Dr. García suggested that the delegates choose one person to present their concerns, someone well known to the administration. Anguiano recalled responding that she had come to share her insights with members of the administration, that they expected to hear from her, and that she would not cede her role to García or anybody else. The proposal died.[39]

"The preplanning conference was an attempt to get a better understanding of the opportunity of programs and . . . to better understand the complaints of the Mexican community," said Armando Rodríguez, who addressed officials of the Department of Health, Education, and Welfare (HEW). Nearly all of those attending agreed that a national White House Conference was imperative, but only if "a prominent Mexican American from outside the Government" helped plan it. They suggested Dr. Julian Samora of the University of Notre Dame. The report recommended that the meeting be held at the White House on a late spring weekend in 1967, with 500–1,000 delegates, a cross-section of the community, who would meet with representative members of the "power structure." Topics should include education, employment, health, housing, the military draft, women, and more Mexican American participation in poverty programs. The report concluded, "The Mexican American community should be discussed both as a locus of problems *and* as a valuable resource to the nation."[40]

Top White House staffers took heed and began planning the spring conference. They came to the conclusion that cooperation of the southwestern governors must be obtained, particularly Governor Connally. Johnson aide James C. Falcon asked the governor to suggest "some Mexican-Americans who would be acceptable to all factions." Falcon called the governor's office twenty-five times between October 15 and November 3 but received no response. Finally Connally told Falcon, "I've got more to do than engage in useless exercises. . . . I'm not going to suggest any names." Writing to the president about Connally, White House Counsel Harry McPherson said, "If he will not agree to having his people take part, we must decide whether to go through with the conference. (If we had a conference and Texas officials were not present, it would certainly intensify problems between the Mexicans and the Governor.)" At the same time Héctor García telegraphed Johnson requesting a personal interview to discuss the situation, but the president was laying low. On the last day of 1966 he told Califano, "We'd better get away from this. I don't want any Mexican meetings at all. The more you have the more trouble you have. I would encourage them to meet—but let's not get into it." [41]

NINE

CLIMAX

As 1967 began, White House aides worried about the negative repercussions of ruling out any White House conference on Mexican American affairs. At a meeting on January 16 top domestic and political staff members came up with the idea of a fact-finding trip through the Southwest to sound out state politicians, corporate executives, and Mexican American leaders on the advisability of such a conference. Johnson agreed, but only on the condition that Governor Connally and other local political officials be apprised of the visit beforehand. Once this had been done, four administration officials hit the road, including two Mexican Americans: Bob Ornelas of the Defense Department and Cris Aldrete of the Democratic National Committee. Afterward Johnson vetoed the White House conference once and for all, calling for "some other type meeting."[1]

BILINGUAL EDUCATION

With no conference on the horizon, Johnson staff members redoubled their efforts to publicize other administration actions on behalf of Mexican Americans. The Department of Labor began a farmworker newsletter, and David North started sending scores of leaders frequent reports describing government programs of benefit to Mexican Americans. "We can supply . . . additional copies," he informed Dr. George Sánchez of the University of Texas. OEO selected a Mexican American boy as its Head Start child of the year and featured him in a film about the War on Poverty. Sargent Shriver wrote to Johnson, "The PANCHO film will be seen by one and one half million Mexican-

Americans and other Texans this coming Sunday, through Dr. Héctor García." These efforts constituted part of an overall counterattack against critics of the War on Poverty, as when an OEO magazine published an article entitled "The Ten Biggest Myths about OEO." [2]

The administration also recruited more Mexican Americans, such as Lupe Anguiano, who stayed on after the preplanning conference to join the Department of Health, Education, and Welfare. She worked to obtain credit on civil service applications for bilingual ability and she proposed ways in which the Census Bureau could lessen the undercount of Hispanics. "My experience with the Johnson administration was that there was this breath of fresh air. . . . I knew that I had the support of the White House. . . . I had a great time. I loved it and I learned a lot."

Anguiano focused mainly on lobbying for the bilingual education bill. She had become a strong advocate after witnessing in California the wholesale labeling of Spanish-speaking children as "retarded." In Washington she visited private schools attended by the children of diplomats, where the students spoke several languages with ease.

A number of educators had briefed the bill's sponsor, Senator Ralph Yarborough, particularly his Austin neighbor and longtime political supporter Dr. George Sánchez. The University of Texas professor had long promoted the goal of exposing all children to a second language. Among other things, this would eliminate the ban on speaking Spanish on school playgrounds, a policy that Albert Peña termed "racist," observing, "In a town like Laredo, everybody is bilingual." Moreover, a 1965 report by the National Education Association indicated that Mexican American children who became literate in their own language developed more confidence as students than those whose language and culture were shunted aside. [3]

On January 17, 1967, Senator Yarborough introduced the bilingual education proposal. Alluding to policy mistakes in Vietnam, he spoke of the hard lessons the United States had learned because of its cultural blunders in the Far East. Now the nation could obtain the best possible cultural ambassadors to Latin America simply by training its "naturally bilingual children to grow up speaking good English and good Spanish." Bilingual education was part of the Southwest Development Bill: one hundred million dollars, in the senator's words, for "programs of education, training, health, leadership, citizenship and other programs designed to assist the Mexican-Americans of the Southwestern United States to overcome the special barriers they encounter." [4]

David North offered Armando Rodríguez the job of setting up a Mexican American unit in the Office of Education. "I didn't think I wanted the job," Rodríguez recalled. The candidate insisted that the appointment be in the civil service and at a high rank: "a career position so as not to be knocked around as a political football." The administration agreed, and Rodríguez worked with White House staffers Jim Jones and Tim Wirth to come up with a job description. "We settled on the concept that it would be a product manager, like in World War II: take a tank and follow it through, making sure . . . everything was done right."[5]

Meanwhile at the House of Representatives Anguiano was talking legislative strategy with the chairman of the education committee, answering Congress members' questions about Mexican Americans, and stressing the president's whole-hearted support for the bill. Anguiano made what she called her "biggest mistake" when she advised her superiors that it would indeed be a good idea to hire a male to run the new Mexican American affairs unit. She assumed that she would continue to conduct the day-to-day lobbying efforts while Rodríguez would handle public affairs. According to Anguiano, as it turned out he took total charge, making all of the decisions. For his part, Rodríguez recalled,

> When I came in, they assigned her to me. She was there almost a year, I think, and she had her own agenda. We got along well for a while, then her agenda [got to] be a pain in my side. I liked her; I thought she was a good person. But . . . either you've got to run the show and be held accountable for it, or let somebody else run it.

"It was very unfortunate," said Anguiano, "but it was also something that I did with very good common sense because in those days the women . . . were just not in the foreground." At the end of 1967 she quit and joined Chávez's union as an organizer.[6]

As soon as the bill appeared, Chávez wrote to Bert Corona, "If there is anything we can do to help the passage of these bills, let us know." George Sánchez sent Yarborough "warmest congratulations on the legislation which you have introduced. . . . I pray for its success." Descended from a family that had lived in the United States for generations but still experienced discrimination, the education professor argued that Spanish, which predated English in the Southwest, be fully integrated into the educational curriculum for the enrichment of all. Sánchez rejected the notion of bilingual education as remediation. He called for a program that encouraged mastery of *both* languages, pointing out the advantage of language learning for all students, regardless of background. "Our public schools have been atrociously negligent in this matter of teaching foreign languages," Sánchez wrote. "Bilingualism *per se* is the gift of the educated man."[7]

Rodríguez recalled, "A lot of my fellow Mexican Americans wanted to teach Spanish." He came to somewhat different conclusions, based upon his experience learning English as an immigrant child and later as the principal of a school with many such students. "[Sánchez] and I were friends, but we disagreed on a lot of things. . . . He was a scholar and he approached things on a scholarly basis. The reality is that the kids have to succeed in their community, and their community is English-speaking and the language of the land is English." When the chairman of the congressional oversight committee pointed out that some states prohibited the teaching of other languages at the elementary level, Rodríguez testified, "Our intent is not to teach another language. Our intent is to teach English." At the same time, Rodríguez parted company with those members of the administration who wanted to stifle the child's native language. "The basic point of this program is to make these children bilingual, proficient in English . . . without having to lose their language. . . We didn't want students to be prohibited from using their language and then having [to] come back ten years later and have to learn their language through a language course. That did not make sense," Rodríguez said. He, along with Anguiano and Congressman Roybal, opposed to no avail the inclusion of bilingual education in a poverty bill, fearing that the program would be stigmatized and not viewed as enrichment.[8]

Congress enacted the bilingual program as part of the Southwest Development Act exactly twelve months after Senator Yarborough had introduced the proposal. While acknowledging that Johnson's poverty and civil rights initiatives helped Mexican Americans, Yarborough stated flatly that the Johnson administration should not be credited with masterminding bilingual education. An Austin reporter concurred, writing, "By now it is well known that the new bilingual education feature of the act was almost wholly a Yarborough achievement."[9]

For his part Congressman Roybal gave the president much of the credit for the original idea, saying that Johnson confided that his own inability to communicate effectively with his young Cotulla students convinced him of the need to use the child's native language. The president told Roybal, "This is the first time in the history of this nation that a president has agreed to sign a bill even before it is passed." At the same time, Roybal recalled that White House aides did not work with him on the bill; it was not a main priority of the administration. In fact, much of the program funding would come from the Hearst Foundation. Rodríguez took a skeptical Randolph Hearst on a whirlwind trip through Spanish-speaking neighborhoods from New York City to Miami to the Lower Rio Grande Valley of Texas. The scion approved the funding after seeing for himself children struggling in vain to understand their teachers.[10]

ESCALATION

While the bilingual education proposal was wending its way through Congress, Mexican American activists were becoming ever more restless. "How about That White House Conference? Latins Wonder," reported a *Los Angeles Times* article that made its way into the White House files. Congressman Kika De La Garza requested a conference as soon as possible, saying that everyone in South Texas was vying for an invitation. Watson reported to the president, "Congressman Roybal said it is boiling up in his district," with local Mexican American leaders harshly critical of the administration. Johnson wanted to meet with Watson to decide on appropriate action but reiterated, "I'll have no conference." A frustrated Califano noted to a colleague, "Where in the world do we go from here?"[11]

Nine days later, on February 12, 1967, the presidents of the major Mexican American organizations in California issued a joint press release that stated "unanimous frustration, disappointment and impatience over long delays, inaction and indecisiveness on the part of President Johnson and his White House staff." As as a result, the leaders pledged to convene their own "White House Conference" on May 5, a Mexican national holiday. At the same time CSO president Alberto Piñón and MAPA president Bert Corona, both leaning toward Robert Kennedy, announced a statewide political conference to be held in March.[12]

In this tense atmosphere Herman Gallegos of the Ford Foundation, Julian Samora of the University of Notre Dame, and Oscar Laurel of LULAC visited the White House on February 16 as members of the President's Commission on Rural Poverty. The three men planned to raise the conference issue with Johnson if he stopped by. Gallegos would sit at one end of the long table in the cabinet room, Samora in the middle, where the president sat when chairing cabinet meetings, and Laurel at the other end.

At the session commission members were chatting informally. "All of a sudden the room was quiet and there were these huge feet standing in front of me. I looked up and realized that it was the president," said Gallegos. Johnson quickly grabbed his elbow, shook his hand, and moved on. With no time to respond, Gallegos made a shrugging gesture to Samora, who motioned that he would say something when his turn came. Samora quickly told Johnson that Mexican Americans were looking forward to their White House conference. "I looked Johnson in the eye while I shook his hand but he didn't look at me." As the meeting continued, Gallegos noticed Cliff Alexander standing in the back. The three Mexican Americans huddled with the Johnson aide, telling him that they strongly desired a conference, that it would be very helpful for both the White House and the Hispanic community. Alexander replied, "You know, we're really struggling with that and we really need to make a decision." He invited them to come to the White House the following morning.[13]

Gallegos and Samora—but not Laurel—showed up for breakfast with White House Special Counsel Harry McPherson. Afterward McPherson reported to the president, "I was evasive and noncommittal." The counsel indicated that he tried unsuccessfully to convince his guests that a permanent office of Mexican American affairs at HEW was preferable to a conference. McPherson characterized the two visitors as

> pretty level-headed activists . . . [who] told me that the Mexican community wants a conference, expects a conference, will be bitterly disappointed without a conference, and that their bitterness would have serious political consequences. . . . The trouble, they said, is that like everything else ever done for Mexican Americans, *an [HEW] office would be imposed from above. . . .* When I said I thought a conference would necessarily be angry and vituperative . . . they said it would, indeed, if we planned it and ran it; if the Mexicans were given a large role in developing it, they thought it would be much more coherent and effective.

McPherson concluded, "The Mexicans are a major political factor in five states and we should not risk losing them; that risk is greater if we deny them the conference . . . than if some hell is raised." Johnson replied, "Keep this trash out of the White House." He may have appointed them to his Commission on Rural Poverty, but he considered them dissidents and, worse, Kennedy sympathizers.[14]

The following week Hubert Humphrey met in California with Gallegos and Bert Corona. The vice president asked them to end the picketing that MAPA and others were conducting in front of post offices, where they were claiming discrimination in hiring. In return, the Postmaster General would meet with them. The two Mapistas said they weren't authorized to end the picketing. Moreover, Corona thought that the deal smacked of "blackmail." Next the vice president asked them to support Johnson's reelection. Despite their active involvement in the president's 1964 campaign they responded that an endorsement for 1968 would be premature.

> Humphrey: "What would it take?"
> Corona: "Well, one of the things is support for the farmworkers' strike."
> Humphrey: "We can't do that." [15]

Corona later wrote, "What happened next only served to impress Herman and me about the tenuous condition of the Johnson administration, as a result of its ill-fated policies in Vietnam." They accompanied the vice president to the site of a speech he was scheduled to deliver at Stanford University. Thousands of people blocked the vice presidential car, which inched forward only with the help of hundreds of police. One of the student leaders, David Harris, spied Corona. Harris and his wife, folk singer Joan Baez, worked with Corona in support of the farmworkers union. "Bert Corona, get outta that goddamned scab car!" yelled Harris.

Corona and Gallegos politely turned aside Humphrey's request to accompany him on the stage. The audience booed for ten to fifteen minutes, only letting him say a few words. The three men returned to the limousine only with the help of a phalanx of beefy Secret Service men. One agent opened the car door and shoved Humphrey inside. Students yelling "warmonger" rocked the vehicle, threw tomatoes, spat, and blocked the route with their bodies. Gallegos commented, "Well at least we turned out nice weather for you, Mr. Vice President." According to Corona, "Humphrey was trembling . . . repeating 'Goddamn Communists.'" Humphrey reported on the melee to the president, describing the hundreds of protesters, including one who "threw a can of urine on three of the agents." The vice president added, "I was not shaken at all." He also made the point, "We are badly lagging behind in working with the Mexican-Americans." Humphrey convinced the administration that it would be prudent to arrange for MAPA representatives to meet with Post Office officials even though the picketing was continuing. As a result of the negotiations, for the first time Mexican Americans were named to a number of postmaster positions.[16]

"The center of attention became the War," said Héctor García. White House special assistant Jack Valenti noted, "The deterioration of the situation began to show its face in the latter part of 1966. . . . And then beginning in 1967 it was all downhill. Everybody was switching." Most of Johnson's close advisors left, including Valenti and Moyers. Years later Moyers recalled, "We . . . went to war on a distant front—against an enemy that would not bargain, compromise, or reason together. The enemy wanted only to win."[17]

By 1967 the administration was spending seven or eight billion dollars on the war. "OEO became a side issue . . . strangled by the war," remembered William Crook. When Crook notified VISTA volunteers that their subsistence allowance would end because Congress had allowed the funding to lapse, he prevailed on them to look for a way to remain on the job. In Cotulla six volunteers were able to continue teaching fifty Spanish-speaking children in preschool programs because community members supported them. According to the local priest, "If the volunteers have to leave, [the children] will be lost."[18]

On December 12, 1966, over one hundred Mexican Americans who were attending a conference in Washington demonstrated in front of the White House against OEO budget cuts. In a letter to Johnson nine days later, the chairman of the Alameda County, California, chapter of the Mexican American Unity Council wrote of "extreme concern at the reduction of anti-poverty funds for rural areas." At its midyear conference in February 1967 the GI Forum membership passed a resolution recommending that the organization withdraw from the SER Jobs for Progress program "unless a major SER project is funded in fiscal year 1967 and tangible efforts are made in fiscal year 1968 towards full implementation."[19]

In April Henry B. González voiced his concern over domestic spending reductions to Cris Aldrete of the DNC. According to a congressional aide, "[González's] view was that the whole thing was wrong." As early as 1961 the San Antonio congressman had warned against what he called "the folly of presidential wars," and aide Kelsey Meeks said, "I think that the greatest regret that he ever felt was that he didn't vote 'no' on the Gulf of Tonkin Resolution. He felt that he had to vote with the president, just as a matter of his own . . . loyalty and faith in the president." González was the president's man in San Antonio, but the congressman tried to keep a low profile and not make statements about the war. Meeks recalled, "He wanted it over, but at the same time, he did not want to criticize his friend the president who had done so much for him." For example, when the congressman celebrated the anniversary of his election to congress, Johnson promised to attend, which guaranteed that Governor Connally and Senator Yarborough, despite their enmity, would come as well. The dignitaries sat before a crowd of twenty or thirty thousand San Antonians. As everyone watched and the television cameras rolled, Johnson leaned over to say a few words to Yarborough and hand the senator something, then they both grinned. Only the people sitting nearby could hear the president say, "Now, Ralph, I'm going to give you this little pen knife. I hope you use it on my enemies as well as you do on me." [20]

While Yarborough criticized the administration's Vietnam policies, González said that withdrawal "would mean the systematic fall of other Far Eastern nations. I doubt the Philippines could last a year." The congressman was not alone. San Antonio political activist Rubén Munguía noted, "The Mexican American has never had any defectors. We volunteered. . . . maybe because we're really patriotic." Although he questioned what he called "the stupidity of some of our leaders," Munguía considered it "wonderful" that his brother and son participated, and he credited the military with offering blacks and latinos the opportunity for advancement. Congressman De La Garza happily reported to the White House that his South Texas constituents were solidly in support of their commander in chief. As for social unrest, a LULAC official blamed it on what he termed "the duping of many Americans by the Communist philosophy." The California State Chairman of the GI Forum sent the president a letter decrying protesters and reminding Johnson, "The American GI Forum has always defended the policies of this country." The organization passed resolutions and led a march in Austin in support of United States involvement in the war. It touted patriotic paeans such as the poem "A Lonely Soldier in Vietnam" by Sergeant Juan Garza Jr. of Corpus Christi, who wrote, "In Viet Nam is where I stand, / Fighting for the rights of the Vietnamese land." Forum leaders pointed out that latino soldiers in Vietnam, like their counterparts in previous wars, earned the most Congressional Medals of Honor of any group. In late 1967 the organization sponsored a seventeen-day tour of Vietnam bases by

Texas entertainers of Mexican heritage. The headliner, Domingo Peña, said, "It's such a good feeling when boys run up to you crying for happiness to see someone from back home." He recorded thousands of soldiers' voices for later broadcast on his radio show.[21]

GI Forum members regularly accompanied families to the airport to receive the coffins of their sons. At the cemetery the local Forum chapter would salute the serviceman, then present a wreath to the mother and the flag to the wife. In Washington, Forum veterans often were joined by administration officials and, on occasion, by the president himself. "He felt a deep responsibility for the wounded and the dead and he translated this into a determination that their suffering should not be in vain," wrote George Reedy, while Joe Califano noted, "Johnson's anguish about the war was heightened by the unfairness of the draft. He saw it as another injustice visited on the less fortunate and minorities." The president recommended the elimination of college deferments and pressured the head of the Selective Service System to appoint more Mexican and African Americans to local draft boards.[22]

An aide to Congressman González recalled, "Every Thursday the casualty list would come in, so we would write these letters of condolence to people which seemed—then and now—to be hollow. . . . [González] finally decided that we would start analyzing these lists." They found that Spanish-surname men comprised 41 percent of the residents in his district but 72 percent of the Vietnam casualties. California Congressman Edward Roybal's office also began looking at casualty rates, spurred in part by Raúl Morín, whose 1963 book *Among the Valiant* featured a foreword by Lyndon Johnson, but who now was questioning the rate of Mexican American participation in the Vietnam conflict.

Roybal came up with some preliminary statistics suggesting overrepresentation of Mexican Americans in combat and underrepresentation as officers, so he visited local schools, urging students to apply to the military academies, saying, "If you're going to go, why not go first class?" Applications rose, many from young men whose relatives had served, and in some cases died, in World War II. At the same time, the congressman made his opposition to the war clear, explaining that he voted for supplies for the soldiers in the field but not for appropriations that would escalate the conflict. He told his constituents, "I don't think we have to prove our patriotism; it's already been proved." He pointed out that the war was undeclared and that "we had no business fighting if we . . . didn't try to win." As for his audiences, "I don't know how many I sold," he said, "but at least I would defuse the spark."[23]

Roybal served as an advisor to the Mexican American Study Project at the University of California, Los Angeles, where political scientist Ralph Guzmán issued a report, "Mexican American Casualties in Vietnam." Guzmán concluded, "In both California and Texas, Chicano war deaths are consistently high and disproportionate to the size of this minority group." The report noted that a high percentage volunteered, often for risky assignments, and he cited several reasons: a "suspect, 'foreign' minority under great pressure to prove their loyalty to the U.S."; a tendency to view the military as a way out of poverty; a paucity of college deferments. Guzmán noted that fewer than 1 percent of the students in the University of California system were of Mexican heritage.[24]

Across the country people were arguing about Vietnam. Hundreds of thousands of protesters were marching on Washington demanding total withdrawal, while public opinion polls that same year found that a majority of Americans wanted increased military pressure. Mexican Americans earnestly engaged in the debate. Sometimes young soldiers who strongly supported the war ran into resistance from their more reluctant parents. Marine Corps Lance Corporal Patrick Vásquez wrote, "It is more communists than a political war," answering a letter from his father, who characterized the war as "senseless." Corporal Vásquez died at Che Sanh. One of Johnson's Cotulla students, Juanita Hernández, became ill upon learning that her only child would be going into the Army. A local attorney provided her with affidavits proving that the young man was her only source of support. When she brought the documents to the Army base in San Antonio and saw her son in his uniform, with his shorn hair, she cried. He refused the legal assistance, telling her, "I'd like to stay, mother. I like it; I passed all of the tests." He served in the army and she noted proudly that he went on to become an FBI agent, but added that her nephew went to Vietnam "and he died and he's the same age."[25]

While some soldiers urged their parents to support the war with more fervor, many others returned disillusioned and embittered. Veterans in the San Antonio barrio told their state senator, Joe Bernal, "The same people that we fight at night will return in the morning, cut our hair, wash our clothes and cook our food." Meanwhile young Mexican Americans who had beaten the odds to attend college were challenging their elders to oppose the war. In Fort Worth Ernesto Cortés, along with several other Anglo and Chicano activists, walked out of a liberal Democratic Party meeting when the organizers refused to call for withdrawal from Vietnam. California student leader Gil Cárdenas said, "I personally thought the war was immoral." In 1967 students at more than five northern California colleges formed the Mexican American Student Confederation, then led a march through the San Francisco Mission district. One participant remembered, "Lots of Chicano soldiers were dying in a foreign war, for the multinational corporations, for the facade of freedom, in disproportionate numbers. . . . So we marched . . . shouting, 'Thanks for what?' It was an idealistic time." [26]

Joan Baez, one of the most prominent antiwar activists, declared, "Browns and blacks are the targets of the most vicious attacks by the state because minorities are the easiest to manipulate. They are the brunt because America needs them. . . . One of the tragedies of war is that the poor people of every nationality are the ones who carry most of the guns, suffer, fight, and die." Although famous for her internationalist perspective, she also takes pride in her ethnic heritage. Baez recalled, "Once somebody called me a dirty Mexican, and a student asked my teacher, 'Is she a Mexican?' My teacher, in an attempt to defend me, said, 'Joan is the very highest breed of Spanish.' I said, 'What do you mean the very highest breed of Spanish? I'm a Mexican.'" [27]

Leaders of the GI generation wrestled with the antiwar arguments. In 1966 the MAPA state executive board passed a resolution opposing the Vietnam War. As word of the vote spread, a number of Mapistas, along with members of the GI Forum, spoke out against the resolution. According to Bert Corona, "They made impassioned pleas, arguing that as the U.S. was involved in Vietnam, we had to support young Chicano men in the military by supporting Johnson's policies. Many of them cried and urged us to be patriotic and not abandon our young men." In the end the board tabled the motion. When police officers bludgeoned protesters at the Oakland, California, induction center, local MAPA leaders debated their appropriate response. "If we encourage those protesters we are lawbreakers and if we discourage them, we automatically send our young men to Viet Nam. It is a very difficult question, laden with contradictions." By 1967 most MAPA chapters had come around to opposing the war, with members joining demonstrations and picketing draft boards and induction centers. MAPA members resisted a total break with Johnson though. In June MAPA president Bert Corona would ask the president to send his greetings to their convention, even though Corona had been speaking at campus antiwar rallies throughout California and in Washington,

D.C., for months and his son had burned his draft card. In March 1967 established organizations such as MAPA and the CSO, along with rising young Chicano groups such as the Brown Berets, met and demanded that "more evident efforts be made for peace in Vietnam and [that] the War on Poverty be stepped up at home." An antiwar resolution failed by one vote; a prowar one lost by a larger margin.

San Antonio County Commissioner Albert Peña remembered, "It took a long time and I did a lot of soul searching about Vietnam." After Pearl Harbor he had led his neighborhood gang to the recruiting station, where they were first in line, but in Vietnam he thought that the United States was destroying a country in order to save it. He found more and more West Side residents nodding in agreement when he said, "Only *our* sons are dying over there," but many of his old GI Forum colleagues disapproved of his statements, dismissing him as a "Kennedy man." [28]

"It tore us up because our people were very supportive of Johnson," said Joe Bernal. Narrowly elected to the Texas senate, Bernal came out against the war despite the political risks of alienating the president and the two most prominent local defenders of Mexican American rights: Congressman González and Archbishop Lucey. The state senator decided to make this announcement not at a press conference or at a university symposium but to his fellow Mexican American veterans, at a GI Forum convention where he was scheduled to appear as the main speaker. He began by reminding the Forumeers that he was a veteran of the Second World War, but went on to characterize the Vietnam War as "a no-win situation." He cited the disproportionate Mexican American casualties: "Young people that I had taught to play baseball and basketball . . . coming back without their arms and legs." Bernal concluded, "You know, it's very hard for me to tell you this but it seems to me that we are in a very unpopular war and we ought to get out of there." When he finished, five hundred people sat in stunned silence. "You could hear a pin drop," he said. Dr. García never raised the issue with him because, Bernal speculated, "they continued to support Vietnam, you see, because he had bought into LBJ and they couldn't go back on their connection." [29]

THE INTERAGENCY COMMITTEE ON MEXICAN-AMERICAN AFFAIRS

On March 4 the president named Héctor García to the revamped National Advisory Council on Economic Opportunity. Formerly headed by Sargent Shriver, it now would supervise him. The new membership consisted mostly of friends of the president and people from the South and Southwest. Johnson also recommended that Congress limit the functions of Community Action Programs and require CAP to name local officials to its community boards. With criticism rising he was circling the wagons.[30]

One week later García wrote to Dave North, warning that without an EEOC appointment Texas would witness the same kind of protests among Mexican American Democrats as in California, "and this has to be prevented." The Forum founder included an article about the recent defeat of Democratic Lieutenant Governor Carr due to disaffection of Mexican Texans. "Unless you help me and my friends, . . . who are the backbone, the main stay, and grass roots of the Viva Johnson clubs," García wrote, "President Johnson will not even carry Texas in 1968." The "good cop/bad cop" routine worked; three weeks later the White House named a Mexican American to the EEOC.[31]

For months the administration had been searching for the right candidate. "Check with me first," the president informed Civil Service Director John Macy in June 1966. Johnson warned Macy that the selection process would be difficult because no single Mexican American organization predominated; a person well respected in, say, Texas might very well be an unknown quantity in California. Finally in the fall of 1966 the president settled on Vicente Ximenes of the GI Forum, who had run the 1964 Viva Johnson campaign and had performed well in various Johnson administration posts. Macy gave him a glowing recommendation as an experienced administrator who had dedicated his life to civil rights and social reform. At the time Ximenes was serving as deputy director of the Agency for International Development (AID) in Panama, and thus had been abroad during the EEOC walkout and the farmworker confrontation with Governor Connally. Moreover, Ximenes was the first choice of Héctor García and grew up in the hometown of John Connally, who characterized the Ximeneses as among "the prominent families in Floresville." Indeed, the candidate's Texas pedigree rivaled that of Johnson; a Ximenes had died in the Alamo. Ximenes's father had visited the president along with Floresville publisher Sam Fore, a longtime ally of Johnson and Connally. "You ought to find something for Vicente," Fore told the president. At the same time, the candidate's decades of residence in New Mexico conveniently obscured these old Texas ties.[32]

The nomination ran into a snag, however, with New Mexico Senator Clinton Anderson because Ximenes had once opposed an Anderson vote. Finally the senator said that he would accede to the nomination, but he was not happy about it, so Macy kept looking, reporting in October, "I have been searching for individuals . . . who are neither so well assimilated that they can be accused of being an Uncle Tom, nor so militant and vitriolic that they cannot bring to the Commission a rational attitude." Macy consulted everyone from César Chávez to John Connally. Several people recommended Grace Olivarez, and Macy called her "one of the foremost Mexican-American leaders," but the Civil Service chief also characterized her as "controversial" and wondered about "the advisability of naming a woman to represent a patriarchal community." Senator Yarborough nominated George Sánchez, but the president rejected the idea and wanted to know who had nominated the professor in the first place. Johnson once summed up his hiring criteria to Bill Moyers: "I want . . . someone who's the best but *indisputably* loyal." Sánchez did not fit the bill. Neither did Herman Gallegos, someone Macy considered extremely able and acceptable to all parties. "Herman, your name is being kicked around for something," a Ford Foundation colleague told him, but cautioned, "You've got to tone down your anti-Vietnam stuff." Gallegos refused to stop marching against the war even though he suspected that the FBI had him under surveillance. When Macy would suggest highly qualified people, but ones with potential political problems, Johnson would complain, "Jesus, he can't find his ass with both hands."[33]

So the nomination process stalled. "There were fewer positions left to fill and all of them were exceedingly important politically to LBJ, and important symbolically to LBJ," Moyers observed. Finally Dr. García prevailed. After Ximenes reiterated his loyalty and his ability to work with Senator Anderson, chief White House assistant Marvin Watson wrote to Johnson on April 3 recommending that Ximenes be nominated the following day. Johnson gave his approval, but just to be on the safe side that same week the White House also named a LULAC leader to a federal post: Oscar Laurel.[34]

Ximenes walked into the Oval Office with his foreign affairs papers, saw John Macy sitting there, and thought, "I'm not here for Panama." Johnson spoke of the EEOC appointment and then made a surprise announcement: he would create a committee consisting of all of the domestic Cabinet officers plus Shriver of OEO, and would name Ximenes as the chairman. "He was just exuberant that he was going to do this and he was waiting for me to say something," said Ximenes, who was stunned, only managing to say,

"*I'm* going to be the chairman?"
"Yup. Call Califano in and let's write up an executive order."
"How am I going to get Shriver, Wirtz, Freeman, Gardner to a meeting?"
"You have your meetings right outside my office, right here, and you put in your little note when you're going to have your meeting that the president will look in on the meeting once in a while."[35]

The White House announced Ximenes's EEOC nomination the next day, but would keep the new committee under wraps until the swearing-in ceremony. Scores of Mexican Americans thanked the president for the EEOC appointment. "Reaction amongst Mexican Americans . . . is one of jubilation and gratitude," declared García in a telegram that was forwarded to the president. The president of LULAC wrote of Ximenes, "While he might not have been my first choice, he is nevertheless a capable and qualified man." Congressman De La Garza told the White House, "The President could have made no better appointment." Even the leading newspaper in Monterrey, Mexico, mentioned the selection, characterizing it as part of an effort by the Johnson administration to woo the Hispanic vote for 1968.[36]

Nonetheless Dave North warned, "Despite the remarkable attention paid to the Mexican American community by the President this week—two Presidential appointments and today's ceremony honoring the late Daniel Fernandez, Medal of Honor winner—the proposed White House Conference for the Mexican American remains a problem." Meanwhile North learned that one of the leaders of the rising Chicano movement, Corky Gonzales, accused Ximenes of going over to "the other side." Gonzales's new poem "I Am Joaquín," a clarion cry for Chicanos to defend their rights and their mestizo heritage, was catching on like wild fire, particularly among young people in the barrios of the Southwest and Midwest. Worried about the increasing militancy of some constituents, members of Congress such as Frank Evans of Colorado and Ed Roybal of California pressed the White House on the conference issue. McPherson sent Roybal a fourteen-page response outlining the numerous administration activities carried out on behalf of Mexican Americans. In the original draft McPherson wrote, "This you will realize is much more meaningful than any conferences or meetings that serve to pinpoint problems but do not supply continuing answers. We know the problems. We are working on the answers." These sentences were omitted from the version sent to Roybal, which simply thanked him for his suggestions and promised to respond.[37]

The items listed in the McPherson letter served as a blueprint for a nine-page press release entitled "The Mexican American: A New Focus on Opportunity," which outlined a number of accomplishments. For the first time the minimum wage covered farmworkers. The Office of Education sponsored adult basic education for 50,000 Mexican Americans in the Southwest and awarded grants for farmworker education, for school districts with a high percentage of Mexican Americans, and for the training of bilingual teachers. Every year the Public Health Service immunized over 1.5 million Mexican Americans, and it supported thirty-eight community health centers in the Southwest. The Migrant Health Act of 1964 provided $7.2 million in health care. Medicare and Medicaid served millions of Mexican-heritage citizens. From Head Start to the Jobs Corps, the War on Poverty helped Mexican Americans across the land. Califano informed the president, "We are preparing speeches for congressmen applauding the report and your interest in the Mexican Americans. We will also background selected reporters on this report." To maximize media coverage, the administration planned to issue the press release on June 9, the day of Ximenes's swearing-in ceremony.[38]

Meanwhile problems were flaring up again between Governor Connally and the farmworkers. On May 31 LULAC President Alfred Hernández wrote to Connally, "Several members of the Texas Advisory Committee to the Civil Rights Commission have been eyewitnesses to illegal arrests by the Texas Rangers." The governor refused to investigate. "We had no abuse by the Rangers in those days," he recalled years later, adding, "I wasn't going to try to intercede and inject myself into the action of an individual Ranger or individual highway patrolman, any more than . . . I was going to . . . tell a university professor what to do." Hernández called David North at the White House. In a letter to Joe Bernal, Hernández wrote, "I trust something will give soon. I tip my hat to you for your effort in trying to get the Rangers out of Rio Grande City. Arriba los hombres con cojones. [Hurrah for men with balls.]" The next day, June 1, the farmworkers union filed suit with the Justice Department against Ranger Captain A. Y. Allee for excessive force after striker Magdaleno Dimas received several injuries, including a cerebral concussion, while in his custody.

Numerous people in the GI Forum, MAPA, and LULAC wrote to the president, urging that the Justice Department investigate. "Connally became a hate figure," Bernal remembered. "The only reason he was halfway acceptable was because of his connection to Lyndon Johnson. . . . Johnson faded out of the scene . . . because of Vietnam."

At the same time that Mexican Texans were confronting the Texas Rangers, tensions in New Mexico were reaching a fever pitch. On June 2 ten members of the land-grant rights organization La Alianza were arrested "probably illegally," according to the *New York Times.* Three days later Reies López Tijerina and members of his Alianza attempted to make a citizen's arrest of the district attorney, Alfonso Sánchez, wounding a police officer and a jailer in the process. Already out on bail, appealing the assault conviction for occupying Kit Carson National Forest, López Tijerina fled, and a full-scale manhunt ensued.[39]

Four days later, on June 9, the same day as Vicente Ximenes's swearing-in ceremony, about 100 people picketed Governor Connally in Laredo, where he was delivering a speech to a LULAC convention. The protesters included union workers, GI Forum members, and some Lulackers. "Connally, get your Gestapo out of Starr County," read one of the signs. Also on June 9 the liberal newsweekly the *Texas Observer* featured an article on Mexican Americans entitled "Three Million Alienated Texans." In the *New York Times,* next to the report describing the Ximenes ceremony, another article quoted United Auto Workers President Walter Reuther, who called for a senate investigation "to help end the brutality and terrorism" against people "whose only crime is that they protest their status as slaves for rent to wealthy farm corporations." Roy Reuther spoke at the Laredo rally along with César Chávez.[40]

At Ximenes's swearing-in ceremony the president praised the Hispanic tradition in this country and characterized his new EEOC commissioner as a "distinguished public servant, a teacher, a war hero, a leader of the Mexican American community." Johnson recalled his teaching days in Cotulla, where he first vowed to use public office to help every American have an equal opportunity in America. "That is . . . the 'Great Society.' It is not great yet, but it has improved a lot . . . and it is going to improve a lot more." He finished with a flourish, announcing, "I am going to establish today the highest level committee a President can create," a cabinet-level group called the Interagency Committee on Mexican American Affairs. "He wanted to really drive home the point that somebody could reach the top," said Califano.[41]

Johnson often followed this pattern: extreme caution in selecting a nominee, then a dramatic, surprise announcement, often of a dual appointment. Luther Holcomb of the EEOC congratulated Watson on the "tremendous" ceremony, writing, "The President was at his best." A staff member told David Jones of the *New York Times*, "This is for real and we're staying with it." Jones reported that Mexican American leaders voiced strong approval of the president's actions but were waiting, with some degree of skepticism, to see the results of the new committee.[42]

Ximenes immediately got to work. As a member of the EEOC he pushed for a new tactic: affirmative action. If an enterprise hired very few minority members or women, he would investigate even if no specific employee had complained of bias. At the same time, as head of the Interagency Committee on Mexican American Affairs he met with the various cabinet members, prodding them, assisting in developing strategies for recruiting Mexican American staff members. "I had the backing of the president," he emphasized, as when Johnson ordered five or six southwestern cities added to the Model Cities list per Ximenes's request, overruling the secretary of Housing and Urban Development in the process.

"I have and had a lot of respect for Vicente," said Armando Rodríguez; "he is a nice guy and hardworking . . . and very bright. . . . I enjoyed working with him." Albert Peña called Ximenes "a good man," but thought that the Interagency Committee could do little. Anguiano credited the committee with bringing Mexican Americans into the federal decision-making process, but she saw very few concrete results. For his part Gallegos considered Ximenes an honorable, dedicated public servant dealing with a Mexican American constituency "that didn't know how to play the national political game. It was still feeling its way."[43]

From the beginning Ximenes noticed that Johnson was the one administration official who invariably took the lead on Mexican American issues. Once Ximenes and Johnson were talking while people were bustling around the White House in preparation for a state dinner. Suddenly Johnson turned to Marvin Watson and asked, "Have you invited any Mexican Americans?" The befuddled aide sputtered, "Well, I don't know." Johnson barked, "Get some! From now on, it doesn't matter who [the honored guest] is, I want some Mexican American

groups and constituencies there." Soon thereafter Armando Rodríguez received an invitation to a dinner honoring the secretary of state
and members of the Supreme Court. "I worked under four presidents
and that was the only time."

Moreover, Johnson realized that they lacked a strong national
lobby, and he urged Ximenes to suggest people for high federal posts,
including the Supreme Court. "Vicente, if you can find me somebody
of the caliber of Thurgood Marshall, I will appoint him," the president said. Unfortunately, at that time only two Mexican Americans
served on the federal bench and they had only recently been appointed. Few had even argued cases before the higher courts. Unlike African Americans, Mexican-heritage people had no colleges of
their own and no legal defense fund. Black professionals honed their
oratorical and leadership skills in their local churches, while non-
Hispanics dominated the Catholic Church. "I looked hard, even for
people who were not on a bench but who were, say, mayors of a city,"
Ximenes remembered.[44]

He was searching for another Gus García. "He would have been
exactly what we were looking for because he did have that legal mind.
Gus García was a genius," said Ximenes, recalling how García successfully obtained the unanimous Supreme Court ruling in the 1954
case of *Hernandez v. Texas*, only to return home unheralded. "Nobody met him. He must have sat there thinking, 'Where are the
troops?'" Meanwhile, the Texas legal establishment vilified García for
his civil rights efforts and applauded his law school buddy John Connally, who was on a fast track to high political office that was closed to
García. Gus García was destroyed by an alcoholism that Ximenes sus-
pects was rooted in bitterness and disappointment. "My brother's
the one that picked him up off the park bench in San Antonio," said
Ximenes. "What a shame, what a tragedy."[45]

By midsummer the president had come around to accepting the
idea of a conference, but somewhere in the Southwest, not in Washington. Ximenes supported this because, he said, "The grassroots have
no way of getting to Washington." (At the same time he knew that
the president had already ruled out a Washington meeting.) When
Ximenes met with the various cabinet members, some expressed concern about possible protests. "Don't worry about it, that's my worry,"
said Ximenes, who advised them instead to bone up on the issues: "Be
prepared for tough questions." After his staff members had scouted
possible sites, including San Antonio, Albuquerque, and Los Angeles,
he went to see the president, who said, "Why don't we have it in El

Paso?" Ximenes replied, "Mr. President, I haven't even *been* to El Paso; I don't even know if they want us there!" Johnson, unconcerned, continued, "Yea, sure, let's have it in El Paso." The president instructed him to call the El Paso Chamber of Commerce right from the Oval Office, telling Ximenes, "Say, 'Get me five hotels' and they'll get five hotels if they have to build them."

Johnson chose El Paso because in late October he and Mexican President Gustavo Díaz Ordaz would be signing a treaty there, returning to Mexico a parcel of land, the Chamizal, that Mexico had lost when the Rio Grande River had changed course. State Department officials resisted linking the two events because they thought it would, in Ximenes's words, "ruin their party." Meanwhile El Paso Mayor Judson Williams opposed what he considered an influx of hordes of minority people. In January residents of El Segundo barrio had erupted in spontaneous demonstrations protesting their impoverished living conditions; the mayor feared a repetition or, worse, an escalation of the unrest. When Ximenes reported these problems to the president, Johnson said, "Don't pay any attention to them."[46]

At a September 12 press conference Ximenes announced the Cabinet Committee Hearings on Mexican American Affairs, to be held in El Paso, Texas, October 27–28. The State Department fell into line and Mayor Williams pledged to make his city a "showplace" by sprucing up El Paso, particularly El Segundo. One thousand Mexican Americans would attend, with a number scheduled to speak. After a general opening meeting, sessions would meet concurrently: Agriculture with Secretary Orville Freeman; Labor with Secretary Willard Wirtz; Health, Education and Welfare with Secretary John Gardner; Housing and Urban Development with Secretary Robert Weaver; War on Poverty with Sargent Shriver; Economic and Social Development with Chairman Ximenes.[47]

FROM MEXICAN AMERICAN TO CHICANO

Ironically, news of the forthcoming conference exacerbated tensions. Ximenes deflected a reporter's question as to whether this substituted for a White House conference; the Los Angeles newsletter *Carta Blanca* wondered the same thing. Dr. Sánchez declined his invitation, saying, "I cannot accept the El Paso conference as a sort of 'consolation prize,' with all due respect to the White House." Representatives of the Mexican American Unity Council—more than 200 activists from the major California organizations—met at a camp outside Los

Angeles to plan strategy. They considered boycotting, but ended up selecting people to testify in El Paso, preferring "someone who is knowl-
edgeable about the subject, but who is dynamic in his or her presentation," in the words of the chairman. They complained that some
important leaders were not invited, notably Corky Gonzales of Denver and Reies López Tijerina of New Mexico. In fact, Ximenes did invite Gonzales, who declined, as did Chávez.[48]

"I wanted desperately for César Chávez to be there," said Ximenes,
who wrote to the farmworker leader, quoting President Johnson to
the effect that "the era of soothing generalities is over," but Chávez
was waiting impatiently for the administration to act on behalf of collective bargaining rights for farmworkers and against Texas Ranger
brutality. He wrote to Ximenes,

> Your and the President's concern for *most* Mexican-American
> problems is commendable. We have not participated in any such
> meetings and are reluctant to do so as we do not want to embar-
> rass the administration. It is our considered opinion that the ad-
> ministration is not ready to deal with specific problems affecting
> farm workers.[49]

Meanwhile the Senate migratory labor subcommittee was conducting
hearings in Starr County similar to those Robert Kennedy held in California. Committee members included Ralph Yarborough—who referred to the Rangers as "Connally's strike breakers"—and Robert
Kennedy's brother Ted. "We expect great things," declared the local
farmworker newsletter. In contrast, union organizer Gilbert Padilla
met for ninety minutes with Governor Connally, with no discernible
results. Albert Peña declared, "We are telling the governor and the
president: 'If you are not going to listen to us in 1967, we are not going to listen to you in 1968. . . . We are demanding that the Rangers be
abolished.'" Peña, representing PASO, planned to boycott the El Paso
meeting but in the end was persuaded to attend in order to present
PASO's demands in person.[50] Ximenes remembered that MAPA President Bert Corona called him demanding to make a presentation before the secretary of the interior, so the under-secretary came to El
Paso "just to meet with Bert Corona!" recalled Ximenes. By that time,
however, Corona had decided to boycott the hearings.[51]

While members of the established organizations debated whether to
accept their invitations, the new Chicano generation was emerging.
In the summer of 1967 José Angel Gutiérrez, a graduate student at

St. Mary's University in San Antonio, held a series of discussion sessions with a handful of other students. They criticized the leaders of LULAC and the GI Forum for "raising substantive issues, but in a nice voice," in the words of one. In a bow to political practicality Gutiérrez and his colleagues named their new group the Mexican American Youth Organization (MAYO) because, said Willie Velásquez, "it sounded 'Boyscoutish.'" Looking back some thirty years later, Gutiérrez said, "We were convinced that we were the generation that was going to recover the land in the Southwest, not by taking the land, but by taking political control of the institutions in the land." In particular they wanted to oust the Anglo leadership that dictated policy for counties with overwhelmingly Mexican-heritage populations, such as in Cotulla, where a distant relative of Johnson's had long served as the county judge, and in nearby Crystal City, the home of one of Johnson's favorite cousins and the hometown of Gutiérrez, who had supported an unsuccessful Mexican American political revolt there in 1963 (see chapter 6). "Oddly enough, José Angel Gutiérrez's political hero was a practical politician by the name of Lyndon Johnson," remarked a MAYO colleague.[52]

Meanwhile in May 1967 southern California students formed the United Mexican American Students. UMAS soon established chapters throughout the Southwest and Midwest. The two most important organizations of the GI generation, LULAC and the GI Forum, originated in Texas, but most of the Chicano groups began in California, reflecting the fact that Los Angeles—with its two million Mexican-heritage residents, many of them young—had eclipsed San Antonio as the center of Mexican-heritage life.

The young activists, wherever they lived, drew inspiration from labor organizers such as Chávez and radicals such as Corky Gonzales, as well as land-grant activist Reies López Tijerina. Many students in Texas and California had marched with Chávez's United Farmworkers, and UMAS chapters drummed up support for the union on campuses. Meanwhile, as Gutiérrez later recalled, "We'd learn about Corky Gonzales and Reies Tijerina, and we'd go find them, or Chávez. We actually read and then went out and got informed first hand." The San Antonians, like others in the rising *movimiento*, rejected English-language ethnic labels. Adopting an old barrio term, they called themselves "Chicanos" and emphasized what they called "cultural nationalism": resistance to assimilation and pride in their *mestizaje*, their blend of European and Indian blood. At the same time, they sought out black nationalists and antiwar activists. UMAS members formed alliances with black and white radicals on campus, while Gutiérrez recalled, "We'd read about [Martin Luther] King, and we'd go look for him; we traveled to Atlanta several times. We'd read about Stokely Carmichael and the SNCC activists and we'd track them down."[53]

Gutiérrez and the UMAS leaders were following a path blazed several years earlier by Chicanas active in SNCC (the Student Nonviolent Coordinating Committee) and in the radical student movement. María Varela—after graduating in the early 1960s from Alverno College in Milwaukee, where she served as student body president—took a seven-dollar per week organizing job for the Young Christian Students, a proworker activist group. "Here I'd been trotting around on Catholic campuses saying that if you're a Christian you really need to *be* there, on the front lines, not lagging behind," she said; she put her words into action by organizing disenfranchised black residents in the Deep South for SNCC. So did Elizabeth Martínez. After serving as book and arts editor at *The Nation* magazine, she joined SNCC in 1963, publishing *Letters from Mississippi* and *The Youngest Revolution.*

Meanwhile Varela participated in founding the Students for a Democratic Society. SDS leader Tom Hayden referred to her in his memoirs as "Mary Varela, a fair-complexioned Mexican-American with deep brown eyes." While they were thrashing out their founding document, *The Port Huron Statement*, Varela quoted from Pope John XXIII's encyclical *Pacem in Terris*: people were "infinitely precious," with "unfulfilled capacities." According to Hayden, "We accepted the pope's formulation and included it verbatim in the document without any citation." In 1967 Varela came to northern New Mexico and began organizing among people whose families had settled there nearly three hundred years earlier. Longtime residents soon merged their small plots of land into a productive farm, La Cooperativa Agrícola del Pueblo de Tierra Amarilla. "There's a reason why there was so much intermarriage between Native Americans and Mexican settlers here," Varela said. "It's because they had the same view of the land; it wasn't a commodity." Elizabeth Martínez came to the area soon thereafter and established the newspaper *El Grito del Norte* (Outcry of the North), where Varela contributed articles on Corky Gonzales and other *movimiento* people.[54]

The weekend before the El Paso conference, land-grant leader Reies López Tijerina held a national convention in Albuquerque. He invited Black Power leaders, the Hopi nation, and members of the New Left to come and form an alliance. Meanwhile Chicanos at the conference used the occasion to plan their first major action. They argued night and day whether to boycott or protest the El Paso meeting. In the end they decide to go and demonstrate against Johnson administration policies.[55]

EL PASO

Meanwhile Chairman Ximenes worked feverishly against the deadline, knowing full well that most of the established leaders welcomed this opportunity to present their views to high administration officials. In a July letter to Cris Aldrete of the DNC Alfred Hernández wrote, "Thank you very much for the picture of the big Jefe. . . . Irrespective of the complaints that many of us have lodged with his office I consider our President Lyndon B. Johnson . . . *el que mas ha hecho por la Raza* [the one that has done the most for our people]." In a matter of weeks Ximenes achieved the seemingly impossible, assembling experts and activists from Chicago to East Los Angeles to rural New Mexico. They would testify on a range of topics that touched on nearly every aspect of barrio life. Most people accepted his invitation, and on October 13 he announced the names of the participants: Cabinet members, public officials, "prominent educators, union leaders, businessmen, and representatives of the Federal, State, and local government . . . from jurists to farm workers," he said, a "virtually unprecedented" assemblage for a meeting held outside of Washington.

Ximenes planned sessions on every topic recommended the previous October by the preplanning conference, with two exceptions: the military draft and women's issues. Ximenes knew of Johnson's concern for minority representation on draft boards, but the president would not risk a full-scale discussion of the issue in this charged political atmosphere. Five of the fifty speakers were women, more than at most governmental conferences, and Ximenes hired several women staff members, including his public information officer. Nevertheless no sessions addressed the women's issues that the planning session had raised. In this respect the hearings were typical of the times.[56]

A number of Mexican American leaders attended the state dinner at the White House for President Díaz Ordaz, then flew to El Paso. The conference opened Friday night, October 23, 1967, with a stirring speech by the vice president, lauding Mexican American contributions to American civic life and calling for redress of their grievances. At the same time, one participant noted, "It was obvious to many of us that someone had ghost-written the speech. The names of the Mexican American leaders were pronounced in such a way as to indicate that Mr. Humphrey did not even know who they were and jokingly apologized for his slight Norwegian accent."[57]

At the hearing participants presented insightful, fully documented information, some the fruit of a lifetime of research, some fresh from the brand-new organizations spawned by the War on Poverty. Delia Villegas, Director of Vocational Training for the Archdiocese of Chicago, described a Manpower Development Training Act program that placed unemployed people in productive jobs. Lorenzo Chávez, an Albuquerque attorney, outlined a $200,000 project that attacked both bad housing and youth unemployment by training young people in construction skills. He called community involvement—from university professors to building contractors to potential homeowners—"the key to success."

At the HEW hearing Secretary Gardner made his opening remarks partly in Spanish. "John Gardner speaks Spanish very well . . . he married a lady from Costa Rica, I think," said Armando Rodríguez, who also addressed the session, at Gardner's request. Faustina Solís presented the findings developed by the health panel she had chaired at the Mexican American Unity Council meeting in Los Angeles, telling Gardner that HEW should collect health data by ethnic group, eliminate residency requirements for federal health programs, establish scholarships for training Mexican Americans, and renew funding for migrant health care. Carlos Truan told Shriver's session that OEO should make better use of the Mexican American organizations. SER was a good start, but where were the centers? Where was the money? Daniel R. López of the East Los Angeles Service Center reiterated this theme, demanding full appropriation of poverty funds, along with better cooperation between programs and more community involvement. Bexar County Commissioner Albert Peña summed it all up by calling for a Marshall Plan for the Southwest.[58]

Labor people placed little hope in the conference. Ernesto Galarza declared:

We who have for thirty years seen the Department of Labor stand by, at times connive, while farm labor unions were destroyed by agribusiness; we who have seen the Immigration and Naturalization Service see-saw with the seasonal tides of Wetbacks; we who are now seeing the Department of Housing and

Urban Development assist in the demolishment of the urban barrios. . . . We who have seen the Office of Economic Opportunity retreat with its shield, not on it, after calling the Mexican poor to do battle for maximum feasible participation in their own destinies. . . . We remain profoundly skeptical.

He demanded collective bargaining rights for farmworkers and withdrawal of government subsidies from growers who imported strikebreakers. The farmworker chronicler implicitly criticized the administration's Border Commission by calling for a new one with membership to include Mexican labor people from both sides of the border, to raise "Mexican levels of income to American standards . . . not . . . lowering American to present Mexican levels." Otherwise, he prophesied, "Goods will be manufactured at Mexican wages and reimported for sale at American prices."[59] Led by Galarza and Corona, activists increasingly stressed alliances with Mexican unions and reform of international economic structures rather than immigration restriction and deportation.[60]

Meanwhile Chicano students demanded to speak, and they called for sessions devoted to the Vietnam War and government ties to corporations. "A number of us went uninvited to the White House conference on Mexican American Affairs, the classic outside agitators," said Gil Cárdenas. (Professor Ralph Guzmán had arranged for the Californians to stay in El Segundo barrio with young people active in LULAC, the Forum, and other local groups.) "I got kicked out of the auditorium when Vice President Humphrey was speaking," said Cárdenas, who was pleasantly surprised to discover that many of the established leaders were dissatisfied as well. Rudy Ramos, attending uninvited, passed out buttons he had designed, proclaiming "Programas y Fondos Primero para La Raza y Después LBJ [programs and funds for our folks first and then LBJ]." Gallegos used funds from the United Auto Workers Union and the Colorado Council of Churches to rent space in the conference hotel for rump sessions. "The meeting rooms were jam-packed with people talking about displeasure with Johnson," he said. He also spotted a number of FBI agents. Gallegos speculated that paradoxically, more protesters could come now that the conference was not in distant Washington.[61]

The next morning, Saturday, when the two presidents arrived at the conference hotel, protesters jeered them and tried unsuccessfully to persuade the invited guests to boycott the breakfast. Inside President

Johnson introduced the official party, saying, "Take a hand, Governor Connally." Boos filled the hall, to the surprise of young Chicanos milling about the corridors. "In the long run that proved more effective than our protest outside," said Cárdenas. The governor saw "no significance at all to the boos." Johnson proceeded with his speech. "I am talking about people I have known all my life and people that I care about deeply," he began. He outlined administration accomplishments, but noted

> it is not enough . . . for too many years, your government paid too little heed to both the status and the hopes of the Mexican American community. Nobody knows better than you how far we have to go. . . . A lesser people might have given up a long time ago. But your people didn't give up. They believed . . . that they were full-fledged citizens . . . even if others didn't always treat them as such.

He pledged to do more. "I'd much rather be controversial than complacent (clapping, hoorahs) or just critical (clapping, laughter.)" The audience applauded their president vigorously, interrupting him some twenty times. People who had worked for civil rights in LULAC and the GI Forum for a lifetime—Mexican Texans, in particular—viewed Johnson's address as a point of departure. This very Texas president, descended from the culture that had subjugated Mexican Americans for generations, had pledged to meet the challenges presented by them in his own conference's testimony. Together they would work to build a better society for their children.[62]

Then the participants learned that the hearings would be canceled so that everyone could be bussed to the Chamizal ceremony. According to Bert Corona, nearly half of the delegates walked out because "the Johnson administration had really gone back on its word." Ernesto Galarza remarked sardonically that the canceled session served as an object lesson in "how the Administration operates."[63] The protesters spilled out of the hotel and joined José Angel Gutiérrez, Corky Gonzales, and Reies López Tijerina, who were picketing in front. Gonzales called the conference participants

> well-meaning, confused, irate middle-class Chicanos who knew they were being had when they were asked to swallow and digest the same old soup and cracker disks fed by the politicians, with Johnson and Humphrey at the head of the line. Lacking any

positive direction or militant action . . . what resulted was a lot of brave words, promises, motions—and no action.

The previous week Gonzales and Tijerina had spoken in the East Los Angeles barrio to one thousand people, including some who had burned their draft cards. Los Angeles mayor Sam Yorty had sent Johnson information on the rally, which the mayor characterized as antiwar and anti-Johnson. Now the demonstrators in El Paso marched together to El Segundo barrio. A Laredo contingent proclaimed, "Today We Protest, Tomorrow Revolution," some Californians carried signs reading "Gracias por Nada!" and a MAYO placard announced, "Mañana is here." Along the way the numbers swelled as barrio residents joined the parade.[64]

Dr. Galarza presided at the protest conference held at Sacred Heart Church. He read a message from César Chávez, who sent prayers and congratulations to all of "La Raza" in their struggle for "social revolution" against "pretty, perfumed sellouts."[65] The conference was abuzz with talk of "brown power" and "chicano power." Speech after speech elicited "Viva"s. Maclovio Barraza of the Steelworkers Union declared that "before we shout 'Viva Johnson,' there better be a 'Viva la Gente Mexicana.' Mañana is too late." Tijerina approached the microphone to applause and the furious strumming of a guitar. His Spanish phrases grew in emotional intensity, carrying the audience along. "We will have to learn from the militants that the government respects nothing but power. . . . The justice we seek with our eyes, our ears, our hearts, is in the land." At a news conference the New Mexican leader demanded that the president investigate the land-grant controversy: "Our life and our blood." LULAC leader Pete Tijerina [no relation] remembered vividly having to pass by a number of bodyguards to reach Reies Tijerina and his wife, "a beautiful woman, brown skin, blazing green eyes, dressed like an Apache." The Lulacker was caucusing with the Alianza and other groups, telling them about a new Mexican American legal defense fund sponsored by the Ford Foundation. Alianza members, in the middle of appealing Tijerina's conviction, were very interested in this possible legal assistance.[66]

For the first time members of the various Chicano movements coalesced. MAYO people concerned with overthrowing Anglo politicians in Cotulla and other Texas towns exchanged ideas with members of the Crusade for Justice who were fighting police brutality in Denver; farmworkers from Chávez's union conferred with land-grant activists from New Mexico. The delegates dubbed their meeting La Raza

Unida—using an old barrio term, *La Raza*, meaning "the people/our folks"—a call to unite for grass-roots political organizing. The delegates approved a manifesto, "El Plan de La Raza Unida"; "Judging our lives with new values," Corky Gonzales called it. Probably coined by Ernesto Galarza, "Raza Unida" connoted the unity of a people. Much of the plan echoed in more general terms the topics discussed at the official conference, including guaranteed employment and training, educational opportunities for all, safe housing "without relocation from one's community," equal representation in government agencies, and an end to gerrymandering.

"La Raza Unida" placed new emphasis, however, on "the right to organize community and labor groups in our own style" and on the enforcement of the land-grant provisions of the 1848 Treaty of Guadalupe Hidalgo. "We affirm our dedication to our heritage, a bilingual culture, and assert our right to be members of La Raza Unida anywhere," it concluded. The "Plan de La Raza Unida" resembled the "Plan of Delano" promulgated by the farmworkers in 1965. Both echoed the plans of the 1910 Mexican Revolution, including the "Plan de San Diego," issued in San Diego, Texas, in 1915, which called for the liberation of the Southwest from the United States (see chapter 2).

Veteran organizers Galarza, Gallegos, and Corona suggested practical strategies for implementing the "Plan." According to Corona, "'Raza Unida' at El Paso . . . was used to encourage the delegates to return to their communities and to organize for political empowerment. . . . We believed that the Democratic Party in particular had to be taken to task for not playing a role in the political empowerment of Spanish-speaking people. We stressed the need to build political organization among our people."[67]

Although a number of women fully participated, including labor activist Polly Baca and women in the UFWOC, La Raza Unida leadership was exclusively male. In this respect the *movimiento* resembled other movements, including black power, antiwar, labor, and Mexico City students, none of which gave women equal stature and all of which influenced Chicanos. With even radical men seemingly unconcerned about gender issues, a number of women began to coalesce around feminist concerns. By the following year Chicanas such as journalists Enriqueta Longeaux y Vázquez of Colorado and Sylvia González of San Antonio were calling for equal rights within the *movimiento*.[68]

La Raza Unida rump conference was, in Julian Samora's words, "the climax." The Chicano movement was on its way. "It was in El

Paso where La Raza Nueva was given form," wrote Frank Moreno Martínez a few months later in the inaugural issue of the Chicano magazine *Con Safos*:

> This independent and inspiring meeting was held in South El Paso in the Sacred Heart Church. It was there that the issue of the Vietnam War was brought out, with the emphasis on the facts that not only were we suffering many social and economic casualties at home, but that we were also being . . . forced to disproportionately suffer almost twice as many deaths and wounds in Vietnam as members of the dominant Anglo group. It was there that La Raza expressed its true feelings and concerns when it resolved not to assimilate and surrender our language and culture.[69]

Johnson's fears had been realized. He had come to El Paso from a Washington teeming with protesters, who on October 20 had struck against the Pentagon. Now MAPA and MAYO members were picketing his El Paso hearing with signs such as "Today We Demonstrate, Tomorrow We Revolt" and "Don't Ask Rich Mexicans to Talk for the Poor." The barrios had remained quiet when hundreds of ghettos had exploded that summer, but now MAYO was putting La Raza Unida bumper stickers—complete with raised rifles—on participants' cars. Chairman Ximenes, attempting to connect with the Chicano activists, called the rump conference "an attempt . . . whereby an organization could be established. And that's fine."[70]

Early in 1968 Ximenes sent the president a report on a number of follow-up activities. In a confidential teletype to the LBJ Ranch a White House staff member wrote, "Ximenes says it will get a lot of mileage in the Southwest."[71] On February 23, after a briefing by Ximenes, Johnson announced the administration's accomplishments. A number of Mexican Americans had joined the administration, notably Héctor García as a member of the delegation to the United Nations. The Department of Housing and Urban Development had established a special task force to recruit more Mexican Americans. The Forest Service promised to ask Congress to open the national forest to grazing by "the smaller rancher." The president highlighted the new $85 million bilingual education act and said that the administration had asked Congress for $1 billion, much of it promised for the barrios.[72]

Nonetheless the president was worried. When Governor Connally was booed by loyal Johnson supporters at the El Paso conference, Johnson remarked, "It's hardly safe to be out in public with you any more!" In the wake of the El Paso events Democratic Party operative Cris Aldrete encountered an increasingly skeptical attitude on the part of South Texas Mexican American leaders. The UFWOC, whose membership was growing there, was accelerating its criticism of Johnson and the Vietnam War. The president had enough problems of his own and did not encourage the governor to run again. In November Connally surprised most pundits by announcing his decision not to run for an unprecedented fourth term. Commentators in the press missed the prophetic nature of this event.[73]

TEN

1968

Mexican Americans mobilized for the 1968 presidential campaign as never before, particularly in Texas and California, two states that the president would need to win in the fall. The Mexican American Political Association (MAPA) targeted 40,000 potential voters in East Los Angeles alone. On January 6 MAPA president Bert Corona told a reporter that California already had some 700,000 to 750,000 Mexican Americans registered, but added that Johnson should not take these voters for granted, despite White House initiatives on their behalf. "Many of our live wires are for McCarthy or Kennedy . . . saying the War is taking our young men and our resources and we get the crumbs." The previous day a disgruntled Corona himself had resigned in protest from the California Advisory Commission to the U.S. Civil Rights Commission because he thought that they had "done nothing significant about the serious violations of the Civil Rights of Farmworkers."[1]

LA RAZA UNIDA

On January 6 some 1,500 activists gathered at John Kennedy High School in San Antonio for the follow-up conference of La Raza Unida. Mexican Americans of every age, region, and political persuasion—from veteran Lulackers to the radicals in MAYO—convened to hammer out an agenda for 1968. A number of Anglo and African Americans also attended. Officials from the Republican and Democratic Parties observed the proceedings, hoping to pick up valuable political intelligence, and a staff member of the Interagency Committee on Mexican American Affairs also attended.

Willie Velásquez of MAYO chaired the conference, which began with a keynote address in Spanish, the official language, by Dr. Ernesto Galarza, who proclaimed "the dawn of a new era for the Mexican American. . . . We are giving notice that we are going to be of service to the community" in a common struggle to combat their "third-class" status. Workshops covered politics, education, community organizing, civil rights, the War on Poverty, and the Mexican American identity. According to the *San Antonio Express-News*, a session on "confrontation with the gringo" did not label all non-Hispanics as gringos, but, rather, "differentiated between the evil gringo and the 'Anglo-Saxon' who cooperated and helped make the lot of the Mexican American a better one."

The newspaper also reported that the conference stressed political participation through voter registration, adding, "Some delegates went as far as requesting that La Raza Unida be transformed into a political organization." In addition to the discussion sessions the meeting featured a number of display booths, including one devoted to materials critical of the Johnson administration, particularly regarding Vietnam. One of the pamphlets declared, "We are cannon fodder, raza." The final conference report, among other things, demanded that Governor John Connally abolish the Texas Rangers and appoint Mexican Texans to the committee revising the state constitution. In the closing address Dr. Joe Bernal exhorted the participants, "Elect your friends and defeat your enemies."[2]

The Young Democrats of Texas endorsed the La Raza Unida report, and people in barrios around the country joined the movement. "La Raza Unida of Michigan" members were active in Great Society programs, including Jane González, who headed the War on Poverty in Muskegon.[3] Some OEO people encouraged Chicano organizing, notably Gonzalo Barrientos, who helped develop the VISTA Minority Mobilization Program. He had watched well-intentioned volunteers from outside Texas spend their whole VISTA stint trying to learn the barrio culture while, at the same time, people in those neighborhoods searched desperately for employment. So Barrientos proposed hiring local residents, teaching them about their cultural heritage—from the Aztecs to *mexicano* Congressional Medalists—and training them in the rudiments of community organizing. MAYO leader Mario Compean participated in the program and recalled, "MAYO had 200 people loose. We had a budget. We had salaries. . . . That really allowed MAYO to expand." Barrientos saw his hopes fulfilled as a lasting network began to take shape, linking the northern Anglos from

VISTA with Chicano activists and, even more, connecting Chicanos all over the state. "You would feed each other's energy levels," he said.[4]

"The VISTA program was a special headache," remembered an aide to Congressman Henry B. González, "because lots of kids who later became Hispanic radicals in the late 60s were involved in those programs." González supported civil rights initiatives such as the Mexican American Legal Defense and Education Fund (MALDEF), but considered the Chicano movement dangerous and racist. When *movimiento* people spoke of land grants owed by the federal government under the Treaty of Guadalupe Hidalgo, González shot back, "Now don't talk to me about land! You're all urban." He advised his friend the president that people such as José Angel Gutiérrez of MAYO had some followers but that none of them could be trusted. González had obtained State Department summer jobs for Willie Velásquez only to see the young man return to San Antonio in late 1967, jump on the MAYO bandwagon, and chair the conference of La Raza Unida, where some people spoke of planting bombs, according to a González colleague. "They were really advocating violence," said the congressman, who pressured the Ford Foundation to cut back on its funding of Southwest Council of La Raza. González characterized the Council as prejudiced against Anglos, according to Julian Samora, who remembered that the press played up what Samora considered a ridiculous charge. González also accused Velásquez of "consorting with my enemies," including Albert Peña and Joe Bernal. Ordinary battles over local political turf became magnified due to disagreements over the Chicano movement and the Vietnam War; while the congressman remained loyal to Johnson, Peña and Bernal leaned toward Robert Kennedy.[5]

VIVA KENNEDY

The president's South Texas political liaison, Cecil Burney, reckoned that although Johnson controlled 1,700 of the 2,600 votes needed for renomination, the turmoil raging within the Democratic Party threatened the outcome. In January liberal senator Eugene McCarthy promised a "vigorous" challenge to Johnson in the New Hampshire Democratic primary, and conservative governor George Wallace entered the California primary.

Then in February "all hell broke loose," said Joseph Califano, when Johnson—concerned about the disproportionate percentage of

poor and minority soldiers—eliminated graduate school draft deferments. This fed the antiwar protests. "There was a sense of siege in the
White House," Califano remembered, as they searched around the
country for places that the president could visit without drawing mass
demonstrations. The children of many of the cabinet officers, including Secretary of Defense Robert McNamara, were among those
marching. On February 27 McNamara, one of the chief architects of
the military escalation, rejected a Pentagon request for 205,000 more
troops, calling it "madness" and conceding that U.S. actions were not
stopping the North Vietnamese but instead were "making us lasting
enemies in Asia." At five p.m. that same day chief White House aide
Marvin Watson sent Johnson a memorandum warning that the Citizen's Crusade Against Poverty was redoubling its criticism of domestic
spending cuts and of a tax system they considered unfair to the middle
and lower classes. The president ordered Califano to call these leaders,
including Héctor García, "and tell them to cut this stuff out." Just a
few hours after Watson sent Johnson the memo, the avuncular Walter
Cronkite, the most popular newscaster in the nation, in a rare personal commentary on the "CBS Evening News," called for reassess-
ment of the United States role in the war.[6]

At this time McNamara confided to a White House colleague that
Robert Kennedy seemed to be leaning toward a presidential bid despite the advice of McNamara and many of the senator's other friends.
Still wrestling with the issue on March 10, Kennedy returned to
Delano to attend Mass with César Chávez, who was marking the end
of a hunger strike. Chávez had fasted as an act of purification when
some striking farmworkers had responded to violence with violence of
their own. The senator came there against the advice of most of his
political people. True, Chávez was the foremost leader of millions of
Mexican Americans, but many, perhaps most, of the migrant workers
in his union did not vote, hampered by state residency requirements.
Moreover the UFWOC had powerful enemies, particularly in the four
billion dollar agribusiness industry.

Kennedy, like Johnson before him, sensed the importance of the
Mexican American constituency ahead of his aides. Moreover the senator greatly admired Chávez's quiet, spiritual strength and his nonviolent credo. After all, Robert Kennedy had lost his own brother to an
assassin's bullet and, like Chávez, received death threats. Years later,
when congressional investigations revealed that as attorney general
Kennedy had approved the use of the Mafia and the CIA to hatch assassination plots, some of his friends could not help wondering

whether the senator blamed himself in part for his own brother's death. After the assassination the younger brother had seemed haunted, much of his famous brashness replaced by a searching openness and an empathy with the most vulnerable in society.

Kennedy first stopped in the East Los Angeles barrio. Wearing a "Huelga" button on his tailored lapel, the senator met with Chicano and Chicana students, a few of the thousands who had recently walked out of their barrio high schools protesting inferior conditions and a curriculum that ignored their heritage. Then in Delano Kennedy reiterated Chávez's nonviolent credo. "Let me say to you that violence is no answer," he proclaimed to the crowd. At the farmworker Mass Kennedy listened intently as a Chávez aide read a statement for the union leader, who was too weak to deliver it himself.

> When we are really honest with ourselves, we must admit that our lives are all that really belong to us. . . . It is my deepest belief that only by giving our lives do we find life . . . in a totally nonviolent struggle for justice. To be a man is to suffer for others. God help us to be men.[7]

Kennedy called Chávez "a hero for our times" and drew strength from the throng that sought to embrace them both. Several Kennedy aides sensed that at Delano the senator made up his mind once and for all. On the flight back east he announced to the other passengers that he had decided to run for the presidency. Aides and old friends once again pointed out the dangers of challenging an incumbent president, of splitting the Democratic party, of reinforcing the press caricature of Kennedy as a ruthless opportunist, but one friend recalled, "He wasn't really listening to us. He was on fire."[8]

"He was intensely interested in *mexicanos* and supportive of our goals in a nonpatronizing fashion. . . . Bobby touched our souls," said Bert Corona, who headed the new Viva Kennedy organization. As in 1960 and 1964 the Viva people developed their own pamphlets, but, more than that, "We and our issues were part of Bobby's national agenda," as Corona put it. For the first time the mainstream materials produced at a national campaign headquarters incorporated issues of particular concern to Mexican Americans. One pamphlet cover, for example, showed the senator with a *latino* boy. The inside text outlined just three issues: poverty, Vietnam, and fair wages for farmworkers. It cited the senator's support of farmworker legislation, charging that Johnson "turned a deaf ear" and that his "close political ally, Governor Connally of Texas, told the farm workers that he had no intention of seeking to help them." Meanwhile César Chávez wrote his last letter to Johnson, wishing "God's blessing on your work during the year" but adding, "unfulfilled promises are a poor substitute for food, wages, and justice." [9]

Corona began working to obtain MAPA's endorsement. Most members had given up on the Johnson administration and some were already working for Eugene McCarthy. Also a Catholic and a liberal, he had spoken out against the war before Kennedy and had been calling for improvements in farmworker conditions for years. While some of these *mapistas* switched to Kennedy once he joined the race, others feared that he might be an opportunistic interloper, and they remembered his role in some of the anticommunist senate crusades of the 1950s. Would he be compassionate or ruthless? Corona and many of his colleagues answered that McCarthy was something of a diffident intellectual who appealed to college students and suburbanites, not poor minority folks, while Kennedy had come to Delano and made a difference. They cited a favorite saying of Chávez's: "Hechos son amor" ["Deeds are love"]. In the end two-thirds of the leaders voted to support Kennedy. Corona got to work and soon Viva Kennedy had established headquarters throughout the Southwest, Northwest, and Midwest, with particular attention to important primary states such as Indiana and, especially, California, which soon had over 100 Viva Kennedy offices alone. [10]

Meanwhile Kennedy called Chávez to ask for an endorsement, but instead simply requested a voter registration drive. "César sounded so ill I didn't have the heart to press him," Kennedy explained to his aide Paul Schrade, who cracked, "This doesn't sound like the hard-headed Kennedy we've all heard about." The senator laughed. Schrade called the farmworker president with the endorsement request, knowing full well that the fledgling union risked alienating the powerful American Federation of Labor, which supported Johnson. At the same time, Schrade brought with him a certain amount of authority, in that he was supporting Kennedy in defiance of his own union leadership. On March 19 Chávez met with his executive board and called Schrade at four in the morning with the news that they had unanimously agreed to have Chávez attend the Democratic National Convention as a Kennedy delegate and to hold a general meeting "at the earliest possible moment . . . for the purpose of considering the possible official endorsement by UFWOC of Senator Kennedy's candidacy."

"We worked our tails off for Bobby Kennedy," said Lupe Anguiano, who had left the White House some months earlier. One of the few other Chicanas in the Johnson administration, Polly Baca, quit as Vicente Ximenes's public information officer and became deputy director of Viva Kennedy. At the same time Kennedy invited a number of Mexican American leaders to a strategy session at his Virginia home. Albert Peña never forgot that moment, as the senator mapped out a coalition of minority people, white liberals, labor rank-and-file, students, and the elderly.[11]

With the Kennedy candidacy Johnson's worst fears were realized. McCarthy had frightened administration officials by nearly winning the New Hampshire primary, but his was a campaign largely of antiwar symbolism, run by amateurs. Moreover, McCarthy had a reputation among his Senate peers as "aloof, indolent, arrogant, and annoying," as political observers from the *London Times* noted. For example, the Minnesota senator proposed extending Social Security benefits to include farmworkers, then allowed the bill to languish. The White House knew all too well that Kennedy possessed the ambition, drive, skill, money, and name recognition to effectively marshall antiadministration sentiment.[12]

WITHDRAWAL

The remaining primaries took on heightened significance, particularly California's, with its large number of delegates and its position late in the primary process. Four days after Kennedy declared his candidacy the president's unofficial California campaign chief Irv Sprague advised the White House that Johnson supporters were demoralized while the Kennedy campaign was picking up support among a number of constituencies. "Kennedy has been cultivating the Mexican community," Sprague warned, adding that Congressman Roybal, one of the few *californios* pledged to the president, was reported to be "disturbed about Vietnam policy." Another Johnson organizer reported that the California barrios were "red-hot for Kennedy." Sprague suggested that Cris Aldrete of the Democratic National Committee (DNC) canvass Mexican American leaders and advise the Johnson people on White House strategy. The DNC also produced a bilingual campaign pamphlet, "Bien Hecho [well done], Sr. Presidente!" featuring numerous Mexican American appointments and programs of benefit to them.[13]

Sprague suggested that the campaign concentrate on those California constituencies where the president remained strong, principally among conservative Democrats. Nevertheless, these votes were also vulnerable. Conservatives disenchanted with the slow pace of the war and angry over domestic social unrest gravitated toward the Republican Party, particularly now that two Californians were its main presidential contenders: Governor Ronald Reagan and the frontrunner, former Vice President Richard Nixon. Both had long opposed the farmworkers union, but Governor Reagan, at least, did not write off the Mexican American vote. He exploited whatever differences could be found, courting the more conservative business sector. The White House noted that Reagan had chosen businessman J. William Orozco to be his personal representative in Los Angeles. Orozco had nearly upset a Democratic Congressman in a solidly Democratic district. Democratic Party chairman John Bailey reported that some of the Mexican American Democratic leadership "is not even on speaking terms with César Chávez . . . who apparently scares the money groups who apparently like to play with the growers." Bailey reminded the president that half of the Mexican American vote went to Reagan in 1966, writing, "This we can't let happen again." [14]

"The unity he sought for the country is imperiled, and he knows it," Bill Moyers remarked later that year, adding that by early 1968 Johnson "recognized that he personally had become the center of the controversy." The president decided to withdraw his candidacy and asked Governor Connally to help draft the statement, which Johnson brought to his State of the Union address but did not use. Instead, on March 31—the date Harry Truman had withdrawn from the 1952 race—Johnson stated that he would not seek reelection. Two days later, at a meeting with his tearful reelection campaign staff, Johnson spoke of his two soldier sons-in-law and of his concern about them raising children amid the wartime dissention, in "this situation we're getting into in the country where we're divided and in trouble. The Negroes are mad at the Mexicans and the Mexicans are mad at somebody else." [15]

When the president made his announcement several Mexican American leaders happened to be with Hubert Humphrey in Mexico for the signing of the Treaty of Tlatelolco, which banned nuclear weapons from Latin America. Just days before the trip Johnson had told Ximenes to invite several Mexican American leaders. "Humphrey didn't think about it. None of his staff thought about it," said Ximenes. Only the president noticed. In Mexico City the news of Johnson's announcement arrived as the formal dinner was ending. Julian Samora heard Humphrey say that he already knew, but the professor wondered about this, because when Humphrey received the news, his face turned ashen. "We were stunned," said Ximenes, who sat in silence along with everyone else on the plane ride home. Humphrey stayed in his cabin.[16]

The vice president soon declared his candidacy, but the nation's attention focused on McCarthy and Kennedy, who were battling it out in the final primaries. Armando Rodríguez, head of the Mexican American Affairs Unit in the Department of Education, recalled, "I was strongly for Kennedy. I did not disagree with anything Humphrey stood for, but I never saw him as a strong person. And, of course, I had worked for the Kennedys early. I owed them a lot of loyalty and I liked what Bobby was doing with César Chávez." [17]

In Indiana, while college students mostly stumped for McCarthy, Viva Kennedy volunteers got to work for their candidate. Some 6,000 people, nearly all Mexican American and Puerto Rican, attended a rally in East Chicago. The well-wishers carried Kennedy on their shoulders to the platform, where Corona stood waiting with other dignitaries. Suddenly Corona felt the platform move as the enthusiastic throng pushed it to the wall. When the senator finally spoke, the crowd cheered so loudly that the MAPA president gave up trying to translate the speech and simply adlibbed.[18]

In Indianapolis Kennedy was campaigning in a black neighborhood when he got word that Martin Luther King had been murdered. The candidate broke the horrible news to the crowd and questioned the nature of American society. Then he reminded his listeners that he had lost a loved one to violence and said, "We can make an effort, as Martin Luther King did, to understand and to comprehend, and to replace that violence, that stain of bloodshed . . . with compassion and love." In contrast, Governor John Connally remarked that King had "contributed much to the chaos and the strife and the confusion and the uncertainty in this country, but whatever his actions, he deserved not the fate of assassination." That evening the president spoke to the nation, urging all Americans to condemn violence and work for "peace and understanding. . . equality and fulfillment for all of our people." [19]

Kennedy won in Indiana, but McCarthy upset him in Oregon. More than ever, all eyes were on California. Within weeks Chávez could report that most Hispanic districts had been covered: "It was just like organizing a strike—hectic. . . . What was new was that we had a good candidate and lots of resources. . . . The drive was a tremendous success." On May 3 the Kennedy campaign manager for California congratulated the UFWOC on its voter registration and mobilization activities. At the end of May, just one week before the election, he wrote to Chávez, "I know you will redouble your effort in these last few days, and make sure that we get every vote for Robert Kennedy to the polls on election day." [20]

The day after McCarthy's Oregon victory Kennedy began a swing through the southern California barrios. Shouts of "Viva Kennedy!" rang through the air as thousands of people filled the streets for the chance to see him, touch him, grab a cufflink. "I have never seen as many *mexicanos* come out for anything," said Corona, who lost his coat in the melee. Journalists from the *Sunday Times* of London reported that Kennedy "seemed almost literally to expand in the exuberance of the crowd. The hooded weariness vanished from his face, the resignation from his eyes. . . . 'If I died in Oregon,' he said, 'I hope Los Angeles is Resurrection City.' " [21]

The real Resurrection City was in Washington, D.C.: the headquarters of the Poor People's Campaign. Organized by Dr. Martin Luther King Jr. and his Southern Christian Leadership Council (SCLC), the Campaign mobilized poor people of all backgrounds to lobby the Johnson administration for a reinvigorated War on Poverty and a de-escalation of the War in Vietnam. LULAC officer Pete Tijerina arranged for Reies López Tijerina [no relation] and Corky Gonzales to meet with Dr. King in March to help plan the agenda. In Washington Gonzales and his Colorado contingent promoted a "Plan of the Barrio," lobbying government agencies for better housing, loans to minority businesses, bilingual education programs, and the return of federal land to Hispanics in New Mexico and southern Colorado. For its part, the Southwest Council of La Raza sponsored Chicano legislative position papers for the campaign.[22] OEO staff members, some of them Mexican American, also participated in the Poor People's march, placing the White House in an awkward position. On May 10 the acting director of the War on Poverty informed the regional directors that although the agency always encouraged poor people to petition their government, agency employees could not lead any such activity. For example, VISTA volunteers could only march if they took leaves of absence.[23]

Meanwhile in California Kennedy won, but only by a small percentage. Journalists covering the campaign concluded that "Mexican Americans contributed most of the slender margin by which Kennedy beat McCarthy in California."[24] As the election day wound down, Herman Gallegos went to pack up the materials at a local campaign office in northern California, just as he had done at the end of previous campaigns. But this day was different. He walked in to find the office nearly stripped of Kennedy items. "It was really strange," he said. "People had taken every last brochure." As he stood there youngsters came in from the barrio streets asking for the posters on the walls.[25]

Lupe Anguiano and the other East Los Angeles organizers told Kennedy that they wanted to hold their own victory celebration. They lined up a mariachi band, only to be informed that headquarters wanted all of the Kennedy folks to celebrate together at the Ambassador Hotel. Exhausted from campaign work, she arrived to find the ballroom jammed with revelers, so she went home, as did an equally tired Chávez, who was chagrined by the attention he received at the ballroom. Moreover, "I must have sensed something was wrong," he said; "I was happy until the time I got to the Ambassador, and then I began to feel melancholy."

In his victory speech Kennedy said,

> I want to thank César Chávez, who was here a little earlier, and Bert Corona who also worked with him and all of those Mexican-Americans who were supporters of mine. And Dolores Huerta, who is an old friend of mine and has worked with the union. Tell her how much I appreciate her coming tonight.[26]

Actually, she was standing just to the senator's right and witnessed his brutal murder firsthand. Corona and other supporters rushed to the hospital and were keeping vigil when Kennedy's death was announced. "It was like they had blown the bottom out of the boat . . . a horrible feeling," said Corona, who worried about all of the poor, unorganized people who had pinned their hopes on this campaign. Instead of enduring the painful funeral he marched in a UFWOC strike, which he considered "good therapy." Anguiano walked around dazed for a week. "Things just haven't been right since," she observed more than two decades later. Chávez agreed, saying, "A vacumn was created when he died. Kennedy was by far the real force for change, and he was willing to take in the poor, and make the poor part of his campaign."[27]

THE POOR PEOPLE'S CAMPAIGN

Meanwhile the Poor People's Campaign caravans were arriving at Resurrection City from all over the country. The main Texas contingent consisted of forty-two Mexican Americans and seventeen blacks. At first the two groups kept to themselves, eyeing each other with a cool politeness, so one of the leaders, Reverend Leo Nieto, assigned seats on the bus, pairing people from each group and asking them to find out one interesting thing about the other person. Reverend Nieto was pleasantly surprised that, when given a chance to return to their original seats, everyone preferred to stay with their new acquaintances. Fed and lodged by churches along the way, they arrived in Washington and set up headquarters in a local public school.[28]

The Texans joined a demonstration in front of the State Department led by Reies López Tijerina. Secretary of State Dean Rusk reported to the White House that he had agreed to meet privately with López Tijerina and a few others for a discussion of the land grants guaranteed under the Treaty of Guadalupe Hidalgo, but canceled when a large crowd came and demanded a public hearing, complete with television cameras. The next day the Texans, along with Mexican Americans from New Mexico and Colorado, joined a Puerto Rican Day rally at the Washington Monument. López Tijerina and Corky Gonzales both spoke, followed by Nieto, who brought a black and an Indian colleague on stage with him in tribute to the triple heritage of Puerto Rico. Afterward most of those in attendance made the long walk to the Kennedy graves at Arlington National Cemetery. Their boisterous conversations subsided as they neared the burial site, where they prayed silently and sang "We Shall Overcome," "Battle Hymn of the Republic," and a Puerto Rican hymn.[29]

A few days later top officials from the Department of Health, Education, and Welfare, including Armando Rodríguez, held a meeting at the request of Gonzales and his delegation. Rodríguez recalled, "Corky and I hit it off real well from way back; I would visit his programs in Denver. . . . He could be radical at times . . . and if that's the way they get it, then that's what they should do." The delegates reiterated demands for equal school facilities for poor children and for the inclusion of minorities in U.S. history textbooks. Then Gonzales said, "We're leaving Armando Rodríguez here in charge. You guys report to him." Rodríguez was, in his words, "being kind and gentle and allocating people to do things." Other administration officials responded, preferring him to Gonzales. "It was guys like Corky who made my job easier," he said.

Meanwhile young Chicanos and Chicanas from the delegation marched toward the White House to protest the draft and the Vietnam War. When stopped, they decided to walk through the police lines, at which point officers began beating the demonstrators, including the daughters of López Tijerina and Gonzales.

At the Justice Department Texas and Colorado Mexican American delegations supported Indian demands for fishing rights in the Pacific Northwest. The Assistant Attorney General and the claimants came to an agreement just minutes before an important Poor People's meeting was scheduled to begin on the other side of town. With no transportation available, Nieto impulsively decided to ask for a ride from the government agents that always seemed to be following them. When approached with this request, the driver ignored the Mexican Americans, started the engine, and in his haste to leave the parking space bumped the other cars. The tired delegates walked to the meeting, where Gonzales, Nieto, and others were named to the newly formed steering committee established to assure multiracial decision making.[30]

The Poor People's Campaign soon petered out. Dr. King's death had demoralized people and hampered the initial planning; Robert Kennedy's assassination cast a further pall on the movement. They ended up petitioning a lame-duck administration whose leader seldom addressed them. The press gave almost no coverage to the positive aspects of the campaign, such as growing racial cooperation among the delegates or agreements reached with government officials. Instead, news reports focused on the problems, from racial tensions to lack of supplies to violent incidents, some possibly caused by government agents. Then it rained. And rained. Mud oozed through the shanties. Demoralized, people drifted home.[31]

VIVA HUMPHREY

As the time for the Democratic National Convention approached, many Mexican Americans refrained from jumping on the Humphrey bandwagon. This despite the candidate's efforts, as when he wrote to the *New York Times* commending its editorial in favor of including farmworkers in the National Labor Relations Act; he pointed out that he had long supported this action and had conducted the first farmworker hearings over fifteen years earlier. MAPA and the UFWOC also were wooed assiduously by Kennedy staffers that supported the candidacy of Senator George McGovern, such as press secretary Frank Mankiewicz, who asked for Chávez's endorsement and added, "It was an honor to talk to your picket line last week. God bless you." [32]

Meanwhile Humphrey and Connally were greeted at the Hemisfair in San Antonio by a sign saying, "Any friend of Connally is no friend of the Mexican American." Undaunted, Congressman Henry B. González introduced the vice president with a warm speech. Nine days later, on the eve of the Democratic convention, Senator Ralph Yarborough stood contentedly at the PASO convention under a banner that read, "PASO Sí, Connally No." Yarborough headed Texas Democrats for an Open Convention (TDOC), liberals who resented the fact that the state delegation was loyal to Governor Connally and that it included people who had forsaken the Democratic Party such as former governor Allan Shivers. Moreover, the few liberal members of the delegation had no voice under the unit rule. Connally's delegates included some Mexican American politicians, such as O. P. Carrillo of the Duval County political organization, which had helped assure Johnson's election to the Senate twenty years earlier. "John Connally was a close friend. . . . He used to come by my ranch and visit all the time," said Carrillo, who worked the convention floor for a Connally vice presidential bid. (At the same time the *mexicano* politician, unlike Shivers and Connally, had always loyally supported the national Democratic ticket.[33])

Yarborough, a McCarthy delegate, led an attempt to replace half of the official Texas delegation and to abolish the unit rule. One of his main lieutenants was Albert Peña, who had headed the Texas Viva Kennedy organizations for both John and Robert Kennedy. Peña and the others told the credentials committee that the Connally delegation was only 5 percent Mexican American and 4.1 percent black, while Texas was 14.8 percent Mexican American and 12.4 percent black, and that the few Texas minority delegates were selected simply because the Democratic Party rules forbade lily-white delegations. State Representative Don Gladden of Fort Worth said, "The few Negroes that were taken think white rather than black, and the few Latin Americans that were taken think white rather than brown." Maury Maverick Jr. pointed out that the challengers were more loyal Democrats than Connally delegates and warned, "Don't shun [our] people or you won't carry Texas." For his part Bert Corona declared, "First-class treatment for the Spanish-speaking must begin right here. We have been taken for granted too long." In later years Connally recalled, "We had people like Barbara Jordan, we had Hispanics, Blacks, labor leaders, we had a good delegation." His right-hand man, Frank Erwin Jr., told the credentials committee that the delegation was broad based in that it included some liberals, but added, "We put them on there because we knew we could control them under the unit rule." [34]

Johnson wanted Connally to win the delegate fight. The president, officially uninvolved in the convention, actually used his position as head of the party to the hilt. White House staffers "organized the convention and virtually dictated the platform" according to Joe Califano. In the administration hotel suite three floors below Humphrey's headquarters and six floors above McCarthy's, Marvin Watson fielded messages between Connally on the convention floor and presidential assistants at the LBJ Ranch. Officially uninvolved, Johnson listened on an extension telephone then wrote his response to an aide who in turn conveyed it to Watson in Chicago. Despite his resignation statement, Johnson hoped that the convention would turn to him, according to Connally, who said, "I personally was asked to go to meet with the governors of the southern delegations . . . to see if they would support President Johnson in a draft movement," but these politicians rejected the idea of a Johnson candidacy, so the president's close associates never found out whether he wanted to run or simply hoped for the draft as a face-saving device. [35]

Connally and other southern leaders got the impression that at least for the 1968 convention, Humphrey would not oppose the unit rule, which the Texas governor called "the very essence of pure democracy." The vice president feared alienating his core supporters and the president, but Humphrey also prided himself on his lifetime of championing equal rights and he needed to win over the McCarthy and Kennedy forces. In the end the candidate came out for the abolition of the unit rule, effective immediately. Connally, as head of the largest delegation still using the rule, felt betrayed. When his vice presidential chances also evaporated he remarked to Texas delegates that he would work against the Democratic ticket. [36]

Connally hinted that he might have the Texas delegation vote for Johnson if the unit rule lost on the convention floor. Frank Erwin began wearing an "All the Way with LBJ" button and saying that maybe the Texas electors should think about voting in November for third-party candidate George Wallace, with his appeals to "law and order" and his southern Democratic Party background. Meanwhile many Kennedy and McCarthy voters might sit out the campaign if the conservatives won the procedural votes. Desperately, Humphrey forces worked out a compromise. The convention voted to seat half of the challengers to the Georgia delegation but none of the challengers from Texas. Lady Bird Johnson remarked, "I couldn't possibly go to bed until Connally had won." Undaunted, TDOCers organized against Connally, publicizing his actions against farmworkers and poverty programs and his remarks about the King assassination. By a voice vote the unit rule was eliminated; the liberal minority within Connally's delegation could now vote its own way. A Connally supporter correctly predicted, "This crumbles the whole foundation of our control." The following year the Commission on Party Structure would order state chairmen to implement open delegate selection processes and insure "that racial minorities, women, and youth be represented in reasonable relationship to their presence in the population of the state."[37]

During the convention the street outside the main hotel became a battleground, with antiwar protesters taunting the Chicago police, who responded by attacking the demonstrators and, at times, anyone in the officers' path: delegates, tourists, reporters. Amid the conflict the Democratic Party nominated Humphrey. Chicano delegates from California responded by standing on their chairs and yelling, "No! No! No!" The nominee worried that the wounds would not heal by November.[38]

To make matters worse, he had to contend with a president who, in Califano's words, "kept a keen eye on Humphrey's words and music on Vietnam, the way a conservative Pope in Rome might monitor each sermon of a liberal American bishop he fears might stray from Vatican teaching." Finally Johnson gave his official blessing to Humphrey at a rally in the Houston Astrodome. Here the president pulled a political coup by convincing both Yarborough and Connally to sit on the platform. Johnson also ordered the Humphrey people to mobilize Texas voters, especially the Mexican Americans in South Texas.[39]

Meanwhile back at the White House Vicente Ximenes arranged the production of a Mexican American film about the administration's programs for use in the campaign. He also issued an updated report on administration accomplishments for Mexican Americans. In the Neighborhood Youth Corps, for instance, almost 40 percent of the trainees were of Mexican heritage. He organized a Midwest conference on Mexican American and Puerto Rican affairs and in his keynote speech at the twentieth anniversary convention of the American GI Forum Ximenes reminded his audience that a brand-new senator named Lyndon Johnson had been the only state official to help the fledgling Forum bury a Mexican American war veteran with honor. The Johnson official cited numerous administration programs for Mexican Americans and then declared, "The time has come when we must rise to the occasion and challenge the critics of the Johnson-Humphrey administration. We must speak to our people and tell them that President Johnson has done more for the Mexican American than all the previous administrations combined." [40]

Viva Humphrey coordinators Héctor García and Rudy Ramos did just that. García once again stumped vigorously in the Southwest for the Party's candidate, while from Washington Ramos sent planeloads of material to Mexican American congressmen. Nonetheless many other Mexican Americans shied away from the Humphrey campaign even after the convention. In September MAPA refused to endorse any candidate. Disgruntled at this, one MAPA member wrote to President Abe Tapia, "Withholding a vote from Mr. Humphrey is a vote for Nixon. . . . the future of every Mexican American in this country is at stake." Humphrey made the same pitch to Tapia, Corona, Peña, and others at a meeting in New York City at the Waldorf Astoria Hotel. The candidate pledged programs targeted for the barrios, endorsed the right of the UFWOC "to represent farmworkers," and promised to "include the Mexican-American and other Spanish-speaking Americans . . . in the total picture of decision-making and the allocation of resources." Some of the activists formed an organization called "La Raza with Humphrey" and promised "to do everything within their means" to drum up support for the vice president, while Henry Santiestevan, former National Coordinator for Viva [Robert] Kennedy, became National Coordinator of Viva Humphrey. [41]

The Democratic campaign continued to woo the farmworkers union. On August 1 Humphrey endorsed the consumer boycott of grapes that the UWFOC was conducting in support of its strike. The following month in San Francisco's Mission District the vice president pinned a UFWOC button onto his lapel and said, "The worker in the fields in entitled to all protection, . . . and when I'm president, he'll have those rights, make no mistake about it." The crowd cried, "Viva Humphrey . . . Viva La Huelga . . . Viva Chávez . . . Viva Mexico."

When Humphrey responded with "Viva America," however, someone countered with "Viva Zapata." On October 19 Secretary of Labor Willard Wirtz went to Delano and met for forty-five minutes with the bedridden César Chávez. "He has done more collective bargaining this year than I have," said the secretary, who reminded Chávez that the Labor Department was apprehending more farmworkers entering illegally from Mexico than ever before. Wirtz also reiterated his call for inclusion of farmworkers in protective labor laws. The union endorsed Humphrey, with 98 percent of the membership voting for the resolution. MAPA also joined the campaign.[42]

With money from the AFL-CIO, MAPA and the UFWOC produced flyers such as one entitled "No Deje Que Nixon Quite Lo Que Usted Ha Ganado" ["Don't Let Nixon Take Away What You've Won"], and "El Corrido de Richard Nixon" ["Richard Nixon's Ballad"]: "You swallowed scab grapes / And now you're choking on them . . . / When the elections are here . . . mexicanos/ Will have no mercy."[43] Nixon made a token attempt to acknowledge these voters. To a crowd of 6,500 in San Antonio he introduced his Cuban servants and said that his daughters studied Spanish. The cliches mattered little, however, for the rally was overwhelmingly white. "They have not been rioting. . . . They have not been breaking the law," he said of Mexican Americans, thus managing to work the conservative "law and order" theme into the speech.[44]

"All over the country, the minority groups Nixon had planned to do without struck back at him," reported the London *Sunday Times* journalists. By election eve Mexican and African Americans had narrowed the Republican candidate's lead in California from 14 percent to 1 percent, or too close to call. Humphrey received his most tumultuous reception when he retraced Robert Kennedy's route through the ghettos and barrios of Los Angeles. That night both candidates held telethons, and a recharged Humphrey projected an energetic optimism that nearly won him California. In Texas, Mexican Americans made the difference. Of the 600,000 or so Mexican Texans, about 400,000 voted and they constituted a majority of the 437,422 new Texas voters. Nixon won with the smallest percentage since 1912, only 43 percent of the vote, to 42.7 for Humphrey and 13.6 for Wallace. If Humphrey had carried California as well as Texas, no one would have won a majority and the election would have been thrown into the House of Representatives.[45]

Nixon did win however, and the Great Society was over. Johnson's dream of the strong helping the weak and all benefiting from a growing economy was dashed, just as he had feared, by "that bitch of a war," as he called it.[46] Military escalation drained funds from poverty programs and polarized the political debate. Johnson's carefully nurtured political coalition ran afoul of racial and class division that came to the surface, forcing him out of office.

ELEVEN

DENOUEMENT

"Unlike Truman and Hoover and Eisenhower, outside the White House Johnson will be nobody," wrote Texas author Robert Sherrill. Indeed, Lyndon Johnson proved to be a moody, difficult retiree who did not fit the role of an elder statesman. His image was not helped by the publication soon after he left office of *My Brother Lyndon*, a tell-all memoir by Sam Houston Johnson. The author devoted the acknowledgement page to one person: his editor, Enrique Hank López, writing, "Since Hank learned politics the hard way (he was the Democratic candidate for Secretary of State of California in 1958, losing by less than one percent after receiving 2,500,00 votes), he had a professional awareness of the various phases of my brother's career" (see chapter 6). Lyndon Johnson's dissatisfaction with the book paled, however, in comparison to his disappointment over his presidency. Congressman Henry B. González felt sorry for him, and another Texas congressman, Johnson's old friend Lloyd Bentsen, noted that the former president was despondent over his inability to do more to help the poor while in the White House.[1]

Johnson threw his impatient energy into the ranch. He "would call us at any hour of the day or night," remembered ranchhand Guadalupe Bravo, but often worked alongside them on the range, ignoring his weak heart, or he would drive up and say, "Let's go to the store," and buy them new clothes.

In a rare public appearance, Johnson addressed a civil rights symposium sponsored by the Johnson Library in late 1972. One last time he prodded his aides to define civil rights beyond African Americans, saying, "Let me make it plain that when I say 'black,' as I do a good many times in this little statement, I also mean brown and yellow and

all other people who suffer discrimination." He popped a nitroglycer-
ine capsule into his mouth, then proceeded to read his short speech.
"We know how much still remains to be done and if our efforts continue and if our will is strong and if our hearts are right and if courage
remains our constant companion, then, my fellow Americans, we shall
overcome."[2]

His daughter remembered, "Fear consumed me . . . and I said, 'I
saw what you did. Daddy, what's happened? How are you?'" After
some prodding he told her,

> The truth is that last night I had an attack of angina and the doc-
> tor told me that I couldn't get out of bed . . . and I said, no, I had
> to go. "My people are going to be there." I had to be with my
> people. And the doctor said, "Well, Mr. President, I don't think
> I can guarantee, as your physician, that you're going to be able
> to walk off that platform." . . . I looked at that doctor and I
> smiled and I said, "Well, then, if I go dying, I will go dying for
> what I've lived for and what more can any man ask?"

She recalled, "A month later, he was dead. . . . He died alone, and . . .
Lyndon Johnson couldn't stand to be alone."[3]

When Dr. Héctor García learned of Johnson's death, the physician
telegraphed Lady Bird Johnson,

> Sorry about your loss. President Johnson's loss will forever be re-
> membered by Mexican Americans as their own loss. After all he
> was also our "presidente." I personally feel that his death is like
> a loss in my own family. May the Lord give you strength. We
> loved him. We love you.[4]

During the funeral ceremony at the LBJ Ranch, García thought back
to previous occasions there "with him in full life in blossom": Johnson
hosting the president of Mexico with banners and serenades, genially
presiding over barbecues, driving guests over the rolling hills at break-
neck speed. Now storm clouds gathered above the somber crowd at
the burial site.

"He understood and knew us," García said later. The GI Forum
founder and his colleagues considered their civil rights activities of the
1970s in part a furtherance of the late president's own agenda. On the
day Johnson returned to Austin from Washington Ed Idar, his wife,

and children had stood along with other well-wishers at the fence at Bergstrom Air Force base in Austin as Johnson passed by. Now Idar was working to expand the coverage of the Voting Rights Act as an attorney for MALDEF.[5]

LA RAZA IN COTULLA

Meanwhile Chicanos were organizing at the grass roots. In 1969 the Mexican American Youth Organization (MAYO) began the Winter Garden Project to mobilize the Mexican American majority that still had virtually no voice in local politics, as in Cotulla, where Mexican Americans constituted 3,200 of the 4,000 residents. Unconsciously echoing Johnson's description of Cotulla in his 1965 Voting Rights speech, a MAYO member said:

> They have been given . . . separate schools, separate health care, separate beatings by Texas Ranger and Border Patrolmen, separate restaurants, in short, separate everything. Their treatment has been separate but not equal. They have paid the price by having only a 49-year life span.[6]

MAYO founder José Angel Gutiérrez convinced War on Poverty administrators to transfer two VISTA volunteers to Cotulla to join those already working in the town. Gonzalo Barrientos of the VISTA office in Austin often came to Cotulla to assist volunteers in training local residents to organize members of their local community around issues of concern to them. The Cotullans began modestly, with clean-up projects in the colonia and helping residents lobby for better recreation programs. These activities, in turn, led to the formation of community organizations such as Nueva Vida and Barrios Unidos.[7]

On January 23, 1970, in La Salle (Cotulla's) County and in two others, MAYO leaders formally registered their new political party, "El Partido de La Raza Unida." In Cotulla Raza Unida activists included one of Lyndon Johnson's former students, Juan Ortiz. By the end of January, Ortiz, La Salle County Raza Unida chairman Raúl Martínez, and Arsenio García had registered two thousand new voters there. La Raza Unida leaders from the party's headquarters in nearby Crystal City came to Cotulla. "They would train people in poll watching and . . . all the things that go along with a campaign," said Cotulla activist Alfredo Zamora.[8]

One problem remained: finding people willing to run for office.

Many a potential candidate feared alienating the Anglo employers, particularly if running for mayor. "We couldn't find any takers," said Zamora, "so at the last minute . . . I decided to file." Born and raised in Cotulla, Zamora had followed the migrant stream with his family. He eventually managed to finish college in Wisconsin, where he was teaching social studies when he received a Ford Foundation fellowship in 1969 to visit alternative educational sites. In the process he met Chicano activists throughout the Midwest such as Gilberto Martínez, a MAYO/La Raza Unida leader in Lansing, Michigan, who was originally from Crystal City. Upon returning home to Cotulla, "I found myself getting involved. For some reason I've always been Raza-oriented, and very, very strong on retaining cultural values. I'm proud of my Mexican heritage. I was full-time on that fellowship, so I had some flexibility to dictate my agenda," said Zamora. Utilizing his background as a professional educator, he spoke to school officials on behalf of some of his friends when their children had difficulties in the classroom. "Then we started looking at Welhausen, that it had not changed since LBJ had been there, that something had to give." As historian Ignacio García has written, "It was a school 100 percent Mexican American in composition, poorly equipped, run-down, and had toilet facilities in an annex room separated from the main building." [9]

The established political leadership obstructed La Raza Unida Party at every turn, according to Zamora, who said, "there was a lot of animosity and a lot of name calling . . . confrontations . . . attempts to dissuade people from voting." Cotulla tax assessor Annie Wildenthal refused to release the voter registration list to La Raza Unida Party, which was forced to file suit to obtain it. From an old Cotulla family, she was related to Mary (Mamie) Wildenthal, who had taught with Johnson, and to John Wildenthal, who had worked on his Senate staff. Fredna Woods, of another important local family, remembered, "There was bitterness." She said that Raza Unida founder José Angel Gutiérrez stated on television that Anglos needed to be hit over the head with a two-by-four. She told some of the Raza Unida "boys" in town that Gutiérrez should "come over and hit me over the head and I'll be a martyr and he'll be a fool." At the same time, unlike many Anglos, she did not oppose Mexican American political mobilization per se; she kept the lines of communication open with Zamora, for whom she expressed "great respect." [10]

Anglo resentment over VISTA/Raza Unida activity in Cotulla was exacerbated by extensive news coverage of a confrontation the year before (1969) in Del Rio, Texas. When Democratic Governor Preston

Smith fired Del Rio VISTA volunteers for assisting in a reapportion-
ment suit, José Angel Gutiérrez and other activists organized a protest
march. The governor responded by deploying state police armed with
machine guns. Undeterred, the demonstrators held a mass rally to pro-
claim the "Del Rio Manifesto," supporting the VISTA program and
demanding racial and economic justice. As a result of this polarized
political atmosphere, Lyndon Johnson was an unmentionable subject
in the Cotulla electoral campaign. Anglo Cotullans were not about to
invoke the name of the man who had sponsored VISTA, while La
Raza Unida opposed the Democrats in general and, in particular, the
Cotulla Anglo leadership that had close ties to him.[11]

Alfredo Zamora was elected mayor in a close vote. In addition,
four of the other five Raza Unida candidates won: two for city council
and two for the school board, including an Anglo, George Carpenter.
In the county elections later that same year, however, the local court
ruled La Raza Party stricken from the ballot, so only one of their candidates—a write-in—was elected. Moreover, in violation of the law,
local election officials administered literacy tests until Raza Unida
people threatened to take legal action.[12]

The new mayor and other Raza Unida leaders persuaded Mexican
American parents to mobilize around their concerns. They pressured
the school board to institute bilingual education and to fully integrate
the schools, with all of Cotulla's children attending Welhausen for first
and second grade, Amanda Burks in the Anglo neighborhood for third
and fourth grade. Some of Johnson's own students, using the tools of
the Great Society, participated in the effort to end the segregated system he had encountered as teacher and principal some forty years
earlier.

At the same time, the school board members, many of them lifelong
supporters of Johnson, refused to hire Zamora, even though he had a
college degree, unlike some of the Cotulla teachers. "The candidates
of La Raza Unida Party are working men and women, most of them
unemployed as the result of a conscious policy of the Anglo-owned
businesses. The mayor of Cotulla, Alfredo Zamora, still can't get a job
in his own home town," wrote Raza Unida founders Mario Compean
and José Angel Gutiérrez. Zamora commuted ninety miles round trip
to teach in Crystal City, which, on top of his mayoral duties, proved
too much. In 1972 Zamora did not run for reelection, but another
Raza Unida candidate succeeded him. Zamora, his wife, and four children returned to the Midwest.[13]

La Raza Unida ran a Texas gubernatorial candidate in 1972 and it established chapters throughout the Southwest and Midwest but never managed to equal elsewhere its political success in the Winter Garden area. By the mid-1970s the party was fading because of hostile lawsuits, intimidation, internal dissension, and antigringo, anticapitalist rhetoric that alienated established Mexican American leaders, notably the highly influential congressman and Johnson's old ally, Henry B. González.[14]

SU VOTO ES SU VOZ

Meanwhile, expensive media coverage was coming to dominate statewide political contests, as with Lloyd Bentsen Jr.'s successful 1970 Senate campaign. Lyndon Johnson had warned his friend not to run in the Democratic primary, saying that Senator Ralph Yarborough was too popular, but Bentsen pulled off a victory, in part by significantly outspending the incumbent. The *Washington Post* reported, "Businessmen's contributions of $5,000 or more seemed to fall like confetti" for Bentsen and Republican candidate George Bush. Only five people donated that much money to Yarborough.[15]

Frustrated by this trend, William (Willie) Velásquez began working to counter the power of money with the power of numbers. A founder of MAYO, Velásquez left because of bickering among the leaders, whom he considered too impulsive. "We didn't read enough," he said. He also feared that the movement was infiltrated by government provocateurs. Mainly, however, he thought that any third party was doomed. Velásquez joined VISTA, where he worked as an administrator and his wife Jane served as a VISTA volunteer. Utilizing the community connections he had established through VISTA, MAYO, and other organizations such as Southwest Council of La Raza, Velásquez founded the Southwest Voter Registration Education Project (SWVREP) in 1974.[16]

SWVREP mobilized Mexican American voters using what civil rights attorney James Harrington has called "the double hammer of single-member district litigation and aggressive voter registration." Many of the SWVREP recruits were women, such as the grandmother who canvassed in Cuero, Texas, registering new voters. She told a reporter that she wanted her ten children and thirty grandchildren to have increased opportunities, and she quoted the SWVREP slogan, "*Su voto es su voz* [Your vote is your voice]." Working with

MALDEF, SWVREP succeeded in extending Johnson's Voting Rights Act to Mexican Americans and in eliminating most other barriers to minority voting. One of the suits culminated with Ed Idar successfully arguing before the United States Supreme Court that at-large legislative districts in Bexar County systematically prevented Mexican American candidates from holding office.[17]

Fittingly, one of the federal examiners implementing the act had known Johnson when she was growing up in Cotulla. "I traveled all over enforcing the Voting Rights Act," Manuela González Contreras remembered. She explained the voting procedures and allayed people's fears, assuring them that no one would test their English and that no immigration official would turn up at the polls. "They were always afraid of something . . . but times have changed," she said.[18]

Ten years after the founding of the SWVREP, the number of Mexican Americans registered to vote and holding office had doubled.[19] Many of the new elected officials had worked in the Johnson administration, including Colorado State Senator Polly Baca Barragán, previously public information officer for the Interagency Committee on Mexican American Affairs, and Texas State Senator Gonzalo Barrientos, formerly a VISTA administrator. Johnson's wife and his daughter Luci campaigned for Barrientos; "Lady Bird is a friend of mine," he said.[20]

Virtually all of the new officeholders were liberal Democrats. Moreover, although the SWVREP has always been rigorously nonpartisan, as a private citizen Velásquez convinced several Raza Unida leaders to become what he called "born-again Democrats" by joining the newly formed Mexican American Democrats (MAD), joking that the "BAD" had "joined the MAD." The following year, 1977, the entire Raza Unida chapter in Cotulla defected to MAD.

Whichever their party affiliation, Mexican Americans have dominated Cotulla politics since Alfredo Zamora's 1970 mayoral victory. "We are the leaders," he said. Zamora returned to Cotulla in 1981 and heads the community health center, which is housed, as it happens, in the former Welhausen school. A number of Lyndon Johnson's students have seen their children become successful professionals, from educators to FBI agents. At the same time, the Anglo-controlled La Salle County Museum has systematically ignored the La Raza Unida story. Zamora complained, "You're taking away probably the most important episode of Mexican American history. . . . What's true is true and should stand. How are we going to teach our kids?"[21]

CLASS ISSUES

Moreover, as in many other rural areas, most young people who left for professional training never returned, while 80 percent of Cotulla's remaining schoolchildren needed remedial help in the early 1990s. This brought the school system's accreditation into question. "We can't blame anybody anymore; it's us," said Zamora, who added that people in the colonia were rising to the challenge, "There's a mood in this locale that's community-oriented." Most colonia residents have few resources, however, and live in tiny, dilapidated houses, such as the one owned by a former student of Johnson's. The home has no air conditioning, even though Cotulla is one of the hottest locations in Texas. A webbed lawn chair and an old couch serve as the furniture in the tidy living room, which is decorated with a small statue of the Virgin Mary and some artificial flowers.

In certain respects the Cotulla economic situation has worsened. Unemployment has skyrocketed as landowners—mostly Anglos—have converted their large farms to ranches, eliminating agricultural labor jobs. Former Johnson student Dan García noted that upwards of 80 percent of the land that used to be cultivated for cotton has been converted to cattle grazing in the last ten to twenty years. The main street of town now looks "sort of desolate," said Rita Worthy, who grew up in Cotulla, and Alfredo Zamora concluded that "Now it's changed; now it's more of an economic situation." Or as sociologist/historian David Montejano has written, "Mexican Americans have taken political control of 'declining farm counties,' much like black politicians have done with 'declining central cities.'"[22]

Montejano has pointed out, "With the weakening of racial divisions as an issue, broadly defined, class issues determine the arena of political discussion and debate." Some Mexican Americans, particularly from the middle class, began to vote Republican; in the early 1990s 15 percent of Mexican Texans switched parties. When he announced that he was becoming a Republican, Texas State Senator Pete Nieto cited the Mexican American tradition of "hard work, self reliance, and family values," which he credited his adopted party with championing. Appearing with him at the press conference was a rising GOP political figure, Congressman Henry Bonilla of San Antonio. As a leader of LULAC, Bonilla had worked with the Johnson administration on jobs programs and other Great Society initiatives.[23]

Professional people continued to be outnumbered, however, by those in the working class, many of whom joined organizations such as Communities Organized for Public Service (COPS), which Montejano has characterized as "the major nonbusiness political entity in San Antonio." Ernesto (Ernie) Cortés founded COPS in 1973. Like his friend Willie Velásquez, Cortés had worked as an organizer for the United Farmworkers and for a project run by MAYO activists, the Mexican American Unity Council. MAUC mobilized voters and obtained a number of OEO grants for projects ranging from housing to business loans to job training. "It did a good job of rebuilding many of the areas of the West Side of San Antonio," recalled a former MAUC organizer. On the other hand, while Velásquez had been a VISTA supervisor, Cortés did not work directly for Great Society programs and came to the conclusion that the Johnson administration's Community Action Programs were inherently contradictory, that the government could not subsidize the organizing of ordinary people against established politicians and their financial supporters.[24]

Cortés found an alternative model for community organizing at Saul Alinsky's Industrial Areas Foundation (IAF). For decades the IAF had been training organizers from Brooklyn to California, including a young farmworker named César Chávez. Upon completion of the Chicago sessions, Cortés returned to San Antonio in the early 1970s determined to educate ordinary people, in his words, "about what politics is all about—public discourse, negotiations, how to argue, when to compromise, not just the quadrennial electronic plebiscite we usually call politics." He did not envision the effort as a Mexican American one *per se*, saying, "This is not about some Mexicans getting some power. This is bigger than that." At the same time, he has written, "If Mexicanos wish to make significant contributions to the transformation of American culture and politics, they will have to have the security that comes with confidence in their own identity and history."

Cortés worked through the Catholic parishes on the West Side, asking the local pastors for the names of the most active lay leaders. Then he spent months listening to them and to people that they recommended, individuals who had made a difference in the PTA or the Little League or a neighborhood celebration. "We tried to bust the stereotypes . . . to see leaders not necessarily as someone who could speak or persuade a crowd. We wanted to see leaders as people who have networks, relationships with other people." Often the people with the most neighborhood connections were women; consequently, many of the COPS presidents have been female, such as Beatriz Galle-gos and Carmen Badillo.[25]

The members drew up a list of common concerns, from inadequate sewers to high utility rates, then investigated the ways in which the city council allocated money. "Just by being on hand for every meeting and keeping score on who votes how, COPS has had a remarkable clarifying effect on what was one of the muddier political puddles in Texas," wrote a reporter for the *Texas Observer*. Moreover, COPS members say that they are dedicated to the organization for the long haul, regardless of the political climate or the obstacles. As Inez Ramírez put it, "This is not merely politics we are engaged in, but correcting injustice, which is God's work and the mission of the Church. . . . Our spirituality embodies a deep concern for the physical well-being of every individual."[26]

IAF-related organizations formed from Houston to El Paso among people of various religious and racial backgrounds, in the process developing into a network that periodically holds "accountability sessions" for public officials. Communities around the state send representatives, often a majority of them female, to question gubernatorial candidates, for example, regarding their positions on issues of concern to the delegates. As Bill Moyers has written about COPS, "Real power comes when people have permission to ask questions." Supported by the legwork and contributions of the neighborhood residents themselves, IAF groups have successfully lobbied for what the *New York Times* called "some of the most important legislation in the state." Among other things, the Texas legislature expanded health care for the poor and allocated $100 million in loans for sewer systems in Rio Grande Valley colonias. By the 1990s the IAF was active in various parts of the country and faced a new challenge: to reconcile the expanding IAF national base with the IAF commitment to local neighborhood agendas. In his book and public television documentary, both entitled, "Who Will Tell the People? The Betrayal of American Democracy," William Greider highlighted the IAF network as part of what he has called "the Democratic promise," amid political processes increasingly in the thrall of monied interests.[27]

LEGACIES

Lyndon Johnson probably would have applauded COPS and its kindred groups for giving voice to people on the margins, for integrating them into the political process. "He really did believe that power was something that was a social invention that democracy could enlarge. And that's rare for a person who had risen to the top playing the game as roughly as he played it," Bill Moyers has said. Moreover, according to Moyers, "the Mexican American community was very important to Lyndon Johnson's political fortunes and . . . formative in his overall outlook on politics, government, and life." For his part, OEO regional director Dr. William Crook considered the Great Society nothing less than an emancipation proclamation for Mexican Americans. White House aide George Reedy wrote about Johnson: "His feelings for blacks, Chicanos, dirt farmers were not feigned. He felt their plight and suffered with them—as long as they did not get too close." Johnson befriended ordinary folks, tried to help them, but on his terms. "He wanted to control everything. His greatest outbursts of anger were triggered by people or situations that escaped his control," wrote Joseph Califano.[28]

Most likely Johnson would have seized the opportunity to work with COPS, all the while warily calibrating the members' political leanings and keeping his other eye on the reaction of his powerful business supporters. While sympathetic to grass-roots organizing, Johnson's own friends tended to be people with close ties to big business, such as Lloyd Bentsen and John Connally, who represented the rancher-politician-elite that had long dominated South Texas. Connally said of Johnson, "He was a man of contradictions . . . he could be whatever he wanted to be." Perennial Connally critic Ronnie Dugger agreed, saying, "I think it's a mistake to try and reconcile the opposites in Johnson. Just leave them there."[29]

Mexican American leaders who knew President Johnson regarded him with a mixture of emotions. Most have tended to evaluate him in light of his legislation, which they credit with giving many people the opportunity to leave poverty and ignorance and discrimination behind. In the opinion of Congressman Edward Roybal, of all the presidents, "he ranks among the top . . . because of the legislation that he passed . . . because there was leadership." Thinking back on his student/activist days, Gil Cárdenas—now a professor and head of the Center of Mexican American Studies at the University of Texas—said that Johnson accomplished more for the poor and minorities even than his own hero, Franklin Roosevelt, and without the impetus of a national economic crisis. Dr. Joe Bernal credited the Johnson administration with policies "that created an atmosphere for change. It was an acceptable thing to be pro change and to fight some of the old established systems that kept people from participating in democracy." Lupe Anguiano—a founder of the National Women's Political Caucus who has gained national attention for her successful programs by and for poor women—remembered her stint working for the Johnson administration as "exciting days. We were so strong in really moving this country to really deal with issues." Judge Albert Peña said of Johnson, "Regardless of my personal feelings of his relationship with Connally, he was doing a good job. . . . He was always very simpático with *mexicanos*." Some, however, thought that in the end Johnson usually sided with the more powerful in society. Sociologist Julian Samora said, "Johnson did do a lot of good things . . . but basically I think Johnson was for Johnson. . . . He was looking for power; he was mainly on the other side." [30]

By welcoming Mexican Americans into the political process, Lyndon Johnson accelerated their integration into national life. Paradoxically, however, this integration also heightened their sense of ethnic identity, which peaked in the cultural nationalism and anti-establishment rhetoric of the Chicano movement. In an even greater paradox, Johnson helped give impetus to Mexican American empowerment even as he pioneered the use of big-money media in his own campaigns and allied himself with powerful people in business and government opposed to the advancement of minorities and the poor. Just as his hero Franklin Roosevelt had created a coalition that included racial enemies, so Johnson hoped to include economic adversaries in that same coalition by means of an expanding economy. When the escalation of a controversial war forced hard economic choices, his contradictory allies turned on one another. Which of his legacies will prevail? Today, in a political climate increasingly dominated by large financial contributors, it remains to be seen whether citizen action movements can serve as an effective counterweight in the formation of public policy.

Aldrete Papers = personal papers of Cristóbal Aldrete, Austin, Texas

Califano Files = Office Files of Joseph Califano, LBJL

FDRL = Franklin Delano Roosvelt Library, Hyde Park, New York

García Papers = Héctor P. García Papers, Texas A&M University, Corpus Christi

García Personal Papers = personal papers of Hector P. García, Corpus Christi, Texas

HRP = House of Representatives Papers

Idar Papers = personal papers of Ed Idar Jr., Austin, Texas

LBJL = Lyndon Baines Johnson Library

Macy Files = Office Files of John Macy, LBJL

McPherson Files = Office Files of Harry McPherson, LBJL

Moyers Files = Office Files of Bill Moyers, LBJL

PPCF = Pre-Presidential Confidential Files, LBJL

Ramos Papers = personal papers of Rodolfo Ramos, Washington, D.C.

Sánchez Papers = George I. Sánchez Papers, Benson Latin American Collection, University of Texas at Austin

Senate Papers = Senate Papers, LBJL

Taylor Papers = Paul Schuster Taylor Papers, Bancroft Library, University of California, Berkeley

Watson Files = Office Files of Marvin Watson, LBJL

WHCF = White House Central Files, LBJL

WHCF-NF = White House Central Files, Name Files

Ximenes Papers = personal papers of Vicente Ximenes, Albuquerque, New Mexico

NOTES

INTRODUCTION

1. Tuchman, *Practicing History*, 18.

2. See, for example, Conkin, *Big Daddy from the Pedernales*; Kearns, *Lyndon Johnson and the American Dream*; Dallek, *Lone Star Rising*; Caro, *The Years of Lyndon Johnson*.

3. See, for example, San Miguel, *Let Them All Take Heed* and Gómez-Quiñones, *Chicano Politics*.

4. Woodward, *Thinking Back*, 56–57; Burns, *The Crosswinds of Freedom*.

5. García Collection; Sánchez Collection; César Chávez/United Farmworker Collection, Reuther Archives.

6. Rose, "Traditional and Nontraditional Patterns of Female Activism in the United Farm Workers of America, 1962 to 1980."

7. Steel, "The Long Shadow of Ambition."

8. Califano, *The Triumph and Tragedy of Lyndon Johnson*; Reedy, *Lyndon B. Johnson: A Memoir*; Moyers, "Epilogue: Second Thoughts."

9. Acuña, *Occupied America*; García, *Mexican Americans*; García, *United We Win*; Muñoz, *Youth, Identity, and Power*.

10. Taylor, *An American-Mexican Frontier* and *Mexican Americans in the United States*; Key, *Southern Politics in State and Nation*; Davidson, *Race and Class in Texas Politics*.

11. Bender, "Whole and Parts: The Need for Synthesis in American History"; Kazin, "The New Historians Recapturing the Flag."

CHAPTER I

1. Goodwin, *Remembering America*, 326–329.

2. "Message on Voting Rights: The American Promise, Remarks of the President to a Joint Session of Congress," March 15, 1965, Ex Sp. 2-3/1965/HU 2-7, box 67, LBJL; U.S. President, *Public Papers*, "Lyndon B. Johnson, 1965," 286; Miller, *Lyndon*, 11; Moyers, auth. int.

3. Steinberg, *Sam Johnson's Boy*, 16; Caro, *Path to Power*, 42, 74; Dugger, *The Politician*, 25–28, 34, 83, 299–300; Baines Scrapbook, Rebekah Baines Johnson Papers, LBJL; White, *The Professional*, 89; Miller, *Lyndon*, 18.

4. J. T. Canales opposed both the poll tax and the primary bill. Porterfield, *LBJ Country*, 32–33; White, *The Professional*, 87, 93–96; Branda, *Handbook of Texas*; Edgeworth, int. by Michael Gillette, LBJL; Dugger, *The Politician*, 53–56, 91–92, 71; Baines Scrapbook, 30; Dyer, "Lyndon B. Johnson and Civil Rights"; Montejano, *Anglos and Mexicans*, 127, 117–125, 143; De León, *Mexican Americans in Texas*; Hunter and Hunter, "'My Dear Friend'"; Paredes, *"With His Pistol in His Hand,"* 138.

5. Kearns, *Lyndon Johnson and the American Dream*, 28–31; Steinberg, *Sam Johnson's Boy*, 24, 29; Caro, *Path to Power*, 45, 20; Conkin, *Big Daddy from the Pedernales*, 23; Ludeman, *La Salle County*, 124; Wildenthal, auth. int.; Pool et al., *Formative Years*, 97, 99; McCoy, "The Education President," 22–23, 48.

6. Perales, *Are We Good Neighbors?*, 213–222; Mitchell, "An Evaluation of Provisions"; Moyers, auth. int.; Foley et al., *From Peones to Políticos*, xxi; Kibbe, *Latin Americans in Texas*, 143; Webb and Carroll, *Handbook of Texas*, I:424, 649; II:31, 351; Meinig, *Imperial Texas*, 84.

7. When *"With His Pistol in His Hand"* was first published in 1958, Paredes was threatened by a Texas Ranger. Cullen, "Lone Star Bibliography," *Texas Observer*, Dec. 10, 1993, 22; Paredes, *"With His Pistol in His Hand,"* 78–82.

8. Durham, *Taming the Nueces Strip*, viii, 42–43; Fisher, "The Life and Times of King Fisher," 238; Robinson, *With the Ears of Strangers*, 166.

9. According to Dobie, his family controlled an additional 200,000 acres. Casto, *The Settlement of the Cibolo Nueces Strip*, 39; Dobie, "Stories in Texas Place Names," in Dobie and Boatright, *Straight Texas*, 11; Guerra, "Rancho Buena Vista," 112; De León, *Tejano Community*, 22; Steiner, *La Raza*, 360.

10. *La Crónica* organized a protest conference attended by representatives of Mexican organizations throughout South Texas, but the dispossession and disenfranchisement continued unabated. Foley et al., *From Peones to Políticos*, 3; Montejano, *Anglos and Mexicans*, 113, 116.

11. Richard White has written of Mexican Americans: "From being a group of farmers, small ranchers, skilled agricultural laborers, and craftspeople they gradually declined into a group of unspecialized laborers." White, *"It's Your Misfortune and None of My Own"*; Montejano, *Anglos and Mexicans*, 113, 248–249; Taylor, *Mexican Americans in the United States*, 362; Ludeman, *La Salle County*, 6, 131, 143; Dobie, *Coronado's Children*, 70–80; Foley et al., *From Peones to Políticos*, 15, 53–54; La Salle County Historical Commission, "A Brief History of Cotulla," 4; Ludeman, *Pioneering in the Faith*, 610; Paredes, *A Texas-Mexican Cancionero*, xviii; Woods, Worthy, Contreras, auth. int.

12. Zamora, *Mexican Worker*, 70; Foley et al., *From Peones to Políticos*, 63; Leininger, *Chicanos in South Bend*, 5.

13. Martin and Martin, "A History of La Salle and McMullen Counties," 4–5; La Salle County Historical Commission, "A Brief History of Cotulla," 1; Montejano, *Anglos and Mexicans*, 107–110, 113–114, 164–166, 176–178, and ch. 9; Wildenthal, Worthy, auth. int.; Taylor, *Dimmit County*, 362, 488; Kibbe, *Latin Americans in Texas*, 195–197; La Salle County Scrapbook, Center for American History; Pycior, "*La Raza* Organizes," ch. 6; Blawis, "Tijerina and the Land Grants," 520.

14. In contrast, in counties along the Mexican border an even more outnumbered Anglo population had long ago accommodated to the ways of a Mexican professional class that dated from the eighteenth century. Pool et al., *Formative Years*, 42–44; Taylor, *Dimmit County*, 357, 370, 379; Wildenthal, Worthy, auth. int.; Smith, "Mexicano Resistance to Schooled Ethnicity," 466; Montejano, *Anglos and Mexicans*, 131, 162, 168, 169, 182–183, 186, 196, 227.

15. At the June 1929 event a contingent of women and children "in luxurious autos" escorted the Consul to the plaza, where Gilberto Leyva's orchestra greeted him with the Mexican national anthem. The talk was followed by a banquet at "El Poblano" restaurant. Foley et al., *From Peones to Políticos*, 16–17, 43–44, 65; Montejano, *Anglos and Mexicans*, 182–187, 196; Robinson, *With the Ears of Strangers*, 170–172; Clinchy, *Equality of Opportunity*, 37; Dugger, *The Politician*, 111, 124; *El Heraldo Mexicano*, April 15, 1928; Meier and Ribera, *Mexican Americans/American Mexicans*, 127; *La Prensa*, June 17, 1929; Paredes, *A Texas-Mexican Cancionero*, 26; "Exodus across Border," *San Antonio Express*, Oct. 20, 1929.

16. Taylor, *Dimmit County*, 370, 379, 388–398, 403–411; Moyers, Wildenthal, Worthy, auth. int.; Ludeman, *La Salle County*, 124; historical marker and grounds, Cotulla cemetery; *La Prensa*, Jan. 1, 1930; *Cotulla Record*, Jan. 1, 1929.

17. Contreras, Ruiz, Dan García, auth. int.

18. David Montejano also noted the variety of Mexican responses: "gratitude, anger, frustration, resignation" (Montejano, *Anglos and Mexicans*, 232). Contreras, Hernández, Woods, auth. int.

19. A few years later Santiago Jiménez recorded the "Cotulla Polka." Phonograph record, Santiago Jiménez, "Cotulla Polka," Cotulla Museum; *La Prensa*, Jan. 30, 1929, Jan. 2, 1930, Jan. 7, 1930, also Jan. 1929–Jan. 1930, inclusive; Worthy, Contreras, Knaggs, Ruiz, Hernández, auth. int.; twenty-six tombstones with "Woodman of the World" inscriptions, all in the old Mexican section, Cotulla cemetery; San Antonio *Express Magazine*, Oct. 11, 1954; Foley et al., *From Peones to Políticos*, 40.

20. Shirley, "Ethnic Music," in Library of Congress, *Folk Music of the United States*, 13–14; Cotulla *Record*, Jan. 1, 1929, and Jan.–Dec. 1929, inclusive.

21. Rock, "Children's Achievement in the Amanda Burks Elementary School," 45; photo caption, "Mamie Wildenthal," Cotulla Museum; Woods and Contreras, auth. int.; Nichols, int. by Michael Gillette, LBJL.

22. Contreras, auth. int.; Sánchez, "Concerning the Segregation of Spanish-Speaking Children in the Public Schools," 28–29.

23. Wildenthal noted the same pattern with truant children of white farm-workers in Travis County. Clinchy, *Equality of Opportunity*, 126–127; Foley et al., *From Peones to Políticos*, 38, 66–67, 111; Montejano, *Anglos and Mexicans*, 191, 193; Wildenthal, Hernández, Dan García, González de Toro, auth. int.; Woods, "Narrative of Welhausen School," 2; Taylor, *Dimmit County*, 373, 378, 383–384, 457; Strickland and Sánchez, "Educational Opportunities," 10–11; Manuel, *Education of Mexican and Spanish-Speaking Children*, 61; Foley et al., *From Peones to Políticos*, 38; Young, "An Administrative Survey," 41, 46–47, 50, 55–56; Gamio, *Mexican Immigration to the United States*, 222–223.

24. Gutiérrez, *Walls and Mirrors*, 49–50.

25. González de Toro, auth. int.—translation by author.

26. Taylor, *Dimmit County*, 372; Young, "An Administrative Survey," 41–42; McCoy, "The Education President," 24; Contreras, Ruiz, Wildenthal, Worthy, auth. int.

27. For the *escuelitas* that flourished in South Texas colonias, see Zamora, *Mexican Worker*, 104–105. Montejano, *Anglos and Mexicans*, 242–243; Dan García, Contreras, auth. int.

28. Caro, *Path to Power*, 172; Smith, "Mexicano Resistance to Schooled Ethnicity," 78, 101–102; Young, "An Administrative Survey," 400–401; Strickland and Sánchez, "Educational Opportunities," 10; Manuel, *Education of Mexican and Spanish-Speaking Children*, 68.

29. Dugger, *The Politician*, 115; Wildenthal, Moyers, auth. int.; Dyer, "Lyndon B. Johnson and Civil Rights," 20; Edgeworth, int. by Gillette, LBJL; Caro, *Path to Power*, 166–171.

30. Dugger, Dan García, Hernández, auth. int.

31. The emphasis on "English only" applied to Anglo children as well, who often arrived from ranches knowing Spanish fluently, only to lose their bingualism at the Amanda Burks school. Pool et al., *Formative Years*, pp. 141, 144; Dan García, Worthy, auth. int.; Steinberg, *Sam Johnson's Boy*, 47; Smith, "Mexicano Resistance to Schooled Ethnicity," 78, 101–102; Manuel, *Education of Mexican and Spanish-Speaking Children*, 150; McCoy, "The Education President," 25, 39, 164.

32. Contreras, auth. int.; Estill, *Beginner's History*, 241, 310; Webb, *The Texas Rangers*, 14; McCoy, "The Education President," 39; Steinberg, *Sam Johnson's Boy*, 16, 20, 24, 47; Miller, *Lyndon*, 18; Samora et al., *Gunpowder Justice*, 2, 66–67; Dugger, *The Politician*, 32; Caro, *Path to Power*, 168; college editorials, LBJA Statements File, April 25, 1928; July 7, 1929, LBJL; Montejano, *Anglos and Mexicans*, 223–224, 231.

33. De León, *Mexican Americans in Texas*, 84, 119–120; Mirandé and Enríquez, *La Chicana*, 225.

34. Dan García, Contreras, Hernández, auth. int.; Miller, *Lyndon*, 33; Steinberg, *Sam Johnson's Boy*, 47; Pool et al., *Formative Years*, 142; Caro, *Path to Power*, 168; Dugger, *The Politician*, 117; McCoy, "The Education President," 24; Ludeman, *La Salle County*, 124.

35. Mamie Wildenthal would spend her career at the Welhausen school.

Manuela González Contreras, when asked her opinion of Mamie Wildenthal, remembered the teacher with mild affection. Woods, "Narrative of Welhausen School," 3; Woods, Dan García, Contreras, auth. int.; Caro, *Path to Power*, 165–168.

36. Worthy, Woods, auth. int.; letter of reference, W. T. Donaho, Feb. 21, 1929, Dorothy Territo Office Files, LBJA Biography File, HRP.

37. Wildenthal, Moyers, auth. int.; Moyers, "Epilogue."

38. Miller, *Lyndon*, 407; Reedy, auth. int.

39. Moyers, auth. int.

CHAPTER 2

1. Miller, an old friend of Sam Johnson and an early hero of Lyndon's, was a well-known lobbyist for the Texas Gulf Sulfur Company and had liberally dispersed money in the San Antonio barrio to influence the vote in favor of Kleberg. Caro, *Path to Power*, 206, 213–214; Joe B. Frantz, "Lyndon Baines Johnson" in Branda, ed., *Handbook of Texas*, 447; Dugger, *The Politician*, 126–128.

2. David Montejano has pointed out that while Texas Mexicans invariably sold their land during hard times, when prices were low, Anglos engaged in land speculation, selling at peak times, when they could maximize their profits. Montejano, *Anglos and Mexicans*, 52, 59–70, 73, 80–81; Taylor, *An American-Mexican Frontier*, 179; Broyles, "The Last Empire," 152, 246; "A Real Cowboy Graces the Halls of Congress," Papers of Richard Kleberg, "1932–1938," LBJL; Key, *Southern Politics*, 271–273, 586, 595, 599; Shelton, *Political Conditions*, 85–86; Mr. Bloodworth, county clerk, Kleberg County, Kingsville, Texas, and Richard King, President of Corpus Christi National Bank, Nueces County, int. by P. Taylor, n.d. (c. 1929–1934), files ZR-4, "Mexican Labor in the United States: Nueces County, Texas," Taylor Papers; "Texas Kingdom That Blocks a Road," *Washington Star*, Oct. 15, 1933, 5–6; Dugger, *The Politician*, 218.

3. Several versions survive; the Spanish original of this version is:

> Esos rinches de la Kineña
> dicen que son muy valientes
> hacen llorar las mujeres
> hacen correr a las gentes
>
> . . . a esos rinches de la Kineña
> les daremos un mal rato.

Taylor, *An American-Mexican Frontier*, 174–175; Broyles, "The Last Empire," 152; Montejano, *Anglos and Mexicans*, 117–125; Longoria, "Revolution, Visionary Plan, and Marketplace"; Paredes, *A Texas-Mexican Cancionero*, 33–34, 72–74.

4. Montejano, *Anglos and Mexicans*, 117–126.

5. According to a resident of the Kingsville colonia, "the board wanted separation, and the Mexicans called an attorney in to fight it." He advised them instead to demand equal facilities. "We got a $45,000 building," the resident said. Taylor, *An American-Mexican Frontier*, 222; Montejano, *Anglos and Mexicans*, ch. 5, 225; Broyles, "The Last Empire," 244; letter, Representative R. Kleberg to U. B. Blalock, May 7, 1933, and letter, Representative R. Kleberg to R. L. Eschenburg, in the *Advance* (Kenedy, Texas), n.d., Papers of Richard Kleberg, "1932–1938," LBJL.

6. García, *Mexican Americans*, 26–27, 30; Andrés de Luna, field interview by P. Taylor, Corpus Christi, Texas, n.d., file ZR-4, "Mexican Labor in the United States: Nueces County, Texas," Taylor Papers; Montejano, *Anglos and Mexicans*, 243; Aldrete, auth. int.; Shelton, *Political Conditions*, 73–74.

7. Many Lulackers also had belonged to *mutualista* organizations, which provided insurance, loans, legal aid, cultural activities, and adult education. LULAC and *mutualista* groups both organized the whole family and voiced pride in their Mexican heritage, but LULAC restricted membership to U.S. citizens, calling for equal educational and civil rights for all people and an end to segregation and child labor. García, "The Making of the Mexican American Mind," 579; Meier and Ribera, *The Chicanos*, 81; *LULAC News*, Sept. 1931, April 1932, May 1932; Pycior, "Mexican American Organizations," in Tyler, *Handbook of Texas*; "LULAC Involved for Mexican Americans," *Corpus Christi Caller*, Feb. 11, 1979; Taylor, *An American-Mexican Frontier*, ch. 21, 243–244; Meier and Ribera, *Dictionary of Mexican American History*, 68; Márquez, *LULAC*, 21; García, *Mexican Americans*, 28, 41–42, 45–46, 55–56; San Miguel, *Let Them All Take Heed*, 78–80.

8. Caro, *Path to Power*, x; Reisler, *By the Sweat of Their Brow*, 232; Montejano, *Anglos and Mexicans*, 167–169; De León, *Tejano Community*, 103; Connally, Ximenes, auth. int.

9. With the connivance of Duval boss Archer Parr, the Klebergs in 1933 convinced the Texas legislature to detour a state road one hundred miles around Kenedy County, which contained a total population of 701 King Ranch employees. Broyles, "The Last Empire," 246; "A Real Cowboy Graces the Halls of Congress," 3.

10. Winston Bode wrote in the *Handbook of Texas*: "With the publication of two books, *A Vaquero of the Brush Country* (1929) and *Coronado's Children* (1931), Dobie became a national literary figure." Branda, *Handbook of Texas*, 248; Montejano, *Anglos and Mexicans*, 82, 250; Caro, *Path to Power*, 294–295; Kearns, *Lyndon Johnson and the American Dream*, 80.

11. Dugger, *The Politician*, 170.

12. In 1933 the new Roosevelt administration, in the person of Secretary of Labor Frances Perkins, discontinued federal involvement in mass repatriation. García, *Rise of the Mexican American Middle Class*, ch. 9; Meier and Ribera, *The Chicanos*, 202–242; *LULAC News*, Sept. 1931, March 1934, March 1938, Aug. 1939; Hoffman, *Unwanted Mexican Americans in the Great Depression*, 123–126; Guzmán, *Political Socialization*, 56; Pycior, "*La Raza* Organizes," 223–227; McCay, "The Impact of the Great Depression on Im-

migrant Mexican Labor," 91–100; Reisler, *By the Sweat of Their Brow*, 209–210.

13. Jackson, "Deportation of Aliens Creating Much Work for Texas Congressman," *Corpus Christi Caller-Times*, Jan. 5, 1932.

14. Dugger, *The Politician*, 170; Miller, *Lyndon*, 40–42, 45; Burns, *Crosswinds of Freedom*, 49, 64–66; Caro, *Path to Power*, 260, 355–356.

15. Foley, "Mexicans, Mechanization, and the New Deal."

16. Tijerina, auth. int.; Meier and Ribera, *Dictionary of Mexican American History*, 370–371; Meier and Ribera, *The Chicanos*, 244; Caro, *Path to Power*, 260; John McQueen to LBJ, Jan. 1939, June 14, 1939, and Sept. 7, 1939; LBJ to John McQueen, June 9, 1939, all in "Correspondence, 1937–1939," HRP.

17. This founder, J. Luz Sáenz, was an attorney in the Del Rio desegregation case and the author of a book on *mexicano* participation in World War I. Idar, auth. int.; García, "The Making of the Mexican American Mind," 597–598; Shannon, *Twentieth-Century America*, 383; *LULAC News*, March 1934, 8; De León, "*Los Tasinques* and the Sheep Shearers' Union," 3–16; *LULAC News*, March 1934, 30–31. For the New Deal coalition, see Lubell, *The Future of American Politics*.

18. The statewide average weekly wage was $5.85 for Mexican American women, $5.95 for black women, and $8.75 for white women. Leininger, "The Chicana Worker in San Antonio," 8–13; Green, "ILGWU in Texas," 156–163.

19. García, *Rise of the Mexican American Middle Class*, 211, 218.

20. Lyndon's brother Sam succeeded him as Kleberg's private secretary and became a public relations man for the King Ranch. Henderson, *Maury Maverick*, 61; Bourgeois, "Lyndon Johnson's Years with the NYA," 13–14; Dugger, *The Politician*, 187; Caro, *Path to Power*, 276–277, 339; Weisenberger, *Dollars and Dreams*, 56.

21. Dugger, *The Politician*, 186, 189; Hernández, auth. int.; Ray Lee and Richard R. Brown, int. by Gillette, LBJL; "Final Report: NYA for the State of Texas," box 6, "Final Reports," NYA Papers, National Archives.

22. "Final Report: NYA for the State of Texas," box 6, "Final Reports," NYA Papers, National Archives; De León, *Mexican Americans in Texas*, 100; Steinberg, *Sam Johnson's Boy*, 91; García, "Mexican Americans and the Politics of Citizenship," 187–204.

23. "Final Report: NYA for the State of Texas," box 6, "Final Reports," NYA Papers, National Archives; Weisenberger, *Dollars and Dreams*, 96–97; Reisler, *By the Sweat of Their Brow*, 246; Robertson, *A Study of Youth Needs and Services*.

24. "Texas Youths Build," *San Antonio Light*, Oct. 7, 1937; *Galveston Tribune*, Aug. 11, 1937; Weisenberger, *Dollars and Dreams*, 79; NYA, Texas. "Administration Projects, July–Sept., 1937," box 87, National Archives; Bourgeois, "Lyndon Johnson's Years with the NYA," 55–56; Rodríguez, *Henry B. González*, 40.

25. One of the San Antonio high school secretaries, Martha López, is the

aunt of Clinton cabinet member Henry G. Cisneros. Contreras, Munguía, auth. int.; Munguía, tel. comm. with author, March 10, 1994; Bourgeois, "Lyndon Johnson's Years with the NYA," 70; Weisenberger, *Dollars and Dreams*, 72–73, 99; Blackwelder, *Women of the Depression*, 118–119.

26. Rebecca Masterson had been a geologist for twenty years prior to the Depression. "Report of Activities of NYA Camp for Unemployed Women, Glen Rose, Texas," "Report of Activities of NYA Camp for Unemployed Women, La Porte, Texas," "Report of Activities of NYA Camp for Unemployed Women, Mico, Texas," "Report of Activities of NYA Camp for Unemployed Women in Mina, Texas," box 51, "NYA, Texas," National Archives.

27. Birdwell, int. by Dorothy Pierce, LBJL. Armstrong, "Report of the NYA of Texas, Oct., 1935," "NYA Administration Reports, 1935–1936," #51, and "Administration Projects, Texas, March 1936," box 3 and "Final Report," NYA Papers, National Archives; García, *Mexican Americans*, 51; Weisenberger, *Dollars and Dreams*, 140–141.

28. In 1934 the Texas legislature established the Texas Farm Placement Service, which told farmworkers where to work, based in part on growers' racial preferences. Montejano, *Anglos and Mexicans*, 212–213, 219; Reisler, *By the Sweat of Their Brow*, 246–248; letters, LBJ to Richard R. Brown, Oct. 10, 1935, and Richard R. Brown to LBJ, Oct. 14, 1935, National Youth Administration, "Correspondence, 1935–1938," box 121, National Archives; *LULAC News*, March 1934, 30–31; July 1937, 17, 19; and Dec. 1938, 3.

29. For the Cotulla version of the anecdote, see above, ch. 1. Dugger, *The Politician*, 187; Richard Brown, int. by Gillette, LBJL.

30. García, *Mexican Americans*, 51; NYA, Texas. "A Report Giving an Individual Resume of Every Employee in the NYA of Texas," box 51 and "Texas Administration Budget and Personnel," July 1936, box 154, National Archives; W. Sherman Birdwell Jr., int. by Eric Goldman, LBJL; "Suggested Labor Supervisory Requests for Johnson City NYA-REA Building," n.d., "Pedernales Electrical Cooperative" file, box 191, HRP.

31. Miller, *Lyndon*, 56; Billington, "Lyndon Baines Johnson and Blacks," 26–42, 29–31; NYA Papers, "Administration Projects, Texas, March 1936," box 3, and "Final Report," 1938, National Archives; Dugger, *The Politician*, 186; Bourgeois, "Lyndon Johnson's Years with the NYA," 81–83; Johnson, *My Brother Lyndon*, 65.

32. Gutiérrez, *Walls and Mirrors*, 27; Dallek, *Lone Star Rising*, 138; Weisenberger, *Dollars and Dreams*, 60, 128, 139–140, 147, 168; LBJ, "Remarks of the President at the Swearing-In for Vicente T. Ximenes," June 6, 1967, file 79, box 95, HPGP.

33. Bourgeois, "Lyndon Johnson's Years with the NYA," 103; Dugger, *The Politician*, 193.

34. Reynaldo Garza, interview by Frantz, LBJL; Bill Douthat, *La Raza*, 24, 26; *Austin Statesman*, Jan. 19, 1940; *Austin City Directory*, 418–419; Olson, *Nonpartisan Elections*, 13–14.

35. Connally, auth. int.; *LULAC News*, Aug. 1938 and Aug. 1939; Shelton, *Political Conditions*, 10–11; "Austin-Prospective" and "Kyle," in "General Lists—Contacts—1937 Campaign," box 2, HRP; *La Prensa*, Sept. 2, 1935.

36. Mary M. Bethune to LBJ, May 3, 1937, box 2, HRP; Caro, *Path to Power*, 407–408, 438, 468, 584, 617, 627.

37. Correspondence, HRP; Caro, *Path to Power*, 494.

38. Connally, auth. int.; Dugger, *The Politician*, 217.

39. Caro, *Path to Power*, 498–501, 519, 531, 766; Billington, "Lyndon Baines Johnson and Blacks," 32–33; Steinberg, *Sam Johnson's Boy*, 125–126, 130; Newlon, *L.B.J.*, 74–77; H. C. Currie, "Folk Festivals, Pageants, Celebrations. Travis County. 1937" (U.S. Works Projects Administration), file #689, Austin Historical Society.

40. Weisenberger, *Dollars and Dreams*, 90–91, 141–142.

41. Fenner Roth to LBJ, May 17, 1939; Sherman Birdwell to LBJ, July 26, 1939; Dan Rose to LBJ, May 23, 1939; LBJ to Dan Rose, June 3, 1939; Dan Rose to LBJ, June 5, 1939; LBJ to Dan Rose, June 10, 1939, all in the "Pedernales Electric Cooperative" file, box 191, HRP.

42. Dugger, *The Politician*, 209–219; *Austin American*, Jan. 22, 1938, Jan. 25, 1938, March 31, 1938; Newlon, *L.B.J.*, 76; *LULAC News*, Sept. 1937, March 1938, Aug. 1939; Caro, *Path to Power*, 496, ch. 20.

43. *Dallas Times-Herald*, June 27, 1939; Miller, *Lyndon*, 72.

44. Patenaude, *Texans, Politics, and the New Deal*, 58; *Christian Advocate* (Houston 1938), "General—Maverick, Maury," House of Representative Papers, box 5; Dugger, *The Politician*, 216; Miller, *Lyndon*, 68–69; Henderson, *Maury Maverick*, 185; Billington, "Lyndon Baines Johnson and Blacks," 32–33; Dyer, "Lyndon B. Johnson and Civil Rights," 64; *LULAC News*, May 1937; García, *Mexican Americans*, 41; "Evergreen cemetery, Section C," June 9, 1938, García Personal Papers; Connally, auth. int.; *LULAC News*, Aug. 1938 and Aug. 1939.

45. Radio address, "Sit-Down Strikers," April 2, 1937, and "Labor Statement," May 24, 1941, both in Statements File, box 1, HRP.

46. Miller, *Lyndon*, 68.

47. García, *The Rise of the Mexican American Middle Class*, 212–213; De León, *Mexican Americans in Texas*, 100; Patenaude, *Texans, Politics, and the New Deal*, 76; Peña, auth. int.; Márquez, *LULAC*, 20.

48. Protests at the proposed conference site in Albuquerque forced the Congreso to cancel the meeting, and Lulacker George I. Sánchez nearly lost his job at the University of New Mexico for agreeing to participate. Undaunted by the Albuquerque fiasco, Moreno—together with Californian Josefina Fierro de Bright—held the meeting in Los Angeles the following year. The delegates conducted panels on labor, racial discrimination, education, and women's rights. Speakers included former Mexican president Adolfo de la Huerta and U.S. union officials. García, *Mexican Americans*, ch. 6.

49. Acuña, *Occupied America*, 317; Emma Tenayuca and Home Brooks, "The Mexican Question in the Southwest," *The Communist* (March 1939),

261; Calderón and Zamora, "Manuela Solís Sager and Emma Tenayuca: A Tribute," 30–40; Green, "ILGWU in Texas," 156–163; García, "The Making of the Mexican American Mind," 273, 279, 474, 494–495; Reisler, *By the Sweat of Their Brow*, 246; Leininger, "The Chicana Worker in San Antonio," 14; García, *Mexican Americans*, ch. 6; Lambert, auth. int.

50. The CIO supported candidates throughout the nation and was the largest contributor to President Roosevelt's 1936 reelection effort. Leuchtenberg, *Roosevelt and the New Deal*; *La Prensa*, Jan. 6, 1938, Feb. 2, 4, 6, 12, 19, 28, 1938; García, "Making of the Mexican American Mind," 273, 279, 474, 494–495; Thomas, *The Spanish Civil War*, 8.

51. *La Prensa*, the largest barrio newspaper, remained neutral, as did the Mexican government. *La Prensa*, Feb. 18, 19, 1938; Blackwelder, *Women of the Depression*, 143; Leininger, "The Chicana Worker in San Antonio," 14–16; Gutiérrez, *Walls and Mirrors*, 27; García, "Making of the Mexican American Mind," 599; García, *Mexican Americans*, ch. 6.

52. After the fact, in 1941, the San Antonio Welfare Commission reported that low wages "tend to perpetuate the racial handicaps under which the Mexicans, especially the pecan shellers and others of low economic status, are forced to live" and expressed the hope of "a growing consciousness of the people in power that discrimination against a strong segment of its population is not wise . . . politically or educationally or economically or socially." García, *Rise of the Mexican American Middle Class*, 204; García, "Making of the Mexican American Mind," 273, 279, 474, 494–495; Dugger, *The Politician*, 215.

53. García, *Rise of the Mexican American Middle Class*, 212–215; Federal Writer's Project, *WPA Guide to Texas*, 333; "The Villita Ordinance," "National Youth Administration, Miscellaneous, 1938–1940," OF44d, box 20, FDRL.

54. Dugger, *The Politician*, 174, 231, 307–317; *New York Times*, Aug. 20, 1939; García, "Making of the Mexican American Mind," 476, 490–494; Maury Maverick to FDR, Oct. 17, 1939, "National Youth Administration, Miscellaneous, 1938–1940," OF44d, box 20, FDRL.

55. García, "Making of the Mexican American Mind," 476, 490–494; Henderson, *Maury Maverick*, 181; Reedy, auth. int.; Caro, *Path to Power*, 584.

56. For the growth of the conservative wing and the demise of the populists in the Texas Democratic Party, see Green, *Establishment*, ch. 2. Dugger, *The Politician*, 215, 222; Caro, *Path to Power*, 556–560, 568, 580, 705; Conkin, *Big Daddy from the Pedernales*, 99.

57. Margaret Johnson Kimball to LBJ, June 12, 1940, "Margaret Kimball," LBJA Select Names, box 22, LBJL; Dugger, *The Politician*, 222–223.

58. Henderson, *Maury Maverick*, 228, 236; Maury Maverick to Aubrey Williams, June 13, 1941, "Williams, Aubrey, Personal File, 1936–1942 M," (file 1), box 2, FDRL.

59. Dugger, *The Politician*, 231; Henderson, *Maury Maverick*, 231; Caro, *Path to Power*, 705.

CHAPTER 3

1. "The Last Hurrah" comes from O'Connor, *The Last Hurrah*. Conkin, *Big Daddy from the Pedernales*, 102; Joseph H. Skiles, int. by Gillette, LBJL; Dallek, *Lone Star Rising*, 215.

2. The machine politics of the traditional cattle ranching counties was a curious blend of the Mexican hacienda system, the Bourbon planter regimes of the post-Reconstruction South, and the urban political tactics brought from the North by settlers such as Richard King. A number of Texas Mexicans had sought political reform, calling in 1891 for the secret ballot in Starr County and in 1892 joining with like-minded Anglos in Duval County to petition for honest elections. The issue became clouded in the following decades, however, as farmers used racist appeals in their campaigns to unseat the paternalistic ranchers. Dugger, *The Politician*, 322; Steinberg, *Sam Johnson's Boy*, 23; "District Office—El Paso," box 18, HRP; De León, *Tejano Community*, 44–45; Reynaldo Garza, int. by Joe B. Frantz, LBJL; Pycior, "Lyndon, *La Raza*, and the Paradox of Texas History," 143; Reedy, auth. int. J. C. Looney, int. by Joe B. Frantz, LBJL; Villarreal, "Voting Participation and Leadership: Chicanos Along the Border," 5; Montejano, *Anglos and Mexicans*, 274–275; Key, *Southern Politics*, 259–260; Dugger, *The Politician*, 324. Aldrete, Reedy, González, Idar, Carillo, auth. int.; E. Idar, int. by Margo Gutiérrez, Benson Latin American Collection, University of Texas at Austin.

3. For more on the Idars, see Zamora, *Mexican Worker*; Limón, "El Primer Congreso Mexicanista de 1911," 85–117; and the Idar interviews. Kunetka, "The Man Who Stuffed Box 13," *San Antonio Express-News*, Aug. 7, 1977, 19; García, *Mexican Americans*, 114; Conkin, *Big Daddy from the Pedernales*, 104; Caro, *Means of Ascent*, 188, 320; Shelton, *Political Conditions*, 47, 51, 59–60; Branda, *Handbook of Texas*, 705; Dugger, *The Politician*, 322–325; Montejano, *Anglos and Mexicans*, 81–82, 253–254, and table 12.

4. Connally grew up adjacent to San Antonio in Wilson County, where politics was something of a hybrid: segregation of schools and public facilities and Anglo political domination of the Mexican majority similar to that in Cotulla, except on the neighborhood level, where the precincts resembled those in the paternalistic *patrón* counties; see ch. 2. Ximenes, Connally, auth. int.; Dallek, *Lone Star Rising*, 222; Connally, *In History's Shadow*, 42–43.

5. Looney, int. by Joe B. Frantz, LBJL; Max Mendlovitz to J. H. Blundell, May 24, 1941, "Webb County"; Quesada, "Judge Manuel B. Bravo: A Political Leader in South Texas, 1937–1957," 55–56.

6. J. T. Canales, a conservative, states' rights Democrat, was an exception to the pro-Roosevelt rule. Hunter and Hunter, "'My Dear Friend,'" 27–28; J. J. Pickle, int. by Joe B. Frantz, LBJL; "Austin Headquarters," box 17, HRP; Connally, auth. int.; Max Mendlovitz to J. H. Blundell, May 24, 1941, "Webb County"; Jacob I. Rodríguez to J. H. Blundell, May 22, 1941, "1941 Campaign," box 19, HRP; Caro, *Path to Power*, 681, 733.

7. Hunter and Hunter, "'My Dear Friend,'" 27–28. Gerald C. Mann, int.

by Joe B. Frantz, LBJL; Munguía, auth. int.; McKay, W. *Lee O'Daniel and Texas Politics*, 402; Caro, *Path to Power*, 677, 688–698; Conkin, *Big Daddy from the Pedernales*, 101, 297, 92–96, 104–105; Dugger, *The Politician*, 276–279; George Brown, int. by Gillette, LBJL; Dallek, *Lone Star Rising*, 215.

8. Green, *Establishment*, 70, 72, 75; Conkin, *Big Daddy from the Pedernales*, 92–96, 101–103, 297; Caro, *Path to Power*, 531, 685, 688–689; Dugger, *The Politician*, 276–279; George Brown, int. by Gillette, LBJL; Dallek, *Lone Star Rising*, 215–216; Burns, *Crosswinds of Freedom*, 166–167.

9. Strickland, *Texans*, 242–243; Gutiérrez, "Under Surveillance," *Texas Observer*, Jan. 9, 1987, 8–10; Meier, *Mexican American Biographies*; Dugger, *The Politician*, 230–233; Conkin, *Big Daddy from the Pedernales*, 103–104; Caro, *Path to Power*, 617; Pycior, "Lyndon Johnson, Mexican Americans, and Public Policy Issues," 28–30.

10. Shelton, *Political Conditions*, 79–81; Caro, *Path to Power*, 718–720, 732–734, 736–737; Caro, *Means of Ascent*, 180–184.

11. See García, *Mexican Americans*, ch. 3; San Miguel, *Let Them All Take Heed*, 76; Simmons, *Anglo Americans and Mexican Americans*, 545–554; García, *Rise of the Mexican American Middle Class*, 213; Dugger, *The Politician*, 321.

12. Conkin, *Big Daddy from the Pedernales*, 105; Caro, *Path to Power*, 734; Connally, auth. int.; Dugger, *The Politician*, 233–235.

13. Caro, *Means of Ascent*, ch. 3; D. B. Hardeman, int. by Gillette, LBJL; Simmons, *Anglo Americans and Mexican Americans*, 549.

14. Margaret Johnson Kimball to LBJ, March (?) 1942, "Kimball, Margaret," LBJA Select Names, box 22, HRP; Wildenthal, Contreras, Dan García, Hernández, auth. int.

15. In 1948 Perales published his findings, with a title that pointedly asked, *Are We Good Neighbors?* Alonso S. Perales to FDR, March 10, 1944, and March 17, 1944; William D. Hassett, March 18, 1944; Edwin M. Watson to Francis Biddle, April 6, 1944; Tom Clark to Alonso Perales, April 18 (?), 1944; Alonso Perales to Franklin D. Roosevelt, Nov. 16, 1944, all in "League of Loyal Americans 1944," OF5529, FDRL; Perales, *Are We Good Neighbors?*, 213–330, 283; San Miguel, *Let Them All Take Heed*, 135; Kibbe, *Latin Americans in Texas*, 78; Acuña, *Occupied America*, 253; tombstones, town cemetery, Cotulla, Texas.

16. Dugger, *The Politician*, 235, 258–261, 266–280; Perales, *Are We Good Neighbors?*, 89, 130–132, 137; Dyer, "Lyndon B. Johnson and Civil Rights," 63–64.

17. Conkin, *Big Daddy from the Pedernales*, 106–110, 113; Green, *Establishment*, 46–50; Key, *Southern Politics*, 644, 657–661, 669–670; Dallek, *Lone Star Rising*, 258.

18. Caro, *Means of Ascent*, 121–122; Idar, auth. int.; monument, dated Sept. 15, 1946, Plaza Militar, San Antonio, Texas.

19. Perales, *Are We Good Neighbors?*, 60–61; Montejano, *Anglos and*

Mexicans, 253–254; Sáenz, *Los México-Americanos en la Gran Guerra*; Christian, "Joining the American Mainstream," 594–595; García, *Rise of the Mexican American Middle Class*, 255–256.

20. Montejano, *Anglos and Mexicans*; *LULAC News*, Oct. 1946, 21; Perales, *Are We Good Neighbors?*, 91, 133.

21. Dan García, auth. int.; De León, *Ethnicity in the Sun Belt*, 127–128, 58, 140; Simmons, *Anglo Americans and Mexican Americans*, 286, 292–293, 303, 548–551; *LULAC News*, Oct. 1945, 5–6, Aug. 1946, Dec. 1946, 16, March 1947, 5, 16, 17; El Paso *Herald Post*, Dec. 14, 1945; Kibbe, *Latin Americans in Texas*, 277; García, *Mexican Americans*, 101–106; Morín, *Among the Valiant*, 166–171; Woods, *Mexican Ethnic Leadership*, 98, 101–103.

22. Voight, Aldrete, Carrillo, auth. int.

23. Dallek, *Lone Star Rising*, 296, 369.

24. Morín, *Among the Valiant*, 278–280; Dugger, *The Politician*, 306; Dallek, *Lone Star Rising*, 7–8, 290–291, 312–315, 335–336, 370; García, *Rise of the Mexican American Middle Class*, 305–307; Márquez, "Politics of Race and Class," 84–101; Connally, Ximenes, auth. int.

25. Truman was the first presidential candidate to send translated campaign information to ethnic newspapers. McCullough, *Truman*, 674–676, 683; Voight, auth. int.

26. Key, *Southern Politics*, 259–260; *LULAC News*, Oct. 1946; Idar, auth. int.

27. Some of Stevenson's forebears had been professionals in North Carolina, but the family was devastated by the Yankee invaders and migrated to Texas, where they struggled to make a living. *Dallas News*, July 2, 1933; Calvert and De León, *History of Texas*, 146; Montejano, *Anglos and Mexicans*, 263, 264, 268–270; McKay, *Texas and the Fair Deal*, 180; Aldrete, auth. int.; Green, *Establishment*, 47–48, 81; Conkin, *Big Daddy from the Pedernales*, 115–116; Dugger, *The Politician*, 309–310; Caro, *Means of Ascent*, 170; Vento, *Alonso S. Perales*, 14; Clifton Carter, int. by Dorothy Pierce, LBJL.

28. Dugger, *The Politician*, 310, 315; Dyer, "Lyndon B. Johnson and Civil Rights," 67–69.

29. Tijerina, auth. int.; Simmons, *Anglo Americans and Mexican Americans*, 549; Dallek, *Lone Star Rising*, 313; Allsup, *G.I. Forum*; Caro, *Means of Ascent*, 322; photographs, "Mrs. Johnson at LULAC National Convention Picnic, Austin, Texas," June 1948, 48-6-30 C, 48-6-31 C, 48-6-32 C, LBJL.

30. Perales, *Are We Good Neighbors?*, 76, 120; Dyer, "Lyndon B. Johnson and Civil Rights," 52; Allsup, *G.I. Forum*, 39; Idar, Aldrete, auth. int.

31. In 1957 Telles would be elected mayor. For the story of Raymund Telles's political career, see García, *Mexican Americans*, ch. 5. Raymund Telles, int. by Joe B. Frantz, LBJL.

32. Allsup, *G.I. Forum*, 30–34; Idar, H. García, Ximenes, Carrillo, auth. int.

33. Cleotilde García, auth. int.

34. H. García, auth. int.

35. Ricardo A. Jiménez to LBJ, July 20 (?) and July 29, 1948; LBJ to Ricardo Jiménez, July 21 and Aug. 10, 1948; LBJ to A.(sic) L. Berry, Aug. 10, 1948; K. L. Berry to LBJ, Aug. 11, 1948, all in box 165, HRP; Dallek, *Lone Star Rising*, 313; Voight, auth. int.

36. Green, *Establishment*, 98, 107; Montejano, *Anglos and Mexicans*, 262–263.

37. Dugger, *The Politician*, 305–306.

38. See García, *Mexican Americans*, ch. 8 (for the history of ANMA and the influence of Mexico's radical tradition on Mexican American activists), 200–204; Urrutía, "Asociación Nacional México-Americana," 177–184; Calderón and Zamora, "Manuela Solís Sager and Emma Tenayuca: A Tribute," 37–38.

39. Green, "Cold War Comes to Latin America," 184.

40. García, *Mexican Americans*, 200, 201, 204.

41. Gabin, "Women's Protests," 369–377; Green, "The Felix Longoria Affair," 24, 44–45n.

42. Montejano, *Anglos and Mexicans*, 279; Malcom Bardwell, interview, LBJL; Dugger, *The Politician*, 321; Acuña, *Occupied America*, 282–283; Simmons, *Anglo Americans and Mexican Americans*, 303; Caro, *Means of Ascent*, ch. 11.

43. The introduction of voting machines did not end bloc voting; political organizers replaced marked ballots with a knotted string in each booth, a knot next to the lever of each of the favored candidates. Dugger, *The Politician*, 321; Voight, Idar, auth. int.; Baum and Hailey, "Lyndon Johnson's Victory," 602, 604, 611–612.

44. Some forty-five years later this neighborhood observer refused to give his name. Anonymous box 13 resident; Idar, Carrillo, auth. int.; Conkin, *Big Daddy from the Pedernales*, 117; Dugger, *The Politician*, 222–232; 322–328; Dallek, *Lone Star Rising*, 326; Caro, *Means of Ascent*, ch. 13.

45. Transcript, Donald Thomas in "LBJ: The Difference He Made," Austin, Texas, June 3–5, 1990; Quesada, "Judge Manuel Bravo"; Baum and Hailey, "Lyndon Johnson's Victory," 610; Dugger, *The Politician*, 328–329; Caro, *Means of Ascent*, 316–317, 391–394.

46. Tijerina, auth. int.; Caro, *Means of Ascent*, ch. 13; Branda, *Handbook of Texas*, 370.

47. Dugger, *The Politician*, 330–339; Caro, *Means of Ascent*, 334–350; Quesada, "Judge Manuel Bravo," 62.

48. Steinberg, *Sam Johnson's Boy*, 272.

49. Cf. O'Connor, *The Last Hurrah*; Branda, *Handbook of Texas*, 705; Montejano, *Anglos and Mexicans*, 262–263, 279, 296; H. García, Connally, auth. int.; H. García, int. by David McComb, LBJL; Dallek, *Lone Star Rising*, 369–370.

CHAPTER 4

1. The town also had a segregated Mexican cemetery that was established in 1924. The mayor told the colonia's spokesman—ironically enough, Félix Longoria's father—that the town cemetery was "too crowded" to include any "Mexican" graves. Green, "The Felix Longoria Affair," 23.

2. As girls' division president Sara Moreno had learned the effectiveness of political pressure. In 1948, when officials refused her request for the use of the Mathis State Park Pavilion, Dr. Héctor García prodded them into rescinding the discriminatory policy. Allsup, *G.I. Forum*, 40–42.

3. For newspaper coverage, see "Longoria, Felix [Newspaper articles]," box 3, PPCF. H. García, auth. int.; Dyer, "Lyndon B. Johnson and Civil Rights," 63–64; H. García, int. by David McComb, LBJL; Green, "The Felix Longoria Affair," 25; Allsup, *G.I. Forum*, 42.

4. Dyer, "Lyndon B. Johnson and Civil Rights," 90–93; Dallek, *Lone Star Rising*, 215, 369–370; Allsup, *G.I. Forum*, 40–43, 369–370; Connally, H. García, auth. int.

5. H. García, auth. int.; memoranda, John Connally, "Re: Felix Longoria," Jan. 11 and Jan. 14, 1949, "Longoria, Felix," box 2, PPCF; Dyer, "Lyndon B. Johnson and Civil Rights," 88, 90–93; Rhonda Smith, "Hector P. Garcia: A Legacy Overlooked," *Austin American-Statesman*, May 22 (?), 1994; Meier, *Mexican American Biographies*, 82.

6. Telegram, R. A. Cortez to LBJ, Jan. 12, 1949, and letter, Dan to LBJ, n.d. (Feb. 24, 1949?), "Longoria, Felix, Correspondence," box 2, PPCF. See this box for letters from Mexican American organizations all over the state and from Anglo Americans all over the nation. Letter, A. S. Vento to LBJ, Jan. 24, 1949, "Longoria, Felix, Statements"; "Longoria, Felix [Newspaper articles]," both in box 3, PPCF; Dyer, "Lyndon B. Johnson and Civil Rights," 94, 97–98; Dan García, Connally, auth. int.; Allsup, *G.I. Forum*, 40–43.

7. Homer R. Long to LBJ, March 4, 1949, "Longoria, Felix, Correspondence, 1," box 2, PPCF; "Resolution, B6, Bexar County American Legion," Jan. 27, 1949, "Longoria, Felix, Statements," box 3, PPCF; Dyer, "Lyndon B. Johnson and Civil Rights," 95–97.

8. Letter, William F. Chesmett to LBJ, Jan. 14, 1949, and letter, Shag Floore to Stanley H. Partridge, Jan. 21, 1949, "Longoria, Felix, Correspondence, 1," box 2, PPCF; Dyer, "Lyndon B. Johnson and Civil Rights," 94–95; Allsup, *G.I. Forum*, 44; Connally, auth. int.

9. Copy of telegram, J. F. Gray to John B. Connally, Feb. 23, 1949, and memorandum, John B. Connally, "Re: Felix Longoria," Feb. 25, 1949; letter, LBJ to Beatrice Longoria, Jan. 13, 1949; letter, LBJ to H. García, Feb. 16, 1949, all in "Longoria, Felix," box 2, PPCF; Galarza, *Merchants of Labor*, 48–51; H. García, Ximenes, Connally, auth. int.; Green, "The Felix Longoria Affair," 26–28.

10. Gus C. García to LBJ, March 16, 1949; LBJ to Gus C. García, March 18, 1949; Gus C. García to LBJ, March 25, 1949; Gus C. García to John B. Connally, March 25, 1949, all in "Longoria, Felix, Investigations by State Leg.," box 3, PPCF.

11. Notarized statement, Juventino Ponce, March 12, 1949, "Longoria, Felix, Investigations by State Leg.," box 3, PPCF; H. García, int. by David McComb, LBJL; Idar, Connally, auth. int.; Allsup, *G.I. Forum*, 45–47, 50, 60–62; Gómez-Quiñones, *Chicano Politics*, 58; Dallek, *Lone Star Rising*, 369.

12. Dyer, "Lyndon B. Johnson and Civil Rights," 71–73, 85, 87; Dugger, *The Politician*, 344–345.

13. Wildenthal, int. by Gillette, LBJL; Conkin, *Big Daddy from the Pedernales*, 300.

14. Telegram, H. García, Chairman, American GI Forum, and Gus García, legal advisor, League of United Latin American Citizens, to LBJ, Feb. 23, 1950, and telegrams, LBJ to Gus García, Feb. 24, 1950, LBJ to H. García, Feb. 24, 1950, all in "Legislation FEPC," Legislative Files, 1950–1952, box 229, Senate Papers; LBJ to Paul Campos, March 8, 1950, "Personal Letters— J," García Papers; H. García to Howard McGrath, April 14, 1951, "Justice— Hector P. Garcia," Departmental Files, Justice, 1949–1951, box 926, Senate Papers; E. Idar to LBJ, May 29, 1952, file 4, box 117, García Papers; LBJ to E. Idar, June 4, 1952, "1952, Department of Justice [3 of 3]," Departmental Files, box 965, Senate Papers.

15. H. García to LBJ, Oct. 20, 1950, "Labor—Garcia, H.," Senate Departmental Files, box 927, Senate Papers.

16. At the same time, the Joint U.S.–Mexican Trade Union Committee, comprised of labor leaders from the U.S. border states and Mexico, met to try to organize and bargain internationally. Sánchez and Saunders, *Wetbacks*; Idar, Schmidt, auth. int.; Allsup, *G.I. Forum*, 107; "The Menace of the Wetback: Peonage by Contract," "Ernesto Galarza," box 6, Sánchez Papers; María de la Paz Torres to LBJ, March 10, 1952, in "Leg. Labor—Migratory," box 233, Senate Papers.

17. Resolutions, American GI Forum, July 6, 1952, "Idar," "I," LBJA Selected Names, box 20, Senate Papers; LBJ to Ed Idar, Nov. 4, 1952, Aldrete Papers, and also in "Political—Travis County," Senate Papers; draft letter, E. Idar to LBJ, Nov. 21, 1952, and E. Idar to LBJ, Dec. 4, 1952, Aldrete Papers; LBJ to R. A. Hightower, July 2, 1952, "Legislation—Labor—Migration," box 233, Senate Papers.

18. Reedy, Yarborough, H. García, auth. int.

19. Some growers opposed the *bracero* program, however, because they wanted *no* government regulation of immigration whatsoever. Cables, LBJ to thirty-three people, May 29, 1951, and J. C. Looney to LBJ, July 13, 1951, in "Legislative Labor (Alien)," box 233, Senate Papers; Oscar Dancy to LBJ, June 30, 1951, and Aug. 9, 1951, "Legislation—Alien Labor," box 232, Senate Papers.

20. Dugger, *The Politician*, 291–294; J. C. Looney, int. by Joe B. Frantz, LBJL.

21. *Forum News Bulletin*, April 1953; LBJ to H. García, July 8, 1953, "Gar–Gat 94," Master File Index, box 66, Senate Papers; Reedy, H. García, auth. int.; telegrams, LBJ to HPG, Oct. 5, 1949, March 23, 1950, May 5, 1950, "Personal Letters—J," García Papers; Allsup, *G.I. Forum*, 57–58;

H. García to LBJ, June 26, 1954, and LBJ to H. García, July 1, 1954, file 15, box 52, García Papers; H. García to LBJ, May 7, 1957, "Garcia," 1957 Case and Project Files, box 1292, Senate Papers; "Hispanic American Recipients of Congressional Medal of Honor," García Personal Papers; LBJ to H. García, May 21, 1954, "Gar–Gat 94," Master File Index, box 66, Senate Papers.

22. Allsup, *G.I. Forum*, 107; *Corpus Christi Caller*, April 22, 1953, and *La Verdad*, Feb. 8, 1952, both in file 50, box 49, García Papers.

23. For Operation Wetback, see García, *Operation Wetback*. Allsup, *G.I. Forum*, 106, 109–110; *Forum News Bulletin*, Oct. 1953; Idar, auth. int.

24. Others who expressed reservations included LULAC founders Alonso Perales and J. Luz Sáenz. Alonso S. Perales to G. Sánchez, Dec. 3, 1951, box 78, Sánchez Papers; Ed Idar to J. T. Canales, Jan. 23, 1952, Idar Papers; Gutiérrez, *Walls and Mirrors*, 167–168, 260 n.38; García, *Rise of the Mexican American Middle Class*, 258–259.

25. García, *Mexican Americans*, 210, 212–213.

26. Dallek, *Lone Star Rising*, 406; Acuña, *Occupied America*, 270; Conkin, *Big Daddy from the Pedernales*, 137–138; *Forum News Bulletin*, July 1953; *Austin American-Statesman*, Feb. 3, 1986.

27. Carleton, *Red Scare*, 124–125, 129; Joey González to G. Sánchez, June 7, 1951, and G. Sánchez to Joey González, June 15, 1951, both in "El Paso Meeting," box 16, Sánchez Papers; C. E. Ayers to G. Sánchez, Dec. 20, 1955, and G. Sánchez to Logan Wilson, Feb. 20, 1956, both in box 21, Sánchez Papers.

28. H. García, Idar, auth. int.; *Forum News Bulletin*, July 1953; *Austin American-Statesman*, Feb. 3, 1986; LBJ to H. García, July 18, 1958, "Personal Letters—L," García Papers; Allsup, *G.I. Forum*, 61–62.

29. Dallek, *Lone Star Rising*, 397; Dugger, *The Politician*, 391, 371–372, 369; García, *Mexican Americans*, 210; Allsup, *G.I. Forum*, 55.

30. González, auth. int.

31. Stambaugh and Stambaugh, *The Lower Rio Grande Valley of Texas*, 203; Lott and Martínez, *The Kingdom of Zapata*, 14; Flores, "Falcon International Dam and Its Aftermath," 25, 29–30, 62–64.

32. The fact that a movie entitled *Viva Zapata* was filmed in Zapata County was a coincidence. The film profiled a major leader of the 1910–1920 Mexican Revolution, while the county was named after a border resident who led a rebellion in the 1830s against the centralist regime in Mexico City. Byfield, *Falcon Dam and the Lost Towns of Zapata*, 2, 4, 5, 9; Flores, "Falcon International Dam," 13–17, 20–25; *San Antonio Express*, Oct. 25, 1936; Branda, *Handbook of Texas*, 433; Federal Writers Project, *The WPA Guide to Texas*, 510; Bailey, "Problems in Relocating the People of Zapata, Texas"; Goodwyn, *Lone Star Land*, 20–21; De León, *Mexican Americans in Texas*, 79; Carmack, "The Tale of Two Cities: One is Old, One is New," *San Antonio Express-News*, Oct. 13, 1973.

33. H. González to LBJ, Nov. 15, 1949; Ed Clark to LBJ, Aug. 26, 1949; LBJ to Ed Clark, Aug. 29, 1949; Francis Adams to LBJ, Aug. 24, 1949, all correspondence in "Falcon Dam Project," Rivers and Harbors Files,

1949–1953, box 845, Senate Papers; Flores, "Falcon International Dam," 74–75; Lott and Martínez, *Kingdom of Zapata*, 13–20.

34. S. H. Holmgren to LBJ, Aug. 21, 1950, and Lon C. Hill to LBJ, Aug. 9, 1950, both in "Rivers and Harbors—Falcon Dam #2," Rivers and Harbors Files, 1949–1953, box 845, Senate Papers.

35. Robert Bobbitt to Lloyd Bentsen, July 9, 1954, and Joseph Campbell to L. H. Hewitt, June 9, 1955, both in "Zapata, City of, Relocation," box 1202, Senate Papers; H. González to LBJ, Nov. 15, 1949, L. M. Lawson to LBJ, R. Bobbitt to LBJ and Lloyd Bentsen, Dec. 15, 1952, and memorandum, Warren Woodward to LBJ, all four in Rivers and Harbors Files, 1949–1953, box 845, Senate Papers; Bailey, "Problems in Relocating the People of Zapata, Texas," 23–26; Flores, "Falcon International Dam," 75; Byfield, *Falcon Dam*, "Conclusions."

36. Allred, a New Dealer, was the former governor of Texas. H. González to LBJ, Nov. 15, 1949; Earl Johnson to LBJ, Sept. 26, 1949; G. Mackenzie to Chairman, Aug. 11, 1950; L. M. Lawson to LBJ, Nov. 30, 1949, all in "Falcon Dam Project," Rivers and Harbors Files, 1949–1953, box 845, Senate Papers; Byfield, *Falcon Dam*, 19, 23, 87; González, auth. int.; Bailey, "Problems in Relocating the People of Zapata, Texas," 27–29.

37. J. T. Canales to LBJ, Feb. 22, 1950; L. M. Lawson to LBJ, Nov. 30, 1949, and March 13, 1950, all in "Falcon Dam Project," Rivers and Harbors Files, 1949–1953, box 845, Senate Papers; Arthur Perry to LBJ, April 25, 1953, "Zapata County," 1953 Case and Project Files, Senate Papers.

38. Bailey, "Problems in Relocating the People of Zapata, Texas," 26–28; *Texas Parade*, vol. 1, no. 9 (Feb. 1937), 24–25; Carrillo, auth. int.; Juan Gilberto Quesada, tel. comm. to author, April 1994; LBJ to Ray Rash, July 31, 1959, and Aug. 6, 1959, "Ran–Raz 1959," Master File Index, box 154, Senate Papers.

39. Flores, "Falcon International Dam," 79n.; S. H. Holmgren to LBJ, Aug. 21, 1950, in "Riv and Har.—Falcon Dam #2," Lon C. Hill to LBJ, Aug. 9, 1950, in "Falcon Dam Project," both in Rivers and Harbors Files, 1949–1953, box 845, Senate Papers; telegram, M. B. Bravo to LBJ, March 12, 1953; Warren Olney III to LBJ, March 21, 1953; M.B. Bravo to LBJ, March 28, 1953, all three in "Zapata Co. Elections," 1953 Case and Project Files, box 1191, Senate Papers; Byfield, *Falcon Dam*, 20; Lott and Martínez, *The Kingdom of Zapata*, 252–254.

40. Bailey, "Problems in Relocating the People of Zapata, Texas," 30–35, 66; Flores, "Falcon International Dam," 87, 93–95, 98; Bill Rudd, "New Zapata Folk Claim Raw Deal," *Houston Chronicle*, May 29, 1955.

41. Bailey, 30–35; Robert Bobbitt to LBJ, Feb. 1, 1954; Robert Bobbitt to LBJ, "Personal," Jan. 23, 1954; Robert Bobbitt to Arthur Perry, Jan. 23, 1954; memorandum, Robert Bobbitt to Arthur Perry, June 23, 1954; LBJ to Robert Bobbitt, June 14, 1954, and June 29, 1954; Robert Bobbitt to M. B. Bravo and Manuel Medina, July 30, 1955; Robert Bobbitt to LBJ, Price Daniel, Joe Kilgore, Zapata County Public and School Officials, July 30, 1955; Robert Bobbitt to LBJ, July 30, 1955; memorandum, Robert Bobbitt to

Arthur Perry, n.d. (July 30, 1955?); Arthur Perry to Robert Bobbitt, Aug. 2, 1955; Arthur Perry to Helen Graham, Aug. 31, 1954; note, LBJ, quoted by Arthur Perry, attached to memo, Arthur Perry to LBJ, June 11, 1954, all in "Zapata, City of, Relocation," box 1202, Senate Papers.

42. Flores, "Falcon International Dam," 7, 71–72, 79, 98; Byfield, *Falcon Dam*, ch. 3; Lott and Martínez, *The Kingdom of Zapata*, 243; Carrillo, auth. int.; Rudd, "New Zapata Folk Claim Raw Deal"; U.S. Department of Commerce, "Tourist and Recreational Programs for Zapata County, Texas," *ARA Case Book*, 1–10.

43. J. Gilberto Quesada, tel. comm. to author, April 1994; note, J. Gilberto Quesada to author, n.d. (April 1994); Carmack, "The Tale of Two Cities: One is Old, One is New."

44. Johnson, who began collecting Salinas's work in the 1940s, was one of the artist's earliest admirers. Dallek, *Lone Star Rising*, 410, 412; Dugger, *The Politician*, 358; Conkin, *Big Daddy from the Pedernales*, 124; Steinberg, *Sam Johnson's Boy*, 572–573; Kearns, *Lyndon Johnson and the American Dream*, 100; Quirarte, "The Art of Mexican-America," 1–9.

CHAPTER 5

1. Reedy, *Lyndon B. Johnson*, 155; Morris, *North toward Home*, 225.

2. Evans and Novak, *Lyndon B. Johnson*, 226; Dugger, *The Politician*, 292, 373–375, 380–381; Voight, auth. int.

3. Munguía is the uncle of Henry Cisneros, San Antonio mayor in the 1980s and Secretary of Housing and Urban Development in the Clinton administration. Munguía, Idar, Peña, auth. int.

4. San Miguel, *Let Them All Take Heed*, n. 49; Stephen A. Mitchell to H. García, Oct. 11, 1952, file 19, box 53, García Papers; García, *Mexican Americans*, 117–118; "Voting Drive for Latins Criticized," *Texas Observer*, Nov. 16, 1955; Tom Sutherland, "Texas Tackles the Race Problem," *Saturday Evening Post*, Jan. 12, 1952, 22–23, 64–65.

5. *New York Times*, Oct. 19, 1952, 1.

6. Voight, auth. int.; Dugger, "Gonzalez of San Antonio," part IV, *Texas Observer*, Oct. 18, 1980; Hunter and Hunter, "'My Dear Friend,'" 35–36.

7. Albert Peña to H. García, Oct. 15, 1952; radio address, H. García, Oct. 17, 1952; J. William Fulbright to H. García, Oct. 11, 1952, all in file 19, box 53, García Papers; Voight, Dan García, auth. int.

8. Peña, Munguía, auth. int.

9. Forum members estimated the crowd at five to eight thousand. Munguía, Idar, auth. int.; James W. Smith, int. by Gillette, LBJL; *El Progreso*, Oct. 1952; *New York Times*, Oct. 19, 1952, 72, 82; Dallek, *Lone Star Rising*, 104, 420, 426; *Forum News Bulletin*, Nov. 1952.

10. *New York Times*, Oct. 19, 1952, 72; *Forum News Bulletin*, Nov. 1952, 2–3; Bernal, Munguía, auth. int.

11. E. Idar to H. García, Nov. 10, 1952, Aldrete Papers.

12. D. Dougherty to Ed Ray, executive editor, *San Antonio Express*, June 2, 1954; press release, D. Dougherty, Beeville, Texas, n.d., 1954, and speech, July 15, 1954, both in "Reedy: D. Dougherty," box 412, Senate Papers.

13. Reedy, auth. int.; *Forum News Bulletin*, Nov. 1954.

14. Idar, auth. int.

15. LBJ to H. García, July 8, 1953, "Gor–Gat 94," Master File Index, box 66, Senate Papers; LBJ to E. Idar, July 8, 1953, "Ia–In 131," Master File Index, box 93, Senate Papers; LBJ to H. García, July 18, 1958, "Personal Letters—L," García Papers; *Forum News Bulletin*, July 1953, 1; address, LBJ to the American GI Forum, Ft. Worth, Aug. 1, 1953, in "Hallway box—L," García Papers; Dallek, *Lone Star Rising*, 442; Idar, Dan García, auth. int.

16. Connally, Idar, auth. int.; George Reedy, "Memorandum," in "Reedy: Memos, 1956 [2 of 2]," Senate Papers.

17. Resolutions, American GI Forum, July 6, 1952, "Idar," "I," LBJA Selected Names, box 20, Senate Papers; Dugger, Yarborough, auth. int.

18. Idar, auth. int.; *Forum News Bulletin*, Nov. (?) 1954, Aug. 1954; memo, "Reedy: Memos, 1956 [1 of 2]," box 419, Senate Papers.

19. Dallek, *Lone Star Rising*, 448, 442; Dougherty, "The Texas Story," and George Reedy to LBJ, June 15, 1954, both in "Reedy: D. Dougherty," box 412, Reedy Files, Senate Papers; LBJ to H. García, July 31, 1954, "Gar–Gat 94," Master File Index, box 66, Senate Papers.

20. Dyer, "Lyndon B. Johnson and Civil Rights," 104–107; Dallek, *Lone Star Rising*, 445, 509; *Dallas News*, Aug. 15, 1954.

21. Allsup, *G.I. Forum*, 70–77; García, *Mexican Americans*, 49–51; Tijerina, auth. int.; Rubén Munguía, introduction to Gus García, "Los Chávez," file 7, box 82, García Papers.

22. In 1961 the Supreme Court would uphold a Florida law that only required male voters to serve. Not until the 1970s, when pioneering lawyers such as Ruth Bader Ginsberg took up the challenge, would the courts address the exclusion of women. García, *Mexican Americans*, 51; *New York Times*, April 20, 1994; testimony, Ruth Bader Ginsberg before the Senate Judiciary Committee.

23. Dallek, *Lone Star Rising*, 369–370; Davidson, *Race and Class in Texas Politics*, 164, 308n.

24. In one of the few letters from a female organizer to the senate staff, the correspondent felt obliged to begin her letter by apologizing; "I didn't mean to be 'bossy,'" she wrote, before making her suggestion that Johnson target female voters, given that in 1960 women would outnumber men by several million. Altavene to Booth Mooney, Feb. 2, 1958, and Altavene to Booth Mooney, n.d.; list, Calixto Mora, n.d., and list, Mrs. Charles F. Falley to Booth Mooney, all in "[Elections] County," 1958 Subject File, box 778, Senate Papers; "District #14, Brooks County," "Senate [2 of 2]," 1958 Subject File, Senate Papers; Cecil Burney, int. by David McComb, LBJL.

25. Contreras had moved from Cotulla to San Antonio in the 1940s. García, *Mexican Americans*, 117–118; Contreras, auth. int.

26. E. Idar to H. García and C. Aldrete, Oct. 27, 1953, "Aldrete" file, Idar Papers; De León, *Mexican Americans in Texas*, 117; G. Sánchez to Simon Gross, March 26, 1953, and Sept. 15, 1954; Simon Gross to G. Sánchez, Sept. 17, 1954; memorandum, G. Sánchez, Feb. 19, 1953; press release, Alianza Hispano Americana, n.d.; R. Soto, C.P.A., to Board of Directors, ACSSP, June 23, 1955, all in box 33, Sánchez Papers; Idar, Reedy, auth. int.

27. García, *Mexican Americans*, 50, 317–318n.88; Meeks, auth. int.; Romo, "George I. Sánchez and the Civil Rights Movement, 1940–1960," 359; G. Sánchez to James A. Dombrowski, May 4, 1955, "Integration," box 21, Sánchez Papers; G. Sánchez to Roger Baldwin, June 2, 1955, and Roger Baldwin to Thurgood Marshall, June 3, 1955, both in box 37, Sánchez Papers; Ralph Guzmán to G. Sánchez, Oct. 14, 1955, box 33, Sánchez Papers; Equal Employment Opportunity Commission, "Administrative History," Biographical Appendix, Administrative History Files, LBJL; *Forum News Bulletin*, Sept. and Oct. 1955, and Nov. 12, 1955.

28. Connally, Idar, auth. int.; Allsup, *G.I. Forum*, 72; memorandum, "Reedy: Memos, 1956 [1 of 2]," box 419, Senate Papers.

29. *Forum News Bulletin*, Feb.–March, 1956.

30. "DAC," Aug. 23, 1955, "V," LBJA Select Names, box 35; Voight, auth. int.; D. B. Hardeman, int. by Gillette, LBJL; Dallek, *Lone Star Rising*, 491–492; memorandum, George Reedy to LBJ, Jan. 16, 1957, "Reedy: Memos Jan. 1957," box 420, and memorandum, George Reedy to LBJ, "Reedy: Memos Fall 1956," box 419, Senate Papers.

31. Green, *Establishment*, 172; H. García to LBJ, March 19, 1956, and LBJ to H. García, March 24, 1956, "Garcia, Dr. H. P.," 1956 Senate Case and Project Files, box 1230, Senate Papers; Davidson, *Race and Class in Texas Politics*, 163–164; memorandum, George Reedy to LBJ, Jan. 16, 1957, "Reedy: Memos Jan. 1957," box 420, and memorandum, George Reedy to LBJ, "Reedy: Memos Fall 1956," box 419, both in Reedy Files, Senate Papers; Voight, auth. int.

32. Green, *Establishment*, 174, 176; Dugger, auth. int.; LBJ to Cristóbal Aldrete, June 9, 1956, Aldrete Papers; Davidson, *Race and Class in Texas Politics*, 164; Reston, *Lone Star*, 172–174; Dallek, *Lone Star Rising*, 504; Ralph Yarborough to G. Sánchez, March 23, 1956, "Judge Ralph W. Yarborough," box 6, Sánchez Papers.

33. The convention eventually nominated Estes Kefauver. Green, *Establishment*, 175–176; Dallek, *Lone Star Rising*, 504; Rubén Munguía, introduction to Gus García, "Los Chávez," file 7, box 82, García Papers; González, Voight, Idar, auth. int.

34. Bard, *LBJ*, 70; Dallek, *Lone Star Rising*, 505–506; memoranda, George Reedy and "History of Texas Dem. Campaign for 1956," both in "Reedy: Memos Fall 1956," box 419, Reedy Files, Senate Papers.

35. In the 1950s the Texas Democrats had a spring convention and a fall convention, the latter sometimes called "the governor's convention." Dallek, *Lone Star Rising*, 505; Green, *Establishment*, 177–178; Dugger, Connally, auth. int.

36. Dugger, "Gonzalez of San Antonio," part IV, *Texas Observer*, Oct. 18, 1980, 4–5; *Austin American-Statesman*, Aug. 15, 1956; Davidson, *Race and Class in Texas Politics*, 164–166; Contreras, Munguía, auth. int.

37. Green, *Establishment*, 178; J. J. Pickle, int. by Joe B. Frantz, LBJL.

38. J. T. Rutherford to Raymund Telles Jr., March 22, 1957, in "Texas Mayors," LBJA Selected Names, box 34, Senate Papers; LBJ to H. García, Oct. 15, 1957, "Personal Letters—L," García Papers; Dallek, *Lone Star Rising*, 166; H. García to LBJ, Nov. 17, 1957, Rufus McLean to LBJ, Dec. 2, 1957, Arthur Perry to H. García, Dec. 5, 1957, all in 1957 Case and Project Files, box 1292, Senate Papers; Allsup, *G.I. Forum*, 100–101.

39. *Giant* won an Academy Award for best direction. Morris, *North toward Home*, 308; Halliwell, *Film Guide*, 550.

40. Allsup, *G.I. Forum*, 63; *Giant*, Warner Brothers, 1956; Ferber, *Giant*, 155–157, 269–270, 274–277, 309, 414–415; Idar, auth. int.

41. Villanueva eventually graduated from Johnson's alma mater, Southwest Texas State. *Scene from the Movie Giant* won the 1994 National Book Award for poetry. Presentation, Tino Villanueva; Villanueva, *Scene from the Movie Giant*, 25–27; Burns, *Crosswinds of Freedom*, 348–352; *Austin American-Statesman*, March 2, 1986.

42. Dyer, "Lyndon B. Johnson and Civil Rights," 113–114; Miller, *Lyndon*, 211–212; "Judiciary Civil Rights," folders, 1957, Legislative Files, 1957–58, box 289, Senate Papers; Conkin, *Big Daddy from the Pedernales*, 140–142; Reedy, *Lyndon B. Johnson*, 113; Dallek, *Lone Star Rising*, 497; George Reedy, "Memorandum," in "Reedy: Memos Fall 1956," box 419, Senate Papers.

43. Reedy, *Lyndon B. Johnson*, 117; Dallek, *Lone Star Rising*, 517–518, 526–527.

44. Dugger, "Gonzalez of San Antonio"; Dugger, *Texas Observer*, May 7, 1957, reprinted Jan. 10, 1985; Robert Sherrill and Ernesto Cortés Jr., both in the *Texas Observer*, Dec. 13, 1991; *Austin American-Statesman*, Oct. 22, 1957.

45. *San Antonio News*, May 6, 1958; *Dallas News*, May 6, 1958, June 1, 1958; Pickle, int. by Joe B. Frantz, LBJL; Dugger, "Gonzalez of San Antonio."

46. "Statements of Lyndon Baines Johnson," index, 61, LBJL; Arturo G. González to LBJ, Feb. 23, 1957, "[Judiciary] Civil Rights—1957," Legislative Files, 1957–58, box 289, Senate Papers; Arturo González to LBJ, Aug. 4, 1958, in "[Elections] Campaign, 1958—County Conventions," 1958 Subject Files, box 599, Senate Papers; LBJ to H. García, Feb. 4, 1959, Feb. 19, 1959, April 22, 1959, and July 14, 1959, all in "Personal Letters—L," García Papers.

47. Alonso Perales to LBJ, April 21, 1958; LBJ to Alonso Perales, April 21, 1958; Luz Salazar to LBJ, June 11, 1958; and Robert Goodwin to LBJ, June 13, 1958, all in "Labor, Mex. Labor," 1958 Subject Files, box 605, Senate Papers.

48. Memorandum, Walter Jenkins to LBJ, May 1, 1958, in "Mexican Labor," 1958 Subject Files, box 604, Senate Papers; transcript, tel. conversation,

Walter Jenkins to Secretary Mitchell, May 2, 1958, in "Labor: Mexican Labor," 1958 Subject Files, box 605, Senate Papers.

49. For the many letters in support of P.L. 78, see the two "Mexican Labor" Senate boxes cited below. Six letters and one telegram: Roy Perkins to LBJ, May 22, 1958; Robert Goodwin to LBJ, June 6, 1958; LBJ to Roy Perkins, June 7, 1958; Wright Boyd to LBJ, Jan. 11, 1958; telegram, Raymond Pribyla to LBJ, June 11, 1957; N. Raymond Hays Jr. to LBJ, May 13, 1958; LBJ to L. L. Coleman, May 2, 1958, all seven in "Mexican Labor [1 of 5]," 1958 Subject Files, box 604, Senate Papers; memorandum, Loyd Hand to LBJ, April 18, 1958, "Bracero Labor: Kleberg and surrounding counties," 1958 Subject Files, Senate Papers; over 100 messages from growers; telegram, LBJ and Joe Kilgore, April 17, 1958, all in "Mexican Labor [4 of 5]," 1958 Subject Files, box 605, Senate Papers; LBJ to C. H. Langford, June 21, 1958, "Mexican Labor [3 of 5]," 1958 Subject Files, box 605, Senate Papers.

50. Telegram, Lionel Kroll to LBJ, "Mexican Labor [1 of 5]," 1958 Subject Files, box 604, Senate Papers; telegram, M. T. Ramírez to LBJ, Jan. 25, 1958; LBJ to William Herndon, Jan. 27, 1958; John Wildenthal Jr. to LBJ, Jan. 30, all in "La Salle County," Correspondence, box 1723, Senate Papers.

51. John Wildenthal Jr. to LBJ, Feb. 4, 1958, "La Salle County," Correspondence, box 1723, Senate Papers; Wildenthal, auth. int.; Mrs. Morris M. Reese to LBJ, Feb. 14, 1958; LBJ to Mrs. Morris M. Reese, Jan. 25 and Jan. 29, 1958; Cotulla mayor to LBJ, Feb. 2, 1958, all in "La Salle County," Correspondence, box 1723, Senate Papers.

52. When Margaret's husband was ailing, Johnson sent her a letter saying, "Margaret, honey, if there's anything in the world that you or Henry need and I can get it, tell me." LBJ to Margaret Kimball Johnson, June 16, 1953, "Kimball, Margaret," LBJA Select Names, box 22, Senate Papers; Ludeman, *La Salle County*, 125, 187–188; Robert Goodwin to LBJ, May 11, 1958; LBJ to H. Sullivan, April 26, 1958, both in "Mexican Labor [2 of 5]," 1958 Subject Files, box 604, Senate Papers.

53. Memorandum, Loyd Hand to LBJ, May 1, 1958, "Mexican Labor [1 of 5]," 1958 Subject Files, box 604, Senate Papers; telegram, LBJ to Lyan Walker, May 1, 1958; telegram, LBJ to Fred Raney, April 19, 1958, all in "Mexican Labor [2 of 5]," 1958 Subject Files, box 604, Senate Papers.

54. Telegram, LBJ to W. C. Mitchell, Jan. 28, 1959; list, "Texas Group. Concerning Bracero," Feb. 9, 1959; Joe Kilgore to LBJ, n.d., all three in "Labor—Mexican [3 of 3]," 1959 Subject File, box 684, Senate Papers; ten items: Doyle L. Ziler to LBJ, March 6, 1959; LBJ to Doyle Ziler, April 7, 1959; LBJ to G. R. White, April 7, 1959; J. C. Looney to LBJ, April 3, 1959; LBJ to J. C. Looney, April 14, 1959; resolution, Texas House of Representatives, June 16, 1959; LBJ to Price Daniel, June 23, 1959; Price Daniel to LBJ, June 12, 1959; Harold C. Nystrom to Frank Schuster, Aug. 31, 1959; memorandum, Arthur Perry to LBJ, Sept. 10, 1959, all in "Labor—Mexican, [1 of 3]," 1959 Subject Files, box 684, Senate Papers; memorandum, Jim Wilson to George Reedy, n.d., and Arthur C. Perry to LBJ, July 11, 1959, both in "Labor—Mexican [2 of 3]," 1959 Subject Files, box 684, Senate Papers; Teodora Olivera to LBJ,

March 10, 1959, and H. García to Sam Rayburn, May 28, 1959, both in "Labor—Mexican [3 of 3]," 1959 Subject Files, box 684, Senate Papers; three letters: Mrs. Glenn Woody and Mrs. William Hassler to LBJ, Feb. 21, 1959; Norma H. Stauffer to LBJ June 21, 1959; LBJ to Norma H. Stauffer, all three in "Labor—Mexican [2 of 3]," 1959 Subject Files, box 684, Senate Papers; six items: Ralph Castillo to LBJ, June 9, 1959; LBJ to Ralph Castillo, June 12, 1959; E. Idar to James Mitchell, July 30, 1959; E. Idar to LBJ, Aug. 4, 1959; LBJ to E. Idar, Aug. 15, 1959; note, Walter Jenkins, n.d. [Aug. 15, 1959?], all six in "Labor—Mexican [1 of 3]," 1959 Subject Files, box 684, Senate Papers.

55. *Texas Observer*, Dec. 14, 1984.

56. Dallek, *Lone Star Rising*, 352; *Texas Observer*, Dec. 14, 1984; Billy Lee Brammer, *The Gay Place*, 146, 165.

CHAPTER 6

1. Bill Davidson, "Texas Political Powerhouse . . . Lyndon Johnson," *Look*, Aug. 4, 1959, 43; Reedy, auth. int.; Evans and Novak, *Lyndon B. Johnson*, 241, 247, 253; Reedy, *Lyndon Johnson*, 52, 128; transcript, Warren Woodward, in "LBJ: The Difference He Made," Austin, Texas, June 3–5, 1990.

2. In private Johnson on occasion referred to some of the northern Democratic operatives as "Those Irish thieves and labor goons." Bill Davidson, "Lyndon Johnson: Can a Southerner Be Elected President?," *Look*, Aug. 18, 1959, 63–64+. 66; Dyer, "Lyndon B. Johnson and Civil Rights"; Davidson, "Texas Political Powerhouse . . . Lyndon Johnson," *Look*, Aug. 4, 1959, 38+. 44.

3. For the voluminous mail against P.L. 78 (including ten GI Forum letters), see "Labor—Mexico," 1960 Subject Files, box 778, Senate Papers; Allsup, *G.I. Forum*, 123–125.

4. H. García to LBJ, May 18, 1960, and LBJ to H. García, July 4, 1960, both in "Labor—Mexico," 1960 Subject Files, box 778, Senate Papers; *Forum News Bulletin*, Nov.–Dec. 1960, 1.

5. Munguía, auth. int.; Henry B. González to LBJ, Feb. 13, 1960, and LBJ to Henry B. González, Feb. 20, 1960, both in "Cas–Caz," Master File Index, box 1872, Senate Papers.

6. Larry Jones to H. García, April 27, 1960, in "Hallway box—L," García Papers; draft, H. García, "Confidential Report for Sen. Lyndon Joynson [sic], June 10, 1960," "Personal Letters—L," García Papers; Dyer, "Lyndon Johnson and Civil Rights," 179, 195.

7. Draft, H. García, "Confidential Report for Sen. Lyndon Joynson [sic], June 10, 1960," "Personal Letters—L," García Papers; *Austin American-Statesman*, March 2, 1986; Hurtado, *An Attitudinal Study*, 50–58; Cecil Burney, int. by David McComb, LBJL; J. C. Looney, int. by Joe B. Frantz, LBJL; H. García, Bernal, Gallegos, Dugger, Connally, auth. int.

8. Evans and Novak, *Lyndon B. Johnson*, 249; Goodwin, *Remembering America*, 79-80, 89.

9. Evans and Novak, *Lyndon B. Johnson*, 249, 265; *Austin American-Statesman*, March 2, 1986.

10. Burney, int. by David McComb, LBJL; Peña, auth. int.

11. Raúl Morín to George Reedy, Nov. 26, 1963, file 5, box 51, García Papers; Meier, *Mexican American Biographies*, 148; Morín, *Among the Valiant*.

12. Johnson had gotten the Texas state legislature to allow him to run for the vice presidency without giving up his Senate seat. State Senator Henry B. González criticized his friend Johnson for this move, which González considered a usurpation of power. Evans and Novak, *Lyndon B. Johnson*, 280, 287-288, 305-308; Banks, *Money, Marbles, and Chalk*, 96-98; Reedy, Meeks, auth. int.

13. Rodríguez, auth. int.

14. Evans and Novak, *Lyndon B. Johnson*, 292; Allsup, *G.I. Forum*, 133; Dugger, "Gonzalez of San Antonio," part IV, *Texas Observer*, Oct. 17, 1980, 2; Rodriguez, *Henry B. Gonzalez*, 110; H. García, auth. int.

15. McCormick's father had long been a leader of the Alianza Hispano Americana. *Forum News Bulletin*, Nov.-Dec. 1969; Ramos, H. García, Idar, auth. int.

16. Dugger, "Gonzalez of San Antonio," part IV, *Texas Observer*, Oct. 17, 1980, 5; Allsup, *G.I. Forum*, 70; Looney, int. by David McComb, LBJL, 18-19; J. J. Pickle, int. by Joe B. Frantz, LBJL; Peña, Ramos, H. García, Carrillo, auth. int.

17. H. García, Idar, auth. int. Reston, *Lone Star*, 198.

18. Rodríguez, *Henry B. Gonzalez*, 111; Marín, *A Spokesman of the Mexican American Movement*, 2-3; Lady Bird Johnson to Mrs. Raymund Telles, Sept. 7, 1960, "Telles," box 588, Macy Files; *Forum News Bulletin*, Nov.-Dec. 1960; Rubén Munguía, introduction to Gus García, "Los Chávez," file 7, box 82, García Papers; H. García to LBJ, Nov. 17, 1960, box 49, García Papers; radio transcript, H. García, 1960, file 53, box 85, García Papers; G. Sánchez to Dr. Goldstein, Oct. 27, 1960, "Viva Kennedy," box 22, Sánchez Papers; Rodríguez, H. García, Idar, Roybal, auth. int.

19. Manuela González Contreras to LBJ, June 30, 1962, LBJA Selected Names, Senate Papers; Rose, "Gender and Civic Activism in California Barrios"; Peña, Contreras, Idar, auth. int.

20. Connally, Idar, Carrillo, auth. int.

21. Hunter and Hunter, "'My Dear Friend,'" 41-44; Carrillo, auth. int.

22. LBJ to H. García, Aug. 25, 1960, and Oct. 21, 1960, both in "Hallway box—L," García Papers; Clifton Carter, int. by Dorothy Pierce, LBJL; H. García, Idar, auth. int.

23. White, *The Professional*; Reedy, *Lyndon B. Johnson*, 52, 130.

24. Moyers, "Epilogue," 352.

25. Johnson biographer William S. White also cited the Mexican-Texan vote as crucial. Telegram, n.d., JFK to Albert Peña, in "What is PASO?" n.d.,

file 1, box 75, García Papers; *Forum News Bulletin*, Nov.–Dec. 1960; White, *The Professional*, 102; Looney, int. by David McComb, LBJL; H. García, Peña, auth. int.

26. E. Idar to Arthur Krock, Dec. 19, 1960, Idar Papers; Dugger, Connally, Idar, auth. int.

27. Calvert and De León, *History of Texas*, 379; Reedy, Moyers, auth. int.

28. *Forum News Bulletin*, Nov.–Dec. 1960; Civic Action Committee [Houston], *Bulletin*, Jan. 1961, 1; Jan. 27, 1961; Albert Peña to "Democrat," "Viva Kennedy," box 22, Sánchez Papers.

29. *Corpus Christi Times*, Feb. 8, 1961; *Harris County PASO Fact Book*, box 9, Sánchez Papers; E. Idar, "Epilogue," April 14, 1961, box 31, Sánchez Papers; Acuña, *Occupied America*, 287; Johnson, *My Brother Lyndon*, "acknowledgment"; Roybal, auth. int.

30. "What is PASO?" n.d. file 1, box 75, García Papers; Acuña, *Occupied America*, 314.

31. Jose Alvarado to JFK, Feb. 11, 1969, box 203, Macy Files; H. García to LBJ, Nov. 17, 1960, box 49, García Papers; Allsup, *G.I. Forum*, 133; *Austin American-Statesman*, March 2, 1986; "Garcia Praises Kennedy Highly," *Corpus Christi Caller*, Oct. [no day given] 1961, and H. García to Manuel Avila Jr., Oct. 28, 1961, both in file 27, box 46, García Papers; H. García, Idar, auth. int.

32. For Dr. Sánchez's foreign policy advice to the Kennedy administration, see "Peace Corps—Corr.," box 16, and "Viva Kennedy," box 22, Sánchez Papers. "High Job Offered Latin American: Hector Garcia in on Talks," *Corpus Christi Times*, Feb. 8, 1961; G. Sánchez to JFK, Jan. 16, 1962, file 56, box 52, García Papers.

33. E. Idar to G. Sánchez, Feb. 27, 1961, "Viva Kennedy," box 22, Sánchez Papers; E. Idar to H. García, Oct. 26, 1959, García Personal Papers; Connally, auth. int.

34. Ezequiel D. Salinas to H. García, n.d., and Ezequiel Salinas to H. García, Jan. 7, 1961, both in box 49, Sánchez Papers; E. Idar to H. García, Oct. 26, 1959, Ezequiel Salinas to H. García and J. A. García, Oct. 28, 1959, García Personal Papers; E. Idar, "Epilogue"; Oscar Laurel to JFK, Feb. 1, 1961, "Viva Kennedy," box 22, Sánchez Papers; *Corpus Christi Times*, Feb. 8, 1961; Burney, int. by David McComb, LBJL.

35. Canales wrote in favor of two other candidates as well, Judge H. A. García and Judge Fidencio M. Guerra, suggesting the three people "not in order of preference, but in alphabetical order." J. T. Canales to Lyndon B. Johnson, Feb. 1, 1961, folder 2, box 430, J. T. Canales Estate Collection; Ezequiel Salinas to H. García, Jan. 7, 1961, LBJ to H. García, March 11, 1960, E. Idar, "Confidential Memo," and E. Idar, "Epilogue," April 14, 1961, all in box 31, Sánchez Papers; E. Idar to G. Sánchez, March 20, 1961, E. Idar to Ralph Yarborough, March 10, 1961, and G. Sánchez to James Boren, March 16, 1961, all three in "Viva Kennedy," box 22, Sánchez Papers; G. Sánchez, "A New Frontier Policy for the Americas," extension of remarks of Honorable

Ralph W. Yarborough, 87th Congress, First Session, *Congressional Record*, vol. 107, no. 41, March 8, 1961; Idar, auth. int.

36. García opposed the Garza nomination even though Garza was a distant relative. Cleotilde García, H. García, Idar, auth. int.; E. Idar, "Epilogue," Idar Papers; Acuña, *Occupied America*, 352; Reynaldo Garza, int. by Joe B. Frantz, LBJL; Teodoro R. Estrada to H. García, March 22, 1962, file 43, box 48, García Papers; H. García to Manuel Avila Jr., July 22, 1961, file 27, box 46, García Papers; H. García to G. Sánchez, June 12, 1961, box 5, "Hector Garcia," Sánchez Papers.

37. "Gonzalez Runs for U.S. Senate," Civic Action Committee [Houston] *Bulletin*, Jan. 1961, 1; Dugger, "Gonzalez of San Antonio," part IV, *Texas Observer*, Oct. 17, 1980, 2–6; Maury Maverick to G. Sánchez, Feb. 2, 1961, box 22, Sánchez Papers. Joe Benham, "Maverick to Back Gonzalez in Race," *Dallas Morning News*, June 14, 1961; Robert Baskin, "Kennedy Writes Gonzalez Letter," *Dallas News*, Oct. 31, 1961; Peña, auth. int.

38. "LBJ Effort Seen to Help Gonzalez," *Dallas Morning News*, Nov. [?] 1961; Rodriguez, *Henry B. Gonzalez*, 115; Cliff Carter, int. by Dorothy Pierce, LBJL; "Gonzalez Lauded, LBJ Draws Fire," *Dallas News*, Nov. 6, 1961; E. Idar [?], "Suggestions—Kenneth O'Donnell," file 44, box 51, García Papers; Manuela González Contreras, auth. int.

39. Carter, int. by Dorothy Pierce, LBJL; *Dallas Morning News*, Nov. [5 or 6], 1961; Reedy, Munguía, auth. int.

40. Terrell Maverick subsequently married historian Walter Prescott Webb, who had worked for a time for Senator Johnson. Terrell Maverick Webb, int. by Joe B. Frantz, LBJL; Carter, int. by Dorothy Pierce, LBJL; Reedy, auth. int.; Daniel Quill, int. Eric Goldman, LBJL.

41. "Gonzalez Lauded, LBJ Draws Fire," *Dallas News*, Nov. 6, 1961; Schmidt, Meeks, auth. int.

42. Dugger, "Gonzalez of San Antonio," part IV, *Texas Observer*, Oct. 17, 1980, 14; Schmidt, Meeks, auth. int.

43. Rodriguez, *Henry B. Gonzalez*, 144; Schmidt, auth. int.

44. Patman had served in the Texas state legislature with Lyndon's father. Dugger, "Gonzalez of San Antonio," part I, *Texas Observer*, April 11, 1980, 1–2; Dugger, "Gonzalez of San Antonio," part IV, *Texas Observer*, Oct. 17, 1980, 14; Schmidt, auth. int.

45. Evans and Novak, *Lyndon B. Johnson*, 317; Conkin, *Big Daddy from the Pedernales*, 162–163.

46. The Forum memo also urged lobbying efforts to get Hispanics on the White House staff and in the attorney general's office. E. Idar [?], "Suggestions—Kenneth O'Donnell," file 44, box 51, García Papers; Albert Peña to Clifton C. Carter, March 14, 1962; memorandum, Cliff Carter to George Reedy, March 19, 1962; memorandum, George Reedy to Cliff Carter, March 20, 1962; Cliff Carter to George Reedy, n.d., all four in "Labor, Equal Employment Opportunity—P," 1962 Subject File, box 4, Civil Rights Papers of the Vice President; Ralph Poblano to LBJ, March 14, 1961; resume, Ralph

Poblano, n.d.; LBJ to Ralph Poblano, March 20, 1961, all three in "Labor, Equal Employment Opportunity, President's Committee, Applicants [2 of 2]," 1961 Subject File, box 1, Civil Rights Papers of the Vice President; George Reedy to LBJ, Oct. 6, 1962, and press release, Nov. 3, 1962, both in "Labor, President's Committee on Equal Employment Opportunity—G," 1962 Subject Files, Civil Rights Papers of the Vice President; H. García to LBJ, March 18, 1963, "Labor, President's Committee on Equal Opportunity [Mar–May]," 1963 Subject File, box 7, Civil Rights Papers of the Vice President; LBJ to H. García, March 25, 1963, file 79, box 51, García Papers.

47. Louis Tellez to LBJ, Jan. 3, 1963, file 34, box 55, García Papers; LBJ to Albert Bonilla, March 31, 1961, in "Labor, Equal Employment Opportunity, Presidential Commission, Case File," 1961 Subject File, Civil Rights Papers of the Vice President; Navy Secretary Korth to LBJ, Sept. 27, 1962, and Louis Lyon to H. García, both in file 81, box 60, García Papers.

48. Conkin, *Big Daddy from the Pedernales*, 162–164; Evans and Novak, *Lyndon B. Johnson*, 317; *Tiempo*, vol. 18, no. 1099 (May 27, 1963) and vol. 18, no. 1100 (June 3, 1963), both in "Equal Employment Opportunity," box 31, Sánchez Papers; Henry Alonso to LBJ, n.d.; Dionicio Morales to LBJ, Jan. 7, 1963; pamphlet, Economic Opportunity Foundation; memorandum, William J. Kendrick to Hobart Taylor, n.d.; LBJ to Dionicio Morales, Feb. 18, 1963, all five in "Labor, President's Committee on Equal Employment Opportunity [Jan.–Feb.]," 1963 Subject File, box 7, Civil Rights Papers of the Vice President, 1961–63.

49. Memorandum, R. Ramos, n.d., Washington, D.C., and Hobart Taylor Jr. to R. Ramos, May 24, 1963, "Pres. Comm. on E. Empt.," Ramos Papers; Ramos, auth. int.

50. "Materials used by Cong. Roybal in introducing V.P. L.B.J." and "Remarks by Vice President Johnson to Mexican American Educational Conference Committee," both Aug. 9, 1963, both in "Statements—Civil Rights," Civil Rights Papers of the Vice President; LBJ to Charles Samario and nineteen others, Aug. [12?], 1963; Carlos Borja to LBJ, Aug. 27, 1963; LBJ to Carlos Borja Jr., Aug. 29, 1963, all three in "Labor—PCEEO—Aug.," box 8, Civil Rights Papers of the Vice President; Gallegos, Roybal, auth. int.

51. Note, LBJ, on "Tentative Prospects, Regional Conference of Community Leaders on Equal Employment Opportunity, Los Angeles, California," and Bill Kendrick to Ivan [Sinclair], Nov. 12, both in "1963, Labor—PCEEO Sept.–Nov.," box 8, Civil Rights Papers of the Vice President; presentation, G. Sánchez, Nov. 14, 1963, box 22, Sánchez Papers.

52. Calvert and De León, *History of Texas*, 381; Clyde Johnson, "Conventional Promise," *Texas Observer*, July 16, 1993.

53. H. García to G. Sánchez, June 12, 1961, "Hector Garcia," box 5, Sánchez Papers; G. Sánchez to E. Idar, Jan. 29, 1962, file 16, box 50, García Papers; R. P. Sánchez and E. Idar to Ronnie Dugger, Jan. 25, 1962, Idar Papers; Dugger, "Gonzalez of San Antonio," part IV, *Texas Observer*, Oct. 17, 1980, 14; Peña, auth. int.

54. González never joined PASO or any other Mexican American organization. E. Idar to G. Sánchez, n.d., "Ed Idar," box 5, Sánchez Papers; *Texas Observer*, Oct. 17, 1980; Peña, auth. int.

55. Sánchez added a favorite aphorism of his, "*A mi no me dan atole con el dedo!* [Don't give me the crumbs!]." G. Sánchez to E. Idar, Jan. 29, 1962, file 16, box 50, García Papers.

56. E. Idar to G. Sánchez, n.d., "Ed Idar," box 5, Sánchez Papers; E. Idar [?], "Suggestions—Kenneth O'Donnell," file 44, box 51, García Papers.

57. G. Sánchez to H. García, April 3, 1962, file 56, box 52, García Papers; Idar, Peña, auth. int.

58. Calvert and De León, *History of Texas*, 381; G. Sánchez to E. Idar, May 16, 1962; E. Idar to G. Sánchez, May 17, 1962; E. Idar to H. García, May 17, 1962, all three in file 56, box 52, García Papers; Idar, auth. int.

59. *Texas Observer*, June 8, 1962; Evans and Novak, *Lyndon B. Johnson*, 330–331; *San Antonio Express*, Oct. 12, 1962; Peña, auth. int.

60. Shockley, *Chicano Revolt in a Texas Town*, 27, 37; Virginia Armstrong, "Nothing Sinister about PASO," *Valley Evening Monitor*, May 27, 1963; Peña, Wildenthal, auth. int.

61. On another occasion Johnson's former students the González brothers, along with their sister Manuela González Contreras, attended an open house hosted by the vice president at his ranch. Ludeman, *La Salle County*, 124–125; "Ludeman Preserves Cotulla History," *Laredo Morning Times*, May 6, 1983; Wildenthal, int. by Gillette, LBJL; Contreras, Dan García, Worthy, auth. int.

62. Margaret Kimball Zimmerman to LBJ, March 1, 1961, and LBJ to Margaret Kimball Zimmerman, March 15, 1961, both in "Kimball, Margaret," box 22, LBJA Select Names, Vice Presidential Papers; Shockley, *Chicano Revolt in a Texas Town*, ch. 2 and 3; "La Raza Unida: The Road to Political Empowerment," episode 4 of Treviño et al., "Chicano! The History of the Mexican American Civil Rights Movement"; Paul Thompson, "Top of the News," *San Antonio News* [?], n.d., file 68, box 63, García Papers; Peña, auth. int.

63. G. Sánchez to John B. Connally, May 2, 1963, box 5, Sánchez Papers; G. Sánchez to William Bonilla, June 17, 1963, file 56, box 52, García Papers; official memorandum, John B. Connally, June 25, 1963, file 70, box 69, García Papers; draft of letter, G. Sánchez to Ronnie Dugger, "Gen. Files—D," box 5, Sánchez Papers.

64. John Mashek, "Senator Not Looking for JFK's Blessing," *Dallas News*, Nov. 19, 1963; Dawson Duncan, "Yarborough Snubs LBJ," *Dallas News*, Nov. 22, 1963; Burney, int. by McComb, LBJL; H. García, Reedy, Connally, auth. int.

65. Translation by Dan William Dickey, *The Kennedy Corridos*, 25–26, 64–65; Reston, *Lone Star*, 289–290; Dawson Duncan, "Yarborough Snubs LBJ," *Dallas News*, Nov. 22, 1963; "LULAC Involved for Mexican Americans," *Corpus Christi Caller*, Feb. 11, 1979; *Forum News Bulletin*, Dec.

1963; Robert Kennedy to José Alvarado, Sept. 20, 1963, file 15, box 61, García Papers; John Herrera to Carlos McCormick, Sept. 21, 1963, Herrera Collection.

66. Carl Freund, "Luncheon Sponsors Ponder Where to Seat Yarborough," *Dallas News*, Nov. 19, 1963; Rodriguez, *Henry B. Gonzalez*, 164; Dickey, *The Kennedy Corridos*, 25–36; Moses Gallegos, "Los Caballos Blancos," file 52, box 75, García Papers; Samora, auth. int.

67. Raúl Morín to George Reedy, Nov. 26, 1963, and Raúl Morín to Bob Rodríguez, Nov. 30, 1963, both in file 5, box 51, García Papers.

CHAPTER 7

1. Dan García, Moyers, auth. int.

2. Transcript, B. Moyers, in "LBJ: The Difference He Made," Austin, Texas, June 3–5, 1990; White House Historical Association, *The White House*, 126–127; Moyers, "Epilogue," 351–352.

3. Conkin, *Big Daddy from the Pedernales*, 208–210; Goodwin, *Remembering America*, 267–271.

4. Conkin, *Big Daddy From the Pedernales*, 210–212; transcript, B. Moyers and Jack Valenti, both in "LBJ: The Difference He Made," Austin, Texas, June 3–5, 1990; Moyers, "Epilogue," 355; Crook, Roybal, auth. int.

5. Meeks, Roybal, auth. int.

6. Goodwin, *Remembering America*, 267–271.

7. Wofford, *Of Kennedys and Kings*, 221; LBJ to Loyd Hand, Dec. 1963, "PL/ST5 Pol. Affairs—Cal. 11/22/63–6/14/64"; Goodwin, *Remembering America*, 285; Conkin, *Big Daddy from the Pedernales*, 211; box 22, Sánchez Papers; Dugger, Samora, auth. int.

8. H. García to LBJ, Sept. 8, 1964, in "Hallway Box—L," García Papers; Ramos, auth. int.

9. Ramos wrote to the White House as early as January 1964, wishing the administration well. Cliff Carter to R. Ramos, Jan. 27, 1964, green notebook, Ramos Papers; R. Ramos, "Report," and R. Ramos to H. García, both June 28, 1964, both in "Misc.—A," box 11, Sánchez Papers; Ramos, auth. int.

10. R. Ramos, "Beginnings of National Mexican-American 'Plan' to Help 'War on Poverty' Program in All Areas with Concentrations of 'Mexican Americans,'" 1964, Ramos Papers; D.C. Forum newsletters, 1964, Ramos Papers; R. Ramos, "Report," Aug. 18, 1964, file 44, box 55, García Papers; R. Ramos, "Report," June 28, 1964, "Misc.—A," box 11, Sánchez Papers; H. García to Fermín Calderón, file 2, box 47, García Papers; Roybal, Ramos auth. int.

11. Rodríguez, *Henry B. Gonzalez*, 115; Dugger, "Gonzalez of San Antonio," part I, *Texas Observer*, April 11, 1980, 1; H. García to Erwin Juraschek, Sept. 5, 1964, file 27, box 50, García Papers; R. Ramos to Willard Wirtz, April 29, 1966, and press release, Nov. 27, 1964, both in "AGIF Information Kit," Ramos Papers; Allsup, *G.I. Forum*, 126; Idar, Gallegos, auth. int.

12. Márquez, *LULAC*, 68–69; Conkin, *Big Daddy from the Pedernales*, 215; Peña, Reedy, auth. int.

13. Joseph Montoya to R. Ramos, May 14, 1965, "National Convention—1972,"; "American GI Forum of the U.S./Washington, D.C. Office," April 30, 1965; D.C. Forum newsletter, 1964; H. García to Robert Weaver, Sept. 14, 1964, all four documents in Ramos Papers; H. García, Reedy, auth. int.

14. Commerce Department, "Status Report," "Human Relations—Equality of the Races [Ex Hu 21]," box 42, WHCF; John Gronouski to LBJ, "Minority Group Employment in the Field Postal Service," Cabinet Meeting, Oct. 5, 1965, and J. Macy to LBJ, April 29, 1965, both in "Federal Government—EEOC," Ex FG 655, WHCF; "Status of School Districts Either Failing or Having Serious Compliance Problems," Sept. 27, 1965, "Human Relations—Equality of the Races: Education/Schooling [Ex Hu 2–5]," box 50, WHCF; Bernal, auth. int.

15. President's Daily Diary Card, Jan. 6, 1964, "Gammal, Alfred–Giles, Lewis," drawer 29, LBJL; "Account of State Department Conference on Equal Employment" in "OEO," "American GI Forum Information Kit," April 1, 1964, Ramos Papers; D.C. Forum newsletter, 1964, and R. Ramos to Jack Valenti, March 13, 1965, green notebook, Ramos Papers; Idar, auth. int.

16. López, "The President and the Spanish-Speaking Vote."

17. H. García and Carlos McCormick to Robert F. Kennedy, 1964, file 55, box 59, García Papers; R. Ramos to Leo Grebler, Aug. 20, 1964, Ramos Papers; pamphlet, "Continuemos Adelante Viva Johnson y Humphrey," in "Hallway Box—L," García Papers.

18. *Forum News Bulletin*, Nov. 1964; Ximenes, Ramos, auth. int.

19. Meier, *Mexican American Biographies*, 62; Meier and Ribera, *Mexican Americans/American Mexicans*, 203; Michael Mosettig, "Latin American Votes Sought by Democrats, GOP," *Corpus Christi Caller*, Sept. 22, 1964.

20. A. D. Azios to Bill Kilgarlin, Sept. 29, 1964, file 29, box 104, García Papers; V. Ximenes to Craig Raupe, file 29, box 107, García Papers; special supplement, *El Diario/La Prensa*, Nov. 2, 1964; Ramos, auth. int.

21. Cleotilde García, Dec. 2, 1964, and V. Ximenes, n.d., to Craig Raupe, file 29, box 104, García Papers; H. García to Dr. Fermín Calderón, Sept. 22, 1964, file 2, box 42, García Papers; Meier, *Mexican American Biographies*, 22; Robert Canino, "Viva Johnson Headquarters," file 29, box 104, García Papers; *Noticias* (Chicago), Nov. 7, 1964; "Viva Girls," in "Hallway Box—L," García Papers; Rhinehart and Kreneck, "The Minimum Wage March of 1966"; Cleotilde García, Connally, auth. int.

22. Rodríguez also was a delegate to the 1964 Democratic National Convention in Atlantic City. H. García, speech, n.d., and H. García to LBJ, Oct. 22, 1964, both in "Hallway Box—L," García Papers; "Message from Dr. Hector Garcia to all his friends," n.d., "Personal Letters—J," García Papers; form speech, n.d., file 51, box 104, García Papers; Rodríguez, H. García, Idar, auth. int.

23. Rodríguez, Gallegos, auth. int.

24. LBJ, Oct. 28, 1964, "Albuquerque" and "Remarks of the President and Mrs. Lyndon B. Johnson," Oct. 28, 1964, Moyers Files, box 28, LBJL; Allsup, *G.I. Forum*, 136; Idar, auth. int.

25. Michael Mosettig, "Latin American Votes Sought by Democrats, GOP," *Corpus Christi Caller*, Sept. 22, 1964; V. Ximenes to Craig Raupe, file 29, box 107, García Papers; *The Eagles* (Los Angeles), Oct. 13, 1964.

26. V. Ximenes to Craig Raupe, file 29, box 107, García Papers; John Bailey to H. and Mrs. García, Dec. 4, 1964, file 29, box 104, García Papers.

27. Wofford, *Of Kennedys and Kings*, 288; Reedy, *Lyndon B. Johnson*, 44, 138; Sherrill, *The Accidental President*, 19; Califano, *Triumph and Tragedy*, 339.

28. Rodríguez, *Henry B. Gonzalez*, 139–140; Schmidt, Meeks, auth. int.

29. Dugger, "Gonzalez of San Antonio," part I, *Texas Observer*, April 11, 1980; President's Daily Diary Cards, under "Gonzalez, Henry B.," "Giles, Robt.–Gordon, Lincoln," drawer 30, LBJL.

30. Dugger, "Gonzalez of San Antonio," part I, *Texas Observer*, April 11, 1980; Wicker, *JFK and LBJ*, 196.

31. Califano, Meeks, Schmidt, auth. int.; Green, *Establishment*, 204.

32. *Oakland MAPA Newsletter*, Jan. 9, 1967, folder 3, box 67, "UFW-President," Reuther Archives; pamphlet, Jobs for Progress, Inc., "Service Employment Redevelopment," Ramos Papers; memorandum, "SER," Ramos Papers; González, Tijerina, auth. int.

33. One photograph featured a community training session led by long-time farmworker activist Dr. Ernesto Galarza. "National Mexican-American War on Poverty Program," in "National Convention—1972," Ramos Papers; "Manpower Opportunity Project, Works for You/el Proyecto de Oportunidades para el Trabajador obra para usted," file 69, box 105, García Papers; D.C. Forum newsletter, Aug. 18, 1964, Ramos Papers; Ramos, H. García, auth. int.

34. R. Ramos to Father Vizzard, Jan. 3, 1965, and "Preliminary Program, National Conference on Poverty in the Southwest, Tuscon, Arizona," both in "National Convention—1972," Ramos Papers.

35. Telegram, H. García [?], file 17, box 47, García Papers; V. Ximenes to Louis Martin, Feb. 15, 1965, Ximenes Papers; V. Ximenes to Craig Raupe, file 29, box 107, García Papers; V. Ximenes to Cliff Carter, Jan. 27, 1965, "Carlos Chavez," box 97, Macy Files, also in file 17, box 47, García Papers; Dr. Fermín Calderón, Sept. 22, 1964, file 2, box 42, García Papers; H. García to Jose Arredondo, file 25, box 45, García Papers; "Jose Maldonado," box 358, Macy Files; Ximenes, Ramos, auth. int.

36. "Keep up the good work," San Jose editor Robert Rodríguez wrote to Ramos, adding that Mexican Americans continued to be overlooked as directors and staff for the California War on Poverty. Robert V. Rodríguez to R. Ramos, April 4, 1965, "Texas—Mexican American Discrimination," Ramos Papers; "Testimony," April 26, 1965, "OEO," Ramos Papers; "War on Poverty List," file 47, box 64, García Papers; R. Ramos, "National Mexican-American War on Poverty Program," in "National Convention—

1972," Ramos Papers; "Observations by Rudy L. Ramos, Director, Washington, D.C. Office, G.I. Forum: 'Manifesto,'" file 42, box 47, García Papers; Ramos, auth. int.

37. Samuel F. Yelte to R. Ramos, July 15, 1965, file 71, box 94, García Papers; Fred D. Baldwin to Sargent Shriver, Oct. 7, 1965, file 43, box 56, García Papers; Schott and Hamilton, *People, Positions, and Power*, 19; William Crook to Hayes Bernard, Dec. 21, 1965, "Aldrete, Cristobal," box 7, Macy Files; Luz Quintero to William Crook, two letters, n.d., box 21, Sánchez Papers; M. Watson to LBJ, June 30, 1965; M. Watson to Fermín Calderón et al., July 2, 1965, and M. Watson to William Bonilla, July 3, 1965, all in box 26, "WE 9," WHCF; Lorenzo Ramírez, personal profile, n.d., "Lorenzo Ramirez," box 473, Macy Files; Marín, *A Spokesman of the Mexican American Movement*, 3; Ramos, Idar, auth. int.

38. Office of Economic Opportunity, "Narrative History," OEO—Administrative History, vol. I, LBJL, 390–395; Roybal, Peña, auth. int.

39. Resolution no. 11, "1965 Resolutions," Ramos Papers; speech, Dr. William H. Crook, Nov. 27, 1965, file 57, box 47, García Papers; "Articles of Incorporation of Jobs for Progress of Washington, D.C., incorporated" and "National Convention—1972," Ramos Papers; Acuña, *Occupied America*, 341; Ramos, H. García, auth. int.

40. César Chávez to Robert Kennedy, July 22, 1967, folder 6, box 3, "UFW—President," Reuther Archives; Schmidt, Bernal, auth. int.

41. Montejano, *Anglos and Mexicans*, 134, 246–247; Kingston, *The Texas Almanac*, 311; González, auth. int.

42. González, auth. int.

43. Memorandum, William Crook to Hayes Redmond, Dec. 21, 1965, "Aldrete, Cristobal," box 7, Macy Files; Bernal, Crook, Cárdenas, Schmidt, Munguía, Carrillo, auth. int.

44. *Cotulla Record*, Feb. 26, 1965; *San Antonio News*, March 18, 1965; *San Antonio Express-News*, March 21, 1965; *Rocky Mountain News*, Sept. 25, 1965; Dan García, Zamora, auth. int.

45. Transcript, John Connally, in "LBJ: The Difference He Made," Austin, Texas, June 3–5, 1990; Smith, "Women and the White House," 123–129; pamphlet, Jobs for Progress, Inc., "SER," Ramos Papers; Lupe Anguiano to R. Ramos, Sept. 6, 1965, and Cecilia Pedrazo to Louis Martin, Sept. 15, 1965, both in "Talent Bank Replies," Ramos Papers.

46. *The Corpsman*, Sept. 1, 1968, folder 11, box 65, "UFW—President," Reuther Archives; Dominga Coronado, "Mexican American Problems and the Job Corps," in Interagency Committee on Mexican American Affairs, *The Mexican American: New Focus on Opportunity*; González, auth. int.

47. Cleotilde García, auth. int.

48. Memorandum, J. Macy to LBJ, Jan. 25, 1968, "Rosita Cota," box 120, Macy Files; Schechter, *Hope Mendoza Schechter*, 115; María Carrizales to Louis Martin, Nov. 5, 1965, "María Carrizales," box 89, Macy Files.

49. Anguiano, auth. int.

50. D. North to J. Califano, May 9, 1967, "Latin American Conference,"

box 6, Califano Files; Mary Drumond, "Dropout Off to Notre Dame Law School," *Arizona Republic*, July 10, 1967; April Daien, "Woman Lawyer with a Mission: To Help Chicanos," *Arizona Republic*, June 24, 1970, and March 27, 1977; G. Sánchez to Ralph Yarborough, Feb. 28, 1967, box 22, Sánchez Papers; memorandum, Marie C. Barksdale to Joan Thornell, May 3, 1966, "Planning Conference—Subject Files," LBJL; Anguiano, auth. int.

51. Conkin, *Big Daddy from the Pedernales*, 216–217; "Message on Voting Rights," March 15, 1965, Ex Sp. 2–3/1965/ HU2–7, box 67, WHCF; Goodwin, *Remembering America*, 229–230, 285; LBJ to H. García, March 24, 1965, "American GI Forum Information Kit," Ramos Papers; press release, Aug. 6, 1965, "P.L. 89–110," in "Task Forces Related to Civil Rights," box 22, WHCF; LBJ to Dan García, March 22, 1965, in "Garcia, Daniel C.," box 28, WHCF-NF; Bernal, Dan García, auth. int.

52. García, *Mexican Americans*, 61.

CHAPTER 8

1. De León, *Ethnicity in the Sunbelt*, 164–165, 170–173; Rodríguez, auth. int.; R. Ramos to Louis Telles, March 18, 1966, Ramos Papers; "Observations by Rudy L. Ramos, Director, Washington, D.C. Office, G.I. Forum: 'Manifesto,'" file 42, box 47, García Papers; Califano, *Triumph and Tragedy*, 136.

2. Hernández's stance was a clear departure from the position of some oldtime Lulackers such as former president Félix Tijerina, who maintained a "whites only" policy in his Houston restaurant until this became illegal under the Civil Rights Act of 1964. Márquez, "The Politics of Race and Class," 97; De León, *Ethnicity in the Sunbelt*, 164–165, 170–173; "M.A.P.A. State Board Executive Resolution," Feb. 11–12, 1966, file 62, box 38, García Papers; "Observations by Rudy L. Ramos, Director, Washington, D.C. Office, G.I. Forum: 'Manifesto,'" file 42, box 47, García Papers.

3. H. García, "Personal," to LBJ, n.d., box 203, Macy Files; LBJ to H. García, Feb. 12, 1966, in "Garcia, Hector P.," box 29, WHCF-NF.

4. United Press International, March 8, 1966, in "Federal Government—EEOC," Ex FG 655, WHCF; report, "Mexican American Situations, March 1966," in "Federal Government—EEOC," Ex FG 655, WHCF; Evans and Novak, "Inside Report," *Washington Post*, March 31, 1966; *Corpus Christi Caller*, Jan. 21, 1966; Franklin Roosevelt Jr. to G. Sánchez, April 26, 1966, and G. Sánchez to Franklin Roosevelt Jr., May 5, 1966, box 10, Sánchez Papers.

5. García, *Memories of Chicano History*; Califano, *Triumph and Tragedy*, 11–12; Goodwin, *Remembering America*, 405–406; Wofford, *Of Kennedys and Kings* 330.

6. García, *Memories of Chicano History*, 232–233; Chester, Hodgson, and Page, *An American Melodrama*, 314–315; Dean, *The Kennedys*; Levy, *César Chávez*, 288.

7. Press release, Southern California Delegation, March 17, 1966, "Federal Government—EEOC," Ex FG 655, MC HU2-1, WHCF; Rodríguez, Ramos, auth. int.

8. "Richard Graham," EEOC, Biographical Appendix, Administrative History"; EEOC, "Administrative History—Technical Assistance, Albuquerque Conference on Job Discrimination," March 28, 1966, 185–189, both in Administrative History Files, LBJL; news release, [April 1966?], American GI Forum, file 67, box 59, García Papers; *Albuquerque Journal*, March 29, 1966; Rhinehart and Kreneck, "The Minimum Wage March of 1966," 31; Ramos, Anguiano, Yzaguirre, auth. int.

9. Secretary of Defense Robert McNamara had refused to hire Roosevelt, saying that Roosevelt was "a drunk and a womanizer"; Kennedy had replied, "I guess I'll have to take care of him some other way." Reeves, *President Kennedy*, 29; Carlos Rivera to M. Watson, March 30, 1966, "Federal Government—EEO," Ex FG 655, MC HU2-1, WHCF; Califano, auth. int.; *New York Times*, April 1, 1966; R. Ramos, "Observations," n.d. [1965?], file 42, box 47, García Papers; *Wall Street Journal*, June 3, 1966; Chairman, EEOC to LBJ, April 7, 1966, "Federal Government—EEOC," WHCF.

10. R. Ramos to J. Macy and Mexican American Ad Hoc Committee on Equal Employment Opportunity, April 22, 1966, and Gilbert Schulkind to R. Ramos, both in file 67, box 59, García Papers; Roybal, Ramos, auth. int.

11. Rowland Evans and Robert Novak, "Civil Rights Concern: Conservative Texas Clergyman May Become Chairman of Rights Enforcement Group," *Washington Post*, June 5, 1966; J. Califano to H. McPherson, Aug. 9, 1966, "Mexican Americans," box 11, McPherson Files; Rowland Evans and Robert Novak, "Inside Report," *Washington Post*, March 31, 1966; Luther Holcomb to M. Watson and Jim Jones, Feb. 17, 1966, in "Federal Government—EEO," Ex FG 655, WHCF; Luther Holcomb to M. Watson, April 27, 1966, "Federal Government—EEOC," Ex FG 166, WHCF; M. Watson to James Moyers, "Federal Government—EEOC," Ex ME 318, FG 655, WHCF; R. Ramos, "Washington, D.C. Report," file 67, box 59, García Papers; "Political Intelligence," *Texas Observer*, Sept. 19, 1966; James Falcon to Jake Jacobsen, Dec. 2, 1966, "Federal Governmennt—EEOC," Ex Hu 2-1, WHCF; H. García to Hobart Taylor, Sept. 8, 1964, file 70, box 61, García Papers.

12. Dick Graham to B. Moyers, April 14, 1966, "Personal," and May 20, 1966, also "Personal," both in "Federal Government—EEO," Ex FG 655; Bert Corona to B. Moyers, April 25, 1966, Macy Files; R. Ramos, "Washington Report," Mexican American Ad Hoc Committee, file 67, box 59, García Papers; César Chávez, "Peregrinación, Penitencia, Revolución," n.d., folder 4, box 48, "UFW-President," Reuther Archives.

13. *New York Times*, Nov. 7, 1965; R. Ramos, "Washington Report," n.d., Mexican Ad Hoc Committee on Equal Opportunity, and R. Ramos, "Washington, D.C. Report," both in file 67, box 59, García Papers; Joan Moore and Ralph Guzmán, "New Wind from the Southwest," *The Nation*, May 30, 1966; *Washington Post*, April 15, 1966; "Planning Conference—

Subject Files" "Recommendations . . .," April 13, 1966, and R. Ramos to Willard Wirtz, April 29, 1966, both in "AGIF Information Kit," Ramos Papers; Dr. William H. Crook, Nov. 27, 1965, file 57, box 47, García Papers.

14. Bert Corona to B. Moyers, April 25, 1966, Macy Files; R. Ramos to LBJ, April 25, 1966, file 67, box 59, García Papers; Califano, auth. int.; press release, May 22 and May 23, 1966, file 71, box 92, García Papers.

15. *Corpus Christi Caller*, May 28, 1966; R. Ramos, "Observations," n.d., file 42, box 47, García Papers; R. Ramos, "Washington, D.C. Report," file 67, box 59, García Papers; Ramos, Yzaguirre, H. García, auth. int.; H. McPherson to Ralph Guzmán, May 25, 1966, "Gen. Hu2 CO190, Hu2/MC," FG 655, WHCF; Roy Elizondo to PASO members, June 16, 1966, box 9, Sánchez Papers; Califano, *Triumph and Tragedy*, 136–137; García, *Memories of Chicano History*, 218–219.

16. *Wall Street Journal*, June 3, 1966; J. Macy to LBJ, "A Latin for the EEOC," June 29, 1966, box 97, Macy Files; Johnson, *Johnson Presidential Press Conferences*, vol. I, 466–467; García, *Memories of Chicano History*, 219; Anguiano, auth. int.

17. Joe Bernal, who had come up from San Antonio, recalled that all of the 1,500 conference participants were black or white, except for about fifteen Mexican Americans, who had no voice because they were considered white. Bernal, Ramos, and some others walked out, joined by a few blacks, who picketed alongside them. R. Ramos, "Washington, D.C. Report"; American GI Forum news release, n.d.; R. Ramos to Agustine Flores, n.d., all three in file 67, box 59, García Papers; Ramos, Bernal, Yzaguirre, auth. int.

18. Report, Aug. 2, 1966, "OEO," Ramos Papers; Wofford, *Of Kennedys and Kings*, 319.

19. Idar, auth. int.; *El Paso Herald-Post*, Dec. 6, 1967; *Corpus Christi Caller*, Dec. 5, 1967; "William H. Crook's VISTA Graduation Speech, El Paso, Texas," Dec. 4, 1967, box 17, Sánchez Papers; G. Sánchez to William Crook, Dec. 6, 1967, "Mexican American Joint Conference," box 18, Sánchez Papers.

20. Gallegos, auth. int.

21. Meeks, auth. int.

22. Gallegos, Cleotilde García, auth. int.; Abe Goertzen to LBJ, Nov. 12, 1965, in "Chavez, A–E," box 186, WHCF-NF; Marín, *A Spokesman of the Mexican American Movement*, 4; Rendón, *Chicano Manifesto*, 123; "Rodolfo 'Corky' Gonzalez," folder 29, box 26, Reuther Archives; R. Ramos to Willard Wirtz, April 29, 1966, "AGIF Information Kit," Ramos Papers; *Rocky Mountain News*, April 21 and 22, 1966; *Denver Post*, April 23 and 24, 1966.

23. Idar, auth. int.; Sargent Shriver to LBJ, "Office of Economic Opportunity," box 56, Moyers Files; Reston, *Lone Star*, 301–304; John Rogers, "Poverty behind the Cactus Curtain," file 3, box 58, García Papers.

24. Father Elizondo is now rector of San Fernando Cathedral, San Antonio, Texas. Elizondo, *The Future Is Mestizo*, 30–31.

25. *Dallas News*, Sept. 25, 1965; *New York Times*, Feb. 15, 1966; Ralph

Yarborough, "The Mexican Americans of the Southwest," *Congressional Record*, vol. 112, no. 75, May 5, 1966, in file 3, box 58, García Papers; Peña, auth. int.

26. Reston, *Lone Star*, 302; Califano, Crook, auth. int.; Califano, *Triumph and Tragedy*, 78; transcript, B. Moyers, in "LBJ: The Difference He Made," Austin, Texas, June 3-5, 1990.

27. Wofford, *Of Kennedys and Kings*, 321; *New York Times*, Nov. 7, 1965; Schott and Hamilton, *People, Positions, and Power*, 121-122; Califano, *Triumph and Tragedy*, 78-80; Wofford, *Of Kennedys and Kings*, 119; Reedy, *Lyndon B. Johnson*, 47-49.

28. "Labor Day in Austin" was the title of the *Texas Observer* issue of Sept. 16, 1966. Montejano, *Anglos and Mexicans*, 284; Carrillo, auth. int.

29. "Washington, D.C., Huelga Committee," Ramos Papers; "Washington, D.C. Report," Aug. 2, 1966, "OEO," Ramos Papers; form letter, Roy Elizondo to G. Sánchez, June 16, 1966, box 9, Sánchez Papers; César Chávez, "Peregrinación, Penitencia, Revolución," n.d., folder 4, box 48, "UFW-President," Reuther Archives; *Sons of Zapata*, n.d., box 9, Sánchez Papers; *Dallas News*, Sept. 1, 1966; *Corpus Christi Caller-Times*, Sept. 1 and Sept. 6, 1966; Cleotilde García, auth. int.; Rhinehart and Kreneck, "The Minimum Wage March of 1966," 27; "King's Aide to Attend Valley Marchers' Rally," *Corpus Christi Times*, Sept. 5, 1966; *LULAC Extra*, vol. I, no. 1, Oct. 1966, 11, in "United Farmworkers Activities in Washington, D.C.," in "National Campaign for Agricultural Democracy—UFWOC," box 8, Reuther Archives.

30. Connally, auth. int.; Rhinehart and Kreneck, "The Minimum Wage March of 1966," 36-37, 39; Greg Olds, "Labor Day in Austin," *Texas Observer*, Sept. 16, 1966.

31. J. C. Looney, int. by Joe B. Frantz, LBJL, 31; Crook, auth. int.; Rogers, "Poverty behind the Cactus Curtain," 23-25; Alan L. Otten, "Two Tall Texans," *Wall Street Journal*, Sept. 28, 1966; M. Watson to LBJ, Oct. 1966, "Pol. Affairs: States—Texas 6/16/66-12/31/67," PL/ST, PL 12-24, LBJL.

32. Johnson, *Johnson Presidential Press Conferences*, vol. 2, 620.

33. Ben Goodwin, "Latin Demos Considering Support of Sen. Tower," *Corpus Christi Times*, Aug. 3, 1966, 1; Rhinehart and Kreneck, "The Minimum Wage March of 1966," 37-38; Reston, *Lone Star*, 70; *Rocky Mountain News*, April 21, 1966.

34. Louis Martin to H. McPherson, Aug. 9, 1966, "Hu2/MC 6/7/66-10/12/66," box 23, WHCF; D. North to J. Califano, Sept. 8 and Sept. 28, "Latin American Conference," box 6, Califano Files; J. Macy to LBJ, Sept. 8, 1966, and "Model Plan of Action," n.d., both in "Mexican Americans," box 11, McPherson Files.

35. Rendón, "La Raza Unida: Today—Not Mañana," 8; D. North to J. Califano, Aug. 18, Oct. 10, and Oct. 11, also telegram, Oct. 28, 1966, all four in "Hu2/MC 6/7/66-10/12/66," box 23, WHCF; D. North to J. Califano, Sept. 28, 1966, and to M. Meier, Oct. 10, 1966, "Hu2/MC 10/13/66," box 23, WHCF; David North to H. García, Oct. 11, 1966, file 58, box 100, García Papers; "Pre-planning for White House Conference," in "Bernal, Joe

J.," box 41, Macy Files. M. Watson to LBJ, Nov. 22, 1966, and Doug Nobles to M. Watson, in "Ernesto Galarza," box 201, Macy Files; D.C. Forum newsletter, Nov. 3, 1966, Ramos Papers; Califano, Samora, Roybal, auth. int.

36. Louis Martin to H. McPherson, Aug. 9, 1966, "Hu2/MC 6/7/66–10/12/66," box 23, WHCF.

37. She also called for MAPA to encourage "more Mexican American and other Spanish-speaking women to run for state and local public offices," in "Mexican American Women," Aug. 17–19, 1966, folder 1, box 67, "UFW-President," Reuther Archives; "Summary of Proceedings—Planning Session of Problems of the Spanish-Speaking People," Oct. 20, Oct. 26, and Oct. 28, 1966, file 64, box 105, García Papers.

38. Blavis, "Tijerina and the Land Grants," in Durán and Bernard, eds., *Introduction to Chicano Studies,* 519, 525; Meier, *Mexican American Biographies,* 219–220; Acuña, *Occupied America,* 340–341; Steiner, *La Raza,* 70–71.

39. Anguiano, auth. int.

40. One notable dissenter was George Sánchez, who considered a White House conference a waste of time; he wanted action, saying, "Do I sound bitter? I am bitter." "Summary of Proceedings," file 64, box 105, García Papers; Rodríguez, auth. int.

41. James C. Falcon, Nov. 3 and Nov. 7, 1966, "Aldrete, Cristobal," box 7, Macy Files; H. McPherson to LBJ, Dec. 1, 1966, and Dec. 13, 1966, "Mexican Americans," box 11, McPherson Files; H. García to LBJ, Dec. 4, 1966, box 100, file 58, García Papers; telephone transcript, LBJ to J. Califano, Dec. 31, 1966, "Ex Hu2/MC," box 23, WHCF.

CHAPTER 9

1. The other two staff members who went to the Southwest were Dave North and Louis Martin. J. Califano to LBJ, Jan. 16, 1967, "Latin American Conference," box 6, Califano Files; Califano, auth. int.; M. Watson to LBJ, Dec. 12, 1966, "Federal Government—EEOC," Ex FG 655, WHCF; M. Watson to LBJ, Jan. 28, 1967, "Ex Hu2/MC 10/13/66," box 23, WHCF.

2. David North to G. Sánchez, April 5, 18, 26, 1967, and June 28, 1967, all in "White House Brochures," box 19, Sánchez Papers; David North to H. García, Jan. 8, 1967, file 67, Feb. 21, 1967, and file 69, both in box 105, García Papers; *The Traveler,* vol. 1, 1967; Hubert H. Humphrey to LBJ, March 1, 1967, "Ex Hu2/MC 10/13/66," box 23, WHCF; memoranda, Sargent Shriver to LBJ, March 22, 1967, and Robert Kintner to LBJ, March 23, 1967, both in "Garcia, Hector P.," box 29, WHCF-NF; Deborah Wager, "The Ten Biggest Myths about OEO," *Communities in Action,* vol. 2, no. 3, April–May 1967, 22–24.

3. Anguiano, Peña, Samora, Bernal, Yarborough, auth. int.; San Miguel, *Let Them All Take Heed,* 192–194.

4. Ralph Yarborough, "Two Proposals," *Congressional Record,* Jan. 17, 1967, vol. 113, no. 5, 21–23; Rodríguez, auth. int.

5. Rodríguez, auth. int.; draft press release, n.d., "Latin American Conference," box 6, Califano Files; *Mexican American Affairs Unit News Bulletin*, file 37, box 95, García Papers.

6. Anguiano, Rodríguez, auth. int.

7. Bert Corona to César Chávez, Feb. 3, 1967, and César Chávez to Bert Corona, n.d., folder 1, box 67, "UFW—President," Reuther Archives; G. Sánchez to Ralph Yarborough, Feb. 1, 1967, and May 26, 1967, box 21, Sánchez Papers; Munguía, auth. int.

8. Califano, Crook, Rodríguez, Yarborough, auth. int.

9. Yarborough, auth. int.; John L. Moore, *Austin American-Statesman*, Jan. 18, 1968.

10. Acuña, *Occupied America* 2d ed., 421n.; Anguiano, Crook, Roybal, Rodríguez, auth. int.

11. Other congressmen inquiring about the conference included John Young of Texas, Frank Evans of Colorado, and Alphonso Bell of California. Jack Jones, *Los Angeles Times*, n.d.; M. Watson to LBJ, Feb. 4, 1967; Congressman Alphonso Bell to Henry Wilson, Feb. 2, 1967, and J. Califano to Jake Jacobsen, Feb. 3, 1967, all three in "Hu2/MC 10/13/66," box 23, WHCF.

12. Press releases, Alberto Piñón, Feb. 12, 1967, "Hu2/MC 10/13/66," box 23, WHCF; press release, Bert Corona and Jess Vela, March 8, 1967, "Mexican Americans," box 11, McPherson Files; "Resolutions of the Mexican and Spanish-Speaking Legislative Conference," March 10, 1967, folder 8, box 67, "UFW—President," Reuther Archives; H. García to David North, March 13, 1967, "Dr. Hector P. García," box 203, Macy Files; Hector Abeytia to "all MAPA Officers and Chapter Chairmen," April 1967, folder 2, box 67, "UFW—President," Reuther Archives.

13. President's Daily Diary Cards, Feb. 16 and April 6, 1967, "Russ, Joseph–Saunders, Stewart," drawer 72, LBJL; President's Commission on Rural Poverty, Feb. 17, 1967, file 69, box 105, García Papers; Gallegos, Samora, auth. int.

14. Secretary Gardner had suggested the HEW office. John Gardner to LBJ, Feb. 11, 1967, and J. Califano to LBJ, Feb. 13, 1967, both in "Latin American Conference," box 6, Califano Files; H. McPherson to LBJ, Feb. 17, 1967, "Mexican Americans," box 11, McPherson Files; memorandum, John Gardner to Jake Jacobsen, Feb. 21, 1967, "Ex Hu2/MC 10/13/66," box 23, WHCF; LBJ to H. McPherson, "Mexican Americans," box 11, McPherson Files; Califano, auth. int.

15. García, *Memories of Chicano History*, 234–235.

16. "César Chávez may provide the best example of strong nonviolent action," said Baez. García, *Memories of Chicano History*, 235–236; Baez, "Thoughts on a Sunday Afternoon," in Ludwig and Santibáñez, *The Chicanos*, 257; Levy, *César Chávez*, 466; Gallegos, auth. int.; memorandum, Hubert H. Humphrey to LBJ, Feb. 23, 1967, "Ex PL/Political Affairs, Aug. 1, 1967–Sept. 14, 1967"; Hubert H. Humphrey to LBJ March 1, 1967, "Ex Hu2/MC 10/13/66," box 23, WHCF.

17. Thompson, *The Johnson Presidency*, 34; Moyers, "Epilogue," 361.

18. Crook, auth. int.; OEO—Administrative History, vol. I, part II [2 of 3], 451–452, Johnson Library.

19. H. García, auth. int.; report, R. Ramos, Jan. 5, 1967, "National Convention—1972," Ramos Papers; Abrahán Tapia to LBJ, Dec. 21, 1966, "Mexe," box 388, WHCF; American GI Forum, Department of California, Feb. 1967, "D.C. Files," Ramos Papers; Dugger, "Gonzalez of San Antonio," part IV, *Texas Observer*, Oct. 17, 1980.

20. All of the members of Congress except for two voted in favor of the Gulf of Tonkin resolution, which gave Johnson authority to take whatever measures he deemed necessary against the North Vietnamese. Cris Aldrete to John Criswell, April 24 1967, "Ex PL/G—Aldrete, Cris"; Meeks, auth. int.

21. Dugger, "Gonzalez of San Antonio," part IV, *Texas Observer*, Oct. 17, 1980; Bernal, Munguía, Idar, auth. int.; memorandum, Cris Aldrete to John Criswell, April 24, 1967, "Ex PL/G—Aldrete, Cris"; Márquez, "The Politics of Race and Class"; Mario R. Vásquez to LBJ, file 49, box 53, García Papers; American GI Forum, "Resolution," 1965, file 42, box 47, García Papers; LBJ to H. García, April 4, 1967, and Aug. 25, 1967, García Personal Papers; "Hispanic American Recipients of the Congressional Medal of Honor," García Personal Papers; poem, Juan Garza Jr., "A Lonely Soldier in Vietnam," file 23, box 49, García Papers; telegram, H. García to LBJ, April 8, 1967, in "Garcia, Hector P.," box 29, WHCF-NF; Idar, auth. int.; *Corpus Christi Caller*, Jan. 20, 1968; telegram, H. García to LBJ, April 8, 1967, in "Garcia, Hector P.," box 29, WHCF-NF; H. García to LBJ, Jan. 2, 1968, file 64, box 100, García Papers.

22. Cleotilde García, auth. int.; report, R. Ramos, Jan. 5, 1967, "National Convention—1972," Ramos Papers; Reedy, *Lyndon B. Johnson*, 147; Califano, *Triumph and Tragedy*, 196–197.

23. Speech, Henry B. Gonzalez, *Congressional Record*, June 20, 1967, file 66, box 92, García Papers; Roybal, auth. int.

24. Other UCLA professors also worked on the issue, including Robert Bullock of the Department of Industrial Relations. Grebler et al., *The Mexican American People*, ix, xiii; Ralph Guzmán, "Mexican American Casualties in Vietnam," n.d., file 67, box 92, García Papers; Mexican American Study Project, *Progress Report #10*, Sept. 1967, "Mexican American Casualties in Vietnam," file 40, box 113, García Papers; Schmidt, auth. int.

25. Miller, *Lyndon*, 418; Patrick Vásquez to P. Vasquez, file 49, box 53, García Papers; Hernández, auth. int.

26. *Texas Observer*, July 16, 1993; Bruce Biossat, "Mexican Americans Seethe over Inaction on Problems," n.d. (1967), "White House Brochures," box 19, Sánchez Papers; Bernal, Cárdenas, auth. int.; e-mail, Juan García Castañón, Nov. 28, 1995, from tmarquez@unm.edu.

27. Joan Baez, "Thoughts on a Sunday Afternoon," in Ludwig and Santibáñez, *The Chicanos*, 256.

28. Bert Corona to LBJ, June 21, 1967, Gen FG 655, WHCF; "Resolutions of the Mexican and Spanish-Speaking Legislative Conference," March 10, 1967, folder 8, box 67, "UFW—President," Reuther Archives; García, *Memories of Chicano History*, 273-275; *Oakland MAPA Newsletter*, Nov. 9, 1967, folder 3, box 67, "UFW—President," Reuther Archives; Ramos, Peña, auth. int.

29. Bernal, auth. int.

30. Press release, White House, March 4, 1967, file 16, box 91, García Papers; *New York Times*, March 23, 1967; William J. Eaton, "LBJ Moves to Outflank Critics of War on Poverty," Chicago Daily News Service, n.d., file 16, box 92, García Papers; H. García, auth. int.

31. García also sent the president an editorial from the South Texas newspaper *La Verdad* that characterized the Vietnam War as "unholy, unconstitutional, and undeclared." H. García to David North, March 13, 1967, "Dr. Hector P. Garcia," box 203, Macy Files; *La Verdad*, April 28, 1967, in "Garcia, Hector P.," box 29, WHCF-NF.

32. J. Macy to LBJ, June 29, 1966, box 97, Macy Files; Connally, Ximenes, Ramos, auth. int.; J. Macy to LBJ, March 10, 1967, "Frank Ortiz," box 437, Macy Files; Ximenes, *Gallant Outcasts*; J. Macy to LBJ, Nov. 3, 1966, "Herman Gallegos," box 201, Macy Files.

33. Other people mentioned for the EEOC post were Ambassador Raymund Telles, regional EEOC director Tom Robles, Ernesto Galarza of the United Farmworkers, and Julian Samora. Ralph Yarborough to LBJ, May 14, 1966, box 21, Sánchez Papers; J. Macy to LBJ, Aug. 18, 1966, and Eduardo Quevedo et al. to LBJ, June 19, 1966, "Raymund Telles," box 588, Macy Files; Albert Piñón to LBJ, n.d., "George Sanchez," box 513, Macy Files; Schott and Hamilton, *People, Positions, and Power*, 23; J. Macy to LBJ, Oct. 14, 1966, "M.A.'s," box 11, McPherson Files; J. Macy to LBJ, Nov. 3, 1966, and M. Watson to J. Jacobsen, Nov. 3, 1966, both in "Herman Gallegos," box 201, Macy Files; Ximenes, Connally, Gallegos, auth. int.

34. Schott and Hamilton, *People, Positions, and Power*, 25-27, 203; Connally, Ximenes, auth. int.; M. Watson to LBJ, April 3, 1967, "April 1967, Appointment of Vicente Ximenes," Ex FG 655, WHCF; Jake Jacobsen to M. Watson, April 3, 1967, in "Garcia, Hector P.," box 29, WHCF-NF; Mike Manatos to M. Watson, July 12, 1966, Ex Co 190, "FG-EEOC," WHCF; J. Macy to LBJ, June 29, 1966, box 97, Macy Files; J. Califano to LBJ, May 11, 1966, Ex FG "Federal Government—EEOC," WHCF; J. Macy to LBJ, Oct. 8, 1968, box 203, "Dr. Hector P. Garcia," Macy Files; J. Macy to LBJ, Oct. 14, 1966, box 11, McPherson Files; LBJ, "Proclamation," García Papers; *Austin American-Statesman*, March 2, 1986; EEOC, *Annual Report*, June 24, 1967, Ex FG 655, WHCF; David North to H. McPherson, April 16, 1967, "HU/MC 10/13/66," McPherson Files.

35. Touching all of the bases, Johnson instructed Ximenes to pay a call on Clinton Anderson. Although the senator did not oppose the nomination, he made his disappointment clear to John Macy. Ximenes, auth. int.; memoran-

dum, J. Macy to LBJ, March 16, 1967, in "Ximenes, Vicente," box X-1, WHCF-NF.

36. For letters lauding the appointment, see "Ximenes, Vicente," box X-1, WHCF-NF; April 6, 1967, "Hu2/MC 10/13/66," WHCF. Press release, March 3, 1967, and C. Aldrete to M. Watson, April 27, 1967, and May 26, 1967, both in "Federal Government—EEOC," Ex FG 655, WHCF; press release, April 4, 1967, "White House Brochures," box 19, Sánchez Papers, also in file 79, box 95, García Papers; Eligio de la Garza, *Congressional Record*, April 4, 1967, file 38, box 88, García Papers; H. McPherson to Armendariz, April 28, 1967, "Mexican Americans," box 11, McPherson Files; Frank Ortiz to LBJ, June 9, 1967, "Ex Hu2/MC 10/13/66," box 23, WHCF; "Memo for the Record" and H. García to LBJ, April 5, 1967, both in "Dr. Hector P. García," box 203, Macy Files; Frank Evans to Irvine Sprague, April 10, 1967, and Dr. Sergio Elizondo to LBJ, April 24, 1967, "Latin American Conference," box 6, Califano Files; Alfred Hernández to LBJ, April 5, 1967, "Gen— EEOC," FG 655, WHCF.

37. David North to H. McPherson, April 16, 1967, and D. North to J. Califano, May 2, 1967, "HU/MC 10/13/66," McPherson Files; press release, June 6, 1967, and H. McPherson to Edward Roybal, n.d. (May 1967?), "Mexican Americans," box 11, McPherson Files; David North to J. Califano, May 9, 1967, and n.d. (1967), both in "Latin American Conference," box 6, Califano Files.

38. J. Califano to LBJ, June 7, 1967, and Office of the White House Press Secretary, "Report to the President: The Mexican American: A New Focus on Opportunity," June 9, 1967, both in "Latin American Conference," box 6, Califano Files, also in box 11, McPherson Files.

39. Meier, *Mexican American Biographies*, 220; Steiner, *La Raza*, 73; Acuña, *Occupied America*, 340–341.

40. Rio Grande City is the Starr County seat. E. Idar to Ramsey Clark, June 3, 1967, file 41, box 47, García Papers; Bert Corona to LBJ and to John B. Connally, n.d., file 2, box 67, "UFW-President," Reuther Archives; Alfred J. Hernández to John B. Connally and Hernández to Joe Bernal, both May 31, 1967, box 10, Sánchez Papers; Bernal, Connally, auth. int.; John S. Díaz to LBJ, May 15, 1967, and Homero Alvarez to LBJ, June 5, 1967, both in "Mexe.," box 388, WHCF-NF; "Rule Bars Green Cards at Strikes," *Corpus Christi Caller*, June 10, 1967; UFWOC, *Sons of Zapata*, box 9, Sánchez Papers; *Corpus Christi Caller*, June 10, 1967; "Reuther Charges Beatings of Texas Farm Strikers," *New York Times*, June 10, 1967, 18; UFWOC, "Ranger Terrorism," in "Rio Grande Newsletter" No. 10, n.d. [June 1967], "National Campaign for Agricultural Democracy," file 33, box 9, Reuther Archives; Greg Olds, "Three Million Alienated Texans," *Texas Observer*, June 9, 1967.

41. Larry Levinson to J. Califano, n.d., and J. Califano to LBJ, 7:15 p.m., May 11, 1967, "Latin American Conference," box 6, Califano Files; "Remarks of the President at the Swearing-in Ceremony for Vicente T. Ximenes,"

June 9, 1967, file 79, box 95, García Papers; *New York Times*, June 10, 1967; *Washington Post*, June 10, 1967; Califano, auth. int.

42. Schott and Hamilton, *People, Positions, and Power*, 203; Sargent Shriver to LBJ, June 19, 1967, box 125, Ex FG 11–15, WHCF; Luther Holcomb to M. Watson, "June 1967, EEOC," Ex FG 655, WHCF; *New York Times*, June 10, 1967.

43. Rodríguez, Anguiano, Peña, Gallegos, Samora, auth. int.

44. Ximenes, Rodríguez, auth. int.; Elizondo, *The Future is Mestizo*, 24.

45. Ximenes, auth. int.; Munguía, "Los Chávez," box 5, Sánchez Papers.

46. Ximenes, Califano, auth. int.; Elroy Bode, "South El Paso and Hope," *Texas Observer*, Oct. 27, 1967, 11.

47. Wirtz was unable to attend and was replaced by Undersecretary James Reynolds. Louis Martin to John Criswell, May 22, 1967, folder 1, "Civil Rights/Negroes," box 18, Aides' Files, Marvin Watson, WHCF; Ximenes, auth. int.; memorandum, Larry Levinson to Tom Johnson, June 17 and June 19, 1967, "Hu2/MC 10/13/66," WHCF; press release, V. Ximenes, Sept. 12, 1967, "White House Brochures," box 19, Sánchez Papers; Elroy Bode, "South El Paso and Hope," *Texas Observer*, Oct. 27, 1967, 11; Interagency Committee on Mexican American Affairs, *The Mexican American: New Focus on Opportunity*, 39.

48. Mexican American Unity Council, Aug. 12, 1967, file 9, box 67, Reuther Archives; G. Sánchez to David North, Oct. 4, 1967, "Mexican American Joint Conference," box 18, Sánchez Papers; "Topic: White House Conference," file 9, box 67, "UFW-President," Reuther Archives; "California Pre-White House Conference," Aug. (?) 1967, "Interagency Committee on Mexican American Affairs," box 65, "UFW-President," Reuther Archives; Rendón, "La Raza Unida: Today—Not Mañana," 9; Marín, *A Spokesman*, 5–6.

49. Chávez's administrative assistant wrote to David North, "It is shocking to consider the suffering of farm workers on strike in Delano and Texas and then to find that our President has not seen fit to endorse and encourage legislation aimed to end such needless suffering." James Drake to David North, March 20, 1967, "UFW-President," file 21, box 45, Reuther Archives; C. Chávez to V. Ximenes, Sept. 27, 1967, V. Ximenes to C. Chávez, Sept. 30, 1967, and V. Ximenes to C. Chávez, Sept. 13, 1967, file 11, box 65, all in "UFW-President," Reuther Archives; press conference, Sept. 12, 1967, "White House Brochures," box 19, Sánchez Papers.

50. "Rio Grande Newsletter" No. 10, "Nat. Campaign for Agric. Democracy," file 33, box 9, Reuther Archives; Dennis Farney, "The Texas Rangers," *Wall Street Journal*, Sept. 13, 1967, 1; John Ford, "End of Rangers asked by PASO," *San Antonio Express*, Aug. 14, 1967.

51. The Federation for the Advancement of the Mexican Americans (FAMA) sent out a call to leaders around Texas to meet on Oct. 16 "to discuss the conference," according to FAMA's president, who wrote, "I am sure that you agree that the effectiveness or ineffectiveness of the Conference will have

long reaching effects on the Mejicano." Fernando Rodríguez to G. Sánchez, Oct. 16, 1967, box 17, Sánchez Papers; Ximenes, auth. int.

52. Navarro, *Mexican American Youth Organization*, 97; Muñoz, *Youth, Identity, Power*, 99; Treviño et al., "Chicano! The History of the Mexican American Civil Rights Movement," episode 4.

53. García, *United We Win*, 15–20; Treviño et al., "Chicano! The History of the Mexican American Civil Rights Movement," episode 4; Acuña, *Occupied America*, 2d ed., 355–356; Romo, *East Los Angeles*, 170–171.

54. At *The Nation* Elizabeth Martínez worked as Elizabeth Sutherland, using her middle name. Martínez and Longeaux y Vásquez, *Viva La Raza*, back flyleaf; Patricia Wright, "Dream Weaver," *Massachusetts Magazine*, 15; Hayden, *Reunion*, 95–96; Steiner, *La Raza*, photographs by María Varela, and 389.

55. Rendón, "La Raza Unida," 8–9, 14–15; Steiner, *La Raza*, 204; Muñoz, *Youth, Identity, Power*, 99–100; *Albuquerque Journal*, Oct. 28, 1967; Cárdenas, auth. int.

56. Alfred Hernández to Cris Aldrete, July 12, 1967, "California 'C'—" General, 1/14/66–4/1/68; press release, Interagency Committee on Mexican American Affairs, Oct. 13, 1967, "White House Brochures," box 19, Sánchez Papers; Henry B. González, *Congressional Record*, June 20, 1967, file 66, box 92, García Papers; Doris Armijo, introduction, Interagency Committee on Mexican American Affairs, *The Mexican American*, xi; Meier, *Mexican American Biographies*, 22; Mexican American Study Project, *Progress Report*, #10, Sept. 1967, file 40, box 113, García Papers.

57. Bernal, Cárdenas, Ximenes, auth. int.; Council on Spanish-American Work, "The Record and Findings . . . ," Phoenix, Arizona, Oct. 30, 1968, 1–2, CHSM-339, "Chicano," Arizona State University Archives.

58. Rodríguez, auth. int.; Interagency Committee on Mexican American Affairs, *Testimony*, 31–33, 65–67, 121–124, 139–142, 149, 151, 173–178, 211–213; Rendón, "La Raza Unida," 16.

59. Ernesto Galarza, "Rural Community Development" and Maclovio Barraza, "Labor Standards," both in Interagency Committee on Mexican American Affairs, *Testimony*.

60. In January 1967 Bert Corona had written to César Chávez—after speaking with labor activists in Mexico—that Mexican Americans needed to "begin to develop a broader understanding of . . . the use of Mexican labor from Mexico . . ." Bert Corona to César Chávez, Jan. 1, 1967, "UFW-President," box 67, folder 1, Reuther Archives; G. Sánchez to V. Ximenes, Feb. 19, 1968, box 10, Sánchez Papers; Norbert A. Schlei to H. García, n.d., file 42, box 48, García Papers; Bert Corona, press release, Aug. 29, 1967, folder 3, box 67, "UFW-President," Reuther Archives.

61. Cárdenas, Ramos, Gallegos, auth. int.

62. Cárdenas, Pena, auth. int.; speech, LBJ, Oct. 28, 1967, "Hum. R-Eq. of R [Ex Hu2]," box 7, WHCF; Charles Ashman, *Connally*, 116–117.

63. Rendón, "La Raza Unida," 10–11; Acuña, *Occupied America*,

331–332; *Albuquerque Journal*, Oct. 28, 1967.

64. Al Ortega to Sam Yorty, Oct. 17, 1967, California "C," General, 1/4/66–1/1/68; García, *Memories of Chicano History*, 226; Rendón, "La Raza Unida," 10–11; Cárdenas, auth. int.; Idar to auth., San Antonio, May 3, 1991; Steiner, *La Raza*, 204, 382.

65. The Chávez text in the original Spanish:

"Felicitamos a toda la Raza reunida en asemblea en esta ciudad de El Paso luchando por el adelantado de si mismo. Que la voz de los pobres, con sus líderes, resalte y borre la mancha de todos los bonitos, perfumados, y vendidos . . . Rogamos a Dios y a la Virgen que triunfen. Viva la Raza!"

César Chávez to Ernesto Galarza, "Chairman—Unity Rally Committee, Hotel Paso del Norte," Oct. 27 (?), 1967, folder 9, box 67, "UFW-President," Reuther Archives.

66. Rendón, "La Raza Unida," 12–14; Armando Rendón, *Chicano Manifesto*, 158–159, 331–332; *Albuquerque Journal*, Oct. 28, 1967; Tijerina, auth. int.

67. Rendón, "La Raza Unida," 12–14; García, *Memories of Chicano History*, 227; Steiner, *La Raza*, 204; Rendón, *Chicano Manifesto*, 331–332.

68. Montejano, *Anglos and Mexicans*, 284; Orozco, "Sexism in Chicano Studies and the Community," in Córdova et al., *Chicana Voices*, p. 12.

69. Samora, auth. int.; Moreno Sifuentes, "The El Paso Conference and La Raza Nueva," *Con Safos*, n.d., 15.

70. Rendón, "La Raza Unida," 10–11; Acuña, *Occupied America*, 331–332; *Albuquerque Journal*, Oct. 28, 1967; Rendón, *Chicano Manifesto*, 183–190.

71. Johnson's former Cotulla student Dan García wrote to congratulate him on the conference and the president sent García a commemorative Chamizal medallion. Clifton Alexander to M. Watson, in "García, Daniel C.," box 28, WHCF-NF; V. Ximenes (?) to LBJ, Jan. 25, 1968, "Hu2/MC 10/13/66," WHCF.

72. Press release, White House press secretary, Jan. 1969; press release, Interagency Committee on Mexican-American Affairs, Jan. 26, 1968, both in Ximenes Papers; *Ft. Worth Star Telegram*, Nov. 19, 1967; V. Ximenes to G. Sánchez, Feb. 23, 1968, "White House Brochures," box 19, Sánchez Papers; Rendón, "La Raza Unida," 10.

73. Reston, *Lone Star*, 323, 330, 339; Banks, *Money, Marbles, and Chalk*; *Houston Post*, Aug. 12, 1967; Kyle Thompson, "Connally Decision to Quit Laid to Break with LBJ," *Houston Post*, Jan. 7, 1968; "Mexican-American Leaders Seek Grass Roots," *San Antonio Express-News*, Jan. 7, 1968; Connally, Ximenes, auth. int.; Califano, *Triumph and Tragedy*, 137; Equal Employment Opportunity Commission, "Administrative History," 188, Administrative History Files, LBJL.

CHAPTER 10

1. The MAPA voter registration notice ended with "Viva La Raza!" *San Antonio Express-News*, Dec. 17, 1967; "Mexican-American Leaders Seek Grass Roots," *San Antonio Express-News*, Jan. 7, 1968; Bert Corona to John Hanna (sic), Jan. 6, 1968, folder 4, box 67, "UFW-President," Reuther Archives.

2. Jorge Lara-Braud and Alfredo Hernández, "Resumen de Resúmenes," Mexican American Unity Conference: La Raza Unida, San Antonio, Jan. 6, 1968, box 10, Sánchez Papers; "'La Raza' to Eye Goals," *Alamo Messenger*, Dec. 15, 1968; "Mexican-American Meet Set Saturday," *Alamo Messenger*, Jan. 5, 1968; "'Raza Unida' ponders bias protests," *Alamo Messenger*, Jan. 12 [?], 1968; Rendón, "La Raza Unida: Today—Not Mañana," 11–12; García, *United We Win*, 20; "Galarza Forsees New Era" and "Mexican-Americans Given Challenge to Up Lot in Life," *San Antonio Express-News*, Jan. 7, 1968.

3. Gilberto V. Martínez to Julie Leininger Pycior, Oct. [?] 1969, Lansing, Michigan; "La Raza Unida," n.d. [1969?], folder 33, box 26, "National Campaign for Agricultural Democracy," Reuther Archives; Young Democrats of Texas, "Resolution on Mexican-American Rights," file 37, box 95, García Papers.

4. García, *United We Win*, 11, 17, 23, 151–154; Barrientos, Wildenthal, Zamora, auth. int.

5. Dugger, "The Politics of Fratricide," *Texas Observer*, Dec. 12, 1980, 6–8; Rodriguez, *Henry B. Gonzalez*, 171; Tijerina, Ximenes, Voight, Samora, Meeks, auth. int.

6. Cecil Burney, int. David McComb, LBJL; Califano, *Triumph and Tragedy*, 203, 257–258; Perini and Grubin, producer, *LBJ*; M. Watson to LBJ, Feb. 27, 1968, and LBJ to J. Califano, March 3, 1968, both in Ex WE9, FI4, FG 11–15, ST 24, box 29, WHCF-NF; James Blum to James Gaither, March 6, 1988, and "Facts and Figures," both in box 290, Macy Files.

7. Chester, Hodgson, and Page, *An American Melodrama*, 313–314; Wofford, *Of Kennedys and Kings*, ch. 12; Muñoz, *Youth, Identity, Power*, 203; Steiner, *La Raza*, 321–322.

8. Wofford, *Of Kennedys and Kings*, 424.

9. García, *Memories of Chicano History*, 236–239, 244; pamphlet, "Citizens for Kennedy-Fulbright in 1968," PL Political Affairs [General], Aug. 1, 1967–Sept. 17, 1967, LBJL; C. Chávez to LBJ, Jan. 8, 1968, in "Chávez, A–E," box 186, WHCF-NF.

10. García, *Memories of Chicano History*, 236–238; Roybal, auth. int.

11. Chester, Hodgson, and Page, *An American Melodrama*, 316–317; United Farmworkers Organizing Committee, "Minutes of the Emergency Executive Board Meeting of March 19, 1968," file 6, box 7, "UFWOC," Reuther Archives; Levy, *César Chávez*, 288–289; Anguiano, Peña, auth. int.; Meier, *Mexican American Biographies*, 22.

12. Chester, Hodgson, and Page, *An American Melodrama*, 71.

13. On Feb. 14 Aldrete attended an off-the-record meeting with Johnson and the Democratic state chairmen. President's Daily Diary Cards, "Albert, Carl–Amb. of Guat.," drawer 2, LBJL; Irv Sprague to M. Watson, March 20, 1968, "California Convention Delegates," and William Connell to Hubert Humphrey, March 19, 1968, both in box 2, Watson Files; "Bien Hecho, Sr. Presidente!," in "Hallway Box—L," García Papers; Ludwig and Santibáñez, *The Chicanos*, 275; Acuña, *Occupied America*, 287.

14. Chester, Hodgson, and Page, *An American Melodrama*, 183–208; "Latin American Conference," box 6, Califano Files; Irv Sprague to M. Watson, March 20, 1968, "California Convention Delegates," John Bailey to LBJ, Feb. 3, 1967, "California-B-Primary (Part One)," and Warren Christopher to M. Watson, March 24, 1968, all in box 2, Watson Files.

15. Janeway, "Bill Moyers talks about LBJ, Power, Poverty, War, and the Young"; Cecil Burney, int. by David McComb, LBJL; Chester, Hodgson, and Page, *An American Melodrama*, 313–317, 335–336.

16. H. García, int. by David McComb, LBJL; H. García, Ximenes, Samora, auth. int.

17. Rodríguez, auth. int.

18. The author, along with scores of other Michigan State students, worked for McCarthy in Fort Wayne. *Latin Times* [East Chicago, Indiana], May 3, 1968, 1–3.

19. Wofford, *Of Kennedys and Kings*, 201, 202; "Connally Denies Criticizing King," *San Angelo Times*, April 6, 1968; Califano, *Triumph and Tragedy*, 273.

20. Bulletin, "Viva Kennedy," April 10, 1968, and memorandum, Bert Corona to National RFK Headquarters, May 1, 1968, both in folder 6, box 7, UFWOC, Reuther Archives; Chester, Hodgson, and Page, *An American Melodrama*, 320; Levy, *César Chávez*, 288–289; Viva Kennedy booklet, folder 14, box 48, "UFW-President," Reuther Archives; R. Ontiveros to César Chávez, April 24, 1968, folder 4, box 67, "UFW—President," Reuther Archives; Cárdenas, Anguiano, auth. int.; Jesse Unruh to César Chávez, May 29, 1968, "UFWOC," folder 6, box 7, Reuther Archives.

21. Chester, Hodgson, and Page, *An American Melodrama*, 335–337; García, *Memories of Chicano History*, 239–240.

22. Tijerina, auth. int.; report, Southwest Council of La Raza, folder 16, box 65, "UFW-President," Reuther Archives; Marín, *A Spokesman for Mexican Americans*, 7.

23. Bertrand M. Harding to OEO Regional Directors, May 10, 1968, file 90, box 90, García Papers.

24. Chester, Hodgson, and Page, *An American Melodrama*, 323–324.

25. Gallegos, auth. int.

26. Anguiano, auth. int.; Levy, *César Chávez*, 289–290; "Transcript of Robert Kennedy's Victory Speech," file 14, box 48, "UFW—President," Reuther Archives.

27. Gallegos, Anguiano, auth. int.; García, *Memories of Chicano History*, 243–244.

28. Confidential report, Leo D. Nieto, "Poor People's Campaign to Washington, D.C.," n.d. [June 1968], folder 17, box 26, "National Campaign for Agricultural Democracy," Reuther Archives; Miguel Barragán, report, n.d. [June?] 1968, folder 16, box 65, "UFW—President," Reuther Archives.

29. Memorandum, Jim Jones, June 13, 1968, "Executive" FG105, HU4, CO190, LBJL; Nieto, "Poor People's Campaign to Washington, D.C.," folder 17, box 26, "National Campaign for Agric. Democracy," Reuther Archives.

30. Rodríguez, auth. int.; *Fresno Bee*, June 19, 1968. Nieto, "Poor People's Campaign to Washington, D.C.," folder 17, box 26, "National Campaign for Agric. Democracy," Reuther Archives; report, "Record and Finding of the Second Arizona Consultation on Mexican Americans," Phoenix, Oct. 30, 1968, p. 5, CHSM-339, "Chicano," Arizona State University Archives.

31. Miguel Barragán, report, n.d. [June?] 1968, folder 16, box 65, "UFW—President," Reuther Archives; Henry Hampton, producer, *Eyes on the Prize*, "The Promised Land."

32. *New York Times*, June 17, 1968; Hubert Humphrey to the editor, *New York Times*, June 18, 1968; Frank Mankiewicz to César Chávez, Aug. 17, 1968, folder 15, box 48, "UFW—President," Reuther Archives.

33. Ashman, *Connally*, 147, 157; *Houston Post*, Aug. 18, 1968; Davidson, *Race and Class in Texas Politics*, 170; Carrillo, auth. int.

34. Davidson, *Race and Class in Texas Politics*, 170–171; Peña, Connally, Bernal, auth. int.; Ed Johnston, "Liberals Blast Connally in Credentials Slugfest," *Austin American*, Oct. 22, 1968; Sam Kinche Jr., *Dallas News*, Aug. 27, 1968.

35. Davidson, *Race and Class in Texas Politics*, 171; Chester, Hodgson, and Page, *An American Melodrama*, 423–424, 556–559; Califano, *Triumph and Tragedy*, 318–321; Reston, *Lone Star*, 353, 356, 364; Connally, in "LBJ: The Difference He Made," Austin, Texas, June 3–5, 1990.

36. Ashman, *Connally*, 160; Reston, *Lone Star*, 348–349, 356; Carrillo, auth. int.

37. Davidson, *Race and Class in Texas Politics*, 171–172; Reston, *Lone Star*, 348–349, 356; Ashman, *Connally*, 159, 172; Bernal, auth. int.

38. Steiner, *La Raza*, 206.

39. Califano, *Triumph and Tragedy*, 323; Reston, *Lone Star*, 374.

40. Extension of remarks, "A New Focus on Opportunity," Edward Roybal, *Congressional Record*, Sept. 4, 1968, E7629, in folder 2, box 21, "National Campaign for Agricultural Democracy," Reuther Archives; "Film Taping, Mexican-American Film," "Executive," "Human Relations—Equality of Races [Ex Hu2]," box 9, WHCF; James Jones to V. Ximenes, Nov. 1, 1968, "Human Relations—Equality of Races [Ex Hu2]," box 9, WHCF; press release, Interagency Committee on Mexican American Affairs, Oct. 7, 1968, Ximenes Papers; V. Ximenes, Aug. 8, 1968, "White House Papers," box 19, Sánchez Papers.

41. Henry Santiestevan to Ted Kennedy, Oct. 10, 1968, and Edward Kennedy to Henry Santiestevan, Oct. 11, 1968, both in folder 13, box 48, "UFW-President," Reuther Archives. Ramos, H. García, auth. int.; Ramón

Castro to Abe Tapia, Sept. 25, 1968, folder 4, box 67, "UFW-President," Reuther Archives; press release, Albert Peña, Abe Tapia, Rudy Ortiz, Joe Huerta, Bert N. Corona, n.d., folder 11, box 65, "UFW-President," Reuther Archives; Chester, Hodgson, and Page, *An American Melodrama*, 750.

42. *El Malcriado*, n.d., "AGIF Information Kit," Ramos Papers; *News American* [San Francisco?], Sept. 27, 1968, in folder 12, box 48, "UFW-President," Reuther Archives; Chester, Hodgson, and Page, *An American Melodrama*, 737, 747, 751, 753, 762–763; *Bakersfield Californian*, Oct. 19, 1968; Don O'Brien to César Chávez, Nov. 5, 1968, file 12, box 48, "UFW-President," Reuther Archives; César Chávez to Beatriz Callejo Rouverol, March 30, 1969, file 10, box 48, "UFW-President," Reuther Archives.

43. In the original the corrido verses are:

Tragastes ubas (sic) esquirolas
Y ahorita te andas hogando . . .
Cuando venga la elección
Ya veras que
Miles de mexicanos
No te tengan compasión

"No Deje Que Nixon Quite Lo Que Usted Ha Ganado," and "El Corrido de Richard Nixon," both in folder 12, box 48, "UFW-President," Reuther Archives.

44. The Republican candidate never remarked on the segregated "Mexican" neighborhood in his hometown, where the colonia residents "just knew they weren't wanted," as one local resident put it. In the 1930s local sheriffs prowled the barrio with machine guns in search of union organizers. Morris, *Richard Milhous Nixon*, 70–71; Chester, Hodgson, and Page, *An American Melodrama*, 751.

45. Chester, Hodgson, and Page, *An American Melodrama*, 737, 747, 751–754, 762–763; Califano, *Triumph and Tragedy*, 328.

46. Wofford, *Of Kennedys and Kings*, 332.

CHAPTER 11

1. Sherrill, *The Accidental President*, 21; Johnson, *My Brother Lyndon*, "Acknowledgment"; Lloyd Bentsen, int. by David McComb, LBJL; Meeks, auth. int.

2. Perini and Grubin, executive producers, *LBJ*; Bravo, auth. int.

3. Transcript, Luci Baines Johnson Turpin, in "LBJ: The Difference He Made," Austin, Texas, June 3–5, 1990.

4. H. García to Lady Bird Johnson, Jan. 22, 1973, "Personal Letters—J," García Papers.

5. H. García, Idar, auth. int.

6. Gómez-Quiñones, *Chicano Politics*, 128; García, *United We Win*, 152.

7. De León, *Mexican Americans in Texas*, 130; García, *United We Win*, 44; Zamora, Barrientos, auth. int.

8. Gómez-Quiñones, *Chicano Politics*, 129–130; Ruiz, Zamora, auth. int.

9. Zamora relinquished his fellowship when he began his political organizing. Gilberto V. Martínez to author, Lansing, Michigan, Sept. (?) 1969; García, *United We Win*, 152–155; Zamora, auth. int.

10. García, *United We Win*, 152; Zamora, Woods, auth. int.

11. San Antonio public official Albert Peña characterized Del Rio as "our Selma," after the 1965 voting rights march in Alabama. Acuña, *Occupied America*, 339; Zamora, Peña, Bernal, auth. int.

12. García, *United We Win*, 69, 154.

13. García, *United We Win*, 156–157; Compean and Gutiérrez, *La Raza Unida Party*, 15; Ruiz, auth. int.

14. García, *United We Win*, 61, 202, 226–227; De León, *Mexican Americans in Texas*, 132; Dugger, "Gonzalez of San Antonio," part V, *Texas Observer*.

15. In a race characterized by massive spending on both sides, Bentsen narrowly defeated Bush in the general election. Davidson, *Race and Class in Texas Politics*, 32, 281 n.41; Gómez-Quiñones, *Chicano Politics*, 110; Bentsen, int. by David McComb, LBJL; Dugger, "Thoughts on Lloyd Bentsen's Election," *Texas Observer*, May 15, 1970; Yarborough, auth. int.

16. García, *United We Win*, 61, 202–203; Greenstein, "Fire in the Belly," *Texas Observer*, July 29, 1988.

17. Tel. comm., James C. Harrington (legal director, Texas Civil Rights Project) to author, Jan. 13, 1995; Harrington, "Power and Responsibility"; Ramiro R. Casso, "Viva Willie!"; and Juan Sepúlveda, "Willie Velásquez, Mentor," all three in the *Texas Observer*, July 29, 1988; Montejano, *Anglos and Mexicans*, 292; Idar, auth. int.

18. Contreras, auth. int.

19. Not that discrimination has disappeared: for example, Congressman Ed Roybal, speaking of the 1980s, said, "A sitting member of congress, chairman of a very powerful committee, said, 'I didn't know Ed Roybal was a Mexican. You know, he speaks pretty good English. I always thought that Mexicans were fat, short, and wore a mustache'" (Edward Roybal, auth. int.). Acuña, *Occupied America*, 417.

20. In 1986 Baca Barragán gave up her state senate seat to run for congress and lost in the Democratic primary. Meier, *Mexican American Biographies*, 22; Acuña, *Occupied America*, 422–423; Barrientos, auth. int.

21. Zamora, Dan García, Hernández, auth. int.

22. Montejano, *Anglos and Mexicans*, 304; Zamora, Worthy, auth. int.

23. Montejano, *Anglos and Mexicans*, 299; Márquez, *LULAC*, 8–9; "GOP Making Gains Among Hispanic Voters," *New York Times*, July 1, 1994.

24. Cortés and Velásquez both were graduates of San Antonio's Central Catholic High School, as was Henry Cisneros, who in 1982 was elected as the

first Mexican-heritage mayor since 1842. Shortly after Velásquez's untimely death, Cortés wrote, "He would often say that since I had hired him to work with the United Farm Workers and then he had hired me to work for M.A.U.C., . . . neither of us knew who was the boss. But we somehow managed to move forward" (Ernesto Cortés Jr., "Willie Velásquez, Beloved Friend," *Texas Observer*, July 29, 1988). Montejano, *Anglos and Mexicans*, 299.

25. Ernesto Cortés Jr., "Willie Velásquez, Beloved Friend," *Texas Observer*, July 29, 1988; Peter Applebome, "Changing Texas Politics at Its Roots," *New York Times*, May 30, 1988; Rogers, *Cold Anger*, 45, 105-109; Greider, *Who Will Tell the People?*, 222-223.

26. Rogers, *Cold Anger*, 122-125.

27. Montejano, *Anglos and Mexicans*, 290, 293, 296-297; *Texas Observer*, Nov. 22, 1990: issue devoted to COPS and the IAF; B. Moyers, introduction to Rogers, *Cold Anger*, ii; Peter Applebome, "Changing Texas Politics at Its Roots," *New York Times*, May 30, 1988; Reverend John P. Duffell to author, Hastings-on-Hudson, New York, Jan. 6, 1995, and New York, New York, April 14, 1996; Greider, *Who Will Tell the People?*, ch. 10.

28. Transcript, B. Moyers, in "LBJ: The Difference He Made," Austin, Texas, June 3-5, 1990; Moyers, auth. int.; Reedy, *Lyndon B. Johnson*, 158; Califano, *Triumph and Tragedy*, 11.

29. Connally, *In History's Shadow*, 61; Dugger, auth. int.

30. Anguiano's successful training projects were featured on the CBS television news program "Sixty Minutes." Cárdenas, Bernal, Samora, Peña, Roybal, and Anguiano, auth. int.; Hartman, *From Margin to Mainstream*, 74-75.

BIBLIOGRAPHY

ARCHIVAL COLLECTIONS

Arizona State University Archives. Chicano Periodical Collection; Graciela Olivarez Collection.

Austin Public Library, Austin, Texas. Manuscript collection.

Bancroft Library, University of California, Berkeley. Manuel Gamio Collection; Paul Taylor Collection.

Benson Latin American Collection, University of Texas at Austin. José Angel Gutiérrez Collection; Ed Idar Jr. Collection; League of United Latin American Citizens Collection; George I. Sánchez Collection.

Center for American History, University of Texas at Austin. Vertical files; Texas Collection.

Cotulla Historical Museum, Cotulla, Texas.

Franklin Delano Roosevelt Library. "National Youth Administration, Miscellaneous, 1938–1940" Collection.

Lyndon Baines Johnson Library. Administrative History Files; House of Representatives Papers; Oral History Collection; Papers of the Vice President; "Papers of Richard Kleberg, 1932–1938" (microfilm); photograph collection; presidential aides files; Pre-Presidential Confidential File; President's Daily Diary Cards; Rebeka Baines Johnson Collection; Senate Papers; "Statements of Lyndon Baines Johnson"; White House Central Files.

National Archives, Washington, D.C. National Youth Administration Collection.

South Texas Archives, Texas A & M University, Kingsville. J. T. Canales Estate Collection.

Texas A & M University, Corpus Christi Archives. Héctor P. García Papers.

Walter P. Reuther Archives of Labor and Urban Affairs, Wayne State University, Detroit, Michigan. "National Campaign for Agricultural Democracy—United Farmworkers Organizing Committee" Collection; "UFWOC" Collection; "United Farm Workers—President" Collection.

PERSONAL PAPERS

Cristóbal Aldrete, Austin, Texas.
Héctor P. García, M.D., Corpus Christi, Texas.
Ed Idar Jr., Austin, Texas.
Rodolfo Loa Ramos, Washington, D.C.
Vicente Ximenes, Albuquerque, New Mexico.

INTERVIEWS BY AUTHOR

Identification of people's occupations as of 1928–1968. Entries marked with asterisks [*] indicate that the interview is available on tape at the Benson Latin American Collection, University of Texas (in the Julie Leininger Pycior interview collection).

* Cristóbal Aldrete (attorney; American GI Forum leader; Democratic National Committee official). Austin, Texas, June 22, 1988, and June 18, 1990.
* Lupe Anguiano (Johnson administration official; educator). Telephone interview, August 10, 1992.
Anonymous resident of Box [precinct] 13, Alice, Texas. July 25, 1993.
* Gonzalo Barrientos (Texas state senator; War on Poverty official). Austin, Texas, June 12, 1991.
* Dr. Joe Bernal (educator; Texas state legislator). San Antonio, Texas, June 14, 1990.
Yolanda Garza Boozer (Johnson secretary). September 16, 1990.
Guadalupe M. Bravo (Johnson ranchhand). June 13, 1991.
* Joseph Califano (attorney; Johnson aide; chief domestic advisor in Johnson White House, 1967–1969). Telephone interview, August 25, 1992.
* Gilberto Cárdenas (a founder of United Mexican American Students, renamed El Movimiento Estudiantil Chicano de Aztlán, or MECHA). Austin, Texas, June 12, 1991.
O. P. Carrillo (Duval County, Texas, official). San Diego, Texas, July 15, 1994.
* John B. Connally (Johnson aide; governor of Texas). Telephone interview, October 16, 1991.
* William Crook (southwestern director of the Office of Economic Opportunity; ambassador to Australia). San Marcos, Texas, June 14, 1990.
* Ronnie Dugger (editor, publisher, *The Texas Observer*; Johnson biographer). Telephone interview, July 1, 1993.
Herman Gallegos (attorney; a leader of Community Service Organization and the Mexican American Political Association). San Francisco, California, January 7, 1994.
Cleotilde García, M.D. (head of Viva Johnson, Nueces County, Texas). Corpus Christi, Texas, July 16, 1994.
* Daniel García (student of Lyndon Johnson; local official). Cotulla, Texas, July 22, 1993.

*Héctor P. García, M.D. (founder, American GI Forum). Corpus Christi, Texas, June 21, 1989.

Ernesto González (Duval County resident; OEO administrator). Telephone interview, June 22, 1995.

Julia González de Toro (Cotulla resident). Cotulla, Texas, July 1, 1993.

Manuela González Contreras (sister of Johnson student; political activist). Telephone interview, August 2, 1993.

Juanita Hernández (student of Lyndon Johnson). Cotulla, Texas, July 21, 1993.

*Ed Idar Jr. (attorney; American GI Forum leader). Austin, Texas, June 22 and 23, 1988.

Latane Lambert (labor activist). Austin, Texas, June 14, 1991.

Kelsey Meeks (aide to Congressman Henry B. González). Telephone interview, September 14, 1995.

*Bill Moyers (Johnson special assistant and press secretary; broadcast journalist). New York City, February 24, 1993.

*Rubén Munguía (printer; political activist). San Antonio, Texas, May 3, 1991.

*Albert Peña (judge; head of Political Association of Spanish-Speaking Organizations). San Antonio, Texas, June 15, 1990.

*Rodolfo Ramos (attorney; head of the GI Forum in Washington, D.C.). Washington, D.C., July 9, 1990; July 28, 1992.

*George Reedy (Johnson biographer, aide, and press secretary). Austin, Texas, June 21, 1991.

Armando Rodríguez (educator; Johnson administration official). Telephone interview, December 7, 1995.

*Edward Roybal (congressman; a leader of the Mexican American Political Association and the Community Service Organization). Washington, D.C., July 31, 1990.

*Julian Samora (sociologist; member of President Johnson's Committee on Rural Poverty). South Bend, Indiana, August 12, 1991.

Clara Santoya Ruiz (sister of a Johnson student). Cotulla, Texas, July 21, 1993.

*Frederick Schmidt (labor professor and organizer; chief aide to Congressman Henry B. González). Fredericksburg, Texas, June 9, 1990.

*Pete Tijerina (judge; LULAC leader; founder of Mexican American Legal Defense Education Fund). San Antonio, Texas, March 26, 1992.

*Kathleen Voight (businesswoman; a leader of the Democrats of Texas). Alamo Heights, Texas, June 16, 1990.

*John Wildenthal (attorney; Johnson aide). Austin, Texas, June 13 and June 15, 1991.

Fredna Knaggs Dobie Woods (member, La Salle County Board of Education). Cotulla, Texas, July 21, 1993.

Rita Binkley Worthy (granddaughter of the first mayor of Cotulla, Texas). Telephone interview, January 19, 1994.

* Vicente Ximenes (attorney; director of Interagency Committee on Mexican American Affairs; member of the U.S. Civil Rights Commission). Albuquerque, New Mexico, November 17, 1990.
* Ralph Yarborough (U.S. senator from Texas). Austin, Texas, June 16, 1990.
* Raúl Yzaguirre (head, NOMAS; director, National Council of La Raza). Telephone interview, August 24, 1992.
* Alfredo Zamora (educator; first Mexican American mayor of Cotulla; La Raza Unida Party leader). Telephone interview, December 8, 1993.

BOOKS, ARTICLES, AND OTHER PUBLICATIONS

Acuña, Rudolfo. *Occupied America: A History of Chicanos.* New York: Harper and Row, 2nd ed. 1981; 3rd ed. 1988.

Allsup, Carl. *The American G.I. Forum: Origins and Evolution.* Austin: Center for Mexican American Studies, 1982.

Almaraz, Félix, Jr. "Carlos Eduardo Castañeda, Mexican American Historian: The Formative Years, 1896–1927." *Pacific Historical Review* 42, no. 3 (August 1973): 319–334.

Alvarez, Rodolfo. "The Psycho-Historical and Socioeconomic Development of the Chicano Community in the United States." *Social Science Quarterly* 53, no. 4 (1973): 920–942.

Alvarez, Rodolfo, and Mario T. García. "American All: Mexican Americans and the Politics of Wartime Los Angeles." In Rodolfo O. de la Garza et al., eds., *The Mexican American Experience.* Austin: University of Texas Press, 1985.

American GI Forum of Texas. *What Price Wetbacks?* Austin: American GI Forum of Texas and Texas State Federation of Labor, 1953.

Ashman, Charles. *Connally: The Adventures of Big Bad John.* New York: Morrow, 1974.

Austin City Directory. Houston: Morrison and Fourmy, 1937.

Bailey, Wilfred C. "Problems in Relocating the People of Zapata, Texas." *Texas Journal of Science* 7, no. 1 (March 1955).

Banks, Jimmy. *Money, Marbles, and Chalk: The Wondrous World of Texas Politics.* Austin: Texas Publishing Company, 1971.

Bard, Bernard. *LBJ: The Picture Story of Lyndon Baines Johnson.* N.p.: The Lion Press, 1966.

Baum, Dale, and James L. Hailey. "Lyndon Johnson's Victory in the 1948 Texas Senate Race: A Reappraisal." *Political Science Quarterly* 109, no. 4 (1994): 595–613.

Bender, Thomas. "Whole and Parts: The Need for Synthesis in American History." *Journal of American History* 73, no. 1 (June 1986): 137–151.

Billington, Monroe. "Lyndon Baines Johnson and Blacks: The Early Years." *Journal of Negro History* 62, no. 1 (January 1977): 26–42.

Blackwelder, Julia Kirk. *Women of the Depression: Caste and Culture in San Antonio, 1929–1939.* College Station: Texas A&M Press, 1984.

Blavis, Patricia Bell. "Tijerina and the Land Grants." In Livie Isauro Durán and H. Russell Bernard, eds., *Introduction to Chicano Studies*, pp. 519–534. New York: Macmillan, 1973.

Brammer, Billy Lee. *The Gay Place*. Boston: Houghton Mifflin, 1961. Reprint, Austin: University of Texas Press, 1995.

Branda, Eldon Stephen. *The Handbook of Texas: A Supplement*. Austin: Texas State Historical Association, 1976.

Brooks, Home, and Emma Tenayuca. "The Mexican Question in the Southwest." *The Communist* (March 1935): 10–12.

Broyles Jr., William. "The Last Empire." *Texas Monthly* 8, no. 10 (October 1980).

Burns, James MacGregor. *The Crosswinds of Freedom*. New York: Knopf, 1989.

Byfield, Patsy Jeanne. *Falcon Dam and the Lost Towns of Zapata*. Austin: Texas Memorial Museum, 1967.

Calderón, Roberto R., and Emilio Zamora. "Manuela Solís Sager and Emma Tenayuca: A Tribute." In Teresa Córdova et al., eds., *Chicana Voices: Intersections of Class, Race and Gender*, pp. 30–41. Austin: Center for Mexican American Studies, 1986.

Califano, Joseph. *The Triumph and Tragedy of Lyndon Johnson: The White House Years*. New York: Simon and Schuster, 1992.

Calvert, Robert, and Arnoldo De León. *The History of Texas*. Arlington Heights, Illinois: Harlan Davidson, 1990.

Carleton, Don. *Red Scare: Right-Wing Hysteria, Fifties Fanaticism, and Their Legacy in Texas*. Austin: Texas Monthly Press, 1985.

Caro, Robert. *The Years of Lyndon Johnson: The Path to Power*. New York: Knopf, 1982.

———. *The Years of Lyndon Johnson: Means of Ascent*. New York: Knopf, 1990.

Carroll, Bailey H., and Walter Prescott Webb, eds. *The Handbook of Texas*. Austin: Texas State Historical Association, 1952.

Casto, Stanley D. *The Settlement of the Cibolo Nueces Strip: A Partial History of La Salle County*. Hillsboro: Hill Junior College, 1969.

Chester, Lewis, Godfrey Hodgson, and Bruce Page. *An American Melodrama: The Presidential Campaign of 1968*. New York: Viking, 1969.

Christian, Carole. "Joining the American Mainstream: Texas Mexican Americans during World War I." *Southwestern Historical Quarterly* 92, no. 4 (April 1989): 555–595.

Clinchy, Everett R., Jr. *Equality of Opportunity for Latin Americans in Texas*. New York: Arno Press, 1974.

Compean, Mario, and José Angel Gutiérrez. *La Raza Unida Party in Texas*. New York: Pathfinder Press, 1970.

Conkin, Paul K. *Big Daddy from the Pedernales: Lyndon Baines Johnson*. Boston: Twayne, 1986.

Connally, John. *In History's Shadow: An American Odyssey*. New York: Hyperion, 1993.

Dallek, Robert. *Lone Star Rising: Lyndon Johnson and His Times*. New York: Oxford University Press, 1991.

Davidson, Chandler. *Race and Class in Texas Politics*. Princeton: Princeton University Press, 1990.

De León, Arnoldo. *Ethnicity in the Sunbelt: A History of Mexican Americans in Houston*. Houston: Mexican American Studies, 1989.

———. "*Los Tasinques* and the Sheep Shearers' Union of North America: A Strike in West Texas, 1934." *West Texas Historical Society Yearbook* 55 (1979): 3–16.

———. *Mexican Americans in Texas: A Brief History*. Arlington Heights, Illinois: Harlan Davidson, 1993.

———. *San Angelenos*. San Angelo: Fort Concho Museum Press, 1985.

———. *The Tejano Community, 1836–1900*. Albuquerque: University of New Mexico Press, 1982.

Dickey, Dan William. *The Kennedy Corridos: A Study of the Ballads of a Mexican American Hero*. Austin: Center for American Studies, University of Texas at Austin, c. 1978.

Dobie, Frank. *Coronado's Children: Tales of Lost Mines and Buried Treasure*. New York: Literary Guild, 1931.

Dobie, Frank, and Mody C. Boatright, eds. *Straight Texas*. Austin: The Steck Co., 1937.

Douthat, Bill. *La Raza*. Austin: Austin American-Statesman, 1981.

Dugger, Ronnie. *The Politician: The Life and Times of Lyndon Johnson*. New York: Norton, 1982.

Durham, George. *Taming the Nueces Strip: The Story of McNelly's Rangers*. Austin: University of Texas Press, 1969.

Elizondo, Virgil. *The Future Is Mestizo*. Bloomington, Indiana: Meyer-Stone Books, 1988.

Estill, Harry F. *The Beginner's History of Our Country*. N.p., n.d.

Evans, Rowland, and Robert Novak. *Lyndon B. Johnson: The Exercise of Power*. New York: New American Library, 1966.

Federal Writers Project. *WPA Guide to Texas*. Austin: Texas Monthly Press, 1986; New York: Hastings House, 1940.

Ferber, Edna. *Giant*. New York: Doubleday, 1952.

Firestone, Bernard, and Robert Vogt, eds. *Lyndon Baines Johnson and the Uses of Power*. Westport, Connecticut: Greenwood Press, 1988.

Fisher, Clark. "The Life and Times of King Fisher." *Southwestern Historical Quarterly* 64, no. 2 (October 1960): 232–247.

Foley, Douglas F., Clarice Mota, Donald F. Post, and Ignacio Lozano. *From Peones to Políticos: Ethnic Relations in a South Texas Town, 1900–1970*. Austin: Center for Mexican American Studies, 1977.

Foley, Neil. "Mexicans, Mechanization, and the New Deal in the Creation of a Texas Agricultural Proletariat." Organization of American Historians, Washington, D.C., April 1995.

Gabin, Nancy. "Women's Protests after the War." In Mary Beth Norton, ed.,

Major Problems in American Women's History, pp. 369–377. Lexington, Massachusetts: D. C. Heath, 1989.

Galarza, Ernesto. *Merchants of Labor*. Charlotte: McNally and Loftin, 1964.

Gamio, Manuel. *Mexican Immigration of the United States*. New York: Dover Press, 1971; Chicago: University of Chicago Press, 1931.

García, Ignacio. *United We Win: The Rise and Fall of La Raza Unida Party*. Tucson: MASRC, University of Arizona Press, 1989.

García, Juan Ramón. *Operation Wetback: The Mass Deportation of Mexican Undocumented Workers in 1954*. Westport, Connecticut: Greenwood Press, 1979.

García, Mario T. *Memories of Chicano History: The Life and Narrative of Bert Corona*. Berkeley: University of California Press, c. 1944.

———. "Mexican Americans and the Politics of Citizenship: The Case of El Paso, 1936." *New Mexican Historical Review* 59, no. 2 (1984): 187–204.

———. *Mexican Americans: Leadership, Ideology, and Identity*. New Haven: Yale University Press, 1989.

García, Richard. *The Rise of the Mexican American Middle Class: San Antonio, 1929–1931*. College Station: Texas A&M Press, 1991.

Gómez-Quiñones, Juan. *Chicano Politics: Reality and Promise, 1940–1990*. Albuquerque: University of New Mexico Press, 1990.

Goodwin, Richard N. *Remembering America: A Voice from the Sixties*. New York: Harper and Row, 1988.

Goodwyn, Frank. *Lone Star Land: Twentieth-Century Perspectives*. New York: Knopf, 1955.

Grebler, Leo, Joan Moore, and Ralph Guzmán. *The Mexican American People: The Nation's Second Largest Minority*. New York: The Free Press, 1970.

Green, David. "The Cold War Comes to Latin America." In Barton Bernstein, ed., *Politics and Policies of the Truman Administration*. Chicago: Quadrangle Press, 1972.

Green, George Norris. *The Establishment in Texas Politics: The Primitive Years, 1938–1957*. Westport, Connecticut: Greenwood Press, 1979.

———. "The Felix Longoria Affair." *Journal of Ethnic Studies* 19, no. 3 (1991): 23–34.

———. "ILGWU in Texas, 1930–1970." *Journal of Mexican American History* 1, no. 2 (1972): 144–163.

Greider, William. *Who Will Tell the People? The Betrayal of American Democracy*. New York: Simon and Schuster, 1990.

Guerra, Fermina. "Rancho Buena Vista: Its Ways of Life and Traditions." In Américo Paredes and Raymund Paredes, eds., *Mexican American Authors*. Boston: Houghton Mifflin, 1972.

Gutiérrez, David G. *Walls and Mirrors: Mexican Americans, Mexican Immigrants, and the Politics of Ethnicity*. Berkeley: University of California Press, 1995.

Gutiérrez, José Angel. *La Raza and Revolution*. San Francisco: R. and E. Publications, 1972.

Guzmán, Ralph. *Political Socialization of the Mexican American People*. New York: Ayer, 1976.

Halliwell, Leslie. *Film Guide*. New York: Scribner's, 1985.

Hamilton, Dagmar S., and Richard L. Schott. *People, Positions, and Power: The Political Appointments of Lyndon Johnson*. Chicago: University of Chicago Press, 1983.

Hartman, Susan. *From Margin to Mainstream: American Women and Politics since 1969*. New York: Knopf, 1989.

Hayden, Tom. *Reunion: A Memoir*. New York: Random House, 1988.

Henderson, Richard B. *Maury Maverick: A Political Biography*. Austin: University of Texas Press, 1970.

Hernández, José Amaro. *Mutual Aid for Survival: The Case of the Mexican American*. Malabar, Florida: Krieger, 1983.

Hoffman, Abraham. *Unwanted Mexican Americans in the Great Depression*. Tucson: University of Arizona Press, 1974.

Hurtado, Juan. *An Attitudinal Study of Social Distance between the Mexican American and the Church*. San Antonio: Mexican American Cultural Center, 1975.

Interagency Committee on Mexican American Affairs. *Testimony Presented at Cabinet Hearings on Mexican American Affairs*. Washington, D.C.: Government Printing Office, 1968.

Janeway, Michael. "Bill Moyers Talks about LBJ, Power, Poverty, War, and the Young." *Atlantic* 221, no. 4 (May 1968): 221–225.

Johnson, George W., ed. *The Johnson Presidential Press Conferences*. New York: Coleman Enterprises, 1978.

Johnson, Sam Houston. *My Brother Lyndon*. Enrique Hank López, ed. New York: Cowles, 1969.

Kazin, Michael. "The New Historians Recapturing the Flag." *New York Times Book Review*, July 2, 1989, 7, 19.

Kearns, Doris. *Lyndon Johnson and the American Dream*. New York: Harper and Row, 1976.

Key, V. O. *Southern Politics in State and Nation*. New York: Knopf, 1949.

Kibbe, Pauline R. *Latin Americans in Texas*. Albuquerque: University of New Mexico Press, 1946.

Kingston, Mike, ed. *The Texas Almanac*. Dallas: Belo Corporation, 1985.

Kirstein, Peter N. *Anglo over Bracero*. San Francisco: R. and E. Publications, 1977.

La Salle County Historical Commission. "A Brief History of Cotulla." Cotulla: La Salle County Historical Commission, 1982.

Leininger, Julie. *Chicanos in South Bend: Some Historical Narratives*. Notre Dame, Indiana: Centro de Estudios Chicanos e Investigaciones Sociales, Inc., 1976.

Leuchtenberg, William. *Franklin D. Roosevelt and the New Deal, 1932–1940*. New York: Harper and Row, 1963.

Levy, Jacques. *César Chávez: Autobiography of La Causa*. New York: Norton, 1975.

Limón, José. "El Primer Congreso Mexicanista de 1911: A Precursor to Contemporary Chicanismo." *Aztlán* 5, nos. 1 and 2 (1974): 85–117.

Longoria, Mario. "Revolution, Visionary Plan, and Marketplace." *Aztlán* 12, no. 2 (1981): 78–83.

López, Henry. "The President and the Spanish-Speaking Vote." *Frontier* (March 1964): 26–28.

Lott, Virgil, and Mercurio Martínez. *The Kingdom of Zapata*. San Antonio: Naylor, 1953.

Lubell, Samuel. *The Future of American Politics*. New York: Harper and Row, 1951.

Ludeman, Annette Martin. *La Salle County*. Quana, Texas: Nortex Press, 1975.

———. *Pioneering in the Faith*. Wichita Falls, Texas: Quanah Press, 1973.

Ludwig, Ed, and James Santibáñez. *The Chicanos: Mexican American Voices*. New York: Penguin, 1971.

Manuel, Herschel T. *The Education of Mexican and Spanish-Speaking Children in Texas*. Austin: University of Texas Press, 1930.

Marín, Christine. *A Spokesman of the Mexican American Movement: Rodolfo "Corky" Gonzales*. San Francisco: R. and E. Publications, 1974.

Márquez, Benjamin. *LULAC: The Evolution of a Mexican American Political Organization*. Austin: University of Texas Press, 1993.

———. "The Politics of Race and Class: The LULAC and American Citizens in the Post–World War II Period." *Social Science Quarterly* 68 (March 1987).

Martin, J. W., and Ora K. Martin. "A History of La Salle and McMullen Counties." Dos Rios Soil Conservation District Number 322, n.d.

Martin, Roscoe. *The People's Party in Texas*. Austin: University of Texas Press, 1933.

Martínez, Elizabeth Sutherland, and Enriqueta Longeaux y Vásquez. *Viva La Raza: The Struggle of the Mexican-American People*. Garden City, New York: Doubleday, 1974.

McCullough, David. *Truman*. New York: Simon and Schuster, 1992.

McKay, Reynolds R. "The Impact of the Great Depression on Immigrant Mexican Labor: Repatriation of the Bridgeport, Texas Coal Mine." In Rodolfo O. de la Garza et al., eds., *The Mexican American Experience*. Austin: University of Texas Press, 1985.

McKay, Seth Shephard. *Texas and the Fair Deal, 1945–1952*. San Antonio: Naylor, 1954.

———. *W. Lee O'Daniel and Texas Politics, 1938–1942*. Lubbock, 1944.

McWilliams, Carey. *North from Mexico: The Spanish-Speaking People of the United States*. Westport, Connecticut: Greenwood Press, 1973.

Meier, Matt S. *Mexican American Biographies: A Historical Dictionary, 1836–1987*. Westport, Connecticut: Greenwood Press, 1988.

Meier, Matt S., and Feliciano Ribera. *Dictionary of Mexican American History*. Westport, Connecticut: Greenwood Press, 1981.

———. *The Chicanos: A History of Mexican Americans*. New York: Hill and Wang, 1972.

———. *Mexican Americans/American Mexicans: From Conquistadors to Chicanos.* New York: Hill and Wang, 1993.

Meinig, Donald. *Imperial Texas: An Interpretive Essay in Cultural Geography.* Austin: University of Texas Press, 1969.

Miller, Merle. *Lyndon: An Oral Biography.* New York: Putnam, 1980.

Mirande, Alfredo, and Evangelina Enríquez, *La Chicana.* Chicago: University of Chicago Press, 1979.

Montejano, David. *Anglos and Mexicans in the Making of Texas, 1836–1986.* Austin: University of Texas Press, 1987.

Morín, Raúl. *Among the Valiant: Mexican Americans in World War II and Korea.* Alhambra, California: Borden Publishing Company, 1963.

Morris, Richard. *Richard Milhous Nixon: The Rise of an American Politician.* New York: Henry Holt and Company, 1990.

Morris, Willie. *North toward Home.* Boston: Houghton Mifflin, 1967.

Moyers, Bill. "Epilogue: Second Thoughts." In Bernard Firestone and Robert Vogt, eds., *Lyndon Baines Johnson and the Uses of Power.* Westport, Connecticut: Greenwood Press, 1988.

Muñoz, Carlos. *Youth, Identity, Power: The Chicano Movement.* New York: Verso Press, 1989.

Nance, John. *After San Jacinto: The Texas-Mexican Frontier, 1838–1841.* Austin: University of Texas Press, 1962.

Navarro, Armando. *The Mexican American Youth Organization.* Austin: University of Texas Press, 1995.

Newlon, Clarke. *L.B.J.: The Man from Johnson City.* New York: Dodd, Mead, 1976.

O'Connor, Edwin. *The Last Hurrah.* Boston: Little, Brown, 1956.

Olson, David M. *Nonpartisan Elections: A Case Analysis.* Austin: Institute of Public Affairs, University of Texas, series 67, 1966.

Orozco, Cynthia. "Sexism in Chicano Studies and the Community." In Teresa Córdova et al., eds., *Chicana Voices,* pp. 11–18. Austin: Center for Mexican American Studies, 1986.

Paredes, Américo. *With His Pistol in His Hand: A Border Ballad and Its Hero.* Austin: University of Texas Press, 1958.

———. *A Texas-Mexican Cancionero.* Urbana: University of Illinois Press, 1976. Reprint, Austin: University of Texas Press, 1995.

Perales, Alonso S. *Are We Good Neighbors?* New York: Arno Press, 1974; San Antonio: Artes Gráficas, 1948.

———. *El méxico-americano y la política del sur de Tejas.* San Antonio: Artes Gráficas, 1948.

Patenaude, Lionel V. *Texans, Politics, and the New Deal.* New York: Garland, 1983.

Pool, William, Emmie Cradlock, and David E. Conrad. *Lyndon Baines Johnson: The Formative Years.* San Marcos: Southwest Texas State Press, 1965.

Porterfield, Bill. *LBJ Country.* Garden City, New York: Doubleday, 1965.

Pycior, Julie Leininger. "Lyndon, *La Raza,* and the Paradox of Texas History." In Bernard Firestone and Robert Vogt, eds., *Lyndon Baines Johnson and the Uses of Power*, pp. 129–143. Westport, Connecticut: Greenwood Press, 1988.

Quesada, J. Gilberto. "Judge Manuel B. Bravo: A Political Leader in South Texas, 1937–1957." *Journal of South Texas* 5, no. 1 (spring 1992): 51–67.

Quirarte, Jacinto. "The Art of Mexican-America." *The Humble Way* 9, no. 2 (1970): 6–8.

Reedy, George. *Lyndon B. Johnson: A Memoir*. New York: Andrews and McNeill, 1982.

Reeves, Richard. *President Kennedy: Profile in Power*. New York: Simon & Schuster, 1993.

Reisler, Mark. *By the Sweat of Their Brow: Mexican Immigrant Labor in the United States, 1900–1940*. Westport, Connecticut: Greenwood Press, 1981.

Rendón, Armando. "La Raza Unida: Today—Not Mañana." *Civil Rights Digest* 1 (spring 1968).

———. *Chicano Manifesto*. New York: Collier, 1971.

Reston, James, Jr. *Lone Star: The Life of John Connally*. New York: Harper and Row, 1989.

Rhinehart, Marilyn D., and Thomas H. Kreneck. "The Minimum Wage March of 1966: A Case Study in Mexican-American Politics, Labor, and Identity." *The Houston Review* 9, no. 1 (1989): 27–44.

Robertson, Jack. *A Study of Youth Needs and Services in Dallas, Texas*. Washington, D.C.: American Council of Education, 1938.

Robinson, Cecil. *With the Ears of Strangers: The Mexican in American Literature*. Tucson: University of Arizona Press, 1973.

Rodríguez, Eugene. *Henry B. González: A Political Profile*. New York: Arno Press, 1976.

Rogers, John. "Poverty behind the Cactus Curtain." *The Progressive* (March 1966).

Rogers, Mary. *Cold Anger: A Story of Faith and Power Politics*. University of North Texas Press, 1990.

Romo, Ricardo. *East Los Angeles: History of a Barrio*. Austin: University of Texas Press, 1983.

———. "George I. Sánchez and the Civil Rights Movement." *La Raza Law Journal* (fall 1986): 88–94.

———. "Mexican Americans in the New West." In Gerald D. Nash and Richard W. Etulian, eds., *The Twentieth-Century West: Historical Interpretations*, pp. 123–135. Albuquerque: University of New Mexico Press, 1989.

Rose, Margaret. "Traditional and Nontraditional Patterns of Female Activism in the United Farm Workers of America, 1962 to 1980." *Frontiers* 11, no. 1: 26–32.

Sáenz, J. Luz. *Los México-Americanos en la Gran Guerra*. San Antonio: Artes Gráficas, 1933.

Samora, Julian, Joe Bernal and Albert Peña Jr. *Gunpowder Justice*. Notre Dame, Indiana: University of Notre Dame Press, 1979.

Sánchez, George. "Concerning the Segregation of Spanish-Speaking Children in the Public Schools." *University of Texas Inter-Americans Education Occasional Papers* 9 (1951).

Sánchez, George I., and Lyle Saunders. *Wetbacks: A Preliminary Report.* Austin: University of Texas Press, 1950.

San Miguel, Guadalupe. *Let Them All Take Heed: Mexican Americans and the Campaign for Educational Equality in Texas, 1910–1981.* Austin: Center for Mexican American Studies, 1987.

Santibáñez, Enrique. *Ensayo acerca de la inmigración mexicana en los Estados Unidos.* San Francisco: R. and E. Publications, 1970; San Antonio: Artes Gráficas, 1929.

Saunders, Lyle. "The Spanish-Speaking Population of Texas." *University of Texas Inter-American Occasional Papers* 5 (1945).

Schechter, Hope Mendoza. *Hope Mendoza Schechter, Activist in the Labor Movement, The Democratic Party, and the Mexican-American Community.* Berkeley: Regional Oral History Office, the Bancroft Library, n.d.

Schott, Richard L., and Dagmar S. Hamilton. *People, Positions, and Power: The Political Appointments of Lyndon Johnson.* Chicago: University of Chicago Press, 1983.

Shannon, David A. *Twentieth-Century America.* Chicago: Rand McNally, 1963.

Shelton, Edgar. *Political Conditions among Texas Mexicans.* San Francisco: R. and E. Publications, 1974.

Sherrill, Robert. *The Accidental President.* New York: Grossman, 1967.

Shockley, John S. *Chicano Revolt in a Texas Town.* Notre Dame, Indiana: University of Notre Dame Press, 1974.

Simmons, Ozzie G. *Anglo Americans and Mexican Americans in South Texas.* New York: Arno Press, 1974.

Smith, Nancy Kegan. "Women and the White House: A Look at Women's Papers in the Johnson Library." *Prologue* 18, no. 2 (1986): 123–129.

Stambaugh, J. Lee, and Lilliam J. Stambaugh. *The Lower Rio Grande Valley of Texas.* Austin: Jenkins Company, 1974.

Steel, Ronald. "The Long Shadow of Ambition." *New York Times Book Review*, March 11, 1990, 1, 24.

Steinberg, Alfred. *Sam Johnson's Boy.* New York: Macmillan, 1968.

Steiner, Stan. *La Raza: The Mexican Americans.* New York: Harper and Row, 1969.

Strachwitz, Chris, and James Nicolopulos, compilers. *Lydia Mendoza: A Family Autobiography.* Houston: Arte Público Press, 1993.

Strickland, Ron. *Texans: Oral Histories from the Lone Star State.* New York: Paragon House, 1991.

Sutherland, Tom. "Texas Tackles the Race Problem." *Saturday Evening Post*, January 12, 1952.

Taylor, Paul. *An American-Mexican Frontier: Nueces County, Texas.* Chapel Hill: University of North Carolina Press, 1934; New York: Russell and Russell, 1971.

————. *Mexican Americans in the United States: Dimmit County, Winter Garden District, South Texas*. Berkeley: University of California Press, 1930.

Thomas, Hugh. *The Spanish Civil War*. New York: Harper and Row, 1961.

Thompson, Kenneth, ed. *The Johnson Presidency: Twenty Intimate Perspectives of Lyndon B. Johnson*. Lanham, Maryland: University Press of America, 1986.

Tuchman, Barbara. *Practicing History*. New York: Knopf, 1981.

Tyler, Ron, ed. *The New Handbook of Texas*. Austin: Texas State Historical Association, 1996.

Urrutía, Liliana. "An Offspring of Discontent: The Asociación Nacional México-Americana, 1949–1954." *Aztlán* 15 (spring 1984).

U.S. Department of Commerce. "Tourist and Recreational Programs for Zapata County, Texas." *ARA Case Book*. Washington, D.C.: Area Redevelopment Corporation, U.S. Department of Commerce (October 1964).

U.S. President. *Public Papers of the Presidents of the United States*. Washington, D.C: Office of the Federal Register, National Archives and Records Service, 1953.

Vento, Adela Schloss. *Alonso S. Perales: His Struggle for the Rights of Mexican-Americans*. San Antonio: Artes Gráficas, 1977.

Villanueva, Tino. *Scene from the Movie Giant*. Willimantic, Connecticut: Curbstone Press, 1994.

Webb, Walter Prescott. *The Texas Rangers*. Boston: Houghton Mifflin, 1935.

Weisenberger, Carol A. *Dollars and Dreams: The National Youth Administration in Texas*. New York: Peter Lang, 1994.

White, Richard. *"It's Your Misfortune and None of My Own": A New History of the American West*. Norman: University of Oklahoma Press, 1991.

White, William S. *The Professional: Lyndon B. Johnson*. Boston: Houghton Mifflin, 1964.

White House Historical Association. *The White House: An Historic Guide*. Washington, D.C.: White House Historical Association, 1964.

Wicker, Tom. *JFK and LBJ: The Influence of Personality on Politics*. New York: Penguin, 1968.

Williams, T. Harry. *Huey Long*. New York: Bantam, 1969.

Wofford, Harris. *Of Kennedys and Kings: Making Sense of the Sixties*. Pittsburgh: University of Pittsburgh Press, 1980.

Woods, Frances Jerome. *Mexican Ethnic Leadership in San Antonio, Texas*. Washington, D.C: Catholic University Press, 1949.

Woodward, C. Vann. *The Strange Career of Jim Crow*. New York: Oxford University Press, 1955.

————. *Thinking Back*. Baton Rouge: Louisiana State University Press, 1986.

Ximenes, Ben Cuéllar. *Gallant Outcasts*. San Antonio: Naylor Publishing Company, n.d.

Zamora, Emilio. "Chicano Socialist Labor Activity in Texas, 1900–1920." *Aztlán* 6, no. 2 (summer 1975): 221–238.

————. *The World of the Mexican Worker in Texas*. College Station: Texas A&M Press, 1992.

THESES AND OTHER UNPUBLISHED MATERIAL

Bourgeois, Christie Lynne. "Lyndon Johnson's Years with the National Youth Administration." M.A. thesis, University of Texas at Austin, 1986.

Castañón, Juan García. "LatinoNET Access Alert!!!" November 28, 1995. CHICLE@unmvma.unm.edu.

Cotulla cemetery, Cotulla, Texas. Historical marker and headstones.

Dean, Elizabeth, executive producer. *The Kennedys*. Public Television System.

Dyer, Stanford P. "Lyndon B. Johnson and the Politics of Civil Rights, 1935–1960: The Art of 'Moderate Leadership.'" Ph.D. dissertation, Texas A&M University, 1978.

Flores, Adela Isabel. "Falcon International Dam and Its Aftermath: A Study of U.S.–Mexican Border Policy Making and Implementation." M.A. thesis, University of Texas at Austin, 1985.

García, Richard Amado. "The Making of the Mexican American Mind: San Antonio, Texas, 1929–1941." Ph.D. dissertation, University of California, Irvine, 1980.

"Giant." Warner Brothers Productions, 1956.

Ginsberg, Ruth Bader. Testimony before the Senate Judiciary Committee. National Public Radio, July 20, 1993.

Hampton, Henry, executive producer. "Eyes on the Prize." Blackside, Inc.

Jiménez, Santiago. "Cotulla Polka." Phonograph record, n.p., n.d., Cotulla (Texas) Historical Museum.

Leininger, Julie. "The Chicana Worker in San Antonio, 1910–1940." Paper delivered at the Conference on the History of Women, St. Paul, Minnesota, October 1977.

McCoy, Charla Dean. "The Education President: Lyndon Baines Johnson's Public Statements on Instruction and the Teaching Profession." Ph.D. dissertation, University of Texas at Austin, 1975.

Mitchell, Nan James. "An Evaluation of Provisions for the Education of Spanish-Speaking Children in San Marcos, Texas." M.A. thesis, University of Texas at Austin, 1946.

Monument, dated September 15, 1946. Plaza Militar, San Antonio, Texas.

Moyers, Bill. *From D-Day to the Rhine with Bill Moyers*. New York: Public Affairs Television, Inc., 1990.

———. *Moyers: Twenty Years of Listening to America*. New York: Public Affairs Television, Inc., 1991.

Perini, Patricia, and David Grubin, executive producers. *LBJ*. KERA Productions, in association with David Grubin Productions, Inc., 1991.

Post, Donald. "Ethnic Competition for Control of Schools in Two Texas Towns." Ph.D. dissertation, University of Texas at Austin, 1975.

Pycior, Julie Leininger. "Lyndon Johnson, Mexican Americans, and Public Policy Issues: The Formative Years." Paper delivered at the Organization of American Historians, Reno, March 26, 1988.

———. "*La Raza* Organizes: Mexican American Life in San Antonio as reflected in *Mutualista* Activities." Ph.D. dissertation, University of Notre Dame, 1979.

Rock, Beryle Rutledge. "Children's Achievement in the Amanda Burks Elementary School." M.A. thesis, University of Texas at Austin, 1951.

Rose, Margaret. "Gender and Civic Activism in California Barrios: The Community Service Organization, 1947–1962." Paper delivered at the American Historical Association, San Francisco, January 7, 1994.

Rouse, Lura N. "A Study of the Education of Spanish-Speaking Children in Dimmit County, Texas." M.A. thesis, University of Texas at Austin, 1948.

Scholarly Resources. "Resources in Latin American Studies." Wilmington: SR, 1996.

Shirley, Wayne D. "Ethnic Music of French Louisiana, the Spanish Southwest, and the Bahamas." Booklet for the phonograph record of the same name. Washington, D.C.: Library of Congress, *Folk Music of the United States*, 1934.

Smith, Walter E. "Mexicano Resistance to Schooled Ethnicity." Ph.D. dissertation, University of Texas at Austin, 1978.

Treviño, Jesús, et al., producer. *Chicano! The History of the Mexican American Civil Rights Movement*. Galán Productions, 1996.

Villanueva, Tino. Presentation, College of New Rochelle, New Rochelle, New York, April 24, 1994.

Villarreal, Roberto. "Voting Participation and Leadership: Chicanos along the Border." Paper delivered at the Southwest Political Science Association convention, Fort Worth, March 28–31, 1973.

Young, Joe. "An Administrative Survey of the Public Schools of La Salle County, Texas." M.A. thesis, University of Texas at Austin, 1939.

Woods, Fredna. "Narrative of Welhausen School," in Woods's and author's collections.

NEWSPAPERS AND PERIODICALS

Alamo Messenger [Archdiocese of San Antonio]
Albuquerque Journal
Arizona Republic
Austin American-Statesman
Bakersfield Californian
Christian Advocate
Civil Rights Digest
The Communist
Corpus Christi Caller
Corpus Christi Caller-Times
Cotulla (Texas) Record
Dallas Morning News
Dallas News
Dallas Times
Dallas Times-Herald
Denver Post
El Diario/La Prensa [New York City]

El Paso Herald Post
Excelsior [Mexico City]
Fresno Bee
Ft. Worth Star-Telegram
Forum News Bulletin [American GI Forum]
Galveston Tribune
El Heraldo Mexicano
Houston Chronicle
Journal of South Texas
Laredo Morning Times
Latin Times [East Chicago, Indiana]
Look
Los Angeles Times
Lulac News [League of United Latin American Citizens]
El Malcriado [United Farm Workers]
New York Times
Noticias [Chicago]
The Nation
La Prensa [San Antonio]
The Progressive
El Progreso
Rocky Mountain News [Denver]
San Angelo [Texas] *Times*
San Antonio Express
San Antonio Express-News
San Antonio Light
Saturday Evening Post
Rocky Mountain News
The Texas Observer
Texas Parade
Tiempo [Mexico City]
The Traveler
[Lower Rio Grande] *Valley Evening Monitor*
La Verdad [South Texas]
Wall Street Journal
Washington Post

INDEX